WITHDRAWN

WITHDRAWN

The Child and His Welfare

THIRD EDITION

The Child and His Welfare

Hazel Fredericksen
CONSULTANT IN CHILD WELFARE

R. A. Mulligan
THE UNIVERSITY OF ARIZONA

W. H. FREEMAN AND COMPANY
San Francisco

Library of Congress Catalog Card Number: 70-172242

International Standard Book Number: 0-7167-0905-8

2 3 4 5 6 7 8 9 10

Dedicated to

Virginia and Paul

*whose
help and encouragement
have enabled us
to complete this book*

Contents

Preface

Our chief purpose is to provide a broad view of the field of child welfare, and to show how it has developed and is constantly changing.

The book is designed for a wide range of interested persons: undergraduate students who are considering a career in social welfare or child care; social workers in public-assistance and child welfare agencies; country supervisors; probation officers; juvenile judges; elementary and high school teachers who wish to learn more about the field of child welfare; board members of public and private agencies; and many others.

The field of child welfare is constantly expanding, and it should be—if we in this country are to develop a better prospect for that third of the population under eighteen years of age, who (we keep reminding ourselves) include our future leaders.

As authors we do not presume to have covered any one area of the field fully, or to have enunciated final principles. Progress in guiding children to effective adult life demands constant evaluation and reevaluation. We cannot say a suggested procedure is *the* way, but only *a* way that we think will help children achieve a happier life.

We have not included a special chapter about children in minority groups, because we believe that all services and opportunities promoting health, education, and welfare should be of equal access to children in all stations of life, regardless of race, creed or color. We have not overlooked the fact that children in minority groups are often at a cruel disadvantage. We are convinced that what produces a happy wholesome life for one group of children should be provided for all.

We wish to express our appreciation to the large number of generous people who have given time and thought to the discussion of materials presented in this book.

January 1, 1972   *Hazel Fredericksen*
                                                      Raymond A. Mulligan

The Child and His Welfare

[*Photo by Christy Butterfield.*]

1

The Child and His Welfare

American society is changing so rapidly today that parents are unable to predict with any degree of certainty what lies ahead for their children. The factors underlying these changes are both technological and social. An example of the social factor is the increasing tendency of young people to speak out on various aspects of our social order, and as a result some of our most cherished social values are being questioned by them.

Social change as an entity neither guarantees progress nor automatically promotes social disorganization. It may either advance the welfare of children or create additional child welfare problems. Its effects are determined by the values of the social system in which it occurs, and how such change is evaluated depends on the judgments of the population making up the society.

Social change—and consequently child development, child welfare problems and the services for neglected, dependent, or delinquent children—are affected at least indirectly and at times directly by economic, technological, demographic or social value fluctuations. If we are to understand the implications of social change for the field of child welfare, we should first look at some of the variables operating in this process.

CHILDREN AND YOUTH IN A CHANGING WORLD

Technological change, generally considered the prime mover in social change, has been taking place in America with increasing acceleration for the past 150 years. It has influenced agriculture, food processing methods, building techniques, modes of transportation, types of entertainment, and communications, as well as many other areas of our society. Technological changes or material inventions have pervasive rather than unitary effects in our social system. For example, a technological change in mode of travel may affect not only our transportation system but, in variant degrees, public education, industry and business, and other types of activity that are interrelated directly or indirectly with that travel.

The causes of social change are not confined to mechanical inventions. Social inventions, too, may bring about social change, though not as much as mechanical innovations. Social legislation is an example of a social invention. Such social inventions as child labor legislation and compulsory school attendance laws are said to have changed some of the authority of the family by reducing the control of parents over their children. Dramatic or profound modifications in social institutions are brought about when clusters of several inventions, either social or material, come together.

The most striking technological change in modern times has been in the methods of production and distribution by means of power machines. As a result, throughout the years industry has been moved from the home to the factory. In turn, the advent of the factory and railroad led to the development of urban centers. In the cities, slum housing and concentrations of economic, racial, and ethnic minorities arose, as did high crime, delinquency, morbidity, and mortality rates.

In subsequent years, manufacturing and other types of production and business were moved from population centers to small towns or to the outlying districts of larger cities. Many middle class families also moved from areas near the inner city to outlying better residential districts or to the suburbs.

The movement of businesses and people from the central city, aided by rapid transportation and the automobile, left behind not only many vacant shops and buildings, but the poor and their children. In past years, the abodes and neighborhoods of the poor and of certain racial and ethnic groups have deteriorated physically and socially so much that they are now commonly referred to as "jungles." Child welfare problems of every type and combination are found in these areas.

Social values as sources or potential sources of human behavior have been influenced in part by the changes in American society. The dynamics of social change, then, may be studied not only from the point of view of inventions, mechanical and social, but also from that of fundamental societal values. Social values change under social influences, and when the fundamental values are affected they exert significant changes in the behavior of individuals and in the organization of social systems.

"Social system" is a generic and relative term. Basically, it is an aggregate of behavior patterns loosely or formally organized on a long-term or short-term basis in order to pursue some group objective.

Society consists of one all-embracing social system. The family, or any other social institution, is a small social system unto itself, or a subsystem within a larger system. In turn, the family's behavior patterns may be more structured than those of a recreational group, but the degree of structuration does not make the family or any other group of interacting individuals any less a social system. We may refer to the behavior patterns of a highly structured social institution as a social system, as well as to the loosely organized and informal behavior of a child's play group that comes together from time to time.

Social phenomena may consist of music, law, religion, science, architecture, literature, folkways, mores, the social organization of the family, the social system of a factory, formal and informal prison systems, and so on.

American society has been described as a society that is undergoing accelerated social change. It has also been described as one whose value system is highly material—in other words, one that is influenced more by sensory values than spiritual. In addition, modern Americans have been described as self-oriented in their drives rather than other-oriented or group-interested. Whether these values and attitudes are the result of inventions or have developed independently of technological change is not relevant to our discussion. What is important is that some of our basic social values are changing in the areas of morals, authority, and power, and that such changes are bound to have significance for the welfare of children.

All societies consist of a multitude of apparently diverse social phenomena and relationships that at first glance appear unrelated to one another. However, upon closer examination and study it is often found that there is some unity to these parts and that they are in harmony with a fundamental principle or basis value. According to sociological theory, the dominant parts of all the important social systems of a society, mores and manners, articulate a basic principle or value.

The dominant basic value in our society today is the belief that true reality is sensory, that only what we experience through our sense organs is real and worthwhile. This principle has been increasingly articulated by our modern society in all its main compartments. In contrast to the "supersensory" principles basic to some other societies, the basic principle of our society is worldly, secular, and utilitarian.

Values bring about social change by expanding into important areas of a society and becoming more dominant than the existing ones. For example, for many years mutual aid was a common practice in the rural areas of our country, but less so in urban settings. But as urbanization has increased, mutual aid has become less common, and individual- or self-interest has become an important theme throughout the nation.

Beside the technological and value changes that influence society, another important source of change is the dynamics of population. Although population changes are affected by social change, they also influence various social institutions, such as business, economics, education, and agriculture.

Population changes have been continually taking place in the United States for years. The national population jumped from 3,929,000 in 1790 to 39,905,000 in 1870, and to 203,185,000 in 1970; the projected figure for 1980 is 272,600,000, and it is 300,000,000 for the year 2000.

One dramatic population change has been in the percentage of children and youths (0–19). In 1900, there were only 33,700,000 in this age bracket, and in 1970, approximately 99,000,000. This increase gives young people a numerical authority, and presents the rest of society with certain problems in controlling the internalization of the prevailing social values. Youth, and what values it does internalize, is vital because it is a potential business market in clothing, cars, entertainment, motion pictures, and older youth is a significant political force.

In spite of the decline in our birthrate, which began in about 1957, evidence indicates a future increasing population for the United States. The number of births in 1969 exceeds the number for 1968. Women in the childbearing ages of 20–29 will increase by 35 percent in the 1970's. Even with a relatively low birthrate we should expect a significant population increase, owing to the increasing number of young women of childbearing age in our society.

In addition, it appears that these large numbers of children and young people will continue to grow at an increased rate for the next several decades. Unless we also attain an ideal society in which we will have no child welfare problems, the increasing numbers of children in out population means our social services for children and youth will have to continue and expand.

In a rapidly changing society rules of behavior are tenuous. Moral codes tend to be very general, if they are to survive, and in the absence of specific guidelines or rules, the individual tends to be guided by the anticipated consequences of intended behavior instead of established social values.

Ideally, a well balanced society is one in which its social institutions and other major behavior patterns are adjusted to one another. When its major components do not complement each other, imbalance results, and the previously harmonious social relationships which were in a state of equilibrium are disturbed.

Sources of a society's problems that may lead to social disorganization are many. However, it is generally felt that the sweeping advances of science and technology in the United States in recent years have been major causes of rapid change in our education, health, and economic systems, thus creating, in certain areas of our society, imbalances such as unemployment in technological fields and increased poverty.

Social change does not affect all parts of a society, and those it does are not affected evenly. Some institutions change faster than others under the impact of outside influence. Since social systems are highly interrelated, a change in one system sets up strains in another. Also, part of a system may start moving in one direction while component parts have not yet adopted any of their functions to the change. This resulting social lag inevitably produces disharmony in the system (such as too large a number of students for an old school), which in turn affects individuals and their community in the realm of social adjustment.

The American family as a component of our society and the one social institution that has the greatest influence on children during their formative years has been directly and indirectly subjected to some of the forces that are generally considered as sources of social change.

The basic or conjugal family in American society consists of father, mother, and children. It is influenced not only by its own members but also by such local outside sources as relatives, primary groups, and the community. Lesser influences might be collective representations, such as the federal or state governments. In addition, certain international developments and problems may have influenced the American family through the news media. Certainly these developments have caused some married couples to debate the wisdom of bringing children into a world of conflict that presents so many future uncertainties.

The family as a social institution is closely related to other institutions in our society, and changes in any one of these institutions are soon felt in the others. For example, fluctuations in our economic, political, or religious systems are transmitted to the family as well as to other social institutions in our society. Social situations that affect adults often influence their social relationships with their children in the course of a short or a long period of time, depending on the valence of the outside agent of change.

At present, American society is stressing not only the rights of minorities, the poor, and women, but also those of youth and students. Of course, for years many middle class families reared their children permissively, and this permissive philosophy may have contributed to the aggression in youth behavior that is prevalent today. Democratically oriented societies carry the ultimate potential of maximum individual rights, but not out of balance with group rights. Permissive child rearing in the modern American family supports the emphasis placed upon individual rights found currently in so many parts of our social system. Whether our society has gone too far in the direction of individual rights at the expense of group rights, such as in concessions for juvenile delinquents, or whether we can push for still more individual rights without destroying our societal equilibrium is uncertain at this time. It is equally uncertain whether the pendulum has begun to move toward group rights or whether a synthesis of our new values on a different social level is in process along with a more integrated society. However, regardless of the direction of change, we know that our society is in a state of flux that has implications for the future of our children and their welfare.

The effects of living in a materialistically oriented society, such as ours, tend to make material goals more desirable than nonmaterial objectives, although naturally not all families are influenced to the same degree. For example, in a family with children, what is more important —the needs and general welfare of the children, or the material desires of the parents? Is a new car every two or three years a more desirable goal for the parents than food in proper amounts and quality for their children? It is a fact that there are fathers who select new cars over the minimum and basic food needs of their own children. Parental self-interest can also take precedence to clothing, medical attention, proper education, leisure time activities, and proper housing, for the children. Whether child neglect increases as a society becomes more materialistic or, inversely, child neglect decreases with an increase of spiritual social values remains to be demonstrated empirically. However, we do know that child neglect and malnutrition occurs in families with relatively good incomes.

Another result of the influence of material values on family life is the emphasis on individual gain, advancement, or pleasure. Parents may not openly neglect their children, but may subtly compete with them for a disproportionate share of the time and money available to the family. For example, it takes time to converse and play with children. It takes time to accompany them to such places as the zoo, the homes of relatives, museums, sporting events, or settings of cultural events. Some parents are not willing to devote a fair share of their free time to their children's activities. Similarly, parents may divert a disproportionate amount of the family's excess income to their own desires, to the detriment of the children's normal needs. In other words, the self-sacrificing immigrant parents of a generation ago and the ambitious lower middle class American parents of the same era appear to have been replaced, in part at least, to less self-sacrificing parents who are not willing to invest blindly all of their time and fortune in their children. This change may be interpreted as being due to our individualistic and materialistic society. In turn, children are not expected to aid their aged parents even when they are in dire need. Mutual aid among neighbors may be dead or decreasing in many communities throughout American society, but at the same time it has been diminishing in our families and in other primary groups.

As the child matures he eventually discovers the community in which his family is living, and he is influenced by it in proportion to the control exercised by his family. By "control," we mean the degree to which the family supervises the child's behavior outside of the home:

Is he allowed to associate freely with all children, or only with children whose behavior is considered by his parents to be desirable? Is the child allowed to leave and return home according to his wishes, or is he kept to a strict schedule and held accountable for his time by his parents? The stricter the parental controls, the less influential uncomplementary community norms will be on the behavior of the child.

The use of the term "community" has been used to designate populated areas from large cities to small towns. The term implies a territorial area, a high degree of interpersonal acquaintance, and a character that may distinguish one community from others or, in large cities, one neighborhood from another.

The influence that a community or neighborhood may have on the behavior of children and the child welfare services children may need in certain localities is quite well documented in sociological and child welfare literature. Various sociological studies of the past forty years have indicated (1) the influence that the social milieu has on the behavior of children and (2) the existence of a spatial distribution of social and child welfare problems in urban areas. For example, in a big city, the neighborhood in which a child's family resides determines to a large extent the possibility that child has of becoming a juvenile delinquent. The family's income determines the type of neighborhood in which a child is to live, and during his most formative years it influences much of his behavior. Social change has increased the rates of juvenile delinquency consistently since World War II.

In our large cities, neighborhoods vary greatly in many ways. Middle class neighborhoods differ from poor sections in housing, the cleanliness of the streets, the quality of schools, the adequacy of playgrounds, the quantity of public libraries, and the rates of juvenile delinquency and crime. Neighborhoods inhabited by the poor have higher mortality, morbidity, crime, and juvenile delinquency rates than do other areas. They tend to have a disproportionate number of high school drop-outs, poor school-attendance records, unemployed people, overcrowded housing units, and large families. The poor and their children in America do not receive adequate medical attention; as a result many have prolonged illnesses, and the average life span is shorter than that in the higher socioeconomic classes.

Rural communities have such advantages as clean fresh air, primary relationships, and low density of population, but they may in fact be inferior to various urban areas in some important ways. For example, the standard of living in nonurban communities is generally lower than that in urban centers. Social class differences are more visible in rural areas, and social class consciousness is prevalent in many types of social interaction, to the disadvantage of those with low status.

Although crime and juvenile delinquency rates are lower in the hinterland than in the city, the services found in rural communities are inferior, limited, or nonexistent. For example, some towns have been without medical doctors or dentists for years. Social service agencies do not exist, and probation services, if present, are usually nonprofessional. Specialists in any field, including child welfare, are not found in rural communities. Professionals and specialists gravitate to the areas offering high standards of living, the large cities and the immediately surrounding areas.

On the whole, rural communities do not offer many opportunities for the economic or social advancement of the poor. In fact, some of them relegate their poor to slow starvation. In recent investigations of economic conditions in selected rural communities, widespread poverty among racial minorities was found in several southern counties. Many school children were living on one meal a day and their family's income was so low that they could not afford to purchase food stamps.

In our changing and contemporary society the poor are still with us. It is true that most American families are experiencing a comfortable standard of living which includes adequate housing, food, medical care, schooling, and leisure time activities. Our inflationary prosperity has enabled united community fund drives to reach and exceed their quotas in many localities throughout the nation. Also, Social Security benefits have been increased from time to time in recent years by the federal government in a belated attempt to keep abreast of the rising cost of living. However, in most states, categorical welfare benefits (which include relief for the aged, the disabled, dependent children, and the blind) have not increased dramatically, and their real purchasing value has decreased.

Thus a society may experience affluency or prosperity in general, but the distribution of its benefits may be uneven among various families or segments of the population. For example, we may have an increasing employment rate in the general population, and yet the number of recipients on public welfare may remain the same. This appears to be an anomalous situation, but it can be explained to a large extent by examining the reasons people apply for public relief.

The conditions leading to dependency on categorical welfare are either independent of economic conditions or largely the result of long-term irreversible trends or conditions. For example, a family may be rendered fatherless by the man's death, desertion, incarceration, or commitment to a mental institution. It is reasonable to assume that the children in such a family have no control over the conditions leading to the father's absence. Any of these conditions, depending on the circumstances of the case, are conceivably independent of the economic cycle or at best remotely related. Aid to Families with Dependent Children has been provided to increasing numbers of recipients in recent years. This is a reflection of population changes, the increasing number of family breakdowns, the rising cost of living, and other causes.

General prosperity does not automatically create either neglectful parents or good and loving parents. Children continue to be neglected, abused, and deserted by their parents under all types of economic conditions. In fact, one type of child welfare problem, juvenile delinquency, tends to increase during periods of prosperity in this country. However, prosperity may also increase the amount of money available for many child welfare problems and services. It may even eradicate or alleviate such problems as poor nutrition, crippling childhood diseases, and poor housing for some children. Nevertheless numerous other child welfare problems will continue to persist because they are not related to economic conditions.

The quality of certain public services available to children in the United States varies with the standard of living in each state. The wealthier states tend to have the best public school systems, adequate public welfare benefits, extensive public recreation facilities, and strict child labor and public school-attendance laws.

Although all states license day care facilities, maternity homes, foster homes, and child care institutions, the best standards for child welfare services are usually introduced by federal agencies having federal funds at their disposal. State departments of public welfare, in their licensing capacity, see to it that children's services are administered under acceptable standards. In order to carry out this function of maintaining adequate standards, welfare departments should also have a staff large enough to provide professional consultation services and leadership for better child welfare services and programs, and to anticipate new services for child welfare problems that are still unmet. However, realization of these goals is relative to a state's political, social, and economic philosophy.

In the web of our changing society, youth is caught up in such social questions as the redistribution of power, status, and authority. Youth protest marches, minority demands for equal rights, the increasing use of narcotics, and our continuous engagement in war for approximately thirty years appear to be the most pressing problems for our nation at present.

It is difficult to determine the exact effect these conditions may have on the welfare of children in general and particularly on children and youth in need of child welfare services. The general assumption is that they are and will be deleterious.

The protest of minority groups against discrimination in housing, schooling, vocational training, and employment has created a national awareness that has brought results, particularly in employment. As more skilled and managerial positions become available, minorities should eventually be able to experience a higher standard of living and thus a better life and opportunity for their children in health, welfare, and education.

In addition, some observers claim that if the federal government spent less money on its defense and national security budget and directed the savings to the general welfare of the lower social classes in this country, many of our social problems in housing, ghettoes, delinquency, race relations, and health would be alleviated. Of course, this concept assumes that the public and Congress and all its lobbyists are willing to spend the same huge sums of money on health, welfare, and educational services that are now used in the production of defensive armaments. Such an official course of action is not likely to come about in the foreseeable future.

The solution of social and child welfare problems with large sums of money sounds feasible, but the public and our legislative bodies have to agree that such a plan would benefit our economy and society. This is no simple stipulation: Many citizens untouched by poverty or other social ills may willingly support a war effort financed by higher income taxes but they may not agree to appropriate public tax funds for the solution of even a few of our social problems.

One group of children deserving of social concern consists of those who have been forced to share their fathers with the armed services. Most of these fathers, as members of one of the branches of the armed services, were separated from their families for long periods of time. As a result, numerous children have suffered deep anxiety for the safety of their fathers overseas, and their economic welfare has been jeopardized by the limited incomes allotted to armed service families. Another problem these children have had to face is the constant mobility of their families throughout the United States and the world. Although these moves may be educational and broadening, they deprive the child of an identity with a particular community of some stability and security. A life of temporary social relationships is not considered ideal for growing children, and may have some influence on a child's developing personality.

Other groups of children all over the world have been adversely affected by international conditions throughout the years. For the most part the United States has been more fortunate than many other countries. To be sure, there are many children in different parts of the country suffering from crippling diseases, relative poverty, sickness, neglect, and broken families as the result of international conflict or economic upheavals, but their numbers are fewer than in many other countries of Africa, Asia, and the Near East, where the effects of famine, war, and pestilence have been severe indeed. The impediments to the solution of child welfare problems in the United States lie not in the lack of basic resources, which so many other countries lack, but rather in our basic values and administrative systems. The resources in money, techniques, and personnel are present in our country; but if we are to mobilize them extensively enough for effective prevention and treatment of child welfare problems, important public welfare policy changes are essential.

THE DEVELOPMENT OF THE CHILD

Childhood is generally described as the happy, carefree time of life. However, for all babies born yearly in the United States to be assured of a happy, carefree childhood, the following conditions would be necessary:

1. Every child would have healthy, intelligent parents fully prepared in advance for the responsibility of parenthood. Parents would have enough income to provide everything necessary to give him a secure home life necessary for his growth and development.
2. Every child would have a chance for education commensurate with his individual capacity, needs, and interests, and a chance to play and to develop a feeling of adequacy and self-sufficiency as a part of a group.
3. Every child would be taught humanistic, moral, social, or religious ideals and concepts in conformity with his background and individual needs.
4. Every child would be protected from exploitation in premature

and harmful labor. If he had special needs, he would have special services and social safeguards ready to help him. Children born out of wedlock could thus find protection. Children who were crippled, deficient in sight or hearing, or mentally deficient, or who were victims of tuberculosis, rheumatic fever, or cardiac or parasitic diseases would be given care and treatment.

5. Children who were suffering personality and behavior disorders would have the benefits of early identification and treatment. Children in depressed areas would have the special help necessary to make their opportunities comparable to those of the more fortunately situated.

Obviously not every child in the United States has all these advantages; but advancements have been made.

Because of a growing belief that every child should have the kind of care he needs, public and private agencies in nearly all communities have developed aids and services to help families to care for children in their own homes. However, there are still children whose families cannot supply the essentials of home life needed for wholesome growth and development. In this event, an agency designed to provide the form of care needed takes over the child welfare responsibilities.

We find that children need more than satisfaction of their physical needs; for their security they need affection, approval, and a sense of belonging. The first needs of the baby are, of course, physical. His personality development consists of instinctual or "id" drives. His earliest manifestations of emotion are related to the sensations of tasting, touching, urinating, and defecating, and to the blocking of these sensations.

Satisfying of hunger is the first pleasure that the baby knows, and it is one of continuing importance. It not only develops him physically and sets a pattern for his future food enjoyment, but it also provides a "mothering" situation in which his ego or "self" functions can develop. The child makes his hunger pangs known. But food doesn't always come to him at once. He discovers that feeding takes on a rhythmical regularity. Mother isn't always available. So he finds that there is a self, apart from the mother. And this self begins to take on a responsibility —of adapting to the wait. The child has begun his personality growth.

His discovery of self expands. He explores his body. Next he explores his surroundings and takes note of people who come and are useful to this self of his. Not until later does he develop affection for the giver of the satisfactions.

Gradually the normal child learns that he must meet some demands of his environment. A tone of voice or other sign conveys to him that something he is doing annoys others; he stops doing it to avoid an unpleasant consequence or to win praise from a satisfaction-giver.

As the baby grows older he develops himself more and more in relationships with others. The kind of self he develops will be determined by the elements that make up his situation. In his give and take with other persons he acquires a sense of individuality in the world. He sees that others recognize in him a dynamic force that is somehow his own. This encourages him to develop the capacity to influence the direction of his relationships.

As his capacity increases he finds that the world not only expects him to grow, but would like him to follow a certain pattern, one in accordance with the norm. Forces urging him to recreate a likeness that others find good are released. Some of these demands are uncomfortable and he resists. He gets attention by this rebellion, and he derives a sense of his own strength from the extent to which he is able to resist the demands or to profit by compliance. The shape of his personality and its rate of growth are strongly influenced in this difficult period, which some persons never outgrow.

Is the child to reach emotional maturity on a normal schedule, or be delayed, or even constantly frustrated and turned back to infantile behavior? The answer usually depends upon the family more than on the many other childhood influences.

In our society, much depends upon the mother. Generally she is the first with whom the child finds a pleasant relationship. Also, however, she is the first to make demands on him and evoke some of his instinctual negative feelings. Because he sees so much of her, and is dependent upon her, she is for him the representative of that culture that is molding him.

She is in a strategic position. She can accept a positive interest and love on the part of the child and return it in such a way that he gets a sense of belonging without being engulfed. By respecting the child as a separate person, she can help him to become a whole one. However, as child welfare workers must constantly keep in mind, a mother may have embarked upon a less fortunate course, with unhappy effects upon the child. She may reject the child and develop an antagonistic feeling toward him, denying him the security from which he gets the courage for growth. Alternatively, she may take advantage of the child's need for protection, overprotecting him because she gets a satisfaction from doing so, only to discover later that she has suffocated him and not allowed him to mature.

Parents, particularly those who have a hard time adjusting to each other, do not find it easy to make further necessary adjustments to each new child. These adjustments are facilitated, though, if the mother is friendly to the father, because then the child will be friendly to the father, too.

If the father is a well adjusted person, the fact that he is not included in the earlier mother-baby relationships causes no complications, but if the father is very dependent upon the mother's affection he may develop antagonisms toward the small being who takes so much of her thought. A rivalry for the mother's attention then develops, and the child shows antagonisms toward the father in later behavior—and toward other persons in a position of authority.

Fathers and mothers should share in the direction necessary to the child's development. Both parents should understand that the ideal of upbringing is not to force a re-creation of themselves but to assist in the creation of a new, effective personality.

Children actually crave direction, in spite of surface signs to the contrary; they find it difficult to bear the entire responsibility for their own actions. They may even welcome punishment as a proof that their parents care enough to direct them.

In our complex society we prolong the period of direction because there is so much that must be learned. But we still must do what we can to help every child achieve growth at what, for him, is a normal pace.

Every child passes through the same growth processes, but at his own rate of progress. Each child will attain his own height, weight, and temperament by following a pattern unique to him, a pattern that is influenced by his parents, his environment, and the way he is affected by all of his experiences.

If a child's emotional needs find satisfaction in acceptable ways, and if he is physically healthy, he will probably pass successfully through the three stages of infancy, childhood, and adolescence to mature into a normal, stable member of society.

THE FIELD OF CHILD WELFARE

Whenever we consider the welfare of any child, we must realize that when services from persons other than his own parents are necessary something has happened in his life which, unless skillfully handled, may leave lasting scars. Some of the reasons that make it necessary for a person outside the home to offer understanding and help to a child seem quite obvious: for instance, a child may be deprived of his own home because of the death, disability, incompetence, or illness (physical or mental) of one or both parents; he may be without normal guardianship of parents as a result of having been abandoned, neglected, deserted, or born out of wedlock; his home may be broken because of economic pressures, unemployment, marital disharmony, or other family discord.

Less obvious reasons that are nevertheless extremely damaging to the development of the child are situations in which parental personalities adversely affect his welfare. These types of problems exist at every socioeconomic level, and children coming from the homes of the well-to-do are as susceptible to tensions and home discords as are the children of parents in low-income status. The child who is rejected by one or both parents is an example. He may develop anxieties and inferiorities that make it difficult for him to enter into easy social relationships. The child who experiences deprivation of emotional security in his own home may demand excessive attention; for example, he may be unable to bear disappointment without being sulky or having a tantrum. If the child has been overprotected, and his parents have never given him a chance to cope with disappointment, he will be totally unprepared to meet the frustrations of later life. There is also the child who suffers because he is being used for the advantage of an unsatisfactory marital partner; and the child who is a rival either of the marital partner or of the parent of his own sex who envies the child's youth, opportunities, or enjoyment. The influence of sibling rivalry may also create serious problems. These and other influences on the mechanism of personality formation are of great importance in determining a child's future adaptation to life.

Each child must be helped to accept his own responsibility for making something useful of his or her life. In addition to the emotional stability, the health, educational, recreational, social, and economic resources that are present in his immediate environment, all affect his growth and development. Some child-welfare problems are directly related to employment, wages, housing, and other factors affecting family life. However, we have found that if a child has the affection and security of his family he may survive serious social and economic deprivations surprisingly well.

The school situation is another aspect of child welfare. Although schools are primarily responsible for the educational training, we are necessarily concerned with all conditions under which all children of a nation live and grow to maturity either successfully or unsuccessfully. When anything less than the best in child welfare is present (in even an individual case), the whole community suffers.

Social institutions become of prime importance for the child's welfare when the family fails to carry out its responsibilities, or is unable to. These organizations include foster families, child care institutions, and financial assistance agencies; they also include other institutions that provide health services and opportunities for recreational education, spiritual guidance, and social relationships.

A sound child welfare program will provide for all factors that will enable children to develop lives that are useful to themselves and to society as a whole. The extent to which a community is considering its own future is indicated by the kind of provision it makes for the welfare of children of all creeds, colors, races, and nationalities, without regard to financial status of the parents.

Services for children are specialized, because certain factors make work with children different from work with adults. For example, adults find it difficult enough to adjust to one another; but children have to adjust to a world controlled, not by their own age group, but by adults, and this adjustment must be made before the child himself lacks the advantage of maturity. Also, if an adult needs help from a social agency, he applies for it; but almost every child is referred to the agency by some adult. These children may resist this adult interest in their welfare although they may be unable to express their feelings in words. They may have to struggle with adults who lack the understanding needed to help them develop.

It has become increasingly apparent that maladjustment in adults is frequently traceable to unhappy childhood experience. Certainly society will gain when our adult population will have had the benefits afforded by a childhood spent in an environment of understanding. Without some basic knowledge of what science has thus far discovered about human beings and the reasons they behave as they do, intelligent planning for children is impossible. The first goal of the child welfare worker should be an understanding of the child and the role he has in his family.

It is impossible to give in a few brief sentences a formula for the child welfare worker to follow for each type of problem. There is no standard prescription for the best method of interpreting one's program to the community. Possession of a certain amount of skill and knowledge does not necessarily enable the worker to solve immediately all the difficult casework situations, or problems of community interpretation and integration assigned to her. Even the best equipped worker, under adequate supervision, cannot hope to be a cure-all for every problem of delinquency, neglect, unhappiness, and maladjustment in children.

There are, however, certain basic conditions that may be considered in all situations.

Most child welfare workers now accept as routine the task of fostering and encouraging the strength that a parent displays when he decides to do something about his child's problem. If the parent wishes to refer his child to a clinic, the worker may do the following: (1) she might try to prepare the child for psychotherapy by discussing with the parent ways in which he might present to the child the plan for coming to the clinic; (2) she might try to maintain the parent's interest in the child's treatment by accepting the ambivalence of the parent's desires, by helping him to decide what he most wants to do about the child's problem, and by discussing with him what the psychiatrist is discovering about the child's problem.

These sessions may lead to a discussion of a parent's own emotional conflicts and may result in the improvement of the parent's own mental health. This, however, is not the main objective. Their principal aim is to help the parent work out a problem in social relationships valuable for the child. Work with the parent and the function of the child welfare worker in that work differ from place to place, depending upon the patient's needs, the psychiatrist's point of view, and the theoretical concept of the child welfare worker's position in the total pattern.

A child welfare worker must know what a request for a placement of the child means to the parent and to the child. She must be able to evaluate the strength and nature of the emotional tie between them. In order to minimize the negative aspects of placement, the parent must be encouraged to participate as much as he is possibly able to. The child welfare worker must also have a recognition of the role that foster parents play in any placement situation. Even though foster parents, by offering their homes, may be meeting some of their own needs, the worker should not overlook the fact that they are primarily meeting the need of the agency. Many of these foster parents have to be helped in their concepts of a "bad" parent and of their own roles as substitute parents. The worker must remember that foster parents are people—not perfect, not always objective—and that they assume great responsibility for very meager returns. A worker's real skill may be shown in the way she keeps triangular relationships of foster parent, child, and parent well balanced.

It is essential that a child welfare worker know that certain types of behavior may be quite normal for a child in various stages of his development. To attain this knowledge, it may be necessary for her to reevaluate some of her own ideas and attitudes on what constitutes acceptable behavior. Feelings of anger, shock, or disgust are then replaced by understanding, and the worker is able to deal with problems in an honest and unaffected manner. She too may have to revise her image of a "bad" parent. A critical feeling toward the parent may prevent her from doing constructive work with either child or parent.

The child welfare worker must feel at ease with children. She must develop skill in interviewing children and in helping the child to reveal himself. Many adults feel self-conscious about being drawn into a behavior web that is normal for a child. They are afraid of "losing face" and, because of this uneasiness, tend instead to push the child into a discussion of his problem. A child, like an adult, has a right to tell his story in his own way, and the worker must let the child assume responsibility for doing this.

A child may try to make the worker a replica of a father or mother person and act out all of his aggressions; or he may try to reduce her to the role of a person younger than himself so he can assume control of the situation. The worker must realize that the child has to have this freedom to project his guilt or hostility, and she must remain calm through the child's struggles, defining the boundaries of action while at the same time helping the child to achieve freedom of feeling.

The child welfare worker will need to remember that casework is a method in itself, but that the the worker makes full use of psychiatric consultation, and thus of psychiatric knowledge and experience. The psychiatrist does not attempt to teach casework therapy. The caseworker has to take psychiatric consultation and translate it into social work concepts and her own method of therapy.

Information about available community facilities and treatment resources will not only aid the worker in evaluating the adequacy of community programs for meeting children's needs, but it will give her insight into that community's personalities and attitudes, which are such a great influence on the course of community action.

A dearth of community resources may leave the worker confused about her areas of responsibility. The need may be so great and the demands upon her services so pressing that she may tend to spread her activities too thin over a broad range of needs. If this situation occurs, she might first determine her principal duties and responsibilities to her agency. Then she should decide what particular areas of the community's child welfare require special services, what specialized knowledge and techniques she has to offer, and how these can be coordinated with existing activities.

In assessing her potentialities for community organization, the child welfare worker may be keenly aware of her limitations. She is not an executive or a director, nor does she control the purse strings; but she can take definite responsibility for promoting the establishment of a planning group to review conditions affecting children, and she can help to clarify the thinking of its members and help them decide what they want for children.

More and more communities are turning to competent child welfare workers for aid in the promotion and advancement of children's well-being. They expect a well trained worker to have an understanding of children and of the ways of handling the difficulties of the child.

It is a field that promises rich interest and gratification, for the child welfare worker is concerned with the substance of life and of living. Opportunity for constructive work is abundant. To enjoy success in the work, those who engage in it must have integrity, stability, and belief in the potentialities for honest endeavor that lie in every individual.

If a child welfare program is to succeed, it must have community understanding and support and whatever legislation is necessary for its smooth functioning. There must be child welfare agencies to give protective services to children in their own homes and under substitute parental care in foster homes and institutions, and to promote high standards of care for all children.

A child welfare worker should go into her job equipped with a background of knowledge on the development of private services and public services, both state and local. She should have acquired sound basic concepts of social casework, as well as the knowledge and special skills needed to perform the functions inherent in a child welfare program.

She will also need to know something of the resources and the pressures of cultural and social patterns of the area in which she is to work, for these will, to a large extent, determine program direction. Much of a child's behavior is conditioned by cultural traditions and beliefs. The worker must know these cultural and social influences if she is to have a sufficient understanding of the individual and his patterns of adjustment. But, although she must understand the group dynamics and their relationship to the individual, she must never lose sight of other influences and thus attribute the blame to "cultural conflicts."

Whether it is the environmental influences that contribute to the child's problem or the emotional attitudes of the parents toward him and the lack of secure affection which he finds in family life, the treatment responsibility rests with the child welfare worker. Social casework embodies the most comprehensive approach to an understanding of the child in his total life situation.

In the treatment of the individual child, the main goal is to determine the needs of the child and try to meet these by improving the child's life situation. This improvement might be modification of the attitudes of adults close to the child, provision of opportunities for satisfying experiences, and perhaps even removal of a child to a new and more favorable environment. The child welfare worker will realize that a child's behavior may be measured in terms of social values and mores which the community understands and accepts. It is therefore important and necessary to understand the significance of any special kinds of environmental influences that might affect the child's behavior and relationships, *before* a worker tries to interpret that behavior and recognize his real needs or problems so that services may be planned to meet them.

Supplementary Readings

Boy Scouts of America. *A Study of Boys Becoming Adolescents*. Boy Scouts of America, New Brunswick, N.J., 1960.

Braithwaite, Edward Ricardo. *Paid Servant*. McGraw-Hill, New York, 1968.

Carroll-Abbing, John Patrick. *But for the Grace of God*. Delacorte Press, New York, 1965.

Gordon, Henrietta L. *Casework Services for Children*. Houghton Mifflin, Boston, 1956.

Jenkins, William A., et al. *These Are Your Children: A Text and Guide on Child Development*. Scott, Foresman, Chicago, 1966. Third edition.

Kadushin, Alfred. *Child Welfare Services*. Macmillan, New York, 1967.

Packman, Jean. *Child Care: Needs and Numbers*. Allen and Unwin, London, 1968.

Price, Arthur Cooper. *A Rorschach Study of the Development of Personality Structure in White and Negro Children in a Southeastern Community*. Clark University, Worcester, Mass., 1962. [Genetic Psychology Monographs, Vol. 65, pp. 3–52]

Pugh, Elisabeth. *Social Work in Child Care*. Routledge & Kegan Paul, London, 1968.

Riis, Jacob August. *Poverty and the Slum in Another Era*. Doubleday, New York, 1968.

Sanders, Wiley Britton, Ed. *Negro Child Welfare in North Carolina*. North Carolina State Board of Charities and Public Welfare, Montclair, N.J., 1968.

United Nations Educational, Scientific, and Cultural Organization. *Toward Mankind's Better Health*. Oceana Publications, Dobbs Ferry, New York, 1963.

Whiting, Beatrice B., Ed. *Six Cultures: Studies of Child Rearing*. Wiley, New York, 1966.

Zietz, Dorothy. *Child Welfare*. Wiley, New York, 1959.

2

The Development of
Child Welfare

In ancient Sparta, the law demanded that any child born deformed must be killed. In Athens, if parents decided they did not wish to raise a child it could be destroyed at birth. A thorough study of codes handed down by religious and fraternal orders of Asia, Europe, and the Near East shows that a philosophy for provision for homeless and neglected children was steadily developed through the centuries. However, it is sufficient for our purpose to center our attention on early English and American practices, since these practices so greatly influenced the development of child care in this country.

EARLY FORMS OF CHILD CARE

The development of various forms of child care in England and the American colonies cannot be outlined in a simple way because a variety of plans of assistance to children developed concurrently.

Statutes Enacted under Elizabeth

It was not until 1601, the forty-third year of Elizabeth's reign, that the earliest known English law providing for the care of children (the famous Elizabethan Act) was devised. This law set a precedent for modern states by defining responsibility for certain classes of children. Under this and subsequent statutes, various provisions were made for the care of children who were homeless, who were grossly mistreated or neglected, or whose parents were destitute.

Among the most important of these was a system of indenture based upon the idea that such children should work. In each parish two to four "substantial householders," plus the church wardens, were to be named by county justices of the peace to be overseers of the poor. These overseers, in dealing with children whose parents (or grandparents) were not able to keep and maintain them, had the duty of binding them out as apprentices to employers for a specified period, usually until they reached the age of 21. During their indenture the employer would pay them "bed, board and required clothing" for their work.

Necessary outlays by the overseers were met by taxes in each county.

In comparison with present-day standards, the varieties of care provided by these early laws were callous and rudimentary; however, the state aid offered was at least a step in the right direction.

To supplement these first tax-supported programs in England and the United States, numerous sorts of private philanthropies developed, some under religious auspices, some supported by fraternal orders or foundations, and others financed by private subscriptions. Thus a complicated body of social institutions, designed to meet the minimum needs of children who lacked families or whose families could not support them, existed long before social work with children came into being.

Indenture

The Elizabethan system of child care was taken to America by the first settlers and was essentially a continuation of English laws. Even though the settlers were venturesome enough to chop out woods, turn sod, and start fresh enterprises in a new country, they remained strong conservatives concerning the laws and social institutions they had carried with them from England. They clung, for instance, to the system of indenture.

The earliest record of colonial notice of a dependent child in America is that of Benjamin Eaton, who in 1636 was indentured for 14 years, by the Governor of Plymouth Colony, to Bridget Fuller, a widow.[1] The child's age at the time of indenture is not given: presumably, since indenture was usually until the age of 21, he was about seven.

Another example of indenture was recorded in the township of Leicester, Massachusetts, in 1747.[2] In this, the selectmen of the township, acting as guardians for a minor child, Moses Love, two years and eight months of age, bound him by an indenture contract to Matthew Scott until the age of 21.

An example of the indenture of a girl is drawn from Virginia records of 1686. The girl, Mary Polly, was "bound out" by her father, Samuel Polly, to work for John Porter for ten years. In return she was to receive food, clothing, lodging, and at the end of her indenture three barrels of corn, one suit of peniston (coarse woven cloth named for the town of Penistone, England), one suit of good serge, one black hood, two "shifts of dowlas" (suits of coarse linen undergarment), and "shoes and hose convenient." John Porter agreed to "use and maintain ye sd Mary no other ways than he doth his own in all things," and Mary was to obey John Porter "in all his lawful commands within ye sd term of years."[3]

These examples illustrate the type of care, if care it can be called, provided by the colonies for homeless, destitute, and neglected children. Early colonists, such as the Puritans and Quakers, regarded idleness as a sin and believed work a necessary part of child training. Since it was considered especially important to teach these children thrift, so that they would not be a financial burden on the town or country, laws were promptly enacted for indenture of child dependents. An example is the New Plymouth Act of 1641. In all colonies dependent children were indentured by local township, city, or county "poor authorities." Laws for indenture are still unrepealed in some states, but are seldom used.

In spite of the grave disadvantages and hazards of pledging the

1. Robert W. Kelso, *History of Public Poor Relief in Massachusetts, 1620–1920.* Boston, Mass., 1922. p. 165.
2. *New England Historical and Genealogical Register.* Boston, Mass., 1880. Vol. XXXIV, p. 311.
3. Philip Alexander Bruce, *Economic History of Virginia in the Seventeenth Century.* New York, 1896. Vol. II, p. 2. Quoted from the *Records of Henrico County 1677–1692*, p. 425, Virginia State Library.

work of a child as pay for his keep and a minimum education, indenture did remove the need for begging on the streets and sleeping under boxes. It provided some sort of private home and must have given, at least to some of the children involved, a feeling of belonging and a certain amount of security in knowing regular food, shelter, and clothing would be provided. It is reasonable to suppose that some of the employers were just and kindly, treating their indentured wards as foster sons or daughters. However, early records of inspections indicate that most indentured children were put to work at as early an age as possible, and worked hard and long to recompense the employer for their keep. Indenture was always in theory a business contract through which the employers expected to receive from the child a full equivalent in work for the expense of his care.

Outdoor Relief

Not all dependent children in the early colonies were indentured. Some "outdoor relief" was given to dependent families. Not infrequently, the care of dependent families or children was awarded at auction under the poor-law method of "public vendue." If there were several bidders, the local poor officials gave the contract to the one offering care at the lowest figure.

Assistance to the poor in their own homes was known as "outdoor relief." Care in almshouses was known as "indoor relief."

Authorization of Almshouse Care

In England, beginning in 1697, a plan for authorizing almshouse care for dependent children developed. In that year an almshouse, called a "workhouse," was built at Bristol, and thereafter almshouses were built in practically every parish. They housed adult derelicts, the aged or diseased, and dependent children who were not indentured.

In the American colonies the first almshouses were built in 1700 at New York, Philadelphia and Boston, and the practice spread as other towns grew in size. Into these almshouses the dependent children were herded with the aged, the feeble-minded, the insane, the depraved, the perverted, and the diseased. Here they suffered from inadequate diet and lack of sanitation, and were deprived of education and all normal experience of family life. Yet for more than a century almshouse care was considered the best and most economical method of care for dependent children, especially when it provided opportunities for work.

In 1824, under the direction of J. V. N. Yates, Secretary of State in New York, a survey was made of the condition of paupers in New York State. Yates' report to the legislature condemned outdoor relief and was enthusiastic about the possibilities of almshouse care. It stated that "the poor when farmed out or sold are frequently treated with barbarity and neglect by their keepers . . . The education and morals of children of paupers (except in almshouses) are almost wholly neglected."[4] The report recommended that every county in New York State be required to maintain a poorhouse and declared that every overseer of the poor had the right to commit "any child under the age of fifteen, who shall be permitted to beg or solicit charity from door to door or in any street or highway—there to be kept and employed and instructed in such useful labor as he or she shall be able to perform." If a child was discharged from the poorhouse at an age when he could make a useful apprentice, he could still be indentured.

There were, however, voices of criticism, and in 1857 a committee of the New York Senate investigated the condition of children in almshouses. They found "at least 1,300 children now inmates of the various poorhouses, exclusive of those in New York and Kings Counties . . . common domestic animals are usually more humanely provided for than the paupers in some of these institutions."[5]

Blows were struck at the almshouse system in 1875 by Charles A. Hoyt, first secretary of the New York State Board of Charities (organized in 1867), and William Pryor Letchworth of Buffalo, a member of the State Board of Charities and a man of wealth who had given up his business to devote himself to social service. After visits to all the almshouses of the state, these two men succeeded in getting a law passed providing that, effective January 1, 1876, "no child over three and under sixteen years of age, of proper intelligence, and suited for family care, shall be committed to any poorhouse of this state, and that all children of this class, shall . . . be removed from such poorhouses."[6]

Dissatisfaction with care of children in almshouses stimulated the development of other state and local public institutions throughout

---

4. *Annual Report of the State Board of Charities of New York, 1900.* Reprint of the "Yates Report of 1824," pp. 951–952.

5. "Report and Other Papers on the Subject of Laws for Relief and Settlement of Poor." *Assembly Journal,* January, 1824. Appendix B, pp. 289–299.

6. For more detailed accounts, see *Select Documents,* University of Chicago Press, Chicago, Ill., 1938. Breckinridge, Sophonisba, *New York Document. No. 8, 1857.* "Public Welfare Administration in the United States." p. 154.

the country, and a number of states granted subsidies to private organizations to care for children removed from almshouses.

Orphan Asylums

One form of care which in the eighteenth century was found superior to the almshouse was the orphanage. These institutions were established by religious groups, charitable societies, and certain public bodies. They were created to meet the needs of large numbers of children who were orphaned by wars and epidemics. Many of these orphans had been the sons and daughters of substantial citizens of the community, and the need of caring for them brought the disgraceful conditions of the almshouses to public attention. Orphanages, as institutions solely for children, at least kept them from being grouped with adults. However, in the first orphanages with their congregate type of care, the individual needs of children were not attended to. Moreover the young were made to devote long hours to work, with little or no time for education or play.

By the end of the eighteenth century four institutions for dependent children had been established in the United States. The first private orphanage was set up in 1727 at the Ursuline Convent in New Orleans and later used as a reufge for orphans after the Natchez Indian Massacre of 1729. In 1738 the Bethesda Orphanage was established in Savannah, Georgia, by George Whitefield, an English clergyman, one of the founders of Methodism. The first separate public institution or orphanage was established in Philadelphia in 1798. These institutions had more to offer in the way of cleanliness and comfort than the mixed almshouse and were a forward step in child care.

The New York City Orphanage, incorporated in 1807, was the first privately run children's institution of any kind to receive a legislative grant. This grant was made in 1811. The precedent it set has dominated the child welfare programs of some states ever since. Public subsidies were at first lump-sum appropriations. Later, subsidies were generally paid on a monthly per capita basis; however, even now, in some states, public funds are granted to private institutions in lump sums.

Somewhat later, fraternal orders began to undertake the care of dependent children. The first institution established for this purpose by a fraternal order was organized by the Masons in California in 1850. The Jewish Orphan Asylum of the Independent Order of B'nai B'rith was founded in New Orleans in 1855.

The number of orphanages supported by public funds was never large. By the beginning of the twentieth century, institutions were supported almost wholly by private funds, and the numbers of private orphanages and institutions were increasing. Even so they could care for relatively few children, and indenture, outdoor relief, and almshouses still existed as methods of care for dependent children. Most orphanages were denominational. Some of the others were for special groups such as infants, and the orphans of Negroes, of soldiers, and of sailors. Following the war between the states there was great interest in the construction of Soldiers' Orphans' Homes.

Among early institutions to provide care for children outside the almshouses were three established to aid the physically and mentally handicapped. They were the Institution for the Deaf, at Hartford, Connecticut, founded in 1817; the Perkins Institution for the Blind in Boston, Massachusetts, 1832; and the Institution of the Feeble Minded in Waverley, Massachusetts, 1848.

In Ohio a law was passed in 1866 permitting counties to establish separate institutions known as county homes. This state eventually acquired 56 such homes. Connecticut and Indiana also established statewide systems of county homes. In a number of other states, public institutions were created in counties or cities, but local care was more often provided by private institutions receiving public funds. In 1874, Michigan opened an institution known as a State Public School, and this plan was followed by several other states.

Notable changes were made in the years between 1930 and 1939 in the soldier's orphans' homes in Ohio, Illinois, and Indiana when the homes made use of social service to aid with intake and various forms of child placing. After the Public Welfare laws went into effect in these states, the Children's Division of the State Public Welfare Departments continued to supervise children who had been placed by the old agencies, but they transferred children as rapidly as practicable to county welfare departments that became equipped to give the necessary service.

Foster Homes

A further development in the move away from almshouses was the initiation of foster home placement. Under this measure, an institution placed a child in a private home for care without the conditions of indenture.

Foster home placement may be said to have begun with the New

York Children's Aid Society, founded by Charles Loring Brace in 1853. This agency specialized in placing children who were deserted, homeless, or in great poverty. It sent them under care of one of its agents to other parts of New York State and to cities in the Middle West, where from a public gathering place they were distributed to farmers or townsmen who might select them. Several years later in 1860, the Henry Watson Children's Aid Society was organized in Baltimore; it operated in similar ways. Other child-placing societies were organized in Boston, Brooklyn, Philadelphia, and Hartford. These societies were for the most part privately financed.

In Massachusetts in 1866, two plans for placing children in private homes and paying for their board in those homes were launched. Under one of these, the State Board of Charities paid board for foster care of children above infant age. Under the other, the Boston Children's Aid Society, a private agency, paid board in foster homes for temporary care of children with behavior problems. The State Board in the same year, and the private agency in 1883, employed a "traveling visitor" to supervise what the aid society called "placed-out children."

Indiana in 1897 set up a state child placing agency using free, wage, and adoptive homes. The Rhode Island State Home for Dependent Children in 1912 began to place children in boarding homes as well as. in free homes. In 1913 state child placing was initiated in Ohio to supplement the work of county children's homes and agencies; the state agency received the guardianship of only those children that could not be provided for by local agencies.

In Illinois, statewide organizations known as "Children's Home Societies" began in 1833, under the leadership of Martin Van Buren Van Arsdale. In 1885 the title was changed to the National Children's Home Society, and the board of this agency began to grant charters to agencies in other states to do child placing in free foster homes. Iowa was the first of the original ten states to receive a charter. By 1916 there were 36 societies in the national organization. They were called State Societies, not because they were publicly financed, but because they had statewide coverage. For many years these agencies received and placed children without acquiring much knowledge of the child or the foster home.

By 1897, when Wisconsin took out a separate charter, a general movement was under way by state societies to break loose from the administrative control of the national society and to regard this organization as a federation of individual state societies through which ideas and services could be exchanged.

SOCIAL ACTION AND THE
WELFARE MOVEMENT

In the course of the nineteenth century, three small but important groups of citizens seriously concerned with problems of welfare in the states attempted, each in a different way, to improve conditions. As a result of their work, modern aspects of social welfare programs and social work education in the United States had their beginnings.

State Boards of Charity

The first group was composed of intelligent and efficient administrators of charity organizations in Massachusetts. They created a central agency for the administration and supervision of all state charitable institutions. The need for such an agency was obvious, because by 1860 the number of institutions for the care of impoverished, dependent, and delinquent individuals had greatly increased within each state, and all of them were under different administrative boards. Each institution followed the policies and procedures designated by its own board for care of inmates, allowable expenditures, and personal standards, and there was no coordination of policies between the different boards.

The first State Board of Charities and Corrections (State Board of Public Welfare) was established in Massachusetts in 1836. This board inspected all state institutions for the care of dependents, delinquents, the poor, and the mentally ill, including orphans' homes and prisons. It set up standards of care, made reports to the state legislature on the kind of care given to inmates, and recommended the amounts of money necessary for the maintenance of each facility.

The advantages of unified administration and supervision of all state charitable institutions were soon recognized by other states. In 1867 New York and Ohio established State Boards of Charities and Corrections. By 1879 16 states had this form of central state charity agency.

The Charity Organization Movement

The second group emerged in New York as the Organized Charity Group, in 1872. In the large cities of several states such groups were organized to supplement the efforts of State Boards of Charities and corrections. The members of the Organized Charity Group were generally wealthy citizens who felt that by giving friendly advice, encouraging the poor in job seeking, or occasionally giving a small loan, they could persuade the poor to become self-supporting, and thus lessen political and industrial unrest. Many members of the Organized Charity Group were dismayed to find that poverty was seldom caused by laziness, mismanagement, drinking or gambling, or other individual faults, as they had believed, but by low wages, scarcity of jobs, poor housing, and unsanitary and unhealthy neighborhoods. Members of the Organized Charity Groups became advocates of social reform and began to press for legislation which would change social conditions. They supported the movement for child labor legislation and the organization of special courts for children and adolescents.

The first Charity Organization Society (COS), modeled on the Charity Organization Society of London, England, was established in Buffalo, New York in 1877. Subsequently, various Organized Charity Groups in the United States were quickly reorganized as Charity Organization Societies.

By then members of these groups had changed their ideas about the causes of poverty and believed it was necessary for those working with the poor to have a deeper understanding of the behavior of individuals and of social and economic problems. In 1897 Mary Richmond, a COS worker in New York City, formulated the first plan for establishing the Training School for Applied Philanthropy, which in 1898 organized the first social work courses. These early courses marked the beginning of a growing recognition that professional education was essential for social workers. In addition to pioneering in the field of social work education, the COS movement fostered and helped to develop the family service agencies of today, the practice of family casework, family counseling, councils of social agencies, employment services, and other programs designed to promote the welfare of children and adults.

The Settlement House Movement

The third group was interested in establishing centers at which people concentrated in impoverished slum areas of the cities could gain some education, participate in leisure and group activities, and receive help with their social and economic problems.

Many workers and their families from various parts of the United States, plus large numbers of immigrants who came to the United

States because they were needed as industrial workers, lived in over-crowded, unsanitary slum areas. There was great need for mutual understanding among these people of many diverse racial and religious backgrounds and different languages.

In an attempt to deal with problems created by this situation, the Neighborhood Guild—now the University Settlement House—was set up on the lower east side of New York City in 1886. In 1889 Hull House was established by Jane Addams on the west side of Chicago on Halsted Street. By 1929 there were 160 settlement houses in the cities of the United States.

Settlement Houses opened day nurseries and kindergartens, playgrounds, and after-school care centers for neighborhood children whose mothers were working. Some of the activities they instituted included clubs for boys and girls, classes in music, dramatics, dancing, and art, and workshops for hobbies of children and adults. Discussion and study groups, legal aid, and recreational facilities were available to all adults of the neighborhood.

Settlement houses, especially Hull House, furnished laboratories for studies of such problems as factory and sweatshop conditions, wages and working hours of women and children, industrial diseases and accidents, the difficulties encountered by immigrants, courts and correctional agencies, prostitution and other community problems. Students of social problems and leaders in social movements worked in Settlement Houses to try to find the causes of the difficulties and the cures.

At present Settlement houses do not have funds to deal adequately with all of the problems that exist in slum neighborhoods. Consequently they must limit their programs to those which best meet the needs of their specific areas. For example, University Settlement House, like a number of others, considers its psychiatric clinic to be among its most important services. Professionally trained group workers develop programs offered by a settlement house. Local people are on the Board of Directors, because their knowledge of the area can help to determine the most useful projects and programs for that special neighborhood. Constant evaluation of programs is necessary to determine whether these programs meet the real needs of a majority of adults, adolescents, and children in the particular neighborhood the settlement house serves.

THE EVOLVING CONCEPT
OF CHILD WELFARE

The development of child welfare efforts in the United States has progressed since Colonial days, though slowly and unevenly. Programs have been altered and extended to meet the changing demands of the times. We no longer indenture or send to the poor house those children whose parents cannot support them; we no longer auction off the care of the needy to the lowest bidder as was done a century ago. Instead we provide public aid to families and dependent children in order to keep children in their homes.

Welfare programs which, a few generations ago, were hardly more than the dreams of a handful of theorists are now an accepted part of our way of life. A number of factors have been responsible for changing concepts of child welfare, and for the progress in welfare legislation to improve child care. But the major reasons for the advancement of the principles and practices in child welfare and their continued progress can be traced to (1) the White House Conferences, (2) the Social Security Act, and (3) organized planning.

THE WHITE HOUSE CONFERENCES

Early in the twentieth century the attention of the whole nation was focused upon the problems of child care in the United States and elsewhere, when a series of national child welfare conferences, called by the President of the United States, were held in Washington, D.C.

The White House Conference of 1909

The first White House Conference, convoked in 1909 by President Theodore Roosevelt, dealt mainly with the problems of the dependent child. Its keynote was that home life is the highest and finest product of civilization, and children should not be deprived of it except for urgent and compelling reasons. Fifteen recommendations were voiced by this conference; some of the more important can be paraphrased as follows:

1. Children should not be taken away from their homes by reason of poverty alone.
2. The causes of dependency should be studied and as far as possible removed or minimized.

3. Foster homes provide the most desirable care for those children removed from their homes.
4. When care for children at an institution is necessary, the cottage plan is recommended.
5. All child-caring agencies should be under state approval and inspection.
6. A children's bureau should be created by the federal government to investigate and report on all phases of child life and welfare.

The first recommendation embraced the belief that private charity was preferable to public relief as the means of keeping children in their homes. However, the recommendation was not unanimous, but was adopted because many feared public funds would tend to be administered in an atmosphere of politics.

A first outgrowth of the White House Conference was the "Mothers' Pension Law" known as the "Funds to Parents Act," adopted by Illinois in 1911. Although the act was based on the principal recommendation that "children should not be taken away from their homes by reason of poverty alone," it did not incorporate the method that had been advocated: assistance through private charity. Instead, this measure was the first state law to provide that the dependent child should be kept in the home by payments out of public funds.

Following the example of Illinois, other states rapidly enacted laws providing for public aid for dependent children in their homes. By 1934 all the states (except Georgia and South Carolina), the District of Columbia, and the territories had enacted legislation of this type. The laws in the different states were known by such varied terms as "widows' pensions," "mothers' pensions" and "mothers' assistance" acts, but they were all founded in the conviction that it was valid use of public money to invest it so that mothers would be able to continue care of their children in their own homes. Eventually this principle was developed into a plan supported by both federal and state funds, and later it was incorporated into the Social Security Act of 1935 as Aid to Dependent Children.

The second and most outstanding result of the first White House Conference was the birth of the United States Children's Bureau. It was the first public agency in the world whose function it was to consider as a whole the conditions, problems, and welfare of children, and to develop a staff and service having nationwide coverage.

Creation of the Children's Bureau was first suggested by Lillian D. Wald, head of the Nurses' Settlement and founder of Henry Street

Settlement in New York City. She broached the idea to President Theodore Roosevelt in 1906. Mrs. Florence Kelly, then secretary of the National Consumers' League, drew up the first statement of the Bureau's proposed work.

The National Child Labor Committee, at the request of the Consumers' League, undertook a campaign for the establishment of the Bureau. Many other influential persons and organizations joined in this campaign. This interest and support led to the introduction of several bills, beginning in 1906. Six years later, the Sixty-second Congress passed one of these measures, sponsored by Senator William E. Borah. The bill was signed by President William Howard Taft on April 9, 1912, and was effective immediately.

The stated reason for establishing the Children's Bureau was "to have a central office where facts of child life may be collected, reviewed, and interpreted to individuals and organized groups, thus making possible intelligent action and reducing needless experimentation."

When Congress passed the measure, it directed the Bureau "to investigate and report . . . upon all matters pertaining to the welfare of children and child life among all classes of our people."

Subsequent Congresses gave the Bureau additional roles—those of administering certain federal laws affecting child welfare. Thus the Bureau administered the first Federal Child Labor Law in 1917–1918, the Federal Maternity and Infancy Act from 1922 to 1929, the child-welfare provisions of the Federal Social Security Act in 1935, and the Act for Emergency and Infant Care in 1943.

On July 16, 1946, the U.S. Children's Bureau (minus its child labor functions, which remained the responsibility of the Department of Labor) was transferred to the Federal Security Agency. When the Agency became the Department of Health, Education and Welfare on April 11, 1953, the Children's Bureau remained in the Social Security Administration section of the Department. In 1963, reorganization of the Department placed it in the Welfare Administration, and in 1967 it was made part of the Department's Social and Rehabilitation Service.

The Children's Bureau continued to administer programs of grants-in-aid to the states for maternal and child health, crippled children, and child welfare services. It carried on an extensive research program and special services for four groups of children: juvenile delinquents, children of migratory workers, mentally retarded children, and children in unprotected adoptions. It also offered technical assistance to public welfare agencies and communities, and cooperated with national, state, and local organizations for the extension of services to children and youth.

The first White House Conference, recognizing that many private agencies existed in the children's field, recommended the creation of an unofficial national organization for the promotion of child care. To this end, the Child Welfare League of America was organized at Baltimore in 1915. In 1928, it was incorporated under the laws of New York State.

There were only 18 persons at the conference that established the League. In June, 1970, the membership was about 385 organizations. These included "children's aid societies," institutions, state, county, and local welfare departments, child protective agencies, day nurseries, and certain other agencies having direct or indirect responsibility for the protection and foster care of dependent and neglected children.

The Child Welafare League is the only voluntary agency whose primary purpose is to protect and promote the welfare of the child. It establishes standards of service for child protection and care in children's agencies and institutions and in community programs. Also, it publishes a monthly journal, *Child Welfare*.

Membership is granted on the basis of standards of care and protection of children and is, therefore, certification of child welfare standards. The membership comprises private Protestant, Catholic, Jewish, and nonsectarian agencies, as well as public children's organizations that are supported by states, counties, and cities.

As a result of the enthusiasm for improving child welfare that had been generated by the first White House Conference, general interest heightened, and as a result some wealthy men established certain philanthropic foundations, such as the Carnegie Foundation, the Julius Rosenwald Fund, the Rockefeller Foundation, the Russell Sage Foundation, and the Commonwealth Fund. These were established for the study and improvement of health, education, social welfare and civic improvement as well as of science, research, and international peace.

The White House Conference of 1919

The second White House Conference was called by President Woodrow Wilson in May, 1919, after World War I. The year 1919 was designated by the President as Children's Year, and he made a special allotment of $150,000 from his War Emergency Fund for the Children's Year activities. Emphasis was placed on a study of standards for child welfare, health and education, and measures to be taken for their improvement. Eight preliminary regional conferences were held, and at the White House Conference guests from England, France, Belgium, Japan, Serbia, and Italy took part in discussion.

As a result of this conference minimum standards were established for the "Protection of Children in Need of Special Care," for "Children Entering Employment," and for "Health of Children and Mothers." Two new notes were added to the principles that had been enunciated at the First conference.

1. Home life cannot be provided except on a basis of adequate family income.
2. Each state needs to give careful consideration at reasonable intervals to its child welfare legislation.

Before this White House Conference only eight states had child hygiene or child welfare divisions. Today every state has one.

The White House Conference of 1930

In November, 1930, the Third White House Conference, entitled "Child Health and Protection" was held in Washington. It was called in 1929 by President Herbert Hoover and was preceded by 16 months of work by approximately 3,000 men and women in the fields of education, medical, and social welfare. The conference, attended by these people, was organized in four sections: Medical Services; Public Health Service and Administration; Education and Training; The Handicapped Child.

The reports presented showed that the standards that had been built up slowly and patiently through the years were becoming expressed in legislation and practice. At the closing session a Children's Charter with 19 points was adopted that stipulated the rights of all children regardless of race, color, location, or situation.

As a result of discussions during and following this conference, those parts of the present Social Security Act concerned with children —Aid to Dependent Children, Crippled Children, Maternal and Child Health, and Child Welfare Services—were written.

The White House Conference of 1940

In accord with the plan of having a White House Conference each decade, President Franklin D. Roosevelt issued a call on April 26, 1939, for the fourth White House Conference, which took place January 18–20, 1940. Frances Perkins, at that time Secretary of Labor, was chairman, and Katharine Lenroot, then Chief of the U.S. Children's Bureau, secretary. A planning committee of 72 persons was chosen, together with small subcommittees. The general subject was "Children in a Democracy." Sections were on the following subjects: Economic Aid to Families; The Family as the Threshold of Democracy; Social Services for Children; Religion and Children in a Democracy; Child Labor and Youth Employment; Health and Medical Care for Children; Children in Minority Groups; Education through the School; Child Development through Play and Recreation.

In every section of this conference, it was recognized that any step taken in a community to coordinate economic and social problems in relation to the whole population necessarily had an effect upon every child in the whole community.

Recommendations of the conference formed a program of action for the welfare of all children. They were concerned with all phases of child life and emphasized in particular the expansion and improvement of activities that already existed for children. In short, they were concerned with legislation, administration, coordination, education, research, and changes in attitude.

The White House Conference of 1950

The midcentury White House Conference on Children and Youth, December 3–7, 1950, was the largest movement in behalf of children in the history of our country. In December, 1946, the National Commission on Children and Youth (a group of 140 individuals widely representative of the nation's interest in children and young people) proposed that a fifth White House Conference be called in 1950. A special committee from its membership was appointed to develop preliminary conference plans. The day following the appointment of this committee, President Truman telegraphed the governors of all states and territories, asking them to appoint White House Conference Committees to work with the National Committee.

By March, 1948, the plans were well under way. Representatives of children's work in 46 states, the District of Columbia, and the four territories met in Washington to develop plans for state and local participation. At the President's suggestion, a Federal Interdepartmental Committee on Children and Youth was formed. This committee represented 37 major agencies, departments, and bureaus of the federal government concerned with children and young people.

The leaders in the planning felt that the greatest contribution this conference could make would be to bring together, systematize, and integrate the knowledge of the behavior of children and young people that had been accumulated in the course of the previous 50 years, and to determine how social institutions and individuals concerned with children were making use of this knowledge. Consequently they examined the work that had been done since 1900 and tried to visualize the major requirements for the half century in order to ensure every child a fair chance to develop the mental, emotional, and spiritual qualities essential to individual happiness and responsible citizenship.

The conference was developed by four advisory councils and four technical and special committees. Every effort was made to achieve the broadest citizen participation possible in addition to professional cooperation. The advice and help of young people was sought by inviting delegates from youth organizations to participate in the planning. Labor union representatives on the committees were especially helpful and through their efforts many thousands of average Americans helped in the development of this conference. Throughout the entire period of preparation, Katharine Lenroot was again secretary of the conference, and a central figure. Melvin Glasser was the executive director.

Five thousand delegates, 400 of them under 21 years of age, attended the three-day conference in Washington, D.C., working together, sharing experience and knowledge, and seeking a common ground on which to build a platform for future action. Two years of preparation, in which more than 100,000 citizens worked in gathering facts, coalescing opinions, and projecting plans for the future, had contributed to the knowledge of these delegates. Housewives, college presidents, high school and college students, farmers, lumbermen, laborers, psychiatrists, teachers, priests, rabbis, ministers, factory workers, and company presidents shared in presenting findings, developing principles, adopting a platform, and making recommendations for their communities to use for a deeper understanding, broader kinship, and opportunity for the maximum development of healthy personalities in all children.

In addition to the 5,000 delegates, 292 international observers from 41 countries were present, so emphasizing the fact that needs of children are universal.

Plans for state and local follow-up conferences were made. It was contemplated that the 1960 White House Conference would present the results of this follow-up.

The White House Conference of 1960

The Golden Anniversary White House Conference on Children and Youth met in Washington, D.C., March 27–April 2, 1960. The purpose of this conference was "to promote opportunities for children and youth to realize their full potential for a creative life of freedom and dignity." The dual theme was "The World Around the Young," and "The Young in the World."

The conference opened and closed with plenary sessions. Each of the 7,000 delegates was assigned to one of approximately 210 work groups. Half of these groups focused their study on nine outward factors influencing the young; the other half studied the inward needs and problems of children and youth. Work groups having closely related topics then met in 18 concurrent forums of about 325 people to hear presentations of facts and issues related to their special subject of study.

At the final plenary session the delegates heard reports on various subjects prepared by elected representatives of each work group reflecting majority and minority opinions. Together, these reports gave a survey of the services and programs that were present—or lacking—in various communities, and thus suggested what immediate action might be called for in many localities.

In large part, the work of the 1960 conference was the result of the continuing activities and local follow-up conferences conducted by citizen groups that participated in the 1950 conference. Ephraim R. Gomberg, attorney, of Philadelphia, was the planning director, assisted by a 92-member committee appointed by the President. Nine members of this committee were young people of high school or college age, selected because of their leadership qualities.

The White House Conference of 1970

Instead of the one traditional Conference, the 1970 Conference on Children and Youth was divided into two meetings. The first, held in Washington, D.C., December 13–18, 1970, was to consider the problems of children (from birth through age 13); the second, held in Estes Park, Colorado, April 18–21, 1971, was on the problems of youths (ages

14 through 24). The general theme for the conference was "Maximizing Human Potentials."

Both conferences were concerned with initiating action rather than merely uncovering facts. Each conference emphasized the need for such measures as health insurance, experimental schools, and the solution of other pressing social needs of children and youth in this country. The children's conference was concerned with the well-being of 55,000,000 children under 14—one-fourth of the population of the nation. It stressed dramatically the urgent need for decent care for the 12,000,000 children whose mothers were working part or full time. In 1970 there were eight times as many working mothers (with children under 18) as there had been 30 years before. The youth conference focused on the need for more enlightened attention and compassionate action in helping to develop the potentials of American youth.

Since both meetings were designed as much for the guidance of private agencies, citizen groups, and professionals, as for government agencies, two-thirds of the $3,000,000 cost was privately financed. More than 4,000 delegates attended the first conference: 915 young people, aged 14–24, and 473 adults. Dr. Joseph H. Douglas was the Staff Director, and Stephen Hess the National Chairman.

THE FEDERAL GOVERNMENT AND PUBLIC WELFARE

After the 1929 stock market crash, the national income dropped from $81,000,000,000 in 1929 to $40,000,000,000 in 1932. The employment index fell from 106 in 1929 to 66 in 1932. Approximately one-fourth of the civilian labor force was unemployed.

Private and public agencies were unable to care for the growing millions of unemployed. Several bills providing federal funds for relief were passed, but vetoed by President Hoover. Finally he signed the Emergency Relief and Construction Act of 1930. It authorized the Reconstruction Finance Corporation[7] to lend a total sum of $3,000,000,000 for relief and public work projects in states, counties, and cities. These loans were to be made on an emergency basis only. Owing to this limitation, projects that could have provided value to a community through the permanent employment of men and women, could not be set up.

---

7. Reconstruction Finance Corporation was a government organization created by the Hoover administration for the purpose of lending money to financial, industrial, and agricultural institutions to help maintain economic stability.

In November, 1932, when Franklin D. Roosevelt was elected president, the depression had reached its lowest depths. Local groups and private social agencies were unable to provide successfully even basic necessities—food, shelter and clothing—for the great volume of unemployed. It was estimated that millions of children were among the groups in need.

The first major legislation passed under President Roosevelt was the Federal Emergency Relief Act of 1933. It presented a new concept: the federal government accepted for the first time responsibility for public welfare. Federal grants were provided to states to help them care for the basic needs of their people.

As plans under this act proceeded, it became evident that relief alone was not enough to take care of the economic insecurity caused by the depression. The solution required a permanent welfare organization with the federal government sharing the expenditures.

On June 29, 1934, President Roosevelt appointed a Committee on Economic Security, consisting of the Secretaries of Treasury, Agriculture and Labor, the Attorney General, and the Administrator of the Federal Emergency Relief Act. Frances Perkins, Secretary of Labor, was chosen Chairman. The primary task of the committee was to prepare legislation that would provide security for the unemployed and the aged. On January 15, 1935, it submitted its report to the President who sent it to Congress under the title Economic Security Bill.

After several amendments, the bill passed on August 14, 1935, and became the Social Security Act, the basic United States federal law in the field of social welfare. At that time approximately 20,000,000 individuals were on relief rolls. Of that number nearly 7,500,000 were children. Not on relief rolls were an additional 300,000 dependent or neglected children, plus some 4,000,000 unemployed youths (16–24), who were roaming the country as destitute tramps.

THE SOCIAL SECURITY ACT

The Social Security Act covered three main programs: (1) Social Insurance, which included the Federal Old Age Insurance system and a federal system of Unemployment Compensation; (2) Public Categorical Assistance, which embraced Old Age Assistance, Aid to the Needy Blind, Aid to Dependent Children, and, by 1950, Aid to the Permanent and Totally Disabled; (3) Health and Welfare Services, which included

Maternal and Child Health, Crippled Children, and Child Welfare Services.[8]

In 1962 the Social Security Act, Title V, part 3 was amended to provide a new definition for child welfare services, and to provide for day care programs, and for an approach that would be more closely coordinated with Family Services. Section 528 gives the new definition of the term "child welfare services" as follows:

> Public social services which supplement or substittute for parental care and supervision for the purpose of (1) preventing or remedying, or assisting in the solution of problems which may result in the neglect, abuse, exploitation, or delinquency of children, (2) protecting and caring for the homeless, dependent, or neglected children, (3) protecting and promoting the welfare of children of working mothers, (4) otherwise protecting and promoting the welfare of children, including the strengthening of their own home where possible, or where needed, the provision of adequate care of children away from their homes in foster family homes or day care or other child-care facilities.

Section 523 provides the following:

> Each State (1) has a plan for child welfare services which has been developed as provided in this part and which (a) provides for coordination between the services provided under such plan and the services provided for dependent children under the State plan approved under Title IV (ADC), with a view to provision of welfare and related services which will best promote the welfare of such children and their families, and (b) provides, with respect to day care services (including the provision of such care provided under the plan) that a satisfactory showing be made that the State is extending the provision of child care services in the State, with priority being given to communities with the greatest need for such services after giving consideration to their relative financial need, and with a view to making available by July 1, 1975, in all political subdivisions of the State, for all children in need thereof, child welfare services provided by the staff, which shall to the extent feasible, be composed of trained child welfare personnel of the State public welfare agency or of the local agency participating in the administration of the plan in the local subdivision.

Two additional programs based on different legal foundations were added later: Vocational Rehabilitation (The Barden-La Follette Act of 1943), and Public Health Services, 1944.

---

8. "Child Welfare Services" was a technical term used to designate preventive and protective activities as distinguished from material aid.

The Social Security Act placed the administration of Maternal and Child Health, Crippled Children, and Child Welfare Services under the U.S. Children's Bureau. Other programs were under a three-member Social Security Board established as an independent agency. The members of the board were appointed by the President of the United States for terms of six years. Not more than two of the members could be of the same political party. In 1939 the Social Security Board was placed under the newly created Federal Security Agency.

In 1946, the Federal Security Agency devised a reorganization plan, under which the Social Security Board was abolished, and replaced by the Social Security Administration, under a single Commissioner for Social Security. The U.S. Children's Bureau was transferred from the Department of Labor to the Federal Security Agency in order to bring the programs administered by the Bureau in closer contact with other programs administered by the Federal Security Agency.

It was decided to keep the Children's Bureau intact within the operating branch of the Security Agency known as Social Security Administration, because it was advantageous to retain a specialized agency charged with the responsibility for promoting all of the interests of children.

In April, 1969 the Office of Child Development was established. The Children's Bureau was transferred to it. At the time of the transfer it was decided that the Children's Bureau would retain many of its former functions, and would have the added work of finding and training foster families to care for children who for some reason needed care away from their own parents. It would also work to increase the availability of adoptive parents for children who were hard to place. In addition it would gather nation-wide information on any circumstances that might adversely affect children, and make it available to the public.

The Office of Child Development had three specific charges: (1) to administer child development programs of high quality; (2) to coordinate federal services for children and to provide leadership to states and localities for the coordination of all services for children; (3) to be an advocate and an innovator of opportunities for children. This office was to have administrative responsibility for the Head Start Program organized in 1965 to increase opportunities for preschool children of the poor by providing an environment in which each child had an opportunity to develop his full potential. Later the Office of Child Development was to become administratively involved in a comprehensive Day Care Program.

As early as 1923, President Harding first tried to have all the federal government's welfare activities gathered together and placed in a department of welfare. Presidents Hoover, Roosevelt, and Truman, in turn, all urged similar action.

Failure to bring this about resulted from inability to reach agreement on these issues: What services should be included in such a department? Should there be one department or separate departments for health, education, and welfare? How should the department be organized internally? Should extensive authority be given the Secretary to organize, regroup services within the department, and appoint and remove bureau heads, or should authority be lodged in the bureaus?

A bill for the creation of a Cabinet department of health, education and security, offered to the Eightieth Congress in 1947, called for a wider coordination of welfare services, including child services, under one administrator. Doubts were immediately expressed: Would the programs already developed by federal agencies be thereby augmented and improved? What policies would be developed to govern the proposed department's activities? Under what conditions would existing agencies be willing to work in an integrated administrative unit?

Supporters, however, were quick to see that the creation of the proposed department would greatly assist the future development of welfare programs including child welfare, since it would help stream-. line the administrative relationship between national and state governments in the welfare field. A Cabinet department, it was declared, could do much to develop and coordinate research, improve the administration of social insurance, insure that grants-in-aid to the states be used (and for the purposes intended), and coordinate the services in child welfare, health, education, and recreation so that they would be available in all areas and to all children.

After 30 years of study, discussion, and agitation about a federal Department of Welfare, a reorganization bill prepared during President Eisenhower's administration, was passed by the Eighty-third Congress, which promoted the Federal Security Agency to departmental level, and gave it cabinet status as the Department of Health, Education and Welfare on April 11, 1953. All functions of the Federal Security Agency were transferred to the Secretary of Health, Education, and Welfare by the reorganization plan. As a secretary of the cabinet, the administrative head would be appointed by the President, subject to confirmation by the Senate. The first Secretary was Mrs. Oveta Culp Hobby.

The Social Security Administration, Public Health Services, the Office of Education, and the Office of Vocational Rehabilitation are important branches of the Department. Old Age, Survivors, and Disability Insurance is the only insurance program administered directly by the Department of Health, Education and Welfare. In all other programs the federal government only approves state plans, establishes rules and standards (based on federal legislation), supervises the operation of the program in states, and shares expenses of operation by grants-in-aid according to statutory provisions.

In order to be eligible for federal funds in Aid to Families with Dependent Children, the state must submit a plan for the use of these funds to the Bureau of Family Services, Social Security Administration, Department of Health, Education and Welfare. When the state's plan is approved, federal funds are authorized for the child welfare program described in the approved plan.

What percentages of costs are paid by federal, state, and local funds varies, but generally the federal government contributes about 57 percent of the total cost, the state, 33 percent, and the local government, 10 percent. In some states local governments do not share in the program costs.

The grants-in-aid formula has been changed several times since the passage of the Social Security Act. Most of the changes tend to increase the amount of federal sharing. This difference in the amount of federal government participation is called variable-grant provision. This provision was adopted to equalize the Aid to Family with Dependent Children payments. These payments were generally lowest in states with below average per capita income, and these states tended to have a higher number of needy children. So the need was greatest in those states that were less able to pay for it.

Amendments to the Social Security Act have eliminated the emphasis on children in rural areas, authorized training and demonstration programs, increased the uniform grant to each state and liberalized the federal formula for apportioning additional funds to states, has encouraged the development of day care services for children whose parents are unable to give them care and protection during the day time, liberalized the payments from Old Age Security and Disability Insurance (OASDI); included provisions not only for financial assistance but for rehabilitation and other services as well.

A Division of Welfare Services was created within the Bureau of Family Services to help the states in their programs of services to children. This division, operating through the nine regional offices of the Bureau of Family Services throughout the United States, offered consultation and guidance, in addition to the general coordination and administrative direction routinely given.

Each state makes a voluntary decision whether or not to operate an AFDC program with federal participation. The state not only administers the program, but it determines whether local governments will share in the financing, and establishes the amount of assistance payments, and the scope and coverage of the program. As a result, of course, administration of the program, eligibility for aid, and the amount of assistance a client receives vary widely from state to state.

The federal government does not insure that children in all states will be treated equally, nor that every child will receive a sum sufficient to provide the minimum necessities of life. Determination of need is left to each state. Need is defined as the gap between the total cost of living essentials set by the state, and the family's income from all sources. To determine the gap, the state establishes a budget, which is the estimated cost of those items it considers essential for human life. If the family's income is less than that budget, the family is eligible for assistance in the amount of the difference between the income and the state budget.

The items and the liberality of a budget vary from state to state. Some states include personal items such as haircuts and toilet articles, and others do not; some include basic supplies such as cough medicine and bandages, while others do not. For example, the computed budgets for New York, Georgia, Minnesota, and California would vary as much as $90 for a monthly grant.

Today public welfare agencies are the largest family service agencies in the United States. They have a strategic role in providing care and social protection for families in our society.

The public agency works within the framework of responsibilities delegated to it by the law or executive order that brought it into being. Its authority is specific, and its field is usually wider than that of the private agency. Because it represents collective action through government, the voters are theoretically the ultimate controlling group, and therefore the community is justified in expressing its interest in public welfare problems and the way they are handled. It is the responsibility of the staff of each public welfare office, state and county, to explain current needs and the methods being used to meet those needs.

Before 1935, a state's problem was how to induce the county boards to provide a public welfare or child welfare unit. Most states provided mandatory laws for its creation but these were of little effect. There was usually no financial assistance from the state. By 1935 nearly all states had laws giving the state some responsibility for the care and protection of children, but in many states such a law had been of little use, because these states lacked personnel to carry out the provisions of the law. In many, the only public state-wide service that was primarily for children was a state institution for delinquent, or, perhaps dependent children. Only 26 states had within their state welfare departments a division responsible for conducting or supervising services for children.

Alabama led the way in developing correlation between the state and county child welfare services. It provided the first grant-in-aid to the counties for the administration of truancy laws. The grant was matched by the county. It enabled the county child welfare commission to provide at least one full-time trained worker for a general child welfare program in 65 out of 67 counties in the state. Only 11 additional states had developed any public services under state leadership.

Once the Social Security Act had been passed, the provision on grants-in-aid to dependent children and child-welfare services required sweeping changes in the state and county relationship. The federal act required the state to participate financially in a statewide program and a state agency had to be given the responsibility for effective administration of the program in the state. Consequently, since 1935, the public social services have undergone reorganization, and the states are now recognizing and assuming their full and proper responsibilities for the welfare of children.

One of the noticeable improvements has been the study and revision of state laws relating to children. Now each of the 50 state jurisdictions has passed laws in which it acknowledges its responsibility for the welfare and protection of children. Every state has a department of public welfare or a separate division or bureau of welfare in some other state department to carry out welfare functions, including those of child welfare.

The stronger state welfare departments operate on the theory that community planning and community organization constitute a basic responsibility of the state agency.

In approximately half the states, county welfare agencies have fairly broad legal responsibilities for services to children who are dependent, neglected, or handicapped. Each of the 50 jurisdictions has a plan which specifies the types of services proposed, the financing of these proposed services, and the methods for implementing them in at least some of the counties or other local subdivisions.

The child welfare laws of the state reflect the concern of the citizens for the welfare of their children who, by virtue of their years, do not have a voice in making their wants known or having their needs met. The laws in themselves create beneficial conditions; they define safeguards for those needing special protection and they give authority for administrative action by a public agency. Money is the key to progress in providing an effective child welfare program on the state level. Without money, the state cannot use its regulatory powers to safeguard the child.

THE INTEGRATION
OF WELFARE SERVICES

During the depression and the recovery years, from 1929 to 1936, many saw public welfare services as aids that were only temporary until the crisis was over. They did not realize that this period was the beginning of a new era in child welfare services. Others suspected that the advance of public services would end the need for private voluntary services. But between these two groups was a large number who saw that welfare services for children were going through a transition that called for an integration of private and public services, with the functions of each clearly defined.

The private agency established by a group of philanthropic, religious, or fraternal volunteers need not be bound by certain rules and regulations that restrict public agencies, so it has greater flexibility. In contrast to the public agency, which is required by law to accept every client who meets the eligibility requirements, private agencies may limit their clientele. Each private agency can determine whether its services will be of maximum effect for a given client, or the applicant himself may decide whether he wishes to use the services.

Private social agencies may be either sectarian or nonsectarian. The former are more numerous, and offer a greater variety of services. The management of both types is vested in an unpaid board of directors, and both may receive support through United Community Funds. Both may also receive contributions from churches, from special bequests or donations, and sometimes from special campaigns. In the United States most of the private sectarian agencies are in one of the following groupings: protestant social work, Catholic social work, and Jewish social work.

The directors of a private agency represent such organizations as a major religious group in the community, labor, influential women's organizations (e.g., the American Association of University Women, Parent-Teacher Associations, the League of Women Voters, the Junior

League), or business and professional organizations. Also, representatives of men's service clubs (such as the Masons, the Elks, the American Legion, and others), of racial groups, of civic clubs, and of schools and recreation departments are often on the boards of private agencies. The many interests represented provide channels through which local child welfare needs and services may be reported and interpreted as a basis for community action.

Private agencies were pioneers in providing social services for children. Their standards in serving children have been improved by the formation of national organizations such as the Child Welfare League of America, the Family Service Association of America, the National Catholic Welfare Conference, the National Conference of Jewish Social Welfare, and other organizations either sectarian or functional in character. These organizations help their member agencies in developing standards of work and personnel, in planning and organization, and in budgeting. This help is given through consultation field service, institutes, workshops, and conferences.

During World War II private agencies began to work more closely with each other and with the government on all levels, forming such amalgamations as the United Service Organizations, the Association of Youth Serving Agencies, and others. This kind of coordination has proved most valuable for the common good.

Sound organization of public and private welfare programs requires not only an integration of functions within the public and private agencies—state and local—but also a coordination of public and private services in order that each community may have the best for its children. Integration means pulling things together, relating the various parts to the whole. If efficiently done by able staffs, such integration will result in a simplified total welfare program for children, with all-inclusive service provisions. Operating on the philosophy which demands that the needs of the whole child be met, we recognize the emphasis upon and the unmistakable trend toward the coordination of all the forces designed to promote the welfare of the child.

ORGANIZED PLANNING AND CHILD WELFARE

The development of child welfare services in the course of the past 50 years indicates a growing realization that there must be planning on a national and an international, as well as on state and local levels.

National Planning

A gradual acceptance of public aid for child welfare purposes, federal legislation, and the growth of various child welfare movements have all resulted in the present vast network of agencies, institutions, and organizations (public and private) that now exist to handle services for children through federal, state, or local funds, or through a combination of these funds.

Goals for programs for youth set forth by many agencies and organizations, have been influenced by the goals adopted by the National Commission on Children in Wartime, 1945. These goals "to realize the full promise of a better and richer democratic life," were the following:

1. to safeguard family life;
2. to extend health services and medical care until they reach all mothers and children;
3. to assure education and employment opportunity and protection to youth;
4. to develop community recreation and leisure-time services for young people;
5. to assure social services to every child whose home conditions or individual difficulties require special attention;
6. to review and revise legislative safeguards and standards relating to children;
7. to enable federal, state, and local governments to share the public responsibility for the health, education, and welfare of children;
8. to train professional personnel and prepare volunteers to render services to children and youth;
9. to provide increased opportunities for youth to share in the planning and development of programs for youth;
10. to educate parents, youth, and all citizens in the importance of providing full security and opportunity for children for the sake of their own happiness and well-being and for the future of the nation.

The National Commission on Children in Wartime was succeeded by the National Commission on Children and Youth, which held its first meeting in December of 1946. The members of the conference felt that they were in complete agreement on goals set in past conferences and decided to devote this conference primarily to plans for attaining these goals. They adopted an eleven-point action program. It urged expansion of the federal-state cooperative program to make child welfare and health services available within ten years to every child. In addition, the action program included these measures: extension of social security; improvement of state laws on adoption, guardianship, illegitimacy, and juvenile delinquency; expansion of mental health programs for children; recreational opportunities; international programs for youth.

Because there exists a wide divergence in the financial resources of the various states, the conference advocated that federal aid in financing child welfare programs be on the basis of need rather than the amount of financial participation by the state.

National planning in the realm of child care has helped to establish some widely held principles. One of these is that the functions of health, education, recreation, and welfare services should be administered by people who are professionally trained in these fields, people who should be capable of giving strong leadership and of developing services.

State Planning

State planning for child welfare must take into account both federal planning, since funds and advisory services can be obtained from the federal government, and community planning, because the local communities are where the children live and where their needs are known. The state is responsible for establishing state-wide standards of child welfare services, for providing leadership in the development of state and local services for children, for helping with funds, when necessary, to establish specialized programs that local units cannot provide, and for supervising both public and private programs of child care.

State planning has been fostered by a number of groups, including child welfare legislative commissions. The first such commission began work in Ohio in 1911. Later other state committees were organized to follow up the recommendations made by the 1930, 1940, 1950, and 1960 White House Conferences on Child Welfare. During World War II, nearly every state delegated the responsibility for state planning to a particular group—a state planning committee, a special committee on the state defense council, or a special state youth commission which included services for children and youth. Regardless of title, such committees have been concerned with the problem of meeting the needs for child welfare. Since 1940, practically all the states have had White House Conference committees or defense council committees.

Community Planning

It is important that state and local planning groups function together. It is through the local body that services are usually administered by the state government; hence the state has a responsibility to assist the local community in the organization of its services.

Most child welfare workers accept the idea that the area to be covered in community planning depends upon the "habits of association of the community under consideration and the governmental units responsible for services for children." The area may be county, city, town, or village and surrounding farms.

The advantages of using the county as the planning area are (1) that the county agencies are usually the channels for programs of the state and federal governments, and (2) that certain functions in regard to children have already been delegated to the county government and county welfare department. In counties containing large cities this use of the county machinery is probably not necessary, because there are usually councils of social agencies or city planning boards that concern themselves actively with child care needs.

International Planning

The United Nations International Children's Emergency Fund (UNICEF) was established in 1946 at the request of the UNRRA Council as a temporary relief measure to carry on child feeding and child welfare services. The United Nations Assembly adopted provisions that UNICEF was to operate for the benefit and rehabilitation of children and adolescents in war-devastated countries, and in countries which had received UNRRA help, and for child health purposes wherever they were needed, without discrimination because of race, creed, nationality status, or political belief.

The funds provided by UNICEF are matched in each country by a government or voluntary agency, which provides native food supplies, transportation, and a staff that distributes UNICEF supplies.

At the end of World War II, UNICEF provided mass feeding

programs, and antituberculosis vaccination for approximately 40,000,-000 children in the Near East, Asia, Africa, Europe, Latin America, and the Philippines. Where needed, these programs are still going on.

UNICEF also assisted in establishing the International Children's Center in Paris which provides training and research in maternal and child health for doctors, nurses, and social workers. In Calcutta, UNICEF supports postgraduate training for doctors and nurses at the All India Institute for Health and Public Hygiene.

In October, 1953, the United Nations decided that UNICEF should continue as a permanent international child welfare organization within the framework of the United Nations. UNICEF is now called the United Nations Children's Fund.

Supplementary Readings

Abbott, Edith. *Some American Pioneers in Social Welfare*. University of Chicago Press, Chicago, 1937.

Abbott, Grace. *The Child and the State*. University of Chicago Press, Chicago, 1938, 2 volumes.

Aries, Philippe. *Centuries of Childhood*. Knopf, New York, 1962.

Bernert, Eleanor H. *America's Children*. Wiley, New York, 1958.

Brenner, Robert. *American Philanthropy*. University of Chicago Press, Chicago, 1960.

Close, Kathryn. "Selected Priorities at the White House Conference on Children." *Children*. March–April, 1971. Vol. 18, No. 2.

Cohen, Nathan E. *Social Work and Social Problems*. National Association of Social Workers, New York, 1965.

Coles, Robert. *Uprooted Children*. University of Pittsburg Press, Pittsburg, 1970.

Friedlander, Walter A. *Introduction to Social Welfare*. Prentice-Hall, Englewood Cliffs, New Jersey, 1968.

Ginsberg, E. *The Nation's Children*. Columbia University Press, New York, 1960.

Harrington, Michael. *The Other America*. Penguin Books, Baltimore, 1962.

Kadushin, Alfred. *Child Welfare Services*. Macmillan, New York, 1967.

Kelso, Robert W. *History of Public Poor Relief in Massachusetts, 1620–1920*. Houghton Mifflin, Boston, 1922.

Mondale, Walter F. "Justice for Children." *Congressional Record*. December 9, 1970. Vol. 116, No. 197.

Schorr, Alvin L. *Poor Kids*. Basic Books, New York, 1966.

Steiner, Gilbert Y. *Social Insecurity: The Politics of Welfare*. Rand McNally, Chicago, 1966.

Thurston, Henry W. *The Dependent Child*. Columbia University Press, New York, 1930.

Wilensky, Harold L., and Lebeaux, Charles N. *Industrial Society and Social Welfare*. The Free Press, New York, 1965.

Zigler, Edward F. "A National Priority, Raising the Quality of Children's Lives." *Children*. September–October, 1970. Vol. 17, No. 5.

[*Courtesy Office of Child Development, U.S. Department of Health, Education, and Welfare.*]

3

Children in Their Own Homes

An ideal home for children provides physical, moral, and social advantages. Love, emotional security and the opportunity for mental and social growth should also be present.

However, many homes, whether they be rich or poor, in one way or another fail to provide or approximate the ideal social and psychological conditions for children who are developing. If the failures of the home are outstanding, the community may intervene on behalf of the child. If the home conditions are serious enough, the child may be removed from the home. Separation of a child from his home, parents, siblings, playmates, and community is a very serious course of action for all individuals involved. It is not a step to be taken lightly. In any case, it should only be the last alternative, after all plans to keep a child in his home have proved to be unfeasible.

In the past, children were readily removed from their homes not only for reasons of neglect or delinquency but because of poverty alone. Modern child welfare workers now follow the principle of being home builders rather than home wreckers, and consider it a serious matter to remove a child from his home for any reason.

Along with the developing principles of child welfare, various services have been established over the years to help keep children in their own homes and to promote their general welfare within their family. Among these services are family counseling, financial aids, day care services, the use of the homemaker as an aide to the mother, and other resources for the promotion of the welfare of children.

Even for the best of parents, there are times when the role as mother or father becomes irksome. At times they experience ambivalent feelings toward their children; they have acceptance feelings tinged with mild hate. The implications of these feelings depend on their intensity. An extreme degree causes inconsistencies in child rearing practices that generally lead to confusion for many children. In such surroundings, the child cannot predict with any certainty how he will be treated by his parents at any particular time.

In some homes, the parents make no attempt to cover their indifferences or hostility to their children. This kind of rejection causes many children to be emotionally insecure in their own homes. There is also some indication that the withdrawal of parental love increases aggressive behavior in children.

At the other extreme, there are also homes in which one or both spouses are overprotective of a child. These parents tend to gratify every desire of the child and thus keep the child dependent upon them. The child may not be given an opportunity to compete with other children or to develop any self-direction or initiative. Such children are not being trained adequately to assume mature roles in society.

The effect of parental attitudes on children is highly significant to the outcome of any treatment plans that may be evolved for the treatment of behavior problem children. Family counselors have learned that beneficial results are not likely to occur if parents refuse to cooperate in a treatment plan that requires them to alter their attitudes toward their problem child.

Discipline is one of the family problems faced by many parents, and more often than not it leads to serious difficulties with the rearing of children. In the attempt to enforce complete obedience from their children in every detail many dominating parents may dictate not only the choice of friends, but also clothes, types of amusements, and life's calling. Child welfare workers do not advocate that parental controls should be removed, but rather that they be practiced with a sense of balance aimed at developing mature and self-directing individuals. Obedience should be to a principle and not to a person. Difficulties in this and other areas may lead a family to seek out professional help in a child welfare or a family counseling agency.

FAMILY COUNSELING

The main purpose of family counseling or family social work is to promote satisfying social relationships for members of a family who may be experiencing difficulties in adjusting to various individuals in their family.

Although families may be faced with many problems deriving from various outside sources, most family difficulties are problems emanating from within the family itself and its internal social system.

Family relationships consist of a web of social relationships that exist between spouses, siblings, father and children, mother and offspring, and between other persons who may be considered members of the family group. Members of a family also have tangential social relationships with persons outside of their immediate family or with persons belonging to other social systems.

When working with a family that is having problems, the counselor must first determine the type of problem the family is seeking to resolve. Does it fall into the realm of family counseling? If not, what is the appropriate agency to send the applicant to?

If it is decided that the problem is appropriate for the family agency, it is then necessary for the counselor to determine the acceptability of the client. Is the client likely to cooperate with the agency and its study, diagnosis, and plan of treatment? Will the client attempt to dominate the agency and direct the counselor? Will the client assume responsibilities and participate in the agency's plan of treatment? The counselor has to answer these and other questions within quite a short period of time before accepting a client for treatment. For example, the client's request for assistance may represent a positive attitude to maintain his family, or it may be only an effort to seek sympathy amidst a disintegrating family. Some clients are better socially and psychologically oriented than others and need only a minimum of counseling. Others have more serious problems in their familial relationships and attitudes that require intensive and prolonged casework.

In family counseling, many types of problems are handled. Counselors may deal with marital difficulties in which one or both partners in a family need help in deciding whether they should separate or try to strengthen their family relationships. Other cases may present problems stemming from the presence in the family of grandparents, parents, or an ill relative who need institutionalization. Many types of problems center on children in their own homes. At times some parents need help in understanding how to cope with their children who are experiencing unsatisfying social relationships within the family. There are also cases of parental neglect with resulting destructive behavior on the part of the child. The family counselor must exercise great skill in dealing with such cases as it can be difficult to convince parents that their behavior and attitudes are related to their child's negative behavior.

The realities that cause family problems are of course relevant to each case. In a given family a child's problem, as we have seen, may be directly influenced by his parents' attitudes toward him. In some cases, a counselor must recognize that although a parent may appear to be overwhelmed by the problem presented by his child, he or she may want at the same time to separate himself from the child.

When a member of a family comes to a counselor for help with a familial problem, he will be given every opportunity to express his opinions on the genesis of the problem and how he feels it should be solved or treated. The relationships between parents and the problem child are studied, as are those between other members of the family. The counselor has to assess the reality of the interpretation of the problem as presented by the parents. In addition, the counselor tries to discern the true parental feelings and attitudes, which may be covert or overt, toward the child, and also the feelings of the child toward his parents. After conducting several interviews and evaluating them, the counselor may be in a good position to make a tentative diagnosis of the parents' ability and desire to participate in the solution of the child's problem.

A particular problem may require a client to face realistically the psychological and social conditions in the family that are causing, or contributing to, their child's problem. A counselor's success with a child's problem often encourages a mother to ask for help with other problems that have been bothering her or other members of the family.

It has been found that many parents find it difficult to admit that their child has problems that may be related to an insecure home life. This is very often true if the family faces problems of unemployment, illness, or limited income. Most clients are reluctant to discuss unhappy family situations with a counselor until a fair amount of rapport has been established between them. Some of the elements of rapport are trust, confidence, interest, and empathy between the counselor and the client. The client must be given time not only to establish rapport but to gain awareness of his problem and reassurance from his counselor before he can participate in the treatment process or feel secure in discussing what he considers to be delicate family matters.

The methods used by the counselor in solving familial problems include assessing the problem and selecting the appropriate treatment procedures in cooperation with the client. The duration of the counselor-client professional relationship varies according to the complexity of the problem involved. The relationship may be of a short duration or extend for a period of at least one year. Cases of long duration are generally limited to families having children with serious behavioral or interpersonal relationship problems. A child's ego and the nature of his problem affect not only the duration of the professional relationship, but also the kind of help parents may need in solving their familial difficulties.

With the use of the study, diagnosis, and treatment process the counselor attempts to isolate the causal factors that are contributing to the problem a child is having in his family. He examines the relationships within the family in an attempt to isolate possible sources of problem conflict. He holds repeated interviews with the various members of the family who are found to be involved in the problem. By counseling, the counselor can bring about attitudinal change and social adjustment, thus solving or adjusting many of the problems facing a family. Sometimes counseling is not enough, and, depending on the complexity of the problem, several services may be employed as casework aids. For example, financial assistance, either short-term or long-term, may be used to enable a family to readjust economically after experiencing a stress situation. Another casework resource may be the introduction of a homemaker into the family to assist an ailing mother or father: if illness or some other problem takes the mother temporarily out of the home, a homemaker is assigned to the family to keep it intact. Others include various types of medical care, referral to a child guidance clinic, vocational or educational guidance, and recreational planning.

In counseling, the setting of the process or interview traditionally has been in the office of the counselor. Occasionally a home visit may be made in order to gain additional insight into the case. If more than one member of the family is involved, it may be necessary at times to counsel them separately.

In recent years, family counseling agencies have been using a "group approach," in which interviews are conducted with various combinations of members of a client's family. Individual office interviews are still conducted from time to time, but the home is used more frequently as the setting for group counseling.

One of the advantages of interviewing families as a group is that the counselor is able to observe the type of social interaction taking place among its members in a real social situation. In addition, through his attentive observations, he may gain insights into the real roles individual members have in the family and the status that is ascribed to them by the group. Also, basic problems are more apt to appear more quickly in family group interaction than in single interviews.

A variation of family group counseling is found in a type of inter-family group therapy in which clients from different families are brought together to discuss their problems under the guidance of a counselor. In such a group situation, many individuals gain insights into treatment plans for their own difficulties by participating and listening to others analyze and offer possible solutions to problems.

Family counseling agencies also treat couples having difficulties in their relationships as husband and wife. These problems like family problems have to be studied in all their ramifications with much care, sensitivity and objectivity. As in all social casework, the counselor makes a diagnosis and devises plans after careful study and repeated interviews. This process requires the close cooperation of the couple and the counselor.

Emotional problems on the part of one or both partners, role change within the family, or the impinging of outside problems that produce unrest or unhappiness within the family may encourage couples to seek out a family or a marriage counselor for help. Some types of problems occur more frequently in the early years of marriage, and others appear as the family grows and its members go through the life cycle. Examples of life cycle crises are the birth of children, the rearing of the children, the marriage of the children, the unemployment or retirement of the head of the household, and sickness or death in the family. All these crises are stress situations for most families. If families are unable to cope with these changes and problems alone, they may seek the aid of a family counselor.

The family counselor attempts to give each partner some insight and understanding of the attitudes and behavior that lead to disharmony in family and marriage relationships. One or both spouses may have emotional problems that are basic to most of their difficulties. Both partners have to recognize basic problems as well as the use they both make of them in their marriage relationships. The degree to which these problems and the defenses that have been built around them are used by a client have to be assessed by the counselor and incorporated in the formulation of any treatment plan. Defenses can be rigidly structured within the individual client.

FINANCIAL AIDS FOR THE CHILD
IN HIS OWN HOME

Many think of child welfare work as the processes that are employed when a child lacks a home of his own. But these are only part of it: child welfare work, in the broadest sense, should operate primarily in the home. We must be increasingly concerned with problems of those millions of children who are living with their own families under conditions thwarting their health, educational, and emotional development. When the home fails, becomes inadequate, or breaks down, the child becomes a casualty. Economic and social hazards which threaten family security are matters of very real concern to all who are interested in a child welfare program.

An important consideration in safeguarding family life is the financial aspect. When we emphasize the maintenance of the family way of life for children we also emphasize the fact that family life is dependent upon stable employment and adequate income to provide ideals of clean, decent, orderly living.

If circumstances—such as illness, unemployment, accidents, death, childbirth and other crises that cause some or all members of the family to suffer either temporary or permanent injury or impairment—disrupt or break the usual course of family life, it is essential that the human needs of the people in the family continue to be met. The family will be broken or weakened unless aided to meet these difficulties.

When parents are assured the essentials of life—food, clothing, shelter—we can expect them to be better able to supply the necessary emotional and psychological values of wholesome family life.

This need for family security does not change, no matter how the world may change. But as the world changes, there are changes, too, in the ways in which family security is maintained.

In the early days of this country's settlement, pioneer families supplied most of their material needs directly by the produce of their own hands. Today our economy is too complex for that. We tend to specialize and look to others to create most of what we use. All of us are dependent on money both for daily necessities and for future security in the form of savings; but, too often, forces beyond our control make it impossible to earn enough money to supply immediate needs, much less to save anything for a rainy day.

Most men, moreover, now work away from their homes, and they are joined in this by a large segment of the women, including wives and mothers. This makes it more difficult for families to give their children adequate care and limits the opportunities for development of a feeling of family solidarity.

For many years the majority of American people seemed to get along quite well without giving much thought to the enormous changes taking place about us in our very homes and in our own ways of living. To be sure, many suffered from want and poverty even in good times; but the country was expanding, work was fairly plentiful, and opportunity—or so we thought—was any man's for the taking. Our "security" was not very well planned, or even very secure, but as long as times were not too bad we did nothing about setting up a more systematic plan of protection.

When the depression of 1929 came, we reaped the bitter harvest of this short-sightedness. People everywhere began to realize that some of the existing conditions, which were bringing suffering to tens of millions and fear to all, were not a sudden development but the result of the far-reaching changes that we had ignored. When the American people as a whole awakened to the fact that these conditions were likely to continue even after the emergency was met, we decided that something had to be done. We began to demand that the federal government cooperate with its states and communities in setting up permanent safeguards against some of the most widespread hazards of present-day life.

If we are to protect all the children of the world, it is necessary to insure every family that these basic essentials will be met in order that economic conditions will not thwart the maintenance of a child in his own home. The Social Security Act is a step in this direction. The Social Security Act was passed by Congress in 1935 and became effective early in 1936. All of the measures included in this act have a tremendous effect upon the security of family life and, therefore, are in their broad aspects, child welfare measures.

The Social Security Act of 1935, and its subsequent amendments, made provisions through Title V, Part 3, for annual federal appropriations allotted to the states through the Children's Bureau for the purpose of "establishing, extending, and strengthening, especially in predominately rural areas and areas of special need, public welfare services . . . for the protection and care of homeless, dependent, and neglected children, and children in danger of becoming delinquent. . . . The amount so allotted shall be expended for payment of part of the cost of child welfare services . . . and for developing State services for the encouragement and assistance of adequate methods of community child welfare organization in areas predominantly rural and other areas of special need . . ."

The original appropriation of $1,500,000 was increased in 1939 to $1,510,000 when Puerto Rico was added to the areas formerly included; in 1946 it was increased to $3,500,000; and in 1950 to $10,000,000. For 1962–1963, Congress authorized an appropriation of $30,000,000 to be increased by $5,000,000 each succeeding year. Programs exist in the 50 states, the District of Columbia, Puerto Rico, and the Virgin Islands. Each state and territory receives a flat amount of $40,000 and shares the balance according to the proportion of its rural population under 18 years of age to the total rural population of the United States under that age.

In other places the act provides for aid to dependent chilldren in their own homes so that greatly increased numbers of children can be cared for by their own kin. By authorizing unemployment insurance to protect the family from starvation during periods of unemployment, it provides an additional element of security and stability for children. In addition, by means of a system of aid for the aged, it relieves many parents of the burden of support of their own parents and thus puts them in a position to provide more adequately for their own children.

It is important to recognize that all of the act's provisions relating to children are in complete harmony with the most important pronouncement of the first White House Conference in 1909, which declared home life to be the "the highest and finest product of civilization" and the conservation of the child's own home to be "the chief aim of child welfare work."

Aid to Dependent Children

Aid to Dependent Children, later known as Aid to Families with Dependent Children, one of the three original categories of public assistance, was established under Title IV of the Social Security Act.

A dependent child is defined as "a needy child under the age of sixteen, or under the age of eighteen, if found by the state agency to be regularly attending school, who has been deprived of parental support or care, by reason of the death, continued absence from the home, or physical or mental incapacity of a parent, and who is living with his father, mother, grandmother, grandfather, brother, sister, stepfather, stepmother, stepbrother, stepsister, uncle, or aunt, in a place of residence maintained by one or more of such relatives as their own home."

In order to get federal Aid to Families with Dependent Children, each state is required to set up a plan, approved by the Social Security Administration, Bureau of Family Services, for the administration of that aid.

The plan must provide for proper methods of operation, including merit systems for all personnel administering it, and for suitable reports by the state agency to the Social Security Administration. The plan must be put into operation in all subdivisions of the state. Most of the states require that a dependent child must have lived in the state for a certain length of time, usually for a year, in order to get this assistance. If the child is less than a year old, his mother may be required to have lived in the state during the year before the birth. No child can be refused aid because he has not lived long enough in a particular town or county. Income and resources available for the care of the child must be taken into account in determining need; there must be provision for fair hearings by the state agency and for the protection of information on applicants for aid.

The physical and social development of children is deeply embedded within the family group, and their needs can hardly be considered apart from the needs of the family as a whole. Therefore, since most of the families need assistance beyond the individual needs of the child, agencies have begun to consider the needs of the child in the context of the family unit.

The amendment authorizing federal participation in assistance to the mother or other person caring for the child has greatly strengthened the financing of the program. Before 1950 the federal government shared only in payments for the children. Since 1950 the average payment has been substantially increased. It is now recognized that the relative who cares for the child may also have needs, and that, if there is no provision for these, the assistance given to the children must meet them. As a result, the proportion of federal financial participation in Aid to Families with Dependent Children is as large as it is for other types of aid to children.

The granting of aid to dependent children immediately brought forth the old arguments quite usually heard when public funds for aid are to be distributed. At such times there are efforts to establish some general standards that will assure the communities that the money is going to the "right" places. So when Aid to Dependent Children programs were launched, it was often asked whether a child's home was a "suitable" or "proper" place and whether his parents or guardians were "fit" or "proper" people. What a family may mean to a child, and the ability of each parent to care for his child, is a very individual matter, and because of this factor of individuality the terms "suitable" and "proper" are still undefined.

Fortunately, just as the needs of the entire family have been recognized, the standards that were set for homes have also been liberalized. In many homes, "suitability" will become a fact only after economic aid is granted. The physical environs, such as crowded conditions, which are unavoidable for many welfare recipients, have receded in importance as deterrents to aid and are being replaced by an emphasis on what the aid can bring to the child.

The criteria determining "fitness of the parent" have been disadvantageous in large part to the unmarried parent. Mothers' Aid laws in many states did not grant aid to unmarried parents. Because of this precedent and the prevailing hostility in many communities, unmarried parents did not at first benefit from aid programs to dependent children. The ideal situation proposed by many is that aid should be granted to eligible applicants as a right, and be considered for the mother's welfare and that of the child.

Community pressure has often caused a mother to give up her child because assistance has been refused. When a mother decides to keep her child regardless of censure, the economic problems which may ensue are often as detrimental as separation of the child from its mother. Rulings on the use of Aid to Dependent Children funds for children born out wedlock vary from state to state and even among the counties within a state. The Aid to Families with Dependent Children program has had a pronounced influence on the relaxing of formerly rigid rulings. In communities in which general assistance would not be granted, AFDC is now the one means of assisting the parents; in others, general assistance is granted in supplementation of AFDC. As more and more communities are accepting the idea of concentrating on what is good for the children and on how their needs will be best satisfied, denial of aid because of "fitness of the parent" is becoming infrequent.

The problem is complicated if the unmarried parents have more than one illegitimate child. Granting of aid in these cases brings up discussion of whether aid to such families only encourages their unapproved conduct. Here, again, the surest way of determining a course of action is maintaining that the child has rights and needs and that the causal basis for deprivation of care and support is not the most significant factor in an individual case. With this philosophy, the worker may help in solving some of the problems within the family and can assure the community that funds are going where they are most needed.

Overlapping this problem are the difficulties that arise because of the racial barriers that result from the economic discrepancies in some communities. It is unfortunate that the states in which the black people, for example, are most in need of assistance are low-per-capita-income states and have therefore, of necessity, set their maximum grants to families with dependent children below that of maximum federal participation in matching what money the state gives to the family.

The states differ widely in the proportion of their child populations receiving assistance from Aid to Families with Dependent Children. Various states make different definitions of what constitutes "incapacity" on the part of a parent; these differences depend on the inclusion in individual state plans of provisions relating to "suitability" of the home, the differences in standards of assistance, prevalence of need, and the protection afforded by the Old Age, Survivors, and Disability Insurance program and other programs benefiting children whose fathers have died.

More than half of all cases accepted for AFDC are due to the continued absence of the parent from the home. Continued absence may be for a wide variety of reasons, among them divorce, desertion, or separation. Before any aid is granted, most agencies wish definitely to establish evidence of absence.

The economic aid programs for dependent children have changed markedly in recent years, in that coverage has increased. When the Social Security Act originally became law, the state Mothers' Aid programs were assisting only small numbers of children, primarily fatherless children. Relatively few children received aid under the old state system if they were deprived of support by the incapacity or absence of parents; furthermore, at that time, social insurance benefits for survivor children were not then available and did not become available until 1940.

Old Age, Survivors, and Disability Insurance benefits as well as veterans' pensions are aiding an increasing number of children whose fathers are dead. The number of survivor children receiving OASDI benefits outnumbers the number of AFDC fatherless children in substantially all states administering state-federal programs.

A provision of the Social Security Act that became effective July 1, 1952 requires a state agency, as a condition to receiving federal funds, to report promptly to the law enforcement authority (usually the district attorney) all cases of children who have been abandoned by a parent. The purpose of this regulation is to facilitate legal action against the father who has deserted the family in order to force him to assume the financial responsibility for support of his child. Most agencies hope the district attorney will use the services of a qualified social worker to attempt to find the missing parent and enlist that worker's assistance for the family. Many mothers feel that legal action may prevent reconciliation and cause a father to seek divorce.

Desertion, or abandonment, is defined differently in various state constitutions, but it presents a difficult problem to assistance agencies. Individual states have, with varying degrees of effectiveness, tried to cope with it. Some have enacted laws that make prosecution a requirement and others have adopted provisions not unlike the one in the Social Security Act.

The primary purpose of AFDC is to strengthen the normal family relationships and so preserve real assurance for the child. However, financial security alone does not offer a complete solution to many of the problems of these children. The problems of anxiety, experience of desertion, death, continued absence of the parent from home, the physical or mental incapacity of a parent, or other conditions which make these children eligible for AFDC add to the usual anxieties of childhood and adolescence.

If a child lives in a home in which a shifting of normal family roles has occurred as a result of the father's desertion, imprisonment, or prolonged hospitalization, he is deprived of the opportunity of the satisfying family relationships necessary to physical, mental, and spiritual well-being. Furthermore, this child may have to face a community attitude of censure or pity resulting from his family situation.

A skilled family or children's worker sees AFDC as one of the most valuable resources extended to keep children in family homes. She also knows that the needs of children encompass many factors besides food and shelter. She realizes that such needs cannot be properly met without recognition of the needs of other members of the family. Placement in a foster home should not be made without taking into account the factors that would enter into any placement of a child.

Unemployment Insurance

Unemployment insurance, otherwise known as unemployment compensation, is designed to provide an income for workers and their families when, through no fault of their own, they have lost their jobs or have been laid off. Unemployment insurance is intended to be a means of support between jobs, thus protecting a family from want. Although unemployment insurance does not generally cover employees in small firms, more and more states have extended coverage to small firms having only one or more employees. It has excluded public employees, domestic servants, agricultural laborers, people serving nonprofit organizations and institutions, and certain other employees. Nevertheless, the system covers about four-fifths of all wage and salary workers, including federal government employees and former servicemen.

Unemployment insurance is a state program, with the federal government paying the costs of administration and setting up certain basic requirements to be incorporated in the state laws. Every state has its own law and benefits are paid out of a special fund set up under that law. To create this fund the Social Security Act levied everywhere a 3 percent tax on the payroll of employers. In most states the tax is paid by employers only. Alabama requires contributions from employees also, and Rhode Island, California, New Jersey, and New York require contributions from employees for special temporary disability insurance benefits. The law of each state specifies who may receive benefits and how workers may qualify.

The amount of weekly benefit payments that a worker may receive also varies from state to state. In theory it is approximately half the employee's full-time weekly pay, except that there is a top and a bottom limit. If we include the dependents' allowances that are provided in eleven states, the maximum amount ranges from $36 to $70 weekly; it is $50 or more in fourteen states. Many state laws establish a maximum amount which may be paid to a person during a given year.

The length of time a worker may receive benefits also is fixed by the different states. It ranges from 10 to 26 weeks. Most states require a one-week waiting period.

In any part of the country, an unemployed worker can learn at the nearest local state employment service office how to file his claim for benefits. Claims may be filed in any state, regardless of where the worker was previously employed.

In addition to registering in a state employment office, an unemployed worker, to be eligible for unemployment benefits, must have accrued a number of wage credits on jobs acceptable to state law in order to establish his unemployment status. Another requirement for benefits is that the applicant is able and willing to accept a suitable position when offered.

All states deny claims if an applicant left his original job without good cause or was fired because of misconduct. If an applicant refuses suitable work that complies with prevailing standards of working conditions, wages, and union standards, this refusal is considered grounds for denying or disqualifying a claim.

Workers who leave the state in which they previously worked are allowed to file claims for unemployment benefits in any other state, the District of Columbia, Canada, or Puerto Rico. However, the first claim for an ex-serviceman's unemployment compensation cannot be filed in Canada.

Old Age, Survivors, and Disability Insurance

The Old Age, Survivors, and Disability Insurance system in the United States is the only program of social benefits under the Social Security Act to be operated entirely by the federal government. It is the basic program in this country for providing income to covered workers and their families when they retire, die, or become permanently disabled.

Approximately 90 percent of all employed workers as well as all persons in the armed forces are covered by OASDI. Federal government employees, who have their own system, irregularly employed farm and domestic workers, physicians in solitary practice, and others, are the major groups of workers not covered by this insurance. To be eligible for benefits a worker must have worked not only in covered employment but for a specific period of time. Workers in their youth may acquire survivors protection for their dependents after six quarters of covered employment. In general, most workers need ten years of covered employment to qualify for old age benefits. To be eligible for disability benefits a worker must have had covered employment five years out of the last ten before being disabled.

Retired workers may apply for old age benefits at the age of 65 or for reduced benefits beginning at the age of 62. A retired worker's spouse is eligible for family benefits when she reaches the age of 62, as are dependent children under the age of 18.

Benefits for a disabled worker are payable after a waiting period of six months. Workers must be so disabled that they are unable to engage in any gainful activity. The disability must also be judged permanent or of indefinite duration.

When an insured worker dies, reaches retirement age, or becomes disabled, his children are entitled to benefits on his Social Security account if they are under 18, unmarried, and dependent on the parent. However, a disabled child over 18, whose disability was incurred prior to his eighteenth birthday, is also entitled to benefits. Legally adopted children as well as illegitimate children are entitled to Social Security benefits if the father was supporting them or had a legal obligation to do so.

A Social Security amendment passed by Congress in 1965 provided that benefit payments could be extended from the age of 18 to 22 for those children who remained in school as full-time students. However, no benefits are paid to the mother of the child if the only child at home is beyond 18 years of age. A dependent child not in school ceases to become eligible for benefits when he reaches 18, as does a child of any age who marries. A disabled child over 18, drawing benefits because of a disability incurred before 18, will face discontinuation of benefits if he refuses to accept vocational rehabilitation service.

If a child's mother is divorced from the insured worker, a child's rights to benefits from the father are not affected. If the mother remarries, the child is still entitled to benefits from his biological father's account.

Children's benefits in more than 90 percent of the cases are paid to the mother. If a child's mother is not available or is judged unfit to manage funds responsibly, or if the child is not living with his mother, a special unit, the Welfare Branch of the Division of Claims Policy, Bureau of OASDI, is organized to collaborate with local child welfare agencies in selecting and evaluating a payee. If a child is institutionalized, the institution may be designated as payee.

General Assistance

General Assistance is the only form of public aid for needy un-employed persons, for persons whose earnings are too low for family or self-support, and for other needy persons and families not eligible for the special types of public assistance.

It is provided under state laws and is financed without federal participation. In about 16 of the states, General Assistance is wholly financed and administered by the local communities without state supervision or other participation.

Because of local tradition, financing, and administration, the amounts of General Assistance vary much more widely among and within states than the other types of public assistance. General Assistance is the first type of assistance to be restricted because the revenue available to small local units of government limits the resources they can obtain. In general, expenditures are greatest in high-income states and lowest in low-income states, although the need in the low-income states is presumably more extensive. Owing to insufficient relief funds, whole families may be excluded from eligibility: examples are families with any employable member, even though not employed, and families receiving any other form of assistance, whether or not it is sufficient. Also the length of required residence based on local settlement laws may prevent a family from receiving General Assistance. As a result of settlement laws, families may be left without settlement in any state or locality because the length of settlement varies from place to place. Also settlement may depend upon status of the parent who is absent from the home; hence settlement of the family cannot be proved. Under these conditions, the children in a family that is dependent upon General Assistance have small chance to attain a feeling of economic security.

General Assistance should be available to any needy person on the basis of need alone. If the federal government at any time participates in General Assistance, as the Social Security Administration has recommended, some satisfactory method to apportion federal and state funds among counties or other subdivisions of the state on the basic of economic ability must be worked out in order that needy people will receive equitable treatment.

Any discussion of the safeguards of family life must necessarily include the difficulties experienced by children of minority groups. In the United States in 1950 slightly more than one-third of the population group under 18 were other than native born of native parentage. Deprivations in the field of education, recreation, housing, health care, income status, and employment, as well as the more subtle and devastating deprivation that comes from social rejection, all create a lack of family security that inevitably becomes an obstacle when we attempt to provide a happy and healthful environment for all children.

Children of minority status are not the only ones affected. All children are jarred by the denial of opportunity to anyone on the grounds of race, citizenship, color, creed, or financial status. Children are born without prejudice and their reactions are influenced by the attitudes of their families and other adults with whom they associate. What they should receive in their early lives is an appreciation of the contributions minority groups have made to the material and cultural development of this country, and they should understand that social and economic status should not be fixed for any person because of race, color, creed, or nationality. Every child must eventually learn that he, and everyone else, has sprung from a minority group.

The Social Security Act contains important provisions affecting all children regardless of race, color, creed or nationality. No discrimination or mention of minority groups is made by the federal government in its grants to states. When standards of care or grants are lowered for minority groups in any part of the country, this is done by the state or local community, not by the nation.

The child welfare worker has a responsibility for two types of service in safeguarding family life: (1) services that aim to improve social and economic conditions for whole groups of people; (2) those services which help people with their individual needs.

Workmen's Compensation

The oldest form of social insurance in the United States is workmen's compensation insurance.

Germany enacted such a program in 1885, and England in 1897. In 1902, Maryland passed such a law, which was declared unconstitutional. The federal government adopted a workmen's compensation law for a limited number of its employees in 1908. By 1948 all states in the union had passed such laws.

Workmen's compensation provides benefits for workers who are injured while working and, in the case of death, compensation for their families. Each state in the Union has its own program as does the federal government. Most states limit their coverage of types of work by excluding agricultural workers, domestic servants, part-time workers, and personnel engaged in work for nonprofit organizations. Seamen, railroad workers, and veterans have their own special programs.

In every state, workmen's compensation laws demand at least medical and cash benefits for the injured workers. In most states medical services have to be provided for as long as necessary. Cash benefits may be awarded for temporary, permanent, partial, or total disability. In 15 states, payments are also made to the dependents of injured workers. Widows and children may also receive survivors' benefits.

Workmen's compensation systems are for the most part financed by employers and are administered by independent agencies or by a state's department of labor.

Veterans' Benefits

The history of providing benefits for veterans of our armed forces can be traced back to our early colonial wars with the American Indian in New England.

By the time of the American Revolution, the concept of relief and services for veterans was well established. The First United States Congress passed a pension law for disabled veterans of the Revolutionary War. In 1811 Congress approved of the establishment of a home for disabled and aged seamen, marines, and officers.

Until World War I benefits to veterans consisted mostly of pensions and homes for their care. In 1917 Congress established additional benefits providing for disability insurance and vocational rehabilitation. These services were administered by such federal agencies as the Bureau of War Risk Insurance, the Federal Board for Vocational Education, and the United States Public Health Service. The diverse responsibility of these programs and their administration proved to be inefficient. On August 9, 1921, Congress established the United States Veterans Bureau and in 1930 it authorized the President to establish the Veterans Administration as the basic agency for administering benefits for veterans and their families.

There are eight major programs under the Veterans Administration: (1) medical care; (2) financial assistance; (3) education and training; (4) insurance; (5) loans; (6) specialized housing; (7) burial benefits; (8) guardianship.

The Veterans Administration maintains a number of hospitals, domiciles, and outpatient clinics in various localities throughout the United States. These facilities are for veterans with service-connected disabilities. Veterans without service-connected disabilities may be admitted to these facilities within the limits of their availability, if they cannot defray the cost of hospitalization. If VA facilities are being used to capacity or if they are not available, other facilities and services may be arranged through contractual agreements with other governmental or private systems.

Compensation is available to veterans whose earning power has been lost either partially or completely as a result of service-connected diseases or injuries. Compensation is paid to widows and dependents of veterans who die as a result of military service. Veterans having non-service-connected disabilities that affect their earning powers may be eligible for a pension. Also if such disabilities end in death, pensions may be paid to widows and children with low incomes.

By means of readjustment training and vocational rehabilitation, the VA helps veterans to readjust to their civilian careers. Disabled veterans are trained for suitable employment. Educational assistance is also available for the children of veterans who died as a result of war service.

The government offers life insurance coverage, up to a maximum of $10,000, at a minimum cost to members of the armed services. Upon discharge from the armed services, a veteran may elect to continue his government life insurance as long as he pays his premiums.

Loans to veterans for housing, business, or farming purposes that are made by private financial institutions may be guaranteed by the VA. The VA itself may also grant loans directly to veterans when private sources are not available. It may also make monetary grants to veterans with service-connected disabilities for the purchase of housing designed or adapted to their needs.

Burial benefits of as much as $250 are available for the burial expenses of deceased veterans. The VA also has a guardian program to protect the interests of veterans' beneficiaries who are minors or have been declared legally incompetent.

The lack of national supervision of guardians of beneficiaries under the old War Risk Insurance program caused widespread abuses of guardianship after World War I. Misuse of funds, embezzlement, and mistreatment of wards occurred. These conditions were brought to the attention of what was then the Veterans Bureau by the American Red Cross, the American Legion, and the Disabled American

Veterans. The demand for some supervision grew, and there was considerable debate on whether this supervision should be a state or federal function. The compromise view was to give the state courts the power to appoint guardians and to give the federal government supervisory power over them. Weak legislation to this effect was passed in 1924.

The American Legion and other service organizations recognized the need for uniform legislation which would make the federal veterans' administrator in each state an agent of the state courts. They sponsored legislation to this effect, which was drawn up by the Commission on Uniform Laws in 1928 for consideration by state legislatures. At that time, the Veterans Bureau stated it was disbursing approximately $40,000,000 annually to about 50,000 guardians for about 52,000 beneficiaries under guardianship. Of the wards, about 23,000 were incompetent veterans and 29,000 were minor children of disabled or deceased veterans. By 1970 there were more than 28,000,000 veterans, including some 350,000 women, to whom benefits under the Uniform Veterans' Guardianship are available if needed.

When the Uniform Veterans' Guardianship Act was first devised, a compromise was made; guardianship was left to the jurisdiction of the local courts, but the Veterans Bureau was to supervise the estates by supplying the machinery necessary for its administration. However, at first the act did not specify the machinery or authority that was necessary to make action effective. Amendments to the act and the development of a more adequate division of guardianship within the Veterans Administration—formerly the Veterans Bureau—have in some measure brought about correction of the abuses. Now the act provides that the supervision and appointment of guardians is left to the local courts, but the U.S. Veterans Administration, which pays the benefits, is a party to the guardianship proceedings. Social workers on the Veterans Administration staff are assisted in their supervision by service organizations, such as the American Legion and Red Cross.

Guardians appointed under the Uniform Veterans' Guardianship Act do not differ from any other court-appointed guardians. The administration of these laws offered the first attempt toward uniformity and utilization of social work in connection with guardianship.

Guardianship is the responsibility of the Veterans Benefits Division of the Veterans Administration. The legal division is responsible for safeguarding the estates of incompetent or minor beneficiaries. This division is directly responsible to the veterans' administrator.

Chief attorneys in each regional office are responsible to the Veterans Benefits Department under the Chief Administrator for guardianship services in that region. He has authority to determine when a guardian is required and to supervise all guardianship activities in the regional territory. However, the chief attorney may decide whether payments shall be made through an institutional or apportioned award or to the person having custody of the child, in those cases in which there is no guardian or payments to the guardian have been suspended because of his failure to comply with the law.

There is no provision in the act to safeguard the person of the ward. Such supervision is left to the local community. Since no clear line of responsibility has been established and supervision is split, the danger is that there will be no supervision of the guardianship of the ward. A uniform social service program is needed to overcome this difficulty.

Several veterans' organizations help former servicemen in the preparation and presentation of claims for benefits. They also are concerned with rehabilitation services, child welfare services, housing, and employment as means of aiding veterans. The American Red Cross has also provided numerous services for veterans.

The armed forces have service departments that administer various benefits to veterans and their dependents. One of the services is a six-month gratuity payment to the dependents of servicemen who have died on active duty.

DAY CARE

In a broad sense the term "day care" means simply that some person other than members of a child's family takes care of a child during part or a good part of a child's day. The care can be administered in the home or out of the home in some other setting. Day care has been used traditionally by working mothers from poor families, but it has also been used by working mothers and nonworking mothers from other than poor families.

In the field of child welfare, the concept of day care implies services for a child during the day that a parent cannot perform because of economic, health or social conditions affecting the home. Day care in the field of child welfare is distinguished from nursery schools or other socioeducational activities for young children by its emphasis on the need of the parent to seek help in caring for the child.

The first day care center for infants and young children was that opened in Paris, France, in 1844, for working mothers. In 1854 the first day care center in the United States was established in New York City.

During the Civil War day care services for children spread throughout America, and the movement continued to grow after the war. The National Federation of Day Nurseries was organized in 1898, and at that time approximately 175 nurseries were in existence.

As a result of the economic depression of 1929, public funds became available through the Works Progress Administration for programs involving child care. Also during this period the mental hygiene movement brought to the attention of the public the importance of early childhood experiences as well as the significance of planning for the welfare of children in their family. However, the numbers of day care programs expanded largely because of the large numbers of women that were added to the labor force during World War II. Before the war, day care facilities had been mainly for children whose mothers worked because of economic necessity and not for a higher standard of living; whether they will continue to be limited to that group in the future remains to be seen.

The idea of programs that aid a mother in handing over her job of mothering to a day care facility has been highly controversial, because it has been traditionally thought that the primary responsibility of women with young children is that of giving suitable care to their children in their own homes. However, although the Aid to Families with Dependent Children program would enable many of them to reject outside employment and stay in their homes, the right to work must also be recognized for those who do not wish to be dependent upon society or to live at a subsistence level.

Two general types of day care have been developed—individual and group. Each type has been established to serve different needs. In individual care, a child may be accommodated by either foster family care or supervised homemaker service, whereas group care of children includes kindergartens, nursery schools, day nurseries, and extended school programs.

The care of a child in a family home other than his own serves many needs which cannot be met by other types of care. For an infant under two years of age, it is considered the best care outside his own home, because it has been found that group care is unsuitable for the very young child's health as well as for his need for individual attention. Care in a foster home is also particularly useful for the child from two to six years of age if his family lives far away from nursery schools or day care centers; then a good foster home near the child's own home eliminates long daily trips to such schools or centers. In addition, certain small children who, because of emotional, physical, or mental disabilities, are unable to adjust happily to group care find the individual care and homelike atmosphere of a good foster family day care most beneficial.

Foster family day care might also be used for large families, so that all of the children could be cared for together in one foster home, and it is especially suited to before- and after-school care of school-age children. Its main drawbacks are that it is difficult to find suitable foster day care homes and that care in them is expensive.

In the other type of individual care, supervised homemaker service, the child receives care in his own home, so that he remains in known surroundings and has a sense of security not always afforded by other forms of day care. A carefully selected homemaker, actually a visiting foster mother, is placed in the home to care for the children when the mother is temporarily incapacitated or absent from the home, or when the child of a working mother is temporarily ill, or when the child or children of a working mother do not fit into a group care program.

Homemaker service is not domestic service. The homemaker is a mother-substitute who does the mother's accustomed tasks, such as giving care to a sick child, assisting the father to run the household on the accustomed budget, marketing, preparing meals, mending, and doing other general routine housework.

The development of competent homemakers is an important function of many social agencies, primarily family welfare agencies, although a number of other agencies that provide foster care for children have made homemaker service available. Homemaker service is generally financed by the social agency, because most families receiving such service are in a marginal or low-income group. However, an increasing number of families are making their own payments, if they can afford to do so.

The placement of supervised homemakers in family homes was started in 1923. This service developed slowly until shortly before World War II, when, owing to large-scale employment of women, the expansion of such service was rapid.

The term "homemaker" seems preferable to "housekeeper" because it emphasizes the broader scope of service, which includes the ability and skill needed in assuming responsibility for directing the activities and development of children. The qualifying word "supervised" distinguishes this service, given under the supervision of an agency, from the unsupervised work of a privately employed house-keeper.

The procedures used by agencies to determine fitness of a woman for homemaker service are, for the most part, similar to those used in selecting foster parents. Criteria for selection are physical condition, education, previous work experience, religion, interests, ability to work with people, flexibility, ease of adjustment in new situations, sensitivity to home attitudes and family situations, attitudes toward various types of behavior, and methods for meeting problems that may arise. Chronological age is not as important as maturity and flexibility.

The caseworker in the agency and the homemaker must work closely together if the homemaker service is to be effective. The case-worker, because of her professional background, should be able to assist the homemaker in her acceptance and understanding of the family; and the homemaker, because of her close association with the family, should be able to contribute to the caseworker's knowledge and perspective in the particular family situation.

Many agencies arrange for training courses for homemakers. These courses include material on behavior and habit training of children; planning, preparing, and serving meals; home nursing; first aid; and household management. Personnel practices, wages, and hours of work vary with local conditions.

Although homemaker service originated in private or voluntary agencies, the funds of these agencies in many communities were too limited to meet all the need for the services. Tax-supported agencies recognized the value of homemaker service and are finding ways of developing programs.

In addition to the United States and Canada, in which homemaker service has been developing quite extensively since 1950, several other countries have also developed services which have a similar purpose— that of preserving the home for children and incapacitated adults. Among the countries having such services are Australia, Canada, Den-mark, Finland, France, Germany, Great Britain, Israel, the Nether-lands, Japan, Norway, New Zealand, and Sweden. In most of these countries the services are sponsored by the governments and are ad-ministered by health, employment, or social welfare agencies.

In 1962, the National Council for Homemaker Services was founded under the sponsorship of the National Health Council and the National Social Welfare Assembly, with the backing of many national health, welfare, and government agencies. Membership in the Council is open to agencies that provide homemaker-home health aide service and to others interested in supporting the Council's work. In 1963, there were approximately 300 homemaker-home health aide services in 44 states. Three years later, there were 800 such programs in 49 states and Puerto Rico.

Federal legislation passed in 1965 provides funding for comprehensive health care of children and adults in poor families as well as of persons 65 years of age and over. Programs of this nature will create an increasing demand for homemaker-home health aide service.

Homemaker-home health aide services appear to have a rightful place in a children's program and to warrant more extensive development. How much they will be developed will depend on how much success agencies have in recruiting suitable personnel and on how much financial support they can get for their part in such a program. Even though homemaker-home health aide services may seem to be only a small part of a child welfare program, that small part deserves recognition and a chance to develop the worthwhile service it has to give the families of a community.

Of the different kinds of group care for children, probably the nursery school and kindergarten are now the most well known, although the day nursery antedates them. Kindergartens accommodate children between four and six years of age, and, since they are usually administered by local school districts, their programs are set up to emphasize educational needs and are adapted to the advancing maturity of the children. Before World War I, most kindergarten classes were for half a day. During the war, many of them adjusted their programs to provide full-day care for children of employed mothers.

The day nursery (also called day care center) and the nursery school, as they exist today, are two distinct institutions with different backgrounds and techniques. The origin of the day nursery can be traced to women's participation in industry outside the home.

Day nurseries in the United States usually operate independently of schools, and their purpose is to offer a harmonious environment in which a schedule of daily activities provides the child with physical safety, healthy enjoyment, and satisfactory habit training. The emphasis in these nurseries is, as a rule, more upon welfare needs than upon education. However, most day nursery programs borrow freely those techniques that have been found to be the best in the care of preschool children.

The need for supervision of school age children before and after school hours increased so much during World War II that many day nurseries extended their age limits to include children as old as 12 or 14 years of age for before- and after-school care.

The nursery school is a later development, and its primary emphasis is on preschool education that will help the child form habits of friendliness, work, and order, in addition to good physical habits. The nursery school is designed for the child from two to four years of age. Operating under the direction of a teacher trained in the field of nursery school education and child development, it provides such things as health supervision, nutritious meals, indoor and outdoor play with other children, experience with constructive materials, plus a program of parent education.

The depression years of the 1930's increased the need for day care in the course of the succeeding years, because even though mother's aid laws tended to keep many mothers in the home, a great number of women felt obliged to go to work, when work was available, to supplement a substandard income. The White House Conference in 1930 classified the nursery service as one of relief to dependent families, and most children were cared for free of charge. The Works Progress Administration sponsored a great number of nursery school projects in the depression years of the late 1930's, and in 1941, 1,500 were operating.

Early in 1941, under the Work Projects Administration (formerly the Works Progress Administration), child care centers were organized to supplement the nursery school program. The establishment of centers was authorized in those communities having dislocated populations due to industrial defense activities, and in urban and rural communities in which low-income mothers of children under six years of age were employed and yet had no child care centers available to them. Work Projects Administration funds continued to finance day care until December, 1942, when the program was terminated.

With the advent of World War II, the United States Children's Bureau recognized that the new influx of women into defense work and related industries would result in a serious need for protection and care of large numbers of children, and it began to outline plans for action and to stimulate states and local communities to develop day care programs. In July, 1941, a conference on the topic of day care was held in Washington. At this conference it was pointed out that mothers should not be encouraged to work unless there was a real emergency, because children needed their mothers more than ever in periods of stress, such as wartime.

In January, 1943, the chairman of the War Manpower Commission announced plans for mobilization of American womanpower for war employment. However, the policy adopted was to defer hiring women with families except as a last resort. If mothers worked, hours had to be arranged to permit the least disruption of family life, and proper child care facilities were to be supplied by the community, since it was the responsibility of the community to provide care for children "if their mothers must work."

It was pointed out by the Children's Bureau in 1942 that there should be, as a part of a unified community program for day care, a counseling service to assist the mother who wished advice on the practicability of the mother's employment and the effects of that employment on the welfare of the children and the stability of the home. After thoughtful discussion with a well qualified counselor, many mothers realized that the monetary considerations could not compensate for the damage that would be done to the child through separation from his own home. However, many mothers who had no place to leave their children flocked to shipyards and factories, leaving children alone at home or locked in cars.

Many employers took it upon themselves to provide day care for children of their employees in order that the employees would have peace of mind and therefore be more efficient workers. The Curtiss-Wright airplane plant in Buffalo opened a nonprofit day nursery in 1942, where children could be cared for from 8:00 A.M. to 4:30 P.M. daily at 50 cents a day. Henry Kaiser opened a group of day nurseries in his West Coast shipyards; the United States Maritime Commission (the agency that regulates ocean-borne commerce) contributed $750,-000 to subsidize the nurseries, without attempting to influence Mr. Kaiser's plan for their operation. A number of other employers undertook similar projects.

The federal government not only assumed the responsibility for promoting day care plans, but it suggested standards and provided financial assistance for the development of adequate programs by the state and local governments.

The functions of the states were to provide legislation for licensing and regulating institutions and agencies that cared for children, to grant state funds to local governments, to provide additional administrative and supervisory staff for carrying out the responsibilities concerned with state plans for day care programs, to appoint committees and conduct surveys for determining where day care programs were needed, and to suggest standards for care.

The importance of the participation by federal and state governments should not be underestimated, but the actual work of organizing planning committees, making surveys of available resources, studying the extent and type of care needed, and then proceeding to make proper facilities for care available was done by the local communities.

The Lanham Act of 1942 made federal funds available to provide day care for the children of mothers employed in defense industries. At the conclusion of the war, federal funds were withdrawn, and with the exception of a few, most of the child day centers were closed. The actions of various governmental bodies in terminating federal, state, or locally supported wartime centers reflected in part the prevailing attitude toward those mothers of young children who worked outside of the home.

A change in the federal government's attitude toward the needs of some children of working mothers was reflected when Congress passed the Public Welfare Amendments of 1962.

Under this law as much as $10,000,000 of federal child welfare funds may be set aside for child day care each year. States participating in this program must use state funds to match the federal grant, and they must limit the care services to low-income families or to areas in greatest need of the services.

Future developments in day care will depend greatly on public opinion, and on the outcome of the controversy on whether a child should stay at home with his mother until he reaches kindergarten age, or whether most young children should begin at an earlier age to engage in group activity and training. Regardless of prevailing opinion, increasingly more emphasis will probably be placed on a program of guidance work with the families, so that knowledge of the care and training of the child is brought to the parents who are directly responsible for him.

The main considerations are not under which auspices day care services should be operated and from what source funds should be obtained; rather, it is important for each community to determine what child care services are needed to supplement what the home and school together can make available.

Supplementary Readings

Ackerman, Nathan Ward. *Treating the Troubled Family*. Basic Books, New York, 1966.

American Public Welfare Association. *The Homemaker in Public Welfare*. American Public Welfare Association, Chicago, 1962.

Beck, Joseph M. *In Aid of the Unemployed*. Johns Hopkins Press, Baltimore, 1965.

Berkowitz, Monroe. *Workmen's Compensation*. Rutgers University Press, New Brunswick, New Jersey, 1960.

Boszormenyi-Nagy, Ivan, Ed. *Intensive Family Therapy*. Hoeber Medical Division, Harper and Row, New York, 1965.

Brinker, Paul Albert. *Economic Insecurity and Social Security*. Appleton-Century-Crofts, New York, 1968.

Cella, Charles P., and Lane, Rodney P., Eds. *Basic Issues in Coordinating Family and Child Welfare Programs*. University of Pennsylvania Press, Philadelphia, 1964.

Committee on Standards for Day Care Service. *Standards for Day Care Service*. Child Welfare League of America, New York, 1968.

Community Council of Greater New York. *Home Aide Service Needs of Health Agency Clientele*. Community Council of Greater New York, New York, 1961.

Cromley, Ray. *Benefits for U.S. Veterans*. Enterprise Publications, New York, 1970.

Fullmer, Daniel W., and Bernard, Harold W. *Family Consultation*. Houghton Mifflin, Boston, 1968.

Glasson, William Henry. *History of Military Pension Legislation in the United States*. AMS Press, New York, 1968.

Graham, James J. *The Enemies of the Poor*. Random House, New York, 1970.

Howard, Donald Stevenson. *Social Welfare: Values, Means, and Ends*. Random House, New York, 1968.

Langsley, Donald G., and Kaplan, David M. *The Treatment of Families in Crisis*. Grune and Stratton, New York, 1968.

Low, Seth, and Spindler, Pearl. *Child Care Arrangements of Working Mothers in the United States*. Children's Bureau Publication, Washington, D.C., 1968. No. 461.

Lubove, Roy. *The Struggle for Social Security, 1900–1935*. Harvard University Press, Cambridge, 1968.

Mackin, Paul J. *Extended Unemployment Benefits*. W. E. Upjohn Institute for Employment, Kalamazoo, Mich., 1965.

Minuchin, Salvador, et al. *Families of the Slums: an Exploration of Their Structure and Treatment*. Basic Books, New York, 1967.

National Council for Homemaker Services, Inc. *Directory of Home-maker-Home Health Aide Services 1966–67.* National Council for Homemaker Services, Inc., New York, 1967.

Nelson, Daniel. *Unemployment Insurance: The American Experience, 1915–1935.* University of Wisconsin Press, Madison, 1969.

Peterson, James Alfred, Ed. *Marriage and Family Counseling: Perspective and Prospect.* Association Press, New York, 1968.

Pitcher, Evelyn Goodenough, and Ames, Louise Bates. *The Guidance Nursery School.* Harper and Row, New York, 1968.

Ruderman, Florence A. *Child Care and Working Mothers.* Child Welfare League of America, New York, 1968.

Rudolph, Marguerita. *Kindergarten, A Year of Learning.* Appleton-Century-Crofts, New York, 1964.

Stein, Calvert. *Practical Family and Marriage Counseling.* Charles C. Thomas, Springfield, Illinois, 1969.

Van Allen, Edward J. *The Trouble with Social Security.* Omnipress, Mineola, New York, 1969.

[*Courtesy Office of Child Development, U.S. Department of Health, Education, and Welfare.*]

4

Children and the
Community Structure

The structure of any community is complicated, and is composed of many parts. Society is concerned with the welfare of its children not only from the day they are born but almost from the time they are conceived. Part of a community's structure functions in behalf of its children, directly or indirectly.

In this chapter, we will discuss such important topics in the life of children and youth as moral training, school, recreation, and health.

THE CHILD AND MORAL TRAINING

Every person has a value system of some type—a quest for what he considers the values of the ideal life. Some make a religion of money, pleasure, or some other purely secular object. But generally, when we speak of a person's religion, we think of his spiritual attitude of reverence for a controlling power and the manifestation of such a feeling in conduct or life. Whatever a person's values, they determine his motives and undergird his behavior toward his fellowmen.

Religion in its broadest sense is an integral part of man's cultural heritage and has played an important part in the development of knowledge, moral standards, ideals, and purposes. Education, law, medicine, and care of the destitute were developed by religious institutions and continued to be administered by them for a long period until some or all of the functions were taken over by secular institutions or agencies. In studying how great works of music, art, literature, and architecture came into being, we can trace the influence of religion on some of the individuals who created them. We can see that this theme is common to many works of humanity throughout the ages, including the present.

Moral values are interpretations of meaning and as such are dynamic. Human beings, especially during the adolescent years, require more than "bread alone" by which to live. A vital part of a child's personality growth is the spiritual values he has learned in early years at home, strengthened by association with groups outside of the family that hold similar views. Although it has been estimated that a considerable number of children in the United States between the ages of five and 17 are not receiving any formal religious instruction, it should not be assumed that the families of these children are without moral, ethical, and religious values.

The practical philosophy of life that every child needs for his satisfactory adjustment must have its moral and ethical side. Such a philosophy may rest upon a perspective that extends beyond his immediate experiences and be based on ultimate reality. Without it, living in a given society may seem to him to be meaningless and without any real purpose. A code of secular ethics is needed to help him to develop personal and social integrity that will satisfactorily aid him in forming a consistent plan of life based on his insight into life's nature and meaning.

A child's every act and dream is motivated by some kind of ideal; his emotions are intimately related to moral values. He needs to be strengthened by a conviction of his own personal dignity and worth; he needs to be furnished with comforting and elevating ideals; he needs to believe in the worth and wholesomeness of human personality; he needs to feel that he has a secure and significant part in a sane world. He can be helped in the fulfillment of all of these needs by moral and ethical training.

The chief, but not the only, responsibility for giving the child an appreciation of spiritual values rests upon the family and the church. The family has primary responsibility, for it is in the home that the child's first attitudes are formed. Families that have functioning sets of spiritual and moral values pass these values on to their children, formally or informally, as a matter of course. Many families neglect or evade giving religious instruction because they are confused, indifferent, or desirous of keeping their children free from indoctrination, but this does not mean that they shirk moral instruction. It is within families that do have functioning sets of spiritual values that the child is first introduced to the religious and spiritual concepts of the larger group into which he was born. This introduction is the more effective precisely because it occurs in the home. Here attitudes are developed, the mother tongue is learned, culture is instilled. Here the child shares many experiences that are traditional with the group.

No other social agency can be substituted for the family in the nurture of the child's personality. First lessons about many aspects of living are taught the child by each member of the family. Here, through family experience, the child learns to be tolerant, sympathetic, flexible. Here he learns to live in such a way that he can be tolerated by groups and individuals outside the family. Consequently it is in the home, where he observes the behavior of every member of the family, that the child develops a code of ethical and moral values. Regardless of the neighborhood in which the child may live, certain attitudes developed within the family may assist or hamper him in his adjustment.

In their early years, children begin to ask questions about the world's creation and about death. The task of the parent, whatever his own religious beliefs, is to answer these questions in a way that will help the child develop a coherent, realistic, and sustaining philosophy. Moral and spiritual values, like culture, are not communicated by the formal process of teaching alone; they may be inculcated in the child as he participates in the life of the family. Family life promotes social standards that may become a guide for conduct throughout the life of the child.

Even if a growing child comes from a family that gives early instruction, however, his spiritual needs extend beyond the facilities of the home, and it is to the resources of other social groups and institutions that he must turn to find expanding spiritual experience.

The problem of the meaning and significance of life is keenly felt in adolescence. The adolescent, in trying to establish independence from his parents, often feels it is necessary to reject their spiritual and moral values also, although he is fearful and unsure. Uncertainty and lack of confidence also assail him in those other dilemmas of adolescence—how to bring about satisfactory relations with the opposite sex, and how to decide upon a vocation. The child's comfortable adjustment in all these situations might be greatly aided by an experience with established spiritual or social groups in the community.

This is readily explainable. In the group, youths acquire a therapeutic benefit through the feeling of belonging, of being needed and liked, of working with a group for common goals. Here, also, they may extend their concept of the community to include national and world neighbors, so that they consider the welfare of others along with their own, work for the eradication of social injustice and racial intolerance, and have the moral support of friendly people who have the same objectives.

There are many ways in which various groups and the church may help in preparing the child to accept his responsibility toward his fellowmen. Attendance at Sunday school and other church services is, of course, one way, if children are made to feel welcome and the program is not one entirely designed for adults.

In many communities, volunteers, ministers, priests, and rabbis have given dynamic leadership to programs of character training. They have provided healthful, supervised leisure-time programs such as summer camps, glee clubs, athletic leagues, dramatic presentations, and discussion groups. Churches and schools have also sponsored Boy Scout and Girl Scout troops and other activity clubs. Young children and adolescents often become interested in spiritual and moral values through participation in some sort of character-building recreational activity.

Many character-building activities can be designed to overcome tensions between groups of adolescents of different races, nationalities, and creeds. There is increasingly more recognition by many group and religious leaders and their members that the application of social and moral values must meet the needs of everyday life.

Regardless of sect or creed, there are common human needs the church should be able to satisfy. The traditional function of the church is to transmit to the new generations the cherished doctrines of their elders. It offers the opportunity to be part of a group of people who think alike on certain questions, and who are loyal to a common cause, and thus it fulfills a most pressing need of all people—young and old—to be respected, approved, and loved.

The church cannot carry on a program in which community forces are ignored. Sometimes ideas and principles taught by church and home conflict with community forces. Such conflicts make life difficult and frustrating for a child or adolescent, who begins to doubt the validity of the teachings of his own home and church. The church should be able to help the young person to face the reality of situations that cause conflict in a community and to handle differences of opinion in such a way that differences will be assets instead of liabilities. Progress frequently comes out of creative tension produced by differences of opinion.

When a young person enters college he may find it difficult to integrate a new philosophy he learns with the training learned in early childhood. The effort to uphold two seemingly unrelated series of concepts creates strains inside the person that tend to negate the values of both. The social caseworker should be able to help him resolve such conflicts so that he will not feel forced to abandon or repress entirely one or the other.

The school and the social service agency, as well as parents, have a responsibility to furnish the child with opportunities for the development of spiritual and moral values. The child welfare worker at times must help the child with the emotional conflicts in which spiritual values are a vital concern. To be of real help, the worker must have achieved a broad practical philosophy of life and a scale of values consistent with this philosophy. She must be able to recognize and appreciate the differences and complexities of religious, spiritual, and moral beliefs, and to help the child to effect a social adjustment to the standards set up by a complex modern society.

The task of all concerned is lightened in the United States by the existence of freedom to worship or not to worship, according to one's own conscience. In the average community in America, children come into contact with the different spiritual beliefs and customs of other children whose families have given to them something of their cherished traditions and spiritual heritage.

Although children may have difficulties understanding the meaning of a philosophy or religion alien to their own, they can learn through contacts with those of other beliefs, by observation of rituals of the church, and by reading. Such observation and study of the cherished traditions and philosophies of different groups should aid in the understanding and tolerance of various religious and moral systems.

Children may learn that ethical and spiritual differences are largely the result of man-made quarrels about human interpretations of truth. They learn, too, that the major requirement of all religions is an attitude of good will and a constant effort to foster good human relations.

CHILD WELFARE WORK AND THE SCHOOL

The whole child, not just his mind, comes to school. Therefore the school cannot say, "We have responsibility only for teaching him subject matter; his emotional and social development is no concern of ours." The school must, in addition to imparting information, help the child to use his mind and body and to develop social relations that are satisfying to himself and others. There must also be integration of his school experience with social environment.

The social environment of the child has a determining influence on his ability to gain the most from school. Hence there is a growing recognition of the need for a child welfare worker or a school social worker who can assist the child in terms of that environment.

Progressive education's basic tenet—respect for the personality of the child—is supplemented by the work of the child welfare worker in making changes in the child's environment, and therefore in him, that will enable him to participate more effectively in his social and school life. This type of achievement bears out an assertion that is commonly made these days—that a close relationship between child welfare services and the school will contribute toward progress in both fields.

Integration of Education and Child Welfare Work

The school is the strategic center of child welfare work. Not only does the child spend many of his waking hours in the atmosphere of the school, but many of his friendships are formed there and his success or failure, according to the school's standards, is likely to be the basis on which he is judged in the community and even at home. The interests of the teacher and the child welfare worker should meet in their concern for the child.

A child's life is a continuous flow, of which home, school, and other activities are component parts, not confined to separate compartments but interrelated and interacting upon each other. The adequately trained teacher is aware that deficiencies in health or food may prevent the child from benefiting fully from school. She also knows that his emotional adjustment affects the way in which he reacts to other children, to his teacher, and to his school work. She recognizes that the withdrawn child or the excessive daydreamer may be in need of help more than the overaggressive child. She is aware that the so-called "smart aleck," the boastful, bullying, and hostile child, is insecure and needs acceptance and attention. She does not overlook the problems of the child who is new to the community and the particular school. She understands why the child from an institution, a foster home, or an economically deprived home may need to tell "tall tales" of his accomplishments and his rich relatives or to experiment with obscene language or drawings. She realizes that truancy is an expression of an individual need, perhaps for something the school has failed to provide. All of these problems she sees. The extent to which she is able to do anything about them depends on her training, experience, and personality, and on the limitations of time.

Large size of classes, lack of teachers, and paucity of school equipment tend to restrict the flexibility of all school programs and to prevent the teacher from helping the individual child in spite of her interest in doing so. She realizes that her major responsibility is to the group and her work will not permit her to devote time to unravelling the behavior tangles of one child while 40 others wait for her attention. Few lay citizens realize that large classes for children in schools are an extravagance, not an economy.

Some recognition that school-age children had individual differences and behavior problems, and that teachers could not be expected to solve all these problems, must have existed in the middle of the nineteenth century, when mothers' groups began to organize spontaneously throughout the country for the purpose of discussing current literature on child behavior. Their interests were largely confined to problems of obedience, punishment, reward, curiosity, and imagination, with emphasis on getting the child to conform to certain well established behavior standards.

Child training was considered the function solely of women, and the few advanced men who dared brave the Mothers' Congress that met in 1897 were considered a humorous touch. Something of the democratic approach to the problems was evident in the welcome accorded the one black delegate.

This folk movement, which had its humble beginning in the

limited interests of these groups, grew until it attained the structure of the Child Study Association of America, a major force today in promoting a program of continuous parental education.

At about the same time that national recognition of need for parental education was demonstrated by the meeting of the Mother's Congress, the American Association of Collegiate Alumnae, now the American Association of University Women, began a systematic study of its members' children. Today, it continues to expand its activities to include local study groups, research in the fields of child development and education for family life, and the provision of research fellowships for women.

The federal government began to take part in parent education at the beginning of the twentieth century, by instituting, in the home economics departments of the land-grant colleges, courses in family life for farm youth. At about the same time, actual data about human behavior became available and replaced the morally charged content of earlier years. Shortly afterward, the importance of the professional social worker was recognized, and private grants and government funds were used to establish research and training centers for social work. In addition, many local agencies were participating in parent education.

In 1928 the National Council for Parent Education was organized. Its purpose was to coordinate the various parent education activities; state and local participation, however, still varies with each individual community. The White House Conference in 1930 also acknowledged the need for parent education and included as a part of the Children's Charter the objective, ". . . and, for the parent, supplementary training to fit them to deal wisely with the problems of parenthood."

Among government departments today that deal in some measure with parent education are the Office of Education and the Children's Bureau (in the Department of Health, Education, and Welfare), and the Federal Extension Service and the Agricultural Research Service (in the U.S. Department of Agriculture). These agencies, usually concerned with a specific aspect of parent education, cooperate with state and local departments of education in their programs, provide pertinent material, and serve as clearinghouses for studies of nationwide interest.

Another important organization is the National Congress of Parents and Teachers, which since 1897 has held a strategic position and given valuable service, not only in educating parents, but also in assisting parents and teachers to work together with greater mutual respect and understanding.

A conservative survey of nationwide groups engaged in parent education lists 73 agencies, and compilers of the survey admit they may have omitted some that are doing excellent work. By 1956, every city and town in the United States and 80 percent of the rural communities were estimated to have programs of parent education. An analysis of the programs would doubtless show much duplication of activities, because there are parent educators at various government levels, some in voluntary organizations formed for the specific purpose, and a large group of others that participate in related activities and functions.

Despite the apparently extensive scope, the range of effectiveness is limited. This limitation is due partly to the voluntary nature of many activities and partly to the plethora of organizations operating independently and with little centralized planning. Parents in the lower economic brackets are not reached to any significant degree despite the encouraging work of the emergency education program set up during World War II. The number of available parent educators is limited and classes consist of those most desirous of learning, and, of these, many are already reasonably well informed. The goals of the educators vary with the agency involved, and the parent confronted by a multitude of theories and practices may be a little lost in the wilderness of the program. There is obvious need for coordinating the work without losing the experimental quality.

Adequate and widespread preparental education would obviate the need for much of the work now being done; however, there will always be a need for parents to have the opportunity of discussing various problems under the guidance of skilled consultants. In other words, if he is to serve the child effectively, the parent must continue his own education.

Many social agencies conduct classes for parent education, employing in their work both individual and group methods. Child welfare workers serve as counselors and guides on matters concerning parent-child relationships, behavior crises, and the influence of social conditions on the welfare of all children.

Parents and educators, in their search for cures of a child's behavior problems, began to realize in the late 1920's that they could not deal directly with overt symptoms of behavior difficulties without giving consideration to their underlying causes. Why was it that all children did not fit equally well into an accepted pattern of conduct? Children, it was found, were frequently unable to gain the maximum value from their school experience because of unfavorable conditions affecting other areas of their lives. Furthermore, changes within the school itself were taking place. As a result of the introduction of compulsory education and child labor legislation, school enrollments increased, and school plants and courses of study expanded. The classroom teacher could not maintain the close personal contacts she had formerly had with her students.

Because of all these changes, concerned people began to feel that it would be necessary to establish a closer relationship between home, school, and the other groups the child belonged to. One way to carry out this task would be to employ a person whose duties would include that of acting as liaison between home, school, and social agency. So began the movement to employ "visiting teachers," now known as school social workers.

School Social Work

The movement began in the school year of 1906–1907 in the cities of New York, Boston, and Hartford, Connecticut. These initial efforts were entirely independent of one another and developed with slightly different emphasis.

In New York, Miss Mary Marot, a teacher who had for many years been interested in the social aspects of education, became a resident of Harley house, a neighborhood settlement. She and representatives of three other social settlements in the city formed a Visiting Teacher Committee and assigned two visitors to three school districts. The purpose was to bring about closer cooperation between the home and the school for the benefit of the settlement children. The committee became a part of the Public Education Association and by the end of two years the staff had been increased to seven. By 1913, the committee had demonstrated its worth, and its functions were taken over by the Board of Education and established as part of the work of the New York public schools.

In Boston, the Woman's Education Association began school social work by establishing a home and school visitor in the Winthrop School. The reason given was that lack of understanding between the home and school often resulted in injustice to the child. The mothers found it difficult to visit the school, and classes were so large that it was impossible for a teacher to know the homes. Neighborhood associations took up the idea of social work in the schools. Through their efforts, seven elementary schools and two high schools of Boston were provided with school visitors by 1923. The work was conducted in an informal manner and there was no centralized organization.

At Hartford, the work began in 1907 under Dr. William S. Dawson, Director of the Psychological Clinic. The visiting teacher was called a "special" teacher. She assisted the psychologist by obtaining histories of the children and by cooperating with the school in carrying out the recommendations of the clinic.

Other cities began to institute some kind of school social work. Organizations in Worcester, Massachusetts, began in 1909 and 1910. The worker there was entitled "supervisor of attendance" and cooperated with the nursing staff and psychological clinic.

Between 1913 and 1921, boards of education in several parts of the United States began to employ visiting teachers for elementary and high schools. The White-Williams Foundation, which provided counselors for the schools of Philadelphia, added the functions of vocational counseling and junior employment service. In 1916, the Chicago Women's Club influenced the establishment of visiting-teacher work in Chicago, where it was placed under the authority of the Employment Certificate Bureau. This women's club was also interested in establishing a Vocational Guidance Bureau and a School Children's Aid Society; the visiting teachers cooperated with both of these.

The greatest impetus to this movement was given in 1921 when the Commonwealth Fund adopted its Program for the Prevention of Delinquency. The National Committee on Visiting Teachers, affiliated with the Public Education Society of New York, was organized and its work was incorporated into this program.

One part of the program was committed to this National Committee on Visiting Teachers, which consisted of leaders in the fields of education and social work. Demonstrations of visiting-teacher work were to be established in approved communities throughout the United States. Thirty such communities, which varied widely in their geographical, social, and educational situations, were chosen from 270 applications. The Committee appointed the teachers, paid part of their salaries and other expenses, and provided supervision. The local communities shared in the payment of salaries, usually providing one-third. The demonstration period lasted for three years, and there was an understanding that if the projects demonstrated their worth they would be taken over by the local communities.

Because the purpose of the program was not only to extend the work of the communities included in the program, but also to furnish a wide variety of illustrations for other committees which might wish to introduce a similar project, significant data and reports interpreting the results of the demonstrations were published. Publications that are of most general interest to both teacher and social worker are "The Problem Child in School" by Mary B. Sayles and "Children at the Crossroads" by Agnes E. Benedict. The first is a group of twenty-six stories of visiting-teacher cases in urban communities. The second is similar, except that its stories are of work done in rural communities.

The National Conference of Visiting Teachers and Home and School Visitors was organized in 1916, and its first conference was held in conjunction with the National Education Association meeting that year in New York City. In 1919, at Atlantic City, a second national conference was held in conjunction with the National Conference of Social Work. At that time, the significance of the visiting teacher to community welfare was emphasized. The group was reorganized as the National Association of Visiting Teachers in that year, and in 1929, it was renamed the American Association of Visiting Teachers. In 1942, this name was changed to the American Association of School Social Workers. In 1955, the Association merged with the newly formed National Association of Social Workers, which became the single professional association of social workers.

The work of the school social worker has varied from city to city, and it has changed and grown throughout the years. Essentially she has tried to help the child attain a full life by supplementing the work of the teacher when the child failed to respond in the accepted manner or appeared to have some other kind of individual problem. She is definitely not an attendance officer, although unquestionably she is at times expected to function as one.

It is unnecessary to review in detail the changes in the work of the school social worker throughout the years. Generally it seems to have followed the development of education and social casework.

The school social worker is a part of the school administration. She is appointed because the teachers and administrators realize that the teachers cannot handle all problems of maladjustment that may arise. Even when a teacher understands motivations for behavior, she has neither the time nor, usually, the necessary training to handle special problems. It has been pointed out that the very emphasis in mental hygiene on seeing children as individuals has caused some confusion for the teacher. She has a responsibility for the whole group and also another responsibility for those children who do not conform. She can be freed from this conflict of duties if the school social worker is available to work with and to assume some responsibility for the child who needs individual attention.

The school social worker works with the child and the teacher. She is concerned also with parents and others, including other social workers, who have a relationship to the child. She is expected to talk with and counsel the child, his parents, and teacher. She is also expected to give the school a picture of the child's out-of-school life, and convey an understanding of the school life to the home and community.

Her work develops and changes to meet different conditions and changing concepts. She may also find it necessary to adapt her program to the wishes and needs of a particular school, remembering always that she is a part of the school even though she does not work in exactly the same manner as the teachers. She cannot be rigid in establishing the limits of her duties. This type of flexibility is particularly important if the service is not readily accepted by others in the school, and she must gain acceptance before she can establish an effective program.

The amount of casework done by the school social worker varies, and there is some feeling that she should refer cases to other agencies if there is need for continued intensive casework. She can do much to relate educational and social goals.

The school social worker is employed primarily in urban areas. Her services are used in few rural communities, although measures passed by the legislatures of two states, Michigan and Louisiana, to employ visiting teachers in state-wide programs seem to indicate the intention of these two states to extend the work into rural areas.

Some of the schools of social work have set up courses for the training of school social workers. The necessary training would seem to be fundamentally in the field of social work, especially in child welfare. However, it is an asset to the person to have experience or training in the field of education.

Vocational Guidance and Counseling

The term "vocational guidance" seems to have been introduced in print in 1908 by Frank Parsons, the founder of the vocational guidance movement in this country. Since then, the definition of the term has undergone several changes, and like the current concept of social work, its primary function today can be said to be that of helping a person to help himself. As first practiced by Frank Parsons, vocational guidance meant counseling a young person to determine whether a job could be found to suit him. This counseling was usually done just before the person was ready to begin his first job, and he had had very little, if any, training for a specific type of work. In 1925, vocational guidance was defined as the "giving of information, experience, and advice." After numerous revisions as a result of study and discussion by the national organization, the 1937 definition states that vocational guidance is the "process of assisting the individual to choose an occupation."

It is the general consensus that the major responsibility for providing youth with needed vocational guidance rests upon the school system. It has charge of the majority of young people at the time when they are most in need of guidance. It is also in a position to assemble material on the qualities and characteristics of youth, both as individuals and in groups. It can bring together the needed occupational information and can use it to the best advantage. Some of the measures which were developed during the 1930's to meet the needs of youth did not concentrate wholly on the provision of work, but also attempted, in part, to fill the gap left by the incomplete functioning of other programs concerned with the education and guidance of youth. The National Youth Administration, the Civilian Conservation Corps, and the United States Employment Service, all had programs of guidance. Although the main objective of the National Youth Administration and the Civilian Conservation Corps was relief, the stimulation of educational interests and the social and economic rehabilitation of youth were also regarded as of major importance. It was expected that, if young people were given work to do, they would be spared the demoralizing effects of idleness and be kept off the streets, and also they would become more employable by obtaining work experience and work habits.

Vocational preparation is part of the school's educational job. To perform this function well, the school must keep in touch with both employers and workers' organizations: with employers in order to know which types of employment are likely to be available in the community, and with the unions and other groups in order to avoid placing youths in competition with already trained workers.

Counseling service should be accessible to the student upon his request. For many students, however, the counselor will have to instigate the interviews and make the student aware of the service available to him. The successful counseling interview is so conducted that the student leaves it feeling that choice of a vocation is a serious undertaking for which he himself is responsible and that the counselor is ready and able to give him further help in the matter.

The complexity of the social and economic scene, and the changing technological requirements for production have for many years made it increasingly difficult for parents and others interested in the future welfare of young people to provide appropriate guidance and counsel in the subject of occupational adjustments. To some extent the schools have supplemented the counsel given by the family. However, those young people who have left school are not in the habit of turning to the schools for guidance and thus are not apt to keep in touch with the schools. The United States Office of Education, realizing the need for occupational information to be presented to the public regularly and efficiently, in 1939 set up the Occupational Information and Guidance Service, which is supposed to keep the country supplied with information on changes in the field.

There are many misconceptions about counseling and vocational guidance. One is that advice and assistance in this field are simple procedures calling, perhaps, for experience but little or no special skill or knowledge. Another is that it is an interesting form of easily learned psychotherapy. Both of these attitudes are dangerous because they invite dilettantism.

The untrained worker may handle interviewing skillfully enough to obtain a vast amount of information and yet not know how to use this information effectively. To recognize that the individual functions as a total organism and that the work or school adjustment may in fact be a life adjustment, it is essential to look beyond the routine, the procedure, or the immediate dislocation. Counseling is basically casework, and there is no substitute for knowledge of personality and behavior, and for mastery of the basic disciplines. Only with professional knowledge can a counselor have enough real skill to help people or to recognize that there are situations that must be left alone.

THE CHILD AND RECREATION

Leisure time is one of the dividends of a mature civilization. The way it is spent reflects to a large extent the values of an individual and, collectively, of a nation.

Recreation, thought of as a leisure-time activity, is widely recognized as an essential factor in the physical, mental and spiritual growth of an individual or a group. Webster, in the *New International Dictionary*, defines recreation as a synonym for play. Others believe it is an attitude or spirit that finds expression in various ways and that brings a measure of rich and joyful living to those engaging in it.

The word "recreation" implies a re-creation of the individual through constructive use of an area of leisure time for activities affording relaxation, release from tensions, and freedom to be one's self.

Therefore, by means of recreation, the individual may find constructive expression for those instinctive urges toward competition, comradeship, and cooperation; a chance to sublimate in a wholesome way the need for adventure, change, excitement, and expression of the gang spirit. Other specific values that recreation may give are these: respect for rules, fair play, and courage; an ability to subordinate the selfish interests of the individual to the welfare of the group; a capacity for team play; and experience in leadership. The social contacts and cooperation fostered by recreation help to free a personality from fears, shyness, and dislikes and to minimize all those mannerisms, edgy differences, and overindulged peculiarities, which set one person off from another.

Play forms a large part of the young child's life. It is usually the center of all his interests and activities. The child, through his play, is preparing for adult life, regardless of how little visible similarity there may seem to be between the spontaneous activities in the play pen and the way he, as an adult, will meet some of the adventures and frustrations of later life. As the child grows older, "play" is distinguished from other types of activity and becomes "recreation." It supplies an opportunity for developing motor, manual, and artistic skills, and for some of the socializing experiences of group life.

Children of all ages need time for play or recreation. The family group may furnish valuable situations for recreation both within and outside the home; in addition, the child needs recreational opportunities outside the family circle.

Recreational Settings

Before 1955, in only a few cities did anyone seem to care where children played. In most, playing in the streets was indirectly encouraged, because schoolgrounds were closed except during school hours and signs at public parks warned children against playing on the grass. Attempts to organize play for children gained no civic support.

The movement for providing children with play space had its real beginning in 1885, when a religious society in Boston placed a heap of sand in its chapel yard for little children to play in. Other private agencies, especially social settlements, became aware of the need for playgrounds.

This activity awakened the interest of cities and gradually public playgrounds were established throughout the United States. By 1900, the recreation movement was well under way. In 1905, Chicago established ten recreation centers which included enclosed grounds for children of all ages, as well as field houses consisting of assembly halls, indoor gymnasiums, swimming pools, club rooms, and even branches of the public library.

The Playground Association of America, now the National Recreation Association, held its first convention in 1907. Since then the recreation movement has steadily expanded. It has broadened to include leisure-time activities for groups of various ages. It is now commonplace to say that play space and an opportunity to spend playtime with other children are essential to the total development of every child.

From the beginning of the playground or recreational movement, the importance of community support was recognized. Leaders realized the need to convince public opinion that provisions for recreation were a proper municipal function. Public cooperation was sought in whatever way possible. Public school authorities were urged to make schoolyards available for play outside of school hours. Pressure was brought to bear upon city park commissioners to turn their ornamental parks into well equipped playgrounds. Progress was slow, but remarkable.

Beginning with the use of schoolyards only, cities then proceeded to establish more children's playgrounds, and to open recreation parks and school buildings for community use. Plans were shaped for year-round community recreation programs for persons of all ages. City recreation departments were established to provide a variety of local facilities and services; areas of various sizes were acquired and developed; funds were provided for recreational leadership and extended leisure-time opportunities in public libraries, museums, and other educational and cultural centers. During the 1930's, the recreation budgets of cities were decreased, but federal funds began to be provided for leadership and facilities, so that recreational services were able to continue in many communities. The federal departments that promote the programs affecting the use of leisure are as follows: Bureau of Outdoor Recreation, United States Department of the Interior; National Park

Service, United States Department of the Interior; Forest Service, United States Department of Agriculture; Federal Interagency Committee on Recreation; Federal Public Housing Authority.

In many states, the state park and forestry departments have acquired and developed large areas for recreational use. Early state laws limited local recreational services to particular types of areas, facilities, activities, and organizations. Later, the institution of home rule in 27 states empowered municipalities to conduct broad recreational programs and appropriate funds, to acquire and equip land for recreational purposes, to conduct programs, to employ personnel, and to designate or appoint recreational authorities. Thirteen states levy a special tax for the support of such provisions.

Recreational programs must be suited to the needs and cultures of the communities they serve. In general, however, municipal planners consider these factors essential to successful services: a full-time, trained recreation executive; a year-round program serving all recreational interests of the people without restriction to race, religion, age or sex; availability for recreation of all suitable city-owned property; a separate recreational budget; a governing board or committee of responsible citizens.

Among those aiding in the development of programs for the community have been voluntary groups such as settlements, youth-serving associations, and boys' and girls' work organizations. These groups have constructed buildings containing gymnasiums, swimming pools, auditoriums, craft and club rooms, campgrounds, and other recreational facilities. In addition, industrial plants, churches, service clubs, and service organizations, have participated in the development of such programs and facilities, as have private groups formed, under national auspices and otherwise, to foster participation of their members in sports, hobbies, music, and so on.

There has also been a tremendous growth of commercialized recreation enterprises. Commercialized recreation may be beneficial if it is wholesome and low in cost, and if it supplements services rendered by community agencies. Generally, its great expansion has merely revealed the inadequacy of community facilities.

In community plans for recreation the greatest asset is a high degree of cooperation between the city departments and voluntary agencies. This cooperation can be achieved in recreation councils, committees or councils of social agencies, and other groups formed to further mutual understanding on this subject.

Each summer finds thousands of youngsters in America packing their bags to go to camp. It is only unfortunate that the joys of the camping experience are not available to many more. The idea of summer camps originated in 1885 when, under the auspices of the Y.M.C.A., Mr. Sumner Francis Dudley operated a camp on Orange Lake, near Newburgh, New York, for seven boys. Since then the movement has grown until today more than 5,000 camps, serving annually about 1,000,000 boys and girls, are maintained by welfare, social, and religious organizations and private interests. In 1934, state and federal park and forest authorities expanded the camping facilities, and made some areas available for year-round use.

During World War II, day camps increased in number. Maintained by a variety of groups and agencies, they made it possible for a parent to bring a child to camp in the morning and take him away in the early evening.

The adequacy and effectiveness of all camping programs, no matter how extensive, are determined by the number and quality of the persons employed as leaders. Because parents have very definite reasons for sending their children to camp and children have very definite objectives in mind when they go there, trained leaders are necessary. They must have a sound philosophy of life and a good knowledge of the basic concepts of child welfare.

Fundamental to any program that seeks to guide the development of boys and girls intelligently must be an awareness of the chief characteristics of the group. However, one should never lose sight of the fact that each child is an individual and that there is never an inflexible universal pattern of behavior.

Social Group Work and Group Therapy

The leisure-time group is one of the most important groups to which the child belongs. Although he learns to relate himself to others first in the family group and later in the school, it is in a dynamic group-work setting under the guidance of a skilled leader that he will learn to relate himself more positively to a group and to other individuals. The child will gain satisfaction from having his accomplishments recognized by the other members of the group and at the same time he will learn to recognize the accomplishments of other members. Identity with the group, an "in-group" feeling, should develop, and this should be followed by the ability to identify with outside groups and interests, so that there may be a resulting growth in personality and social adjustment.

The group may be a natural one brought together, say, by common interests, age, proximity, or cultural background, or it may be a selected group of individuals chosen by a group-work agency. Group work may take place in any of the community's group-work agencies, such as the Y.M.C.A., the Y.W.C.A., the Girl Scouts, the Boy Scouts, a Boys' Club, or a settlement house.

Many special groups have been set up on the group-work principle, such as groups for children who are especially handicapped physically or socially. A special club was developed for a group of diabetic boys and girls. Here they were able to overcome insecurity, develop responsibility for their own diets and injections, and have fun by planning social events in which they could all participate. As a result of their ability to relate themselves more easily to one another, they were able to become members of outside groups of "normal" individuals.

Community agencies have tried to confront the problem of juvenile gangs through a group-work approach. Early attempts were made to break up gangs and persuade the children to join some "nice character-building club." This method was not successful; the boys and girls found their gang life much more exciting than a "character-building" club. As a result of this failure, a new approach has been tried —that of working with the gang. The gang itself is the initial group, and the interests of the children are noted and directed into more positive channels in terms they can understand. Later the group can affiliate with one of the community agencies if it so desires.

It was only recently that group workers came to recognize the relevance of casework to their own work. Then group-work agencies began to work on the principle of development of the individual, using the concept of "self-help" in their programs as a tool to accomplish this end.

The term "social group work" first appeared in the 1920's, but it was not until 1935 that group work became a major division in the National Conference of Social Work. Soon after this, the National Association for the Study of Group Work was formed. In 1955 it merged with the newly formed National Association of Social Workers.

The modern objectives of social group work are personality growth and social adjustment. If these goals are constantly maintained, group work becomes in fact a program of mental hygiene. Workers in every type of agency are using somewhat informal educational procedures to help develop desirable personal qualities and to improve conditions under which children live. To achieve these aims, it is necessary to apply principles of psychology and the social sciences, and also to use the democratic principle of "self-help."

Group workers tend to state their purpose as threefold: (1) personality growth and social adjustment of the members of the group through voluntary association and group activity; (2) group development and achievement, including group integration and socialization; (3) the development, in members, of a widened social consciousness.

The ultimate objective of all group work is to help the individual become a social being. In this process, he learns to adjust himself to a constantly changing society. He will learn to use some of the changes to meet his own needs and the needs of the community. The development of skill in a certain craft or art is an objective in itself because it brings satisfaction to the individual and an increase in ego. It also becomes the means of broader association with fellow members who have the same interests.

Natural groups are formed in interesting ways. Several studies have shown that boys tend to associate with and form attachments to other boys of similar age, size, maturity, and levels of intelligence, and that girls choose friends of similar scholarship ability. Many other factors can cause groups of considerable heterogeneity to come together: proximity of homes; common experiences; similarity in economic level or cultural background; religion, race, or nationality; athletic interest. As a result, a natural group having just one or two common interests may be formed, but other factors in the group can be very dissimilar.

Groups directed by trained leaders may vary in size, but should be small enough so the leaders will be able to have considerable knowledge of the individuals and the members will have the opportunity to know one another. These groups, whether discovered or created by group-work agencies, should meet somewhat regularly. The program of activities should be developed by the group as a whole.

Except for the special groups, such as those for the handicapped, social group work concerns itself with the more or less "normal" boys and girls. It does not invade the field of group therapy, although in mild cases of maladjustment, the agency may provide individual counsel and guidance.

To distinguish social group work from group therapy, we may say that group therapy uses the group for the treatment of "maladjusted" children. Group therapy utilizes a variety of activities, such as psycho-drama, puppet shows, and psychiatric conferences, in group treatment of individual behavior problems under a trained leader.

The field of group work was just beginning to get itself organized into a profession, when some members of the group who were psychiatrically oriented saw in groups certain possibilities for treatment. Since this method utilized treatment in groups, rather than individual treatment, they called it group therapy to distinguish it from the individual interview.

Therapy is the concept that is currently being adapted to the needs of the patient, and recently it has been popularized by the new, scientifically introduced treatment for war casualties. Just as group workers have used the terms vocational therapy and occupational therapy to describe some of their duties, they and others have now come to use the phrase "group therapy."

Because authorities disagree on the theory underlying the technique of group therapy, any description of that term in these pages must necessarily be general, the only purpose being to define it and differentiate it from the term "group work." According to Webster, "group" means, "two or more figures forming a design or unit in a design, an assemblage of persons or things forming a separate unit"; and "therapy" means, "medical science which treats of the application of remedies for diseases, curative, pertaining to the healing art."

The external features of group therapy for children are (1) children in the presence of other children, (2) tools and work materials, (3) one or more adult leaders. This type of group is unique in its purpose, relationships and atmosphere. The techniques of applied psychotherapy specify a certain type of adult leader, a permissive atmosphere, and a preoccupation with the aims of psychiatry so that the child is exposed to a therapeutic or healing process. It is implicit that the child is emotionally sick and needs help. The means by which the extent of maladjustment or need for therapy is measured depends on many factors, which must be defined for each child by the agency and the therapist.

The purpose of the permissive atmosphere is to provide a situation in which the patient is freed to act out hostilities in the presence of an adult and other children without fear of discipline, censure, or restraint, although at the same time he is restrained from physical violence or dangerous destructiveness. From a sick child, the adult must accept behavior which would ordinarily bring punishment, in order to break the vicious circle of destructiveness—followed by rejection—followed by destructiveness. The tension of the sick child is released and his conviction that the world is hostile and persecuting is exposed to doubt; assurance of acceptance can counterbalance inner indictments that he is worthless, "bad," unwanted, and alone.

The illness in the patient is created and enforced by outer pressures which may become so unbearable that the child is unable to react in a healthy, acceptable manner and is no longer amenable to the usual educative processes, counseling, or discipline. To the intensely deprived child, the slightest denial is a major rejection so that an atmosphere which can relieve anxiety is essential.

When intrapsychic tensions are broken down, the patient becomes accessible to emotional reconstruction and the extreme behavior is no longer utilized as self-defense. The patient is enabled to establish a positive relationship, first with the therapist, then with members of the group, and finally with his family and the world. The successful treatment will bring the child to the point at which he can withstand more of the controls and denials imposed by the world.

The function of the psychotherapist is to make the patient more accessible to an educative process and in that way to recondition the personality structure so that the child can participate in the regular influences of the home, school, club, church, and general recreation. The need for therapy is indicated if the child blocks his own emotional development.

The play interview, used by psychoanalysts, psychiatrists, and psychiatric caseworkers, is seldom applicable for older children who are unable to obtain pleasure from symbolic play which would lead to interpretation. The child who avoids any form of fantasy expression and play is also inaccessible, as is the child who finds a play situation between child and adult unnatural.

Children who undergo vehement developmental changes view adults as representatives of societal and all other pressures and they resist "advice-seeking" or "problem-awareness." Often the parents, teachers, and other educative influences are hostile to a casework or psychiatric approach, and this hostility is reflected in the child's attitudes during interviews. In certain types of cases and under certain circumstances, the effect desired cannot be achieved through interviews as well as it can through group pressures exerted by contemporaries, but under controlled conditions.

Selection of the group for therapy is not random. It is carefully made on the basis of the individual problems, the anticipated interaction among personalities of the individuals, and the leader's own theory on the kind of group experience that can be therapeutic. If a therapy group has been developed by means of close analysis and discussion of the total personality of each patient, the records of the interviews, the case histories, and the nature and source of each difficulty are used intensively.

Since the purposes and techniques of the psychiatrist, psychologist, and caseworker differ radically from those of the teacher and group worker, a great deal of mutual interpretation is necessary to clarify the uses and value of these different types of group treatment.

SAFEGUARDING THE HEALTH OF CHILDREN

In past centuries the children of the world were considered pawns of society. The weak or deformed were ignored or left to die. The strong were reared as fighting men or public servants. It was not until the time of the French Revolution that the child was recognized as an individual with an inherent right to live. Today, most modern societies have adopted measures that give the child a better chance of living to maturity than he has had ever before. In the United States organizations have been set up to maintain standards of medical care and protection that in general give to every child his fair opportunity for health.

Maternal and Child Health

It is well recognized that health starts in prenatal life. Therefore, if a child is to be given the best possible chance of starting with a well developed body, his mother's health, mental as well as physical, must be protected during pregnancy, and the infant must have the opportunity for safe delivery into the world.

When the United States Children's Bureau was established in 1912, one of the greatest public national health problems was the high mortality among women in childbirth and among their newborn babies. The actual death rate was unknown because births were not registered everywhere in the United States. The records that were available showed shockingly high loss of life. It was believed that at least one baby out of every ten born alive failed to survive his first year of life.

Today carefully compiled records show that only 2.2 out of 100 die, but in some states the infant mortality rate is lower.

In the early days of the Children's Bureau, for every 10,000 live births, some 61 mothers died of causes related to childbirth. Today the number has decreased to 2.7 mothers out of every 10,000 births. The seriousness of death of the mothers cannot be measured by their deaths alone. It must also be measured in the numbers of children who are left motherless. Other mothers, because they lack proper care during pregnancy or at childbirth, may be left with damaged health, which makes them unable to function as happy, wholesome individuals and parents.

To help mothers and children, the Children's Bureau had to have factual material on which to base its requests for better health services. Therefore, in 1918, its representatives went to carefully selected communities and called at each house, wealthy and very poor alike, in which a baby had been born within the year. They asked questions about care of the mothers and babies, and on the basis of the material they had gathered it was decided that, if the lives of mothers and babies were to be saved, help had to be given early in pregnancy. In communities where help was most needed, the local and state governments were least able to provide it; therefore help had to come through the federal government.

In 1921, the Sheppard-Towner bill was passed by Congress, in spite of strong opposition. It provided for the establishment of federally financed health services for mothers and children throughout the states, particularly in rural communities. Public health nurses began to appear, calling from house to house, teaching mothers how to take care of themselves and their babies. The idea of clinics, too, began to take hold—clinics where expectant mothers could go regularly for examination and instructions, and other clinics where babies could be checked in and examined regularly as a step toward keeping them healthy.

This help from the federal government—it amounted to only $1,240,000 a year for all the states—was short lived. In 1929, it was cut off. The ground had been broken, though; it had been shown what could be done if more money were available, and at the same time more facts could be presented that demonstrated why federal aid was needed. Those facts were obtained in a Children's Bureau study of maternal deaths that occurred in 1927–1928. This study was made in cooperation with physicians in 15 states. The doctors helped to find out how many of the mothers died from causes directly related to childbirth. The simple word "childbirth" given on a death certificate was not enough; doctors determined the actual causes, and these records showed that mortality among women during pregnancy, childbirth, and the post-partum period was unnecessarily high and could be reduced.

Then, in 1935, the Social Security Act was passed, and, as the result of the groundwork that had gone before, Title V, Part I contained a provision for maternal and child health services of the kind the Children's Bureau had long sought. Funds were once again made available through the Bureau to help the states develop maternal and child health programs. Moreover, for the first time, federal help was to be given for the care and treatment of crippled children. Today, some 238,000 physically handicapped children are being helped each year by state crippled children's programs, and these programs are supported in large part by Social Security funds.

The program has since been expanded, although still only a small proportion of all those in need of these health services can be reached. As in other state-federal programs, the state plan must meet certain requirements set forth in the federal act. The states have to share the expenses and administer the program through the state health agency. The amount of each state's share in the federal funds that have been authorized depends on the ratio of live births in that state to the total in the United States, and on how much financial assistance the state requires in order to carry out its program of maternal and child health. The state must provide an amount equal to half of the federal funds supplied to it. Part of the other, unmatched half of the federal funds is used for special projects and emergencies.

Many of the services provided are preventive health services—to help healthy mothers and keep children healthy. These services include prenatal clinics, public health nursing services, well-child clinics, immunization, and examination of school-age children by physicians and dentists.

In 1935, before the passage of the Social Security Act, 31 states had child hygiene divisions or divisions of maternal and child health in their state health departments, but in only 22 states was the director a physician who was employed full time. Almost half the states had either no special funds or less than $10,000 a year for maternal and child health services. Fourteen states spent less than $3,000 a year or nothing at all for this work. In contrast, by 1945, the states used $4,800,000 of state and local funds in maternal and child health programs, or almost as much as the total federal funds then available. All of the states, the Dis-

trict of Columbia, Puerto Rico, and the Virgin Islands are now participating in such programs, and all of the state departments of health now
have maternal and child health divisions.

Public Health Education

Many of the public health nurses—they are now familiar figures even
in rural areas—are paid in part from maternal and child-health funds
made available under the Social Security Act. In this program the public health nurses give health supervision and health education service to
mothers and children, whereas the local practicing physicians provide
medical supervision to mothers in prenatal clinics and to children in
child-health clinics. As part of her work, the public health nurse con-
ducts classes and makes home visits. In a limited number of areas, home-
delivery nursing service is provided at the request of attending physicians. Nurses may give supervision to midwives, and in some states
nurse-midwives are provided to train and supervise midwives and to a
limited extent to give this kind of service. In a few places in the United
States, midwifery functions independently of good medical supervision.
This is to be discouraged; but until adequate medical and hospital
facilities are made available at a price all patients can afford to pay, the
practice of midwifery will probably continue in certain areas, and the
best that can be hoped for is eliminate the most incompetent practitioners and to extend careful supervision over the others.

Each year some 160,000 women now go to the prenatal clinics for
advice and help during pregnancy. These clinics, conducted by competent physicians, greatly increase the mother's chance of a safe and
normal delivery. Many localities also have postnatal and well-baby
clinics, to which mothers can take their babies and young children for
regular health examinations.

Medical services vary greatly from one vicinity to another, but
in general they are greatly superior in urban centers. Of the small cities, 25 percent lack child-health clinics, many are without prenatal
clinics, or diagnostic and treatment clinics, and a great number have no
hospital. Provisions for children who require prolonged institutional,
sanatorial, or convalescent care are generally inadequate throughout
the country. In many localities, the services that are available are not
reaching the people who need them the most. There is a great demand
for more intensive case-finding projects and definitely more need for

informing the public about what facilities are available in certain areas. The facilities for the care of black children are greatly inferior in many states to those for white children.

In the course of the next few years, a well designed and well organized plan, the construction of more hospitals, clinics, and health centers, and the training of more personnel will be required to meet the great and continuing needs of mothers and children in all cities and counties.

Better facilities for care of expectant mothers, particularly those in rural areas, have been established as a result of the Hospital Survey and Construction Act passed by Congress in August, 1946. This act authorizes the federal government to provide financial assistance to states, local governments, and nonprofit agencies to defray part of the costs of construction of hospitals, rehabilitation facilities, diagnostic and treatment centers, nursing homes, public health centers, and related health facilities. Federal funds for the project match between a minimum of one-third and a maximum of two-thirds of the funds provided by the state or local government. The act made available to the states $75,000,000 a year for a five-year period. Since that time some budget increases have been made. Today about half the money spent for the construction of medical facilities has come from public funds.

The amount of money appropriated for the functioning of nearly all types of medical programs in the United States is far less, in proportion to the need, than the amount appropriated for buildings and equipment.

In March, 1943, an emergency program was authorized by Congress to bear all or part of the cost of maternity and infant care for families of lower-income service men of World War II. The Children's Bureau was named the federal administrative agency. EMIC, as it was called, was the largest public health program for mothers and children undertaken in this country, up to that time.

Crippled Children

In ancient times, cripples were left to the rigorous forces of nature and the fittest survived. As recently as 100 years ago, there was no socially organized plan for the treatment of the crippled child. Public schools did not make provision for him, and vocational rehabilitation was unknown.

The first attempts to provide medical care for cripples were sponsored by private organizations and funds. In 1897, the first state-sup-ported hospital for the care of crippled children was established in Minnesota. From that time, progress in the care of this segment of our dependent population has continued, but current programs and facilities remain pitifully inadequate for the actual need.

One of the important milestones in the development of public responsibility was a provision in the Social Security Act that permitted allocation of federal funds to states wishing to organize programs for the diagnosis and treatment of crippled children. This was a permissive rather than a mandatory law and, as a result, even now the state plans are extremely varied in their services, coverage, and adequacy.

Until the state departments of public health, or whatever state agency may have been designated to handle the crippled children's services, began their case-finding programs very little was known about the number of children needing care. For a long time, the Children's Bureau had been conducting surveys which gave estimates but, since most state departments of public health kept statistics only on deaths and communicable diseases, these surveys were limited in scope.

As states began their crippled children's services they realized their available funds were a mere pittance compared to what was needed, so they dared not publicize the program too highly for fear of arousing futile hope in parents whose children could not be helped. For this reason their registers of handicapped children do not include all of the children who really need care. Most of the figures quoted in the paragraphs that follow are not the totals of the state registers; rather, they are approximations compiled from intensive surveys carried on in varied selected areas, made more accurate by medical knowledge of the ratio of the incidence of the disease or condition to geographical areas and age groups.

Several years ago the proportion of cripples was estimated to be six out of each 1,000 of the population under 21 years of age. Of each 100 crippled children, 24 had been so from birth, 11 had been the victims of accidents, ten were suffering as a result of nutritional deficiencies, and 55 were crippled as a result of disease. Poliomyelitis at that time was responsible for three out of ten crippling conditions. However, in recent years the use of the Salk vaccine has brought about a dramatic decline in crippling caused by poliomyelitis.

Since the 1950's we have come to recognize that conditions less obvious than paralysis, deafness, blindness, amputation, and malformation can disable and can result in adults who are physically and emotionally unable to be independent.

The most consistent national trend has been the broadening of the definition of a crippling condition. States first concentrated on providing services for orthopedic handicaps. Next, projects for disabilities amenable to plastic surgery such as cleft lip and palate were added. About 1941, several states began demonstration projects for children with rheumatic fever, rheumatic heart disease, and hearing impairment. Soon after this cerebral palsy cases began to receive special attention in several states. Projects were developed to provide physical, occupational, and speech therapy, plus medical, psychological, and social supervision simultaneously with the education of the child. Other conditions receiving special attention in state programs today are sight defects as well as eye disorders amenable to surgery, speech disabilities of all types, congenital heart disease, epilepsy, nephrosis and nephritis, diabetes, asthma, severe orthodontic defects, and even clinical aspects of reading disabilities.

One of the most outstanding contributions of the state crippled children's programs has been the insistence on a high quality of medical care. This high quality has been mandatory for the qualifications of professional personnel, the facilities used, and the organization of services: consequently, children can be moved freely from rural areas to medical centers and back, from hospitals to long-term institutions, and to their homes again, with needed services available to them at each place.

Private agencies have tended to adopt the standards of care set by state agencies for both treatment and personnel. Federal money has been used to provide special training such as courses in pediatric nursing, cleft palate surgery, audiology, the care and treatment of epileptic or rheumatic fever patients, and various aspects of physical therapy, and to provide for medical social work field practice in agencies for crippled children.

It will take time to locate the children who need help, to train personnel, and to develop programs for care. In some states, a court order is still required before the child can be accepted for treatment under these programs. Court action should not be necessary when the agency and the parents are eager to work out a treatment plan.

Under a state crippled children's program, diagnosis is arranged for at a crippled children's clinic—it may be a permanent clinic in a hospital or health center, or an itinerant clinic in a smaller more remote area—or, if a child is acutely ill, the physician will go to the home. For any crippled child, examination and diagnosis are absolutely free, regardless of family ability to pay. Care and treatment are usually expensive. If the family cannot pay for the needed services, they are furnished by state and federal funds. Sometimes, if a family is able to do so, it pays a part of the cost of care. Eligibility for medical care is based upon the child's need, not upon the parents' ability to pay.

An important feature of a crippled children's program is the effort to keep children from causes that cripple. Individual and community effort is important in this respect. Parents must guard children against accidents and disease. Children must be taught how to avoid accidents. Better obstetric care for mothers will reduce birth injuries and crippling due to syphilis. Periodic medical examination of children, especially in the preschool period, will reveal injuries and disease in their early stages, when treatment can be most effective.

The Children's Bureau of the Department of Health, Education, and Welfare administers several services for crippled children. These services include case finding, diagnoses, medical care, hospitalization, surgery, therapy, and other services. Grants are made to states for crippled children services. From 1961 to 1962 federal, state, and local funds expended for crippled children amounted to more than 78 million dollars.

Child Health Services

In spite of all the work done by national organizations, private persons, and the medical profession, there is still great evidence of need throughout the country for improved medical care for children of school age. The most striking factor brought to public attention in recent decades was the figure from the United States Army Selective Service System showing that two out of every five men called for service in World War II were rejected on physical or mental grounds. Of these, thousands were rejected for causes that could have been remedied in childhood.

In too many public health programs, more emphasis has been placed on medical examinations and the diagnosis of diseases than on follow-up care. There is evidence in school records that the same diagnostic finding has been noted in an individual's record year after year. Many parents have been told of their child's troubles without being offered any advice or help on how they can procure help to treat the problem. Such a procedure overlooks the educational aspects of the health examination.

Programs of health education, guidance, and services for school children are being continually developed—in some cities, under the education department; in other cities and in rural areas, under the health department. These programs include careful physical examinations (unless evidence of examination by family physician is submitted by the parents), tests of eyesight and hearing, with recommendations for remedial measures if necessary, and immunization and vaccination if these shots have not already been given. For children participating in athletics there are special medical examinations.

Health examinations in schools should be given by competent physicians and dentists assisted by well trained school nurses. When parents are unable to be present during the physical examination of their child, the school nurse reports and interprets to the parents the result of the examination and any indicated need for correction. The nurse should also be responsible for follow-up treatment of children whose defects can be remedied by a nurse's skill. In small communities and rural areas, school nursing service may be provided by nurses from the health department.

It is hoped that, as a part of the school health program, more adequate provision will be made for immunization against those communicable diseases of childhood which can be prevented by this treatment. Diphtheria, scarlet fever, poliomyelitis, and typhoid fever are almost under complete control now in some communities; but measles, whooping cough, and others of the communicable diseases cause many deaths each year among children from one to five years of age. Rheumatic fever, influenza, pneumonia, tuberculosis, and appendicitis take approximately 5,000 lives annually from children of five to 15 years of age. (Rheumatic fever is the highest single cause of death in school-age children.) All of these prevalent diseases could be curtailed immeasurably by the proper medical help. In the decade from 1930 to 1940 alone, according to the Bureau of Census figures, the death rate from contagious diseases for the five- to 14-year-old group was cut to one-third of that of the preceding decade.

Part of every child's care should be a complete periodic health examination by a pediatrician. The frequency should depend upon the child's age, his growth, and evidence of deviation from satisfactory physical and mental condition.

Nearly 1,500,000 children now have some medical care available to them through the Aid to Families with Dependent Children program. Under the Social Security Act, the state public welfare agency may use either or both of two methods of paying for medical care to families receiving funds through AFDC. By one method, the agency includes the amount to pay for such care in the money payments to the family. By the other it makes direct "vendor payments" to doctors, hospitals, and others providing the care. Most states provide financially for some medical care through this program. In some states the care provided is comprehensive; in others relatively slight.

Periodic dental examination, dental education, and service should be a part of the health service for all children. Dental education and services should be provided throughout their school years. Parents should begin their children's program of care in the preschool years.

A program of mental health for all children actually begins with the formation of wholesome attitudes and the acquisition of suitable knowledge by the parents before the child's birth. There should be courses for all expectant parents on the physical and emotional needs of the child.

Many mothers and fathers do not actually know or understand that from the time a little human being comes into the world his mental health depends upon his physical comfort, his happiness, and a chance to express himself without too much unnecessary frustration. Birth itself is a traumatic experience for the baby. It brings a sharp and severe change to him.

If he comes into a home where he is wanted, if he is made comfortable through the feeding process, if he is given reassurance by affectionate care and cuddling, he has the kind of start necessary for becoming an optimistic, hopeful, secure person. If, however, he comes into the world unwanted, or neglected—either physically or by a cold indifferent parental attitude—it is very difficult for him to function as a happy, wholesome little person.

As a child grows, he is constantly faced with the continuous necessity of adjusting himself to living and so he is bound to have problems. And at some time in his development he is bound to show evidences of some disturbance in greater or lesser degree. He may be rebellious and unreasonable; he may quarrel with other children; he may refuse to eat; he may develop fears or become preoccupied with sex practices to the exclusion of other interests; or he may show other behavior symptoms that are disturbing while they last. But, if the parents' attitude is understanding and helpful, the child usually emerges with success.

Many parents content themselves with hoping that their children will work out such difficulties in their own individual ways and that time will cure all—that the child will grow up and the problem will disappear. By adopting this attitude, parents sometimes seek to avoid the responsibility of fully facing the fact that there are basic underlying causes that must be eliminated. Unless help is obtained for the child, he may grow out of one particular problem, only to assume another. This exchange of one symptom for another is something that parents may fail to recognize. A child may become docile and well-behaved and yet develop night terrors; he may stop sucking his thumb and take to nail biting; he may suppress his jealousy of the new baby and start to wet his bed; he may quit being overaggressive but lose interest in the outside world by becoming absorbed in daydreams. Thus, the basic underlying cause still remains.

Parents, often unconsciously, regard disturbances in their children as a reflection on themselves; hence they become panicky at the mere notion that their children might have problems and will go to any lengths to blind themselves to what is often a genuine "distress signal." But when a maladjustment is already so deeply rooted that it impairs the emotional functioning of the child and severely cripples the personality, the individual problem is one for the psychiatrist or the child guidance clinic, and the parents must be able to turn to professional counsel. For not all behavior difficulties can be successfully treated just by a combination of sympathy and common sense; these qualities are of fundamental importance to the sound growth of the child, but they are not a guarantee against emotional disturbances any more than against physical illness. The underlying cause of such a disturbance may be in the relationship between parent and child, and treatment of one or both parents, as well as of the child, may be required; cause and treatment can be determined only by study.

Parents must have some place to turn for expert guidance when signs first indicate that the child is emotionally upset. Symptoms, a few of which have been mentioned, show that these children need help quite as much as the child we ordinarily think of as being ill. Yet outside of large urban areas, few communities are equipped to give the necessary assistance.

The schools are in a strategic position to conserve the mental health of children and to recognize the child in need of help. However, parents cannot leave the solution of mental health programs to the teachers, even if they were trained for this, because by the time the teacher comes into contact with the child, some of the most important things that fix a child's behavior have already happened to him.

The child is never an isolated person. He is not born with mental health. Whether he attains and maintains it depends upon his immediate family, his home, his school, his recreational activities, his companions, and his own attitudes towards all these.

Parents living in both urban and rural areas need to have available to them the services of good child psychiatrists and children's workers with sound psychiatric training. The development of mental hygiene programs in the states should serve to point out the existing needs and the available facilities and trained personnel, and to coordinate and integrate all work for the mental health care of the child.

The National Mental Health Act, approved July 3, 1956, includes children in its scope. Its stated purpose is to improve the mental health of the people in the following ways: (1) by conducting, assisting, and fostering and promoting the coordination of research relating to the cause, diagnosis, and treatment of psychiatric disorders; (2) by training personnel in matters relating to mental health; (3) by developing and assisting states in the use of the most effective methods for prevention of psychiatric disorders, and for diagnosis and treatment of persons with such illness. The act is administered by the National Institute of Mental Health of the United States Public Health Service in the Department of Health, Education, and Welfare. Its governing body is the National Mental Health Council, which consists of the Surgeon General, who acts as chairman, and six members appointed by him (selected from outstanding authorities in the field of mental health) for three-year terms.

Three programs have been developed under the National Mental Health Act: (1) research; (2) training of personnel (psychiatrists, psychologists, psychiatric social workers, psychiatric nurses, and laboratory technicians); (3) development of community resources for mental health protection and treatment.

The National Institute of Mental Health at the Bethesda Medical Research Center in Maryland provides facilities and staff for research studies of emotionally disturbed children. Federal grants are allocated to states that will provide matching funds for the establishment of local diagnostic and treatment facilities and for mental hygiene and child guidance clinics. Funds are distributed in each state by a state mental health authority. In most states this authority is the health department or department of mental hygiene, but in a few it is the department of public welfare.

The first appropriation made by Congress on July 8, 1947 to implement the measure was $7,500,000. Since that time the federal appropriation has more than doubled.

Under Title V of the Health Amendments Act of 1956 an additional method was introduced to deal with the problem of mental illness. The National Institute of Mental Health was authorized to provide support for mental health research grants.

In 1955 the Mental Health Study Act was passed by Congress. As a result of the act, some 20 professions cooperated in sponsoring a Joint Commission on Mental Illness and Health for conducting studies. After these studies had been completed, Congress in 1963 then provided funds for the construction of mental health centers and facilities for the retarded. In addition, in the years since the mid-1950's, several states have also enacted legislation providing grants to localities in their state.

At the present time, one person out of seven can be expected to seek help for a mental problem during part of his life. This figure can be greatly decreased if we can get skilled care to the "behavior problem" child in time.

The child welfare worker can and should play an important role in all phases of any handicapped child's existence from the time the handicap is recognized until the maximum benefits of treatment have been realized and rehabilitation has been completed.

In case finding, a number of professions have a part. A doctor probably makes the original diagnosis; the teacher in the public school may be the first to notice the symptom and to suggest to the family that something be done; the public health nurse, either as a visiting nurse or as school nurse, may first spot the difficulty; or the child welfare worker, as a member of the staff of a public or private agency, may be the first outsider to learn that something is wrong—especially if the child is of preschool age. The worker should know of the facilities available for competent medical or psychiatric care and be able to refer the family properly.

The child welfare worker's responsibilities do not end with the referral. Her next task is to learn the parental reactions to obtaining care, the family financial status, and at least an inkling of the parents' attitudes toward the child. It may be that much work with the parents will be necessary before they are willing to cooperate in a plan for the child's care, and a worker already known to the family can probably do this more effectively than one unknown to them. It is also her place to present a summary of her knowledge of the total family situation to the medical agency so that it may have the most complete possible picture of the problem ahead.

In the actual treatment of handicapped children, parental attitudes can be either constructive or destructive. Some parents can accept the problem and the child, secure treatment, recognize the child's need for compensations, and let the handicap make little difference in family relationships. Others react by rejecting the child because of what they regard as his imperfections, and by developing various forms of guilt mechanisms to cover the rejection. Some manifestations of guilt mechanisms are overanxiety, overprotectiveness, and overstimulation of the child to achieve things beyond his ability.

Most of the destructive attitudes arise in parents who are immature or inadequate emotionally and thus unable to rise above an additional strain. Occasionally a person who has seemingly adjusted well to all other phases of living will show an unexpected weakness when confronted with a deformed or otherwise handicapped child. True parental attitudes are often uncovered during or after a disabling illness. One parent may have a destructive attitude and so negate some of the emotional gain made by a child during treatment.

In the treatment of a very young child, especially, the parental attitudes must be constructive if anything is to be accomplished, since the emotional development and maturation of the child depend so completely upon the atmosphere in which he lives. With the many strains of physical illness and handicaps pulling him in different directions, he could not be expected to make a satisfactory adjustment without the security of parental affection and approval.

Knowledge of parental attitudes and evaluation of them may determine how long a child should be kept in the hospital and whether he is to return to his own home or go to a convalescent or foster home for further treatment.

The child welfare worker helps the physically handicapped patient in any age group to reach a nice balance between being aware of (and reconciled to) the handicap, and striving for as much independent living as can be achieved. Occasional patients do themselves physical damage by refusing to admit their need for help, and instead they resign themselves to self-pity and helpless invalidism, which make needless misery for themselves and those upon whom they depend.

It is a duty of the worker to be watchful of the health of children in foster homes and in institutions for which she is working. Foster parents and others who are caring for children are required to have physical examinations; often it is left to the worker to evaluate the resulting medical information.

Supplementary Readings

Armor, David J. *The American School Counselor*. Russel Sage Foundation, New York, 1969.

Batten, Thomas Reginald. *The Non-Directive Approach in Group and Community Work*. Oxford University Press, London, 1967.

Beal, George M., Bohlen, Joe M., and Raudabaugh, J. Neil. *Leadership and Dynamic Group Action*. Iowa State University Press, Ames, 1962.

Benedict, Agnes E. *Children at the Crossroads*. Commonwealth Fund, New York, 1930.

Berne, Eric. *The Structure and Dynamics of Organizations and Groups*. Lippincott, Philadelphia, 1963.

Bonney, Merl Edwin. *Mental Health in Education*. Allyn and Bacon, Boston, 1960.

Brown, Sheldon S. *Guidance and Counseling for Jewish Education*. Bloch, New York, 1964.

Burmeister, Eva Elizabeth. *Tough Times and Tender Moments in Child Care Work*. Columbia University Press, New York, 1967.

Collins, Barry E. *A Social Psychology of Group Processes for Decision-Making*. Wiley, New York, 1964.

Davis, James H. *Group Performance*. Addison-Wesley, Reading, Mass., 1969.

Ellis, Richard W. B., Ed. *Child Health and Development*. Churchill, London, 1966.

Ferguson, Donald G. *Pupil Personnel Services*. Center for Applied Research in Education, Washington, D.C., 1963.

Glennen, Robert E. *Guidance*. Pruett Press, Boulder, Colorado, 1966.

Hill, Margaret. *What to Expect from School Counselors*. Public Affairs Committee, New York, 1967.

Humphrey, James Harry. *Elementary School Health Education*. Harper, New York, 1962.

Johnson, Arlien. *School Social Work—Its Contribution to Professional Education*. National Association of Social Workers, New York, 1962.

Jones, Mary Gwladys. *The Charity School Movement*. Archon Books, Hamden, Connecticut, 1964.

Klubard, Herbert M. *Religion and Education in America*. International Textbook Company, Scranton, Pennsylvania, 1969.

Konapka, Gisela. *Social Group Work*. Prentice-Hall, Englewood Cliffs, New Jersey, 1963.

Langdon, Grace, and Stout, Irving W. *Teaching Moral and Spiritual*

Values: A Parents' Guide to Developing Character. John Day, New York, 1962.

Lee, Grace, Ed. *Helping the Troubled School Child.* National Association of Social Workers, New York, 1959.

Lundberg, Horace W., Ed. *School Social Work—A Service to Schools.* Office of Education, Washington, D.C., 1964.

Mayshark, Cyrus. *Health Education in Secondary Schools.* C. V. Mosby, St. Louis, 1968.

Millar, Susanna. *The Psychology of Play.* Penguin Books, Baltimore, 1968.

Montessori, Maria. *The Child in the Church.* Catechetical Guild, St. Paul, Minnesota, 1965.

McCullough, M., and Ely, P. J. *Social Work with Groups.* Humanities Press, New York, 1969.

McLaughlin, Raymond. *Religious Education and the State: Democracy Finds a Way.* Catholic University of America Press, Washington, D.C., 1967.

Nebo, John C., Ed. *Administration of School Social Work.* National Association of Social Workers, New York, 1960.

Pheffer, Leo. *Church, State and Freedom.* Beacon Press, New York, 1964.

Pickard, P. M. *The Activity of Children.* Longmans, London, 1965.

Quattlebaum, Virginia, Ed. *School Social Work Practice.* National Association of Social Workers, New York, 1958.

Ruitenbeek, Hendrik M. *Group Therapy Today.* Atherton Press, New York, 1969.

Sayles, Mary B. *The Problem Child in School.* Commonwealth Fund, New York, 1927.

Vermes, Hal G., and Vermes, Jean. *Helping Youth Avoid Four Great Dangers: Smoking, Drinking, V. D., and Narcotics Addiction.* Association Press, New York, 1965.

Wallace, Helen M. *Health Services for Mothers and Children.* Saunders, Philadelphia, 1962.

Wessel, Janet A. *Fitness for the Modern Teen-Ager.* Ronald Press, New York, 1963.

[*Courtesy Office of Child Development, U.S. Department of Health, Education, and Welfare.*]

5

Selected Community Services for Children

Labor is an important influence on social behavior and on the social relations of the community. In all of its manifestation, it is closely associated with the economic structure of any community.

The use of child labor in Western society, including the United States, has had a long and depressing history of cruelty and exploitation of children and youth. In this chapter we will trace some of the more important legislative efforts in this country to control unregulated child labor, and we will discuss employment of young workers and the use of the volunteer as a community resource.

Aside from labor, another important factor influencing child welfare is the type of community, which demographers divide into two major categories, rural and urban. These designations include not only density of population but also ways of life, values, and subsocial systems. The significance of the rural community for child welfare, the family, children and types of social services will also be discussed.

EMPLOYMENT PROTECTION
FOR THE YOUNG WORKER

Unregulated child labor has been recognized as a social evil in the American economic order for years, but progress in controlling it has been laborious and slow. All of the states and territories have regulatory laws of a sort, but efforts for a uniform national law have been fought tooth and nail.

Few persons, if any, would take the position that a child should not be permitted to do any work; it is commonly recognized that the welfare of the child may benefit from some types of work (those which are well within his capabilities), because that type of employment can give him purpose, freedom, and an opportunity for self-development. However, it is generally agreed that a child should be protected from overwork and from types of work that crush or stultify him.

It is a fact that children have been exploited and abused by ruthless and inconsiderate employers whose sole concern has been mercenary gain. By law a minor is considered too immature to bind himself in the responsibilities of a contract, but the law permits him, if he has the consent of a parent, to assume responsibility for his own safety, health, and future in undertaking to labor for another. Hence many children have stunted their physical and mental growth, exposed themselves to serious physical and moral hazards, sacrificed their opportunities for education, and even lost their lives by working in unfit places under improper conditions at too young an age.

Child labor laws are society's protection of children from these adverse conditions, against which children alone are neither mature enough nor responsible enough to protect themselves.

In the early American colonial period, most of the work performed by children was about the houses of neighbors or relatives and could hardly be considered child exploitation in the present sense of the term. It was with the advent of factories in the United States that great changes came in the economic status of children. The early manufacturing establishments used such simple mechanical operations that children could do the work of adults and yet be paid lower wages.

The idea that children should work was generally accepted for several reasons. First, work was thought to be morally desirable and economically necessary. The Puritan tradition against idleness was so powerful that little time was set aside for play and leisure. Children were supposed to learn discipline and responsibility at an early age; life was a very serious matter. Second, the labor of children and women was considered to be a valuable asset to the colonies.

The colonies wished to become independent (especially economically) from the Old World and every pair of hands was needed. As early as 1790, Samuel Slater, founder of the cotton industry in the United States, hired nine children between the ages of seven and 12 in his first experimental cotton mill at Pawtucket, Rhode Island.

The first spinning machines were so simple to operate that a small handful of adult supervisors could oversee several hundred children as they tended the spindles. Then, as the industry expanded, the local supply of children proved to be insufficient, and the mills advertised in newspapers, by letter, and in leaflets for families with five or six children to settle near the mills, guaranteeing "constant employment and encouraging wages." The employers preferred boys and girls between the ages of eight and 12. And citizens considered it an act of public service to direct such children to the mills!

An advertisement appearing in *The Federal Gazette* of Baltimore on January 4, 1808, is an example of the enticing methods used to lure families and little children to the mills:

BALTIMORE COTTON MANUFACTORY

This Manufactory will go into operation in all of this month where a number of boys and girls from eight to twelve years of age are wanted, to whom constant employment and encouraging wages will be given: also, work will be given out to women at their homes, and *widows*, will have preference in all cases, where work is given out, and satisfactory recommendations will be expected.

This being the first essay of the kind, in this city, it is hoped that those citizens having a knowledge of families who have *children* destitute of employ, will do an act of Public benefit, by directing them to this institution.

Applications will be received by Thomas White, at the Manufactory near the Friend's Meetinghouse, Old Town, or by the subscribed. (Jan. 4, Isaac Burneston No. 196 Market Street.)

The figures of the *Digest of Manufacturers* in 1820 revealed the large percentage of youthful workers in the textile mills, the majority under the age of 12. In Rhode Island, children under 12 made up 55 percent of the labor force of the mills; in Connecticut, they made up 47 percent; in Massachusetts, 43 percent. Even the youngest children were not barred from industrial employment.

Early Child Labor Laws

Public attention was first focused on child labor when the long hours of toil interfered with education. A legislative remedy, sought in Connecticut in 1813, attempted to revive for that state the remarkable Massachusetts universal compulsory education law of 1647 by requiring from three to six months' schooling per year for all youth. Even before 1813, many of the mill owners felt impelled, because of public opinion and their own moral convictions, to provide religious instruction and elementary libraries for their young employees. Strange to say, few people seemed to question a child's ability to learn after toiling for 12 hours a day.

In 1836, Massachusetts provided that children under 15 could not be employed in manufacturing concerns unless they had been to school for three months of the year preceding. The workingmen's associations, or labor unions, exerted considerable pressure against the working of young children, and were to a very large degree responsible for this law of 1836.

The regulation of hours of work was the next step in child labor legislation. Massachusetts led the way in 1842 by prescribing a maximum ten-hour day for those under the age of 12; Connecticut followed suit the same year for children under 14. Several other states soon adopted similar measures. In 1853, a legislative committee in Rhode Island learned by investigation that many youngsters were working 12 hours for 11 or 12 months of the year. Immediately, an act was passed that restricted child labor to 11 hours per day and that set a fairly strong educational requirement for working children.

In about the middle of the nineteenth century, legislation began to be enacted to prohibit the employment of children, under certain ages, in manufacturing industries. Pennsylvania began in 1848 by barring children of 12 and under from working in factories. One year later the age was advanced to 13.

Other states followed. Rhode Island fixed the minimum age for factory work at 12 years in 1853; Connecticut, at nine years in 1855; Massachusetts, at ten years in 1866. By and large, however, these child labor prohibitions were ineffective because of the poor drafting of the laws, the inefficiency of enforcement, and also the lack of cooperation from either the employers or the parents. Evidently the parents did not understand that the presence of children in the labor market, at low wages, acted to lower the rates of pay for the adult workers.

Because their own wages were low, they felt that the wages of all members of the family were needed.

In the period following the war between the states (1861–65), tremendous advances were made in transportation and communication, in the expansion of factories, and the growth of cities. Many new opportunities for the employment of children arose because of this great and rapid industrial progress, particularly in the East. Children began to infiltrate the cigar-making and wood-working trades in such numbers that the skilled craftsmen in these trades became very fearful of the competition of cheap child labor. As labor-saving devices became more numerous and efficient, young, untrained workers entered other than the textile industries. Child labor was not confined to manufacture; there were openings, for instance, in messenger work, clerking, and the street trades (errand and delivery boys, news vendors, and so on).

Little, if any, attention was given to the educational and physical well-being of the young workers. Illiteracy increased alarmingly because the youngsters started working at such tender ages as seven or eight years.

People of all ages, down to the very young, began to undertake "homework"—small manufacturing tasks that could be done in the home—from 1885 on. Some of the homework conditions (in tenements and other undesirable places), hours, and wages of that era seem fantastic to the citizen of today.

Indications appeared in the last third of the nineteenth century that the federal government had begun at last to take cognizance of the child labor problem. In 1870, the Census Bureau of the United States began to gather information on the employment of persons over ten years of age, instead of only on those of 15 years and older, as before. The first convention of the American Federation of Labor, in 1881, adopted as one of its goals the complete abolition of labor by youngsters under 14. In Senate hearings of 1883, union spokesmen strongly pointed out that child labor was an injustice to a growing person, that it was inefficient, that the ultimate social costs were much too high, and that child employment was harmful competition to adult breadwinners.

Some years later, the various states began to realize that better child labor legislation was needed. The laws already passed lacked uniformity and seemed to attack the problem without any plan. When a state adopted a strict child labor law, it placed itself at an economic disadvantage because some of its industries were bound to move else-where. The wonder was that a few states had courage to make some attempt at regulating child labor. However, the laws usually lacked adequate coverage and their enforcement was lax.

Sincere advocates of child labor laws in the United States favored nationally unified laws. As early as 1888, the American Federation of Labor urged congressional action to control child labor. However, those favoring states' rights seriously questioned the power of Congress to pass laws for the direct and exclusive control of child labor. In 1899, the National Consumers League was formed. One of its main purposes was the elimination of child labor and industrial homework. Then, in 1905, the National Child Labor Committee was formed. Besides being largely responsible for the creation of the United States Children's Bureau in 1912, this pioneer private welfare agency is still working with public and private groups and with individuals to better the lot of children under the title of the National Committee on Employment of Youth of the National Child Labor Committee.

The first actual proposals for national regulation of child labor in the United States were made in Congress in 1906 in an effort to pro-vide uniform and effective control in the various states. Since then, this goal has been only partly attained. For the main part, two means of instituting national child labor laws have been explored: one is Constitutional amendment, and the other is the liberal interpretation of existing congressional powers under the interstate commerce clause of the Constitution. To date, the first method has been blocked and the second has afforded only limited results.

The initial federal proposals were made in December 1906 when Theodore Roosevelt was president. Nothing materialized immediately.

In 1907, the Bureau of Labor of the United States Department of Commerce and Labor conducted an extensive investigation of workers under the age of 16. Children of this age group composed 20 percent of the operatives in the textile industries in the South, 23 percent of those in the silk industries in Pennsylvania, and 10 percent of those engaged in the glass enterprises of the United States. Amazingly enough, it was found that, in families connected with the glass, textile, and silk industries, 84 to 96 percent of the children who were 14 or 15 years of age were at work.

During the years following, child labor bills of various kinds were proposed in each successive Congress, but none of them became law. The first ones were killed in committee; later, a few others were reported out of committee, but either they were never brought to a vote, or they were passed in one house but sidetracked or defeated in the other.

When national legislation on child labor finally became a fact, it was at first directed at the oppressive industrial labor of children in regimented industries such as mines, factories, and mills. Other child labor occupations, such as the street trades, appeared more difficult to regulate and therefore remained uncontrolled. Because of the many related legal, economic, and social issues, the achievement of uniform federal child labor legislation was slow indeed.

In September, 1916, the first national legislation was enacted when the Owen-Keating Bill regulating and restricting child labor was passed by Congress. This law did not become effective until September 1, 1917; employers had a full year in which to make necessary changes in their labor force.

This first law invoked the powers of Congress over interstate commerce to regulate the industrial labor of children. It prohibited the shipment in interstate and foreign commerce of goods produced in the following industries: in mines or quarries in which children under 16 were employed; in mills, canneries, workshops, factories, or other manufacturing establishments in which children under 14 were employed; or in those in which children of 14 to 16 years of age worked more than eight hours a day or six days a week, or between the hours of 7 P.M. and 6 A.M.

Although this law was an attempt in the right direction for the protection of young laborers, it had no provision covering the young agricultural worker. It made no mention of the many who laborered on farms to the detriment of education, health, and welfare—those who would be just as much a part of future society as the young workers needing protection from the hazards of mechanical and industrial labor.

This act was met with opposition organized and led by representatives of southern textile industries. In the summer of 1917, opponents argued that, since the United States had entered World War I, the military conscription and the demand for ships, munitions, and war supplies were creating a serious labor shortage; they urged that, therefore, the enforcement of the act should be postponed until after the war. However, Congress felt that curtailment of nonessential industries would provide a sufficient labor force for war industries. This position of the federal government did much to prevent state legislatures from passing ill-considered acts by giving state officials moral backing to oppose any demands for relaxation in state laws. Indications were that in the winter of 1917–1918 there was less rather than more employment of children, in violation of state laws, than in previous years.

The Owen-Keating Act provided that the power to make rules and regulations for carrying out its provisions be given to a board composed of the Attorney General, the Secretary of Commerce, and the Secretary of Labor. It provided that this board should decide the conditions under which, and the persons by whom, federal work permits or employment certificates for minors should be issued. The child labor laws in each state were examined to determine whether they met minimum standards of the federal law. If they did, the state was permitted to serve as an agent of the federal government in the issuance of work permits for minors and in the making of enforcement inspections.

This law went into effect in September, 1917, and was administered by the U.S. Children's Bureau. On June 3, 1918, however, it was declared unconstitutional by a five-to-four decision of the U.S. Supreme Court in the *Hammer vs. Dagenhart* case. The decision stated that the attempt of Congress to bar the products of child labor from interstate commerce was an unconstitutional attempt to control the processes of production and manufacture, which were supposed to be a subject of state or local concern.

The second attempt at federal regulation of child labor was a tax law that imposed a tax of 10 percent on the profits of mines or manufacturing establishments that were employing children in violation of the standards originally set forth under the Owen-Keating measure. This tax law was included in the Revenue Act of February 1919 and remained in operation until May, 1922. On that date, by an eight-to-one decision in *Bailey vs. Drexel Furniture Company*, the United States Supreme Court held the tax to be unconstitutional because it was not a valid exercise of the taxing power of Congress.

The supporters of child labor reform then sought an amendment to the Constitution of the United States in order to achieve federal control and afford protection to the hundreds of thousands of child laborers who had not been reached by the sporadic and ineffective legislation of the states.

Accordingly, President Warren G. Harding recommended an amendment to the Constitution that would directly give Congress unquestionable power to legislate for the regulation of child labor. However, the amendment was not presented to Congress until 1924, when Calvin Coolidge was president. The proposed amendment was introduced in the Senate by Samuel M. Shortridge from California and in the House of Representatives by Israel M. Foster from Ohio. The House passed the amendment on April 26, 1924, by 61 to 23.

The proposed Child Labor Amendment declares the following: Section 1: the Congress shall have power to limit, regulate and prohibit the labor of persons under eighteen years of age; Section 2: the power of the several States is unimpaired by this article except that the operation of State laws shall be suspended to the extent necessary to give effect to legislation enacted by the Congress.

Despite the large vote in its favor—more than four-to-one in the House and nearly three-to-one in the Senate—the proposed amendment is not yet a part of the Constitution. The necessary ratification by three-quarters of the states has not been accomplished, although more than four decades have passed. When the amendment came up for ratification, it met with tremendous campaigns of opposition. Because of this opposition, only four states ratified in 1924 and 1925. The adversaries propagandized the nation so effectively that interest waned, and only two more states acted favorably.

During the depression, children were working at deadening and hazardous occupations for extremely low wages while adult men were unemployed and standing in bread lines. In 1933, President Franklin D. Roosevelt wrote to the governors of many states prevailing upon them to encourage their states to ratify the Child Labor Amendment, and in that year 14 more states ratified.

To this outstanding success, the opposition retaliated by organizing a well planned campaign, concerned primarily with resisting ratification of the amendment. Opponents have even claimed that the proposed amendment would make it illegal for a mother to ask her daughter to wash the lunch dishes or her son to bring in an armload of kindling.

Because of this counterthrust, only eight additional states ratified between 1934 and 1938, bringing the total to 28. The refusal of certain state legislatures to ratify is directly opposed to public opinion as was seen in a nationwide poll conducted by the American Institute of Public Opinion in the early part of 1937. This poll showed that a majority of the citizens of each of the 48 states favored the Amendment, and that in the country as a whole 76 percent favored ratification. This indicates the effectiveness of the opposition. Following is a list of the states that have ratified the Amendment and the year of the action:

Arizona 1925	Maine 1933	Ohio 1933
Arkansas 1924	Michigan 1933	Oklahoma 1933
California 1925	Minnesota 1933	Oregon 1933
Colorado 1931	Montana 1927	Pennsylvania ..1933
Idaho 1935	Nevada 1937	Utah 1935
Illinois 1933	New Hamp-	Washington ..1933
Indiana 1935	shire 1933	West Virginia .1933
Iowa 1933	New Jersey ..1933	Wisconsin 1925
Kansas 1937	New Mexico ..1937	Wyoming 1935
Kentucky 1937	North Dakota .1933	

After 1937, little effort was made to secure additional states for the ratification of the amendment, because its objective was in large part achieved through the Fair Labor Standards Act of 1938.

Later Child Labor Laws

During the depression years of the 1930's, when employers preferred cheap child labor to more expensive adult labor, the public demanded regulation, not so much for the protection of health and welfare of children as for the economic purpose of decreasing adult unemployment.

The National Industrial Recovery Act was passed by Congress on June 13, 1933, for the stated purposes of meeting the emergency of national unemployment, eliminating unfair competitive practices, improving standards of labor, and increasing purchasing power. The act provided for the national organization of industry into a kind of cartel plan. Each industry was asked to submit a detailed plan of its organization, pricing, labor, and competitive practices to the President of the United States for approval. These plans were called codes, and the President was authorized to prescribe a code for an industry in any given area of the United States that failed to submit one of its own.

When the National Recovery Act was passed, only four states had previously required a minimum age of 16 for labor. Most of the codes fixed the general minimum age at 16 years for employment, and a higher minimum age at 18 for hazardous work. The codes differed widely throughout the country and local enforcement was often weak and ill-defined; nevertheless, child labor decreased to a considerable extent for a period.

The Supreme Court in May, 1935 ruled that the Act was unconstitutional, abruptly ending the operation of these codes. Child labor again increased notably, the increase being as high as 150 to 182 percent in some areas.

Within two years after the nullification of the National Recovery Act, more than 30 bills affecting child labor were introduced in Congress. The most notable were the Barkley bill, the Wheeler-Johnson bill, and the Black-Connery Labor Standards bill. Some of the bills dealt directly and exclusively with the employment of children. Others, such as the Walsh-Healy bill, included provisions concerning minors along with general labor regulations.

The Walsh-Healy bill, passed by Congress June 30, 1936, was concerned primarily with government contracts in excess of $10,000, and it specified conditions of employment, labor, and wages that contractors working on federal contracts must meet. This law is still in effect. Its exact provision pertaining to the subject of child labor is as follows:

> That no male person under sixteen years of age and no female person under eighteen years of age and no convict labor will be employed by the contractor in the manufacture or production or furnishing of any of the materials, supplies, articles or equipment included in such contract.

In the years 1936 and 1937, the various other bills introduced in Congress that sought the regulation of child labor contained one or a combination of principles. Some proposed to implement the states to enact uniform child labor laws that would embody the principles of the first child labor legislation; others proposed new child labor amendments to the Constitution, most of them setting a minimum age and devising some substitute for the word "labor." All of these bills were prevented from becoming law.

The 1937 Sugar Act had direct application to agricultural child labor. Under its provisions federal benefit payments were denied to those producers of sugar beets and sugar cane who employed children under 14 years of age or who worked children between 14 and 16 years of age for more than eight hours a day. The protection did not apply to the children of anyone who legally owned at least 40 percent of the crop at the time the work was performed. But it set a precedent for the protection of young agricultural workers employed elsewhere than on their families' farms. And the greater portion of young workers in agriculture do not work on the home farms.

In 1941, the provisions of this act were extended and also amended to provide that the Secretary of Agriculture could make benefit payments to a grower who had failed to comply with the child labor provisions, but that a deduction of $10 would be made for each child for each day or portion of a day during which that child was employed or permitted to work contrary to the provisions.

The Sugar Act of 1948, like the earlier Sugar Act, which expired at the end of 1947, provides for payment benefits to growers of sugar beets and sugar cane who comply with certain conditions. One of these conditions is that such growers do not employ children under 14 years of age in cultivating and harvesting, and do not employ children between 14 and 16 years of age in such work for more than eight hours a day. Benefit payments are still subject to deduction in case a child is employed or permitted to work contrary to such standards. The Sugar Act is administered by the United States Department of Agriculture.

Although the beet and sugar cane products are only two agricultural products from a vast array, the sugar acts exemplify the somewhat circuitous means that federal legislation has had to employ in order to control, and to a very limited extent at that, the youth labor problem in agriculture.

The Fair Labor Standards Act of 1938 was the result of a great amount of attempted legislation and controversy pertaining to child labor laws and labor laws in general. During its consideration by Congress, it was known as the wages and hours bill. Attention was centered on the wage and hour provisions; the child labor provisions met little opposition.

This act, passed in June, 1938, also invoked Congress' power to control interstate commerce in much the same manner as did the Owen-Keating bill. It constitutes a major victory in the battle against child labor. The act sets minimum ages for the employment of minors in interstate or foreign commerce, or in the production of goods for shipment in interstate or foreign commerce. The child labor requirements of the Fair Labor Standards Act now also apply to agriculture. These requirements apply to the employment of migratory children as well as local resident children, but not to the employment by a farmer of his own children on his farm.

The measure fixes 16 as the basic minimum age for general employment, and 18 as the minimum in occupations that are declared hazardous. For minors of 14 and 15, special provision is made for limited employment outside of school hours in a few occupations. For example, most of the employees in the communications industry (including telegraph companies) and in transportation, public utilities, and some construction are subject to the child labor provisions of the act because they engage in commerce. Employers are directly prohibited from employing children who are under the minimum age limits in commerce or in the production of goods for commerce. An exemption of employees engaged in the delivery of newspapers to consumers is added, and the exemption for actors and performers has been broadened to include radio and televison productions in addition to motion picture and theatrical productions.

The conditions of work applying to children of 14 and 15 are the following: no work may be performed during school hours; when school is in session these children may work a maximum of three hours a day and 18 hours a week; when school is not in session they may work a maximum of eight hours per day and 40 hours per week; all work must be performed between 7 A.M and 7 P.M

By an amendment of August 6, 1942, the following exception to the foregoing was put into effect for the duration of World War II: children of 14 and 15 might be employed in perishable fruit and vegetable packing sheds (but not in canneries) until 10 P.M. for a period of not more than eight work weeks in any calendar year. For such employees, the following conditions were mandatory: a maximum six-day week; a meal period 45 minutes; there was to be no employment on days when school was in session; records of the names and addresses of children employed after 7 P.M., and of the work weeks in which they were so employed were to be kept.

Another wartime provision of the same amendment said that children 14 and 15 years of age could be employed in cutting pears, peaches, and apricots in fruit-drying yards under the following conditions: maximum six-day week; a meal period of 45 minutes; a 15-minute rest period in each half day; provision for seats to be used while working, pure drinking water, washing facilities, and toilet facilities; no employment in which there was risk of exposure to sulfur-dioxide fumes. (This amendment was revoked on September 28, 1945, and the nullification became effective October 31, 1945.)

Under the Fair Labor Standards Act, the Children's Bureau was charged with administering a system of granting age certificates or employment permits to employed minors. In states and territories equipped to administer such a plan in their own geographical areas, this responsibility is delegated to local school authorities, state departments of labor, or state departments of education.

Under the President's reorganization plan, effective July 16, 1946, the powers formerly exercised by the Chief of the United States Children's Bureau were transferred to the Secretary of Labor, who has designated the Wage and Hour and Public Contracts Division as the administrative agency. The federal government, through the Wage and Hour and Public Contracts Division of the United States Department of Labor, issues age certificates and employment permits directly in these states because state facilities either are not available or are not organized to administer such a program.

The Fair Labor Sandards Act holds employers of minors responsible for obtaining and keeping on file age certificates and employment permits showing that each minor employee is old enough to engage in the occupation in which he is working. The Children's Bureau drew up a standard recommended form and method of procedure for the granting of work permits, which it encouraged the states to adopt. Whenever state standards for employment of children are higher than federal standards, the state standards prevail.

Since 1938, a great body of administrative rules and regulations concerning enforcement of the child labor provisions of the Fair Labor Standards Act has developed. These administrative refinements of the broadly written act have been necessary to meet the hundreds of perplexing situations encountered in enforcement. Many have been formulated by the exercise of powers granted the Children's Bureau by the act.

The 1949 amendments to the Fair Labor Standards Act extended the application of child labor provisions to employment in commerce or in production of goods for commerce. Thus the employment of telegraph messengers is now subject to these provisions, and the minimum age for such employment is 16. It has been ruled that occupations in many industries are included within the definition of interstate commerce, so they are thus subject to the act. For example, the manufacture of men's shirts for local sale within a state is considered interstate commerce if even the buttons used are made in another state.

The Wage and Hour and Public Contracts Division of the Department of Labor makes all investigations for compliance in the wage and hour provisions and in the child labor provisions of the act. Investigation is done by regional federal inspectors with business and

accounting backgrounds. These inspectors are responsible for all provisions of the act, not only the child labor provisions. Other inspections of industrial establishments, such as an audit of payrolls and
personnel records and personal inspections of the premises, are made
periodically. There is an attempt to make at least an annual inspection
of every established industry; and, in addition, all new establishments
are inspected when they begin operations. When irregularities in the
employment of minors, overtime work, and wage computation methods for overtime work are revealed in industries engaging in interstate commerce, the provisions of the act are explained to the pro-
prietor and a warning is given. A follow-up inspection is made in a
few months; if violations are found to persist, legal action is taken.

In 1941, the question of the constitutionality of the Fair Labor
Standards Act was taken before the United States Supreme Court in
the case of the *United States versus Darby Lumber Company*. In
sustaining the act, the Court clearly overruled its earlier decision in
the case of *Hammer versus Dagenhart*.

In August, 1946, when the Children's Bureau moved to the Federal Security Agency, its Industrial Division remained in the Department of Labor. It is now known as the Child Labor and Youth Employment Branch of the Division of Labor Standards. This branch is
the administrator of the child labor provision of the Fair Labor Standards Act, and it will promote standards in the field of youth employment. The wage and hour provisions are administered by the Wage
and Hour and Public Contracts Division of the department.

We have said that all states and all territories have some provisions
governing child labor. These laws vary widely in content and application: one might be a statement in minute detail of the conditions
for the employment of minors; another, the barest legal framework
on the subject. Similarly state child labor laws vary widely in effectiveness.

Most state laws regulating child labor are closely coordinated with
the compulsory education laws of the state. In fact, all but two states,
Idaho and South Carolina, maintain some sort of accounting procedure
to determine that a child is either attending school or working. It is
for this reason that laws pertaining to the employment of minors are
to be found in either state labor codes or state school codes, or in
both.

The state employment certificate requirements follow a general
pattern, though of course there are variations. In general, to obtain an
employment certificate, the child must submit proof of his age and a

statement from the employer agreeing to give him a job. (This statement is the promise of employment.) The certificate will not be issued unless the child is permitted to leave school for work. In some states, the child may also be required to have parental consent and to pass a physical or medical examination showing his fitness to do the job.

In more than half of the states, minors up to the age of 16 are legally required to present promise of employment as a condition for obtaining certificates. Practically all of the remaining states require this promise in practice. The employer's statement is essential, because it prevents a young person from leaving school unless he has a job.

There is usually no educational requirement for a certificate in those states that have established a 16-year minimum age for work during school hours. A school record is often required, however, and completion of the sixth or eighth grade is commonly required in those states in which the minimum age for work during school hours is 14. Every state, except Wyoming, has a minimum age: in 23 states, it is 16 years; in two states, 15 years; and in 22 states, 14 years. In Wyoming there is no provision except that children whose attendance at school is required by law shall not be employed at any occupation or service during school hours. Every state except South Carolina, which repealed its law in 1955, has compulsory school attendance laws.

In most states, the local school authorities issue the work permits or age certificates for employed children. However, in a few states, the county superintendent of schools or the state labor commissioner is charged with this responsibility.

In many states, the state labor department is responsible for the enforcement of state child labor laws. In other states however, such laws are enforced by the state department of industry or industrial welfare. Only five states authorize the state education authority to enforce child labor regulations, and 15 states have made enforcement a joint responsibility of both the state labor department and the state education authority. In practice, enforcement is effected by many kinds of public officials, teachers, truant officers, probation officers, county agriculture agents, sheriffs, factory inspectors, and county judges, to name a few.

Some states have assumed the responsibility for providing a program of rehabilitation for children suffering industrial or other work injuries. Too many children in need of retraining do not get it. The laws of New York, Oregon, and Arizona provide a stipulated amount of maintenance and other expenses incidental to rehabilitation. Virginia fixes a maximum amount at $800. Every child should be given the opportunity to be retrained at a new job if, because of an accident, he can no longer earn his living at the job he knew.

The children engaged in agricultural labor pose one of the most serious of all child labor problems. Very little responsibility has been taken by the states for this greatly exploited group, which includes a large number of very young workers. Children who should be in school or at play are put into the fields to work long hours at hard and monotonous chores for a pittance. However, now that the Fair Labor Standards Act applies to agriculture, these conditions should be eliminated.

The problem of transient children is serious in some states. The abuses to the migratory worker, especially the child, are known to all. The local community feels no responsibility for this group because they are not local residents. Therefore it is especially important that the state assume its responsibility and protect this group of people. Often the state disclaims responsibility because the workers do not have state residence. A child in need of care should not be denied it simply because he happens to come from another state, nor should his family.

There is special need for states to enforce school attendance laws, whether or not the parents of the child are legal residents, and thus accomplish the dual objective of educating the child and of taking him out of the agricultural labor market at least during school hours.

The children of minority groups are especially in need of protection, which only the state can give them. Yet despite the urgency of legal protection, the need goes unmet. There is need for the development of rural welfare services and for strengthening of those services now provided. Once adequate social services have been developed for the rural child, the protection of the child from abuses in the fields and farms will be made easier. More adequate rural educational programs will also help. Rural school truancy laws are frequently not enforced.

It is the responsibility of the state to pass adequate child labor laws to regulate hours of work, working conditions, pay, minimum ages of children, recruitment of children, living conditions in work camps and homes, and health provisions for the child. The coverage of these laws needs to be complete, so that every child who is in the labor market is under state supervision and control. The Fair Labor Standards Act does not cover intrastate industries. Unless children under 16 years of age are protected by state labor laws, therefore, they can be employed in hotels, restaurants, bowling alleys, theaters, and many other establishments.

A central system of reporting should be developed so that states will know about every child that is employed—his age, physical condition, conditions of work, and so on. There is need for the appropriation of adequate funds to permit the effective administration of good child labor laws. Also needed are revised methods of penalizing the employer who disregards the law. He should be prosecuted as the law provides he should be. He should be placed upon probation and further infringements of the child labor laws should bring punishment. Too often, the payment of a fine means little or nothing to the employer, because the fine to be paid is so small that it can be just deducted as a business loss, so that in effect it is not punishment at all.

The laws should be enforced throughout the state; they should be just, but strictly enforced. The National Child Labor Committee and the American Association for Labor Legislation have set up minimum standards for working children. In general, these standards require that state laws specify the following: a minimum age of 18 for hazardous employment; a minimum age of 16 for all children placed in farm work away from home; a minimum age of 14 or 15 for work during vacations or after school for any employment; a maximum of eight hours a day, and a maximum 40-hour week; a requirement that a child's schooling not be interrupted for periods of time with certain exceptions; special protection for girls; elimination of night work and overtime work; adequate pay, and vacations; complete physical and medical examination; documentary proof of age; work permits; the establishment of a state agency responsible for child labor protection, such agency to have copies of all work permits and a registry of all minors employed in the state; adequate protection for compensation; an adequate program of rehabilitation.

It is the duty of every child welfare worker to know the federal child welfare laws and the laws of the state in which she is working. She should also know whether they are being enforced. She must interpret the laws and the reasons for their enforcement to citizens who, once they understand the need, can and will help to obtain better laws and work for their enforcement.

The child welfare worker is also in a strategic position to work for improvement in the laws and for a sound employment certificate system.

It is estimated that by 1980 there will be more youth between the ages of 14 and 17 in the population than there are at present if the present population trends prevail. The percentage of youth enrolled in school in October 1954 was higher than it had ever been: 96 percent of those 14 and 15 years of age, and 78 percent of those 16 and 17 years of age were enrolled in school. This was partly due to the advance in education of youth resulting from the agricultural provision in the Fair Labor Standards Act.

The social costs of child labor are the following: (1) impairment of health, both mental and physical; (2) lack of the normal child development that is a consequence of play and rest; (3) such severe curtailment of education that many do not even absorb the bare rudiments; (4) poverty and unnecessary dependency; (5) delinquency; (6) industrial waste; (7) social and political loss (loss of potential leaders and good citizens).

International Efforts

Unfortunately, World War I interrupted the operation of the International Association for Labor Legislation, whose offices were in Basel, Switzerland. This quasi-official organization was financed by various governments, and it collected statistics and published reports. Under its auspices, the Berne Conferences of 1905 and 1906 formulated the first multilateral labor conventions, which prohibited night work for women. Also, the International Secretariat of Trade Union Centers, made up of the national federations of trade unions in 19 countries, worked closely with the International Labor Organization in promoting legislation designed to improve the working conditions of children; but World War I interrupted this splendid work also. In order to survive, European powers as well as other nations relaxed their hard-won standards for child labor in order to swell the numbers of industrial workers. In World War II, a similar move took place.

The International Labor Organization, formed as an adjunct of the now defunct League of Nations, gave new hope to those who were carrying on the crusade for child labor regulation. This organization functions through three agencies: (1) the International Labor Conference; (2) the Governing Board; (3) the International Labor Office. The International Labor Conference is the parliamentary assembly to which each country annually sends four representatives: two from government, one employer, and one from labor. Sixty-six nations are now represented by such delegates. The Governing Board is the executive council of the ILO. The director, appointed by the governing body, in turn appoints the staff. In general, the staff is organized in sections, of which the main ones include Official Relations, Conference, Administrative, Safety, Economic, and Industrial Hygiene. The annual budget is financed by assessment upon member states. The International Labor Office, its secretariat, has its headquarters in Geneva. In 1919, the General Conference of the ILO met in Washington, D.C. to organize, and, since this initial meeting, it has maintained its office in Geneva, Switzerland, close to the former headquarters of the League. The United States did not join the ILO until August 20, 1934.

The functions of the ILO are to draft conventions embodying standards for labor legislation, to maintain official contacts with member governments and other member bodies, to collect and publish information concerning labor conditions and legislation in the various countries in general and about child labor in particular. The ILO has also compiled comparisons of national child labor laws.

The official languages used are French and English, but the more important publications are put out in other languages also. The ILO issues a number of periodicals. The weekly publication, *Industrial and Labor Information,* gives news notes from all over the world and brief reports of the governing body, whereas the other publications are highly specialized.

Among the major international conventions drafted for labor have been those relating to the employment of children, to an eight-hour work day; and to a 48-hour week.

One of the conventions fixes the minimum wages in trades in which they were low. Nine countries have ratified this so far.

Another convention sets a minimum age of 14 years for employment in industry, agriculture, and at sea. Twenty powers have thus far ratified this. In addition, France, Italy, Germany, Sweden, and Austria ratified, but with reservations allowing child employment in case of family poverty.

A convention prohibiting night work in industry by those under 18 years of age has been ratified by 25 countries, including Great Britain, Belgium, Netherlands, Austria, Poland, Italy, and France. Many other conventions have been ratified by from 13 to 25 nations.

The International Labor Organization was instrumental in helping some of the countries of Latin America to enact their first child labor regulations. Peru, in 1918, had passed its initial child labor measure; Argentina and Chile passed theirs in 1924; Guatemala, in 1926; Brazil and Colombia, in 1927; Ecuador and Venezuela, in 1928; Costa Rica, in 1932.

In general, it might be said that in many foreign countries, compulsory school attendance keeps the children in school until they are 14; however, the laws of some nations excuse younger children if the family is destitute, if the distance to school is too great, or if the child has attained a certain degree of proficiency. Employment of 12-year-old children outside school hours is permitted. Also, in many countries, it is the general rule not to regulate the hours of minors apart from those of adults.

Canada has fairly progressive regulations. Its Child Welfare Act of 1936 says that those under 18 shall not be employed between 9 P.M. and 6 A.M. except by a special license issued by the municipality. It also states that no license to work shall be granted to a child under 14 without written consent from parent or guardian, and that no work license shall be issued to a child under 12.

Conferences on international labor have been held quite regularly since the founding of the International Association for Labor Legislation in 1900 in Paris. The first International Labor Conference was held in 1919 at Washington, D.C.

When the representatives of 48 nations gathered in Paris, October 15, 1945, for the twenty-seventh session of the International Labor Conference, the first postwar meeting, considerable emphasis was placed on the problems of children and youth. This was indicative of the growing international interest in child welfare that is so prominent today.

Twelve meetings of the Committee on Protection of Children and Young Workers were devoted to a draft resolution on the protection of children and young workers and another resolution on youth of liberated countries. The text of the first resolution had been prepared after consultation with the experts who met in Montreal in May, 1945. This resolution aimed to present a coordinated scheme of various measures for the realization of the essential objectives of the International Labor Organization on the protection of youth, which had been formulated in its constitution in the Declaration of Philadelphia. The draft resolution was approved.

Two other resolutions were adopted: one is concerned with regulating the underground work of young persons in mines; the other requests the governing body to set up an advisory committee for studying the problems of young workers.

The results of the work of ILO to date are most gratifying. When it was organized in 1919, few countries in western and central Europe had social insurance laws. The ILO recommended and worked for several insurance laws, modern social assistance statutes to replace the old laws for relief of the poor, laws for the protection of unmarried women and children born out of wedlock, child labor laws, and laws for maternity and infant protection. It succeeded in having established in member nations such programs as workman's compensation laws, health insurance, unemployment compensation, old age insurance, and family allowance programs.

The ILO works in close cooperation with the Economic and Social Council (ECOSOC) to develop a comprehensive system of social welfare for the protection of families and children.

If sound preventive measures could be put into effect all over the world, society might approach the ideal state for the care of its children. They would have an opportunity to be in school and would be given a chance to develop to mental and physical maturity. Let us exert ourselves in this direction.

CHILDREN IN RURAL AREAS

The term "rural," as used in the United States Census, includes all persons living on farms and in incorporated places having a population of less than 2,500. Places of more than 2,500 in population are counted as urban. Thus the term "rural" would also include mining towns, small factory towns, and suburbs.

The words "rural area" evoke a definite picture, but the details depend entirely upon the type of rural area. To one person, it may mean cornfields stretching to the horizon; to another, stony hillside lots that are mean in yield and size; to some, a coal camp; and to others, the suburban area in which city workers have their homes. It is obvious that in four such regions local problems differ widely. However, we will use the term rural in a restricted sense, basing the classification on the type of social system in which the individual finds himself. This will exclude those people who live in rural districts but whose work and social connections are urban. For our purpose, then, the basis of rural life in its restricted sense is the farm family and the village that serves the family.

The Rural Area as a Social System

Villages of 2,500 or less in an agricultural area and the life of the farm family are inseparable since the villages are dependent upon the income from goods of which the farmer is the consumer, and the farmer is dependent upon the facilities of the village for marketing his produce.

Everything distinctive in American rural life, as contrasted with the life of the cities, is in some way a product of the family-farm organization. If the occupation of agriculture were generally carried on under a factory system, the problems would be but slightly differentiated phases of the social and industrial problems which characterize urban life. One can see this trend now in the large corporation farms in different parts of the United States.

The personalities of the villages are as varied as the personalities of the people who live in them. The geography of the area determines to some extent the nature of the economy (rural Arizona and rural Vermont present widely different pictures), and that economy may to a large extent influence culture.

Culture is said to include man's heritage of material goods, his intellectual knowledge, his system of moral, spiritual, and economic values, his social organization, and his language.

The complexity and multiplicity of factors—history, region, economy, degree of isolation from urban centers—make generalization a hazardous task. However, certain characteristics differentiate rural areas from the urban centers.

The rural village is a compact and relatively simple unit. The physical distance from the homes of the wealthy citizens of the town to the shacks "across the tracks" is comparatively short. The banker's wife will patronize the same grocery store as does the wife of the section hand on the railroad. The son of the town's leading doctor goes to high school with the son of his mother's laundress. This does not necessarily mean that the social distance between people may not be great; but it does mean that they see and know one another in a manner not found in the city with its more numerous subdivisions of schools, shopping districts, and residential areas.

Rural people listen to the same radio and television programs, read the same magazines, and see the same movies as do their city brethren. Along the business streets of the villages are branches of the well known chain stores of the city; the goods on the shelves display the same standard brands; the corner drugstore sells the cigarettes the city dweller smokes, and the gas station handles his favorite gasoline. Where, then, does the difference lie?

The difference can be illustrated in this way: the gas station is not just the filling station with the familiar red, white, and blue sign. It is Don Dawson's station. Don walks into the drugstore for a package of cigarettes and Ed Anderson, with whom he has gone to grade school and high school, says, "Say, Don, Ethel called up and wants you to bring home a bottle of this new mosquito repellant. Figured you must be going up on the Gunnison fishing this Sunday. How are the fish biting now?" In other words, the townspeople know one another; they know the habits of one another.

The area may be one of those in the United States in which various groups are isolated from general community life—in which social patterns, rigid traditions, and customs influence the culture of the people holding them, and weld them into a unit even in the midst of others.

Groups like the Acadians—more commonly known as "Cajuns"—of south-west Louisiana, a fairly homogeneous people of French descent, resolutely resisted the cultural influences of surrounding groups until World War II. The German-Russian groups of several middle western states have retained some old customs but have not successfully repelled outside influence in recent years. The Navajo Indians of the southwest have tended to perpetuate their own social heritage best of all, but have not been immune to outside influences.

Not only these groups that are held together by language, race, or nationality present distinct cultural patterns; but in certain sections there is inflexibility of religious belief and a community moralistic attitude and prejudice toward the ne'er-do-well, the unmarried mother, the child born out of wedlock, or the alcoholic. For example, Elva M. might come to the child welfare worker for help. The worker sees her as an insecure and emotionally immature youngster from a deprived home, who is going to have a baby out of wedlock. The attitudes of the people in the area may range from an apathetic attitude to outright hostility toward Elva and her problem. They see her as that wild M. girl, old F. M.'s oldest. Everybody knows old F. M. is a no-account loafer who hasn't done a lick of work for years. Didn't Elva's mother run away with a ranch hand? Wasn't her grandma a little wild before that? Sure, what can you expect? Runs in the family.

It would be unfair to imply that attitudes in the rural areas are unsympathetic. They vary from place to place with the rigidity of the mores. People are closely concerned with the troubles and triumphs of one another. When death occurs, there is a genuine sympathetic response of neighbors to the bereaved family. When Ted wins a scholarship to the state university, the village weekly paper writes a feature article about him, and the whole community is proud of its product. In certain situations, the overwhelming response of the countryside may occasion the use of diplomacy of the highest order on the part of the child welfare worker in the selection and rejection of suggestions and offers to help.

The disparity between farm income and the cost of living, and the great effort required to wrest a living from submarginal land or from a farm of uneconomic size not only present problems due to an unbalanced agricultural economy but also may produce personality problems engendered by the struggle for survival. This definitely affects decisions by township trustees on who should receive financial assistance, and under what circumstances. Frugality, thrift, and moral standards are apt to enter into the decision.

This majority of children living in rural areas have far less than a majority of the resources of the nation for their needs in health, education, recreation, and adequate housing.

The most striking characteristic of family-farm life is without doubt the closely knit organization of the family. Two forces are responsible for the high degree of solidarity which exists. First, there is the factor of physical isolation. Because there are fewer opportunities on the farm for contacts with the outside world than there are elsewhere, the individual members must depend upon the remainder of the family group very largely for their social life. Second, the nature of the occupation is such that all members must spend a considerable part of their working hours together. The family farm is really a family undertaking, and the farm father is the head of the family in a more real sense than are many fathers who are in other occupations.

Farm-family solidarity is frequently exhibited throughout a larger group than that made up simply of the parents and the children. The grandparents on one side or the other may exert considerable influence in the determination of family procedures. Farm parents are forever faced by work to be done. This may be one reason that child labor seems to be tied up with the family farm. When parents think of child labor, it may seem to be a natural part of their life. Many who see no justification for child labor in industry see nothing but good to be derived from child labor on farms, giving such reasons as the benefit of fresh air and the wholesome contact with parents.

A fairly high proportion of men on farms in America never seriously considered entering any other occupation. They did not choose, but simply proceeded through their childhood apprenticeship until in the natural course of events they became farmers. Another group is made up of those who at one time or another really desired and possibly planned to enter some other occupation, but who remained on the farm because they were needed and the force of circumstances seemed to prevent them from realizing other ambitions. The smallest group is that which chose the occupation of farming rather than some other which they might have taken on equal terms. Women are more apt to leave the farm and go to the city to find a job. Consequently there is a higher percentage of men than women on the farms.

The farm girl realizes that if she remains on the farm and becomes a farm wife she will not lead a life of luxury. She will pay her way as a member of a working unit. Choice of wife or husband is limited in regions of relatively high degree of physical isolation; it is often manipulated by parents. The acquisition of a daughter-in-law who will make a good farm wife—or a son-in-law who will add one more worker to the farm labor force—is usually given careful consideration by parents. The farmer's wife shares the family occupation with her husband. In the urban family, the woman shifts more of the housekeeping to outside establishments such as bakeries, laundries, and food shops. It is a traditional ideal that many household tasks remain in the farm home even if the farm families can well afford to have work done outside the home.

The age of marriage in rural life is younger than that in urban areas and the rural birth rate is higher than the urban. The urban population may consider children a luxury and sacrifice their desire for children in an economic and social struggle for success. The arrival of children in the farm family does not tend to interfere so much with farm life. There is, however, a woeful lack of good maternity care in rural areas. Medical care and hospital services have lagged far behind programs in urban areas. Many farmers are not aware of what services can be given to them and their families by hospitals, clinics, and medical skill. Because of this lack of knowledge, they have not demanded adequate health services.

Distance from a local doctor's office and lack of money to pay for care are two principal reasons why treatment of children's illnesses is often delayed until it is too late. In many rural areas, improperly balanced diets, due to the inability to secure proper foods, result in malnutrition and vitamin deficiency among children.

The opportunity for help through the aid of a child guidance clinic or a psychiatrist seldom exists in rural areas. Sometimes a mobile clinic may be available to a few sections of a state, but this is the unusual situation. If the rural area is close enough to an urban area where mental health facilities exist, a child may be taken to the clinic or hospital for diagnosis and treatment. This procedure is usually an attempt to care for a condition that might have been prevented if help had been available closer to home.

Often farm housing is substandard. Although the house may be large enough so there is not undue crowding, sanitary facilities may be entirely lacking, and although much more work related to the home function is carried on in the farm house than in the urban home, the typical farm home is less adequately supplied with modern conveniences than is the average urban home. Although many farming communities now have available to them electricity, motorized equipment, and other modern conveniences, these are far from common to rural homes, or within the purchasing power of many. Income is uncertain, owing to unexpected loss of crops or stock, fluctuating prices, and limited bargaining power.

Education

Perhaps one of the greatest differences between urban and rural communities is found in their school systems. Presumably the United States has one of the best systems in the world, but a considerable number of children from five to 17 years of age are not enrolled in school. Most of these are children of migrants, farmers, and some minority groups from the poorer rural areas. What were some of the reasons for this?

Distance is one factor. Hundreds of rural homes are far from paved roads or well maintained highways. Dirt roads are at times impassable because of snow or flood or mud. Washouts and blizzards may prevent communications and travel, thus causing children to miss school. In rural areas where schools are open only five or six months of the year, two weeks of absence becomes a serious loss.

In some sections, children of 14 and 15 have never been to school. They live beyond the three-mile limit of compulsory attendance and there may not have been money enough to establish a school for them to attend, even though one may have been recommended.

The structure of public school systems in rural and urban areas differs greatly. In many rural areas, finances are lacking to supply buildings, equipment, competent teachers, and a normal school term. State and federal aid should be provided to reduce the educational inequalities between rural and urban areas and, in rural areas, among communities.

Textbooks present a problem. Who is to pay for them if the state does not and the family cannot? Food and clothing are also problems. Insufficient food at home for the child who walks several miles to school, and a cold lunch of unbuttered bread and "salt side" do not give a child "boundless energy and vitality" to expend in study or play.

It is absolutely necessary that a child have clothing that is adequate for comfort and is similar in quality and design to that worn by the majority of children in the particular school area. A child so poorly clothed that he suffers from cold or rain or snow, or that he cannot keep his self-esteem because other children remark about the poor quality of his clothing, cannot be in a very receptive mood for education.

The increasing consolidation of small rural schools has not done away entirely with the one-room schoolhouse. In some areas, consolidation has aggravated the problem of rural school attendance; many children are so far from the school that they cannot reach it unless they travel by bus, and snow in side roads may prevent school bus travel during stormy days.

Rural schools are seldom able to make provision for the very young child or the older adolescent or for pupils with special abilities or disabilities.

Many teachers in rural schools are not much older than their oldest pupils and have had only high school education or less; they are completely inexperienced, and unfit for dealing with a group of children of varying ages and abilities. It is apparent that a teacher is not capable of awakening or stimulating leadership or breadth of vision if her own training and experience are not much beyond those of her pupils. The teacher who has better training and is more gifted is drawn to a school system that pays a better salary and provides better equipment for work than do the majority of rural schools.

Increases in school budgets would mean better educational opportunities for rural children.

Recreation

The problem of rural recreation is not easy to solve. Rural families may feel that children do not need to be taught to play. Farm work is demanding. Owing to seasonal needs for specific work schedules, parents and children expect to work long hours. Long hours mean that when, at last, the child does have leisure time, he is just too tired to enter into any form of activity that will call for physical exertion or mental alertness.

Although farm work provides for an abundance of physical exercise in the open air, observation seems to indicate that farm boys and girls do not develop symmetrically. It is therefore necessary to supplement the ordinary routines of farm life with recreational activities which will offset this deficiency. There are certain farm occupations which are deleterious to the health of rural youth—such as cotton picking, onion and sugar beet weeding, and other forms of seasonal agricultural labor which require a difficult and unnatural posture and demand almost the same degree of monotonous attention as that of simple machine labor of industry. Many rural youths live in a sparsely populated, isolated, or stranded village community. Many live on little eroded farms, distant and removed from normal human companionship and contacts other than those afforded by the child's immediate family. Still others live in a tiny rural community that is slowly dying out—the factory has closed and the local trade has been transported to other areas.

If one family is the only representative of a particular race, creed, or color in a rural area, the children of this family may be isolated from whatever limited opportunities exist.

The average farm boy does not receive much in the way of cash remuneration, and consequently he lacks spending money. Many young persons living at home on the farm are family workers receiving no pay whatever. And yet, many of the simple, free outdoor amusements of earlier years are no longer in vogue. Home amusements are not as easy to plan as they once were. The average rural youth has more time on his hands than his parents had when they were the same age; and today he has but little choice other than to look outside of his home for fun. In certain sections of rural areas, solitary roadhouses or taverns are the only places where rural people may gather and mingle with others.

More rural leaders in recreation should be trained, and funds from larger units of government should encourage a more extensive recreation program. Such activities as the 4-H Clubs and Future Farmers of America are of great value in providing activities for rural youth.

The Rural Child

The rural child lives in a neighborhood which may be abundant with animal life but contains few people, particularly of his own age. He uses the animals about him for playmates and companionship because distance makes it difficult for him to find playmates outside of his own immediate family. This is one of the factors that must be given consideration by the child welfare worker in her relationship with the child. The limited contact with people gives the rural child little experience in knowing and understanding strangers. He will be sensitive to differences and be puzzled, curious, and perhaps frightened by them. His general lack of experience with strangers will make it hard for him to move quickly into new relationships. This often makes him appear awkward, shy, reserved, and surrounded by an intangible barrier. It may also cause him to appear less intelligent than he actually is.

The worker may, in turn, find herself puzzled by this barrier and unable to penetrate it unless she has quite a clear understanding of its cause.

Another important characteristic of rural life which is of special significance for the children is the relative immobility of the population. A child most often grows to maturity in the same community where he was born. The community itself has a high degree of homogeneity in that its members do similar kinds of work, and have approximately the same social values, moral standards, and religious beliefs. A child who, for whatever reason, finds himself in conflict with the accepted mores of the community, will have limited opportunity to find acceptance and approval. It will not be easy for him to allow himself differences of opinion which are disapproved by the people with whom he is identified. If he finds himself in conflict with the standards of his immediate family, he will probably find that his family's opinions are supported by others in the community. Minor differences, however, may be more easily tolerated because he is not in constant contact with many people.

At home, the child experiences considerable freedom and acceptance. He is welcomed to the family group as an economic asset in a comparatively noncompetitive society. There are simple as well as complex tasks to be performed on the farm, and the young, the slow, the dull, or the handicapped child can find a useful function there. This gives the child a sense of basic security in that he can feel wanted and useful.

Migrant Farm Children

The problems of education, health, and social adjustment of children whose families follow the crops from Florida to Maine, from Texas to Washington, from New Mexico to Minnesota, have been of widespread concern. However, these problems at present are not fully met. Thousands of children of migrant laborers—white, black, and others—lack decent housing, school opportunities, facilities for play, and the pleasures of participating in the club and group activities available to children of permanent residents.

According to the U.S. Department of Labor, migrant farm laborers compose about 20 percent of the seasonal agricultural work force in the United States. Nationally, their average annual earnings are below the poverty level yearly income. The inadequacies of the migrant's wages are compounded by his long periods of seasonal unemployment, the average annual employment being only 122 days. Because the harvesting of many fruits and vegetables still requires hand picking, these migrant workers are needed members of the labor force.

Beginning in early spring, the migrant workers follow the maturing crops. At the crop season's end, if they have been able to save enough money, they tend to drift back to the places they started from, where there may be some beginning picking to be done.

Thousands of workers with children join the migrant group each year; some of them are lured by the prospect of work for the entire family. The lives of these children are a kind of endless chaos. They live in the most primitive conditions: housing consists of cabins or shacks with no running water or sanitary facilities; there is little furniture, often not even chairs and beds; there is little or no privacy; the only toilet facilities are a few outhouses for the use of all the people living in the migrant camp.

Children of migrant workers sometimes work in the fields at hard labor that requires constant stooping. Often local officers are unaware of this, and moreover state laws controlling child farm labor are concerned only with the time the child works (specifying that work hours be restricted to before and after school), and not with the difficulty of the work. These children find little fun, few laughs, and a lack of planned recreation in a migrant camp where they see struggle, misery, and the hardships of poverty.

Because the family moves with the crops, children are apt to enter school at a later age than normal; their attendance is spotty and their school progress is slow. As a result, most migrant children are put in grades with children chronologically younger. Because the language and culture of these children may differ from that of the children in local communities, the migrant child is frequently shunned by children of permanent families living in the community, and this alienation helps to make him drop out of school at an early age.

These conditions have existed in greater or lesser degrees since the early 1920's. For years sporadic efforts were made in some states to provide services for these children. In some places, voluntary agencies tried to offer some educational and day care facilities. County health and education departments made some progress in providing services.

Early in 1954 a Joint Committee on Migrants was established by three divisions of the U.S. Department of Health, Education, and Welfare: the Children's Bureau, the Office of Education, and the Surgeon General's Office. Its purpose was to work with a group of states in a cooperative effort to improve health, education, and welfare services for all children whose families follow the crops. The Wage and Hour and Public Contracts Division and the Bureau of Employment Security, both in the Department of Labor, give valuable help to this committee.

The general plan of the committee requires the state agencies to identify the children in families expecting to migrate each spring. They are to see that the children receive physical examinations and immunization, and to set up health records to be used en route; they get the children into school and give them traveling report cards; they identify pregnant women, and provide initial services for them. State agencies along the migration route are notified in advance of their coming; these continue health and education services, and add their recordings to the health and education report cards.

Since most of the migrant children are retarded by two or three years because of lack of schooling, it is necesary to prepare educational material that is suitable for them. They can carry their special books with them to show each successive teacher their progress, and they can complete some courses at the end of each year.

The plan seems soundly conceived and illustrates once again the importance of federal initiative. In general, the states will not get special funds for the project, because the objective is to "supply the children of migrants only those services that all other American children have available."

Congress passed the Health Services Act in 1962, granting appropriations of as much as $3,000,000 per year for the establishment of clinics for improving the health of migrant families. In the same year two additional bills for the alleviation of rural poverty were passed by Congress, thus hopefully reducing the mobility rate of the poor farm worker. These bills were entitled the Area Redevelopment Act and the Manpower Development and Training Act, and the Rural Areas Development Program.

Comprehensive programs to meet the needs of migrants, and their families and children are badly needed. The interest and leadership of government on all levels, as well as communities, social agencies, and agricultural interests, should be instigated and progressively supported by the public. The migrant laborer is important to our economy and desires more recognition and public services than he has received.

As a result of the 1954 plan, a number of jurisdictions organized state and local councils or advisory committees on migratory and seasonal farm laborers. These committees, aided since 1963 by federal funds from the Migrant Health Branch of the U.S. Public Health Service, the Office of Education, and the Office of Economic Opportunity, have set up projects in a number of states for the health care of children and adults. Among these projects are Head Start and preschool care for young children, tutoring in school subjects for older children, and basic education courses and training in non-agricultural work for adult migratory farm laborers.

However, the needs of migratory laborers are still not met. Federal and state services are limited by lack of adequate legislation, coverage, and enforcement. There is a general lack of appropriations to implement health, education, and welfare programs for their benefit. The limited coverage of present legislation does not protect the migratory farm laborer legally, socially, educationally, or physically. At best, present services for migratory laborers and their children are fragmented and superficial. Citizen involvement (consumer, grower, legislator) is necessary to see that these workers obtain the rights and powers most citizens take for granted.

There are more than 500 rural counties in the United States in which public agencies now employ child welfare workers to give services to all children whether they be from migrant farm families or not. Theoretically, there are no fundamental differences in either the preparation for, or the practice of, child welfare work, whatever the area. Practically, however, there are some difficulties between social worker and client, many of which center on the personality of the worker practicing in rural areas. Much depends upon her ability to relate and adapt her professional training to the realities of a rural community.

The Rural Child Welfare Worker

The rural child welfare worker will need the same definite background of information about the area and its resources that she would if she worked in an urban area. She will need to learn something of the occupation of farming, as she would of any of the industries operating in the region where she worked. She may find that the difference between this occupation and others is primarily that the farm is a family enterprise. She need not have the knowledge of an expert in agriculture, but she should have an understanding of the people who farm and of those who live in rural villages.

She should be familiar with the rural school program. A good working relationship with the teaching staff is of inestimable advantage to her. She should know the extent of child labor, and the composition of the population—its ethnic and racial groups. Some of this information she will obtain by reading and inquiry before she starts to work. Much of it, however, she will secure gradually, as the opportunity avails itself, after her work has begun. She will need information on state and county resources and knowledge of how to obtain needed assistance and services from these resources. The facilities and resources of the rural area are not those of the urban center. This must be faced realistically by a worker going into rural work.

It would be unrealistic to expect to find, in a rural area, a court dealing with juveniles exclusively. The judge who handles juvenile cases must handle other business of the court. The judge is often the leading citizen of the community as well as a public official. In both his official and his unofficial capacity, his support of the worker is an asset. As much as it is to be desired, many judges will not be cognizant of the newer methods of dealing with young offenders, nor in sympathy with them. The worker may have to move slowly and be satisfied with small gains until she has demonstrated her effectiveness and willingness to cooperate with him.

The task of the child welfare worker in many rural areas is primarily interpretation of services for children, their advantages, and limitations. She will need to explain why she is in the area, what services she has to offer, and how she can give this service. What she needs in the way of help and support from the community must be clearly presented. Her contact with people in a rural community is much closer than it is in the city. The people among whom she works will seek to know her as a person. They will want to know who she is, where she was born, and how she was raised, and unless they accept her, they will probably not accept the work she represents, no matter how well qualified she is professionally. She is professional, yes, but she must be a friend, too. In the city, a worker leaves her clients when she leaves the office at the end of the day. In the country, she lives with her clients, sharing pleasures and work with them.

Traveling great distances modifies the worker's ability to plan her work. Limited supervision, or total lack of it, places the burden of difficult decisions upon her. She needs to be aware that it is going to be one of her tasks to find ways of helping rural people to feel they know her. It is possible that the worker as a "stranger" will feel herself trapped in isolation until this experience takes place. The worker, with her wide experience and understanding of people, is in a position to bring this about while the rural people themselves may actually be unable to do so.

The rural child welfare worker is obliged to keep simplicity in her technique because of the inaccessibility of other individuals or organizations with whom she could share responsibility. She must be especially careful of the confidences of her clients. In a community so closely interwoven, private affairs need scrupulous guarding.

The job of the child welfare worker in a rural community gives her a rare opportunity to see and appreciate the innate courage and dignity of human beings. It takes a gallant endurance, energy, and vitality to rebuild and start again, to fortify one's home against destruction. Even the normal maintenance of a farm, stock, tools, fences, ample water supply, and fuel supply places heavy responsibility on the rural family, and requires strong effort.

What the worker accomplishes in a rural setting is the more remarkable because of the imagination, initiative, and resourcefulness it represents on the part of the worker. She has to rely on strengths within the family group and to capitalize on them because of the lack of outside resources. She must be alert to every possible constructive opportunity offered through rural home demonstration agents, agricultural extension services, churches, and farm organizations.

She must be especially alert to the needs of that one large group of rural folk who can almost be designated as a "forgotten people"— the migratory agricultural workers. As we have shown in preceding pages, the children of these workers need everything—from decent housing and sanitation to opportunities for health services, education, recreation, and nursery schools. It is not within the power of the child welfare worker to provide for all their needs, but it is part of her job to interpret the needs of these children to the community in which migratory labor is used, and to enlist the efforts of the people in the community to marshal and develop resources for the welfare of these children.

The rural child welfare worker must take a broad view of her responsibilities and carry them out with courage and conviction. There are potentials for both romance and challenge in the job. However, if she is to realize the power for good and for progress which lies within her capabilities, she must allow herself maximum vision so that this power is given full scope.

VOLUNTEERS FROM THE COMMUNITY

During any emergency situation—war, fire, flood, or other disaster— more people volunteer to work for their community than at any other time. There are, of course, two obvious reasons for this: first, the personal sense of urgency, self-sacrifice, and responsibility; and, second, the opportunity offered to all people in times of distress to work for their community on equal terms with others.

Another element that enters into the satisfactions of volunteer work during emergencies is the fact that volunteers are assigned to essential tasks. Their time is not wasted on mere "busy work" but devoted to relief of community disaster. People derive dignity and interest from doing necessary work and thus becoming a part of important services.

Community loyalty and good will that has developed in times of stress should be preserved and redirected to further wholesome and desirable community planning and action. Even when conditions are normal, community agencies need the participation of large numbers of individual volunteers in community service. Those who may still think of volunteer service in terms of the "lady bountiful, carrying a basket" should recall the important tasks performed by thousands of volunteers during World Wars I and II. It is inevitable that, in the period following a war, many find less interest and appeal in the idea of volunteer service than they did when a sense of necessity, pressure, and self-denial prevailed. Conversely, many wartime volunteers found new satisfactions in their community activities and did not wish to lose these satisfactions. Wartime publicity on volunteer participation also helped to sustain interest in postwar activity.

Many of the communities throughout the nation have recognized the value of continuing volunteer services. They also recognize that the postwar volunteer program must be broadened to cover a wider range of community service activities than health, welfare, and recreation fields only. It is of interest to note the number of new opportunities that arose during wartime for work on community projects which are almost entirely manned by volunteers. Examples are campaigns, surveys, and the like.

In some communities, a permanent volunteer service bureau, created as a central place for the recruitment, registration, and guidance of volunteers, is in operation, established as a department of the community welfare council, financed by the United Community Fund. In other communities, the volunteer service bureau is an independent agency that holds membership in the United Community Fund and council, and its governing body is broadly representative of the whole community.

The volunteer may participate as an individual in selected services of an established welfare agency in the community, or he may work on a project which is community, not agency, centered.

Recruiting volunteers is not an easy matter. The informal method utilized by most agencies is not always satisfactory, either in producing the numbers of volunteers needed or in securing the services of those persons best suited for volunteer work. In order to develop a sound program of volunteer service, it is essential that an agency give thought to job classification, and the delegation of specific jobs, and, that it decide on the number of days per week and hours per day the volunteer should work. It is necesary to plan an orientation course and a training course for volunteer workers, and to select a supervisor of volunteers who is adequate in the field of supervision and also sees the value of volunteer services. There should be provision for recognition and promotion within the volunteer ranks.

A placement bureau which will organize community-wide recruitment and referral of volunteers is effective in handling volunteer services. When community projects are planned, the bureau should provide a service that is actually useful, and that does not overlap or compete with other established services; the administrative responsibility of the volunteer service should be clearly defined, and official sponsorship guaranteed.

Volunteers in Action

The story of the experience of one county in the use of volunteer services illustrates some of the strengths and weaknesses in such a program.

In this particular county, the county welfare department has used volunteers for a number of years. The budget was insufficient, and the workloads of the staff were much heavier than was desirable. Realizing that it was but the agent of the community and that it could only do what the community would let it do, the department decided to share the knowledge its staff had gained on the job with the citizens. This would mean seizing every opportunity to tell the secure in the county about the insecure, and, once this task had been accomplished, asking citizens to share with the agency the responsibilities for the inadequacies of the welfare program.

The best way to inform the community was to let citizens work side by side with the staff. During the first five years, at least 45 women and men in the community and 130 university and high school students served with the staff. The amount of service contributed by two or three individuals ranged from a few hours to three-year periods. Housewives, club women, members of the Junior League, teachers, wives of college professors, college students, and classes from various Sunday schools have participated in the volunteer work of the agency.

Recruitment of volunteers was both a planned part of the program and incidental to the main work of the agency. Among the first volunteers were two boys who were majoring in business administration in the local high school. The agency's office gave them the opportunity to get the 150 hours of work experience required by the high school for business majors. Each year, two high school students have worked in the office on a volunteer basis.

For several years, the professor of sociology at the university has invited the agency director to speak to his sociology class. Usually several students volunteer as a result of these tasks. These student volunteers often bring other students with them. Their time is scheduled with the understanding that if this volunteer work interferes with their studies, the time spent at the agency will be reduced.

Talks made by professional staff members and, in recent years, by some of the volunteers before the League of Women Voters, the Junior League, the American Association of University Women, parent-teacher associations, church groups, women's clubs, and men's service organizations always bring volunteers. Stimulated by a desire to do something, many women and men with limited ability, as well as many who are highly skilled have come to the agency. A way has been found to use each.

Volunteers are introduced to the work of the department by the director, who relates a brief history of the organization and its objectives. He discusses policies and the various services offered, and tries to impress upon the volunteer a sense of his own responsibility to the agency and to the clients. In this initial conference, the mutuality of the arrangement is stressed. It is pointed out that a volunteer is free to withdraw any time; however, previous notice of his intention to do so is expected by the agency. Furthermore, the director makes it clear that the agency cannot consider employing the volunteer if a vacancy in the staff should occur. The confidential nature of the work is always stressed. One of the valued assets of the agency is its reputation in the community for keeping confidences inviolate. The director attempts to answer any questions which may occur to the volunteer and to explain reasons for procedures used. A simple outline of all office procedures is given out to each volunteer. Both the agency and the volunteer profit from the material.

What can a volunteer do in a local public agency? They are usually assigned first to some clerical duty in the office. This is because clerical work is a mechanical process which can be readily understood; the novice sees and handles the records, realizes that social work is work with individual people, and that the financial operations are carefully recorded. She also becomes familiar with technical terms used in the field of social work.

Volunteers may want to do casework with clients; however, most of them have accepted gracefully the explanation given at the beginning of their work—that the only persons in the agency equipped to do social casework are those who have had professional training; therefore, the volunteer cannot be permitted to participate in this field.

Many volunteers have become excellent receptionists, learning the names of the clients, putting them at ease, and directing them with little lost motion. Several have become so skillful that they can assist in a preliminary interview with a client when the number of people waiting is large. Volunteers have been invaluable in investigating and answering correspondence from out of town.

No secret has been made of the agency's affairs. If the volunteers are in the office at a time when staff meetings are scheduled, the volunteers, as a matter of course, attend and participate in the discussions if they so desire.

As a whole, the volunteers have gained understanding of the problems, courage, weaknesses, and limitations of families in the community, about whose existence they were formerly only dimly conscious. They know too that behavior problems occur in children of the banker and the psychiatrist as well as in the children of the section hand and the street cleaner.

If poor interpretation of agency work has been made by volunteers, reports have not resounded. It seems probable that, since they have been included in staff meetings, their questions have been answered with frankness, and their relationship with staff and clients has been honest at all times, misinterpretation has been at a minimum.

Within every community, there are untouched community resources which could be used if the community was aware of the need. Volunteers can and do tell the community about the agency and help the agency to do the job more adequately. The work of this agency has gone more smoothly because volunteers have donated more hands and more brainwork to various tasks.

When the Child Welfare Division of the State Department of Public Welfare, in cooperation with the school of social work of the university, established a training unit in this county agency, the supervisor and six graduate students in child welfare fitted smoothly into the agency because the staff had previous experience with volunteer workers and was not disturbed by the addition of outside people.

This county agency believes the services which a volunteer can render an agency are limited only by the aptitude and skill of the volunteer and by the planning ability of the staff.

From the example of this one agency, and there are many similar ones, it is obvious that the group of professional workers (too small in number for the amount of work that has to be done) needs the assistance and support of men and women in the community who have time they are willing to give community services. The need of services for children is so great that volunteer help can be of constant help in carrying out certain functions and expanding the total program.

Volunteers in Child Care

Volunteers in child care are being effectively used in all parts of the country, both urban and rural, by agencies and communities that have given thought and direction to programs of volunteer service. If a child welfare agency decides to use volunteer service, the first consideration is to determine what services may be assigned to the volunteer; here, "volunteer" refers to any person who gives services, without pay, to supplement the services of the paid staff. Whether volunteer participation is to be sought depends primarily on whether there is real constructive work that can be allocated to a volunteer. Since programs of child welfare differ with different agencies and in the various communities, no attempt will be made to specify types of services that can be performed by volunteers. Generally, agencies find that volunteers can work as aides to nurses or supervisors in routine care of children, and also as playground assistants, library aides, receptionists, office workers, interpreters of foreign languages, hospital aides, committee members, seamstresses, assistants in publicity programs, and suppliers of transportation. Volunteer services may also be used to lead groups in such activities as athletics, hiking, dancing, cooking, puppetry, sketching, music, woodwork, and photography. Other opportunities for volunteer services will suggest themselves to alert citizens.

It is necessary to establish some general qualifications for volunteers who are to work with children. Patience, an understanding of children, good physical health, and emotional balance are always essential, and additional qualifications may be necessary for a particular job.

The method used in recruiting volunteers for agencies concerned with the well-being of children determines to some extent the success of the program. An initial interview of each person wishing to give his services should be held, and the qualifications for the job should be stressed. Volunteers need to feel the job is important and constructive; they must be able to accept direction from regular qualified staff members, and also be willing to assume delegated responsibilities. A sincere interest in children, as well as calmness, poise, and a pleasant voice are essential in the work with children. Special skills in handicrafts, art, music, story telling, or playing games are advantageous.

In the initial interview, the mutuality of the arrangement is stressed, and the policies as well as the various services offered are outlined. The responsibility of the volunteer to the agency, the client, and the community, as well as the limitations of the program and the reasons for them, are outlined. At this time, it should be possible to determine the suitability of the volunteer for work with children. The importance of this interview is great. The volunteer who seems to lack ability to work with children may be able to do an excellent job in some other type of volunteer activity. Help in locating other opportunities for services should be offered, so that the volunteer's help will not seem unimportant or unwanted.

The agency should design a good basic training course to prepare volunteers to work with children. Some volunteers may have had previous professional training; others, no former special experience or training in child welfare. The course should be broad enough to include a series of lectures or discussion periods on such material as the protection of a child's physical well being and mental health, the growth and development of wholesome attitudes, the social needs of children, and community resources for children. A session for discussion of the volunteer's role in the agency should be included in the course. There should also be an opportunity for planned field observation visits to other agencies in the community. The content of any course will depend on local conditions and available leadership and it will vary to suit conditions. The background and experience of the volunteers will also help to determine the content of the course. An alert supervisor will use every opportunity to help the volunteer develop his potentialities for growth in handling assigned tasks, and understand the importance of his part in the agency program.

Supplementary Readings

Brooks, Melvin S. *The Social Problems of Migrant Farm Laborers.* Department of Sociology, Southern Illinois University, Carbondale, 1960.

Burchinal, Lee G., Ed. *Rural Youth in Crisis.* U.S. Department of Health, Education, and Welfare, Washington, D.C., 1965.

Burchinal, Lee G., et al. *Career Choices of Rural Youth in a Changing Society.* Agricultural Experiment Station, St. Paul, Minnesota, 1962.

Coles, Robert. *Uprooted Children.* University of Pittsburgh Press, Pittsburgh, 1970.

Committee Appropriations, U.S. Senate. *Children in Migrant Families.* U.S. Children's Bureau, Washington, D.C., 1961.

Conant, James B. *Slums and Suburbs.* McGraw-Hill, New York, 1961.

Feldman, Lloyd, and Peevey, Michael R. *Young Workers: Their Special Training Needs.* U.S. Department of Labor, Washington, D.C., 1963.

Gurin, Gerald. *Inner-City Negro Youth In a Job Training Project.* Survey Research Center, University of Michigan, Ann Arbor, 1968.

Herman, Melvin, Sodofsky, Stanley, and Rosenburg, Bernard. *Work, Youth and Unemployment.* T. Y. Crowell, New York, 1968.

Ireland, Thomas. *Child Labor As a Relic of the Dark Ages.* Putnam, New York, 1937.

Landis, Benson Y. *Rural Welfare Services.* Columbia University Press, New York, 1949.

Levitan, Sar A. *Antipoverty Work and Training Efforts.* Institute of Labor and Industrial Relations and the National Manpower Policy Task Force, Ann Arbor, 1967.

Loamis, Charles P., and Beegle, Allan. *Rural Social Systems.* Prentice-Hall, New York, 1950.

Metzler, William H., and Sargent, Frederic O. *Incomes of Migratory Agricultural Workers.* Agricultural Station, College Station, Texas, 1960.

Ogburn, William Fielding. *Progress and Uniformity in Child Labor Legislation.* AMS Press, New York, 1968.

Reynolds, Bertha C. *Social Work and Social Living.* Citadel Press, New York, 1951.

Sills, Dorothy H. *Volunteers in Social Service.* National Travelers Aid Association, New York, 1947.

Spargo, John. *The Bitter Cry of Children.* Johnson Reprint Corporation, New York, 1969.

Taylor, Miller Lee. *Urban-Rural Problems.* Dickenson, Belmont, California, 1968.

Weeks, Christopher. *Job Corps: Dollars and Dropouts.* Little, Brown, Boston, 1967.

Weissman, Harold H. *Employment and Educational Services in the Mobilization for Youth Experience.* Association Press, New York, 1964.

Woodson, Carter Godwin. *The Rural Negro.* Russell and Russell, New York, 1969.

Wyckoff, Florence R. *Health Projects for Migrant Farm Families,* National Consumers Committee, Washington, D.C., 1963.

[*Courtesy Office of Child Development, U.S. Department of Health, Education, and Welfare.*]

6

Children in Need of Special Services

The normal child is generally considered to have the ability to adapt himself to average patterns of behavior in the community and to conform to what is considered average in physical and mental characteristics for the mass of population. If a child possesses either fewer or more of the abilities necessary for this self-adaptation, he is exceptional and provision must be made for him so that he can develop his potentialities as fully as possible.

In the past century it has become generally recognized that the exceptional child needs specialized training. We recognize that the child who deviates from the general concept of normal cannot be stereotyped with all other children having the same type of handicap as his. Every child is an individual with a personality of his own; services cannot be identical for each one in a particular group.

If it is positively determined that neither home nor local school can provide the training and services to enable the exceptional child to attain his utmost in development, then it is the responsibility of the state to fill the gap.

In this chapter we shall not try to discuss all of the crippling conditions that cause children and youth to deviate from average or typical. We believe that exploration of conditions such as epilepsy, cerebral palsy, rheumatic fever, and emotional disturbance should be left to persons who are expert in medical and psychiatric fields.

We will, however, discuss a few of the most generally recognized groups that have psychological or physical problems which tend to set them apart for special attention and services: children who are mentally retarded or mentally superior; the deaf and hard of hearing; those who are blind or have defective vision; those with defective speech. We will conclude the chapter with a discussion of the special legal service of guardianship. Chapter 7 will deal with other types of special social services—those protecting children and the unmarried mother.

THE EXCEPTIONAL CHILD

In this section we will discuss the mentally retarded children and mentally superior children. Both of these terms are broad and inclusive: one referring to all children who develop some or all of their mental functions at a subnormal rate; the other, to all who develop these functions at an accelerated rate.

Mentally Retarded Children

It is estimated that approximately 3 percent of the population of the United States is mentally retarded, either severely or mildly. This means that approximately 6,000,000 persons are handicapped to some degree by lack of innate capacity; of these, 200,000 are institutionalized.[1]

Statistics show that mental retardation is not more common among children of any one race or nationality, nor does poor housing and environmental deprivation have any particular relation to the incidence of mental retardation. Poor nutrition and environmental deprivation may cause a slowing of mental process owing to lack of stimulation, but this is not true retardation.

---

1. MR-69. *Third report of the President's Committee on Mental Retardation,* PCMR, Washington, D.C.

There are so many degrees and types of mental retardation that no single definition or classification is possible. Some mentally retarded children are educable to a certain degree; others are not. Some are maladjusted, but so are some normal and mentally superior children. Some are noisy and belligerent; others quiet and happy. Some may have speech or language impediments; others do not.

Experts differ slightly in the range of Intelligent Quotient (I.Q.), as measured by the Stanford revision of the Binet-Simon Intelligence tests, for classification, but generally all agree that the I.Q. of an average child ranges from 90–110. The classification of mentally superior children begins at above 110. A child with an I.Q. of 75–90 is a slow learner, but educable to varying degrees. A child with an I. Q. of 35–75 may be trainable. The child with an I.Q. of 35 or under will never reach more than a maximum mental age of three years at maturity, and should be considered for custodial care. We know, however, that classification based upon intelligence quotient alone is not valid. We must take into account the individual's capacities for learning, for self-responsibility, and for social adaptability. Studies show that about 30 children of every 1,000 are retarded, but of the 30 only one is so severely retarded that he needs custodial care. About four can be trained to do simple tasks under supervision, and about 25 are educable to some degree.

Mental retardation today is no longer regarded as the curse of an evil spirit, or as a disgrace, but rather as one of nature's errors. Studies of mental retardation among children show no single cause of mental retardation; rather, many causes may be responsible—infections, birth abnormalities, prenatal conditions, heredity. Much more research is necessary and it is being constantly carried on by professional men and women.

Not until the eighteenth century was science applied to education of the mentally retarded. Pereire, a French physician whose sister was a deaf mute, taught the child to speak through touch and sight. In 1798 Itard, also a French physician, brought science to the aid of the mentally retarded by developing and training the senses. Itard's pioneer efforts were carried on by his pupil Seguin, who also based his work on developing the senses, and in 1837 he founded a center in Paris for care and development of the mentally retarded. Three years later the first such center was opened in England. In 1866–67 the Germans started two schools for mental defectives at Halle and Dresden.

In 1848 Seguin came to the United States and assisted in setting up three outstanding institutions for the mentally retarded; one each in Massachusetts, New York and Pennsylvania. These institutions provided training centers for children and staff members, but they could serve only a small number of children. As a result of the knowledge gained in these three institutions for the care and training of retarded children, large state institutions were built throughout the country, and between 1850 and 1900 institutional care became widely accepted and waiting lists for each institution were long.

Then came the development of the first intelligence tests by Dr. Alfred Binet who established the first psychological laboratory in Paris in 1900, for the scientific diagnosis of retarded intelligence. In 1905 the first Simon-Binet intelligence tests appeared. Now, after years of work on improving these tests, we know them as the Stanford-Binet Intelligence Scale. Through the years we have learned that a child's potential capacity can not always be measured even by the best standardized tests.

Since the 1940's, there has been a shift from institutional care to the use of foster homes for mentally retarded children who could adjust better in a foster home than in an institution.

In 1911 New Jersey became the first state to establish in its public school system special classes for retarded children. People were beginning to understand for the first time that mentally retarded children might have potential abilities to lead lives of socially acceptable self-support in a limited environment, provided they were given the help they need.

Now as a result of new laws or amendments, all of the 50 states have expanded services in public schools for the exceptional child. These offerings vary widely from state to state, and it is estimated that only about 50 to 75 percent of all mentally retarded educable children are actually receiving aid through special classes in public schools.

At a time when our schools are overcrowded and understaffed, it is practically impossible to work out in each classroom the special, individual instruction needed for a mentally retarded child. Special schools or classes meet the need much more adequately. They offer a diversified program of work, because mentally retarded children vary in interests, skills, and potentialities as do normal children. The work in special schools or classes is so planned that each child will have a chance to feel the satisfaction of accomplishment. At present most cities and large towns have either special classes or schools to provide for the mentally deficient child, but the education and training of similar pupils in rural districts are usually neglected.

The tragedy of mental retardation is usually felt more keenly by the parents than by the child. If the child is well cared for and loved, he is often a happy little person unaware of his misfortune.

In a child's infancy or first year, parents often suspect he may be mentally retarded, but will put off facing the reality of the situation by reassuring themselves that the child is just a little slow in development and will "outgrow" this. During this time they struggle with the emotions of doubt, hope, shock, guilt, shame, bitterness.

When at last they can no longer excuse this retardation as only slowness, they take the child to a physician, psychologist, or psychiatrist, if they live where such services are available.

If the diagnosis of the professional person confirms the parents' suspicion, it is still a shock and some parents are unable to accept the facts and try to convince themselves the diagnosis is wrong. Sometimes there is a long period of additional search for a hopeful diagnosis, before parents can face the reality of their child being mentally retarded. Parents of epileptic children have been relieved to learn that epilepsy and mental retardation do not necessarily go hand in hand. Many epileptics are not mentally retarded. Since parents of the retarded child differ, as do other individuals, in emotional and mental stability, their reaction to the fact differs. They may reject a mentally subnormal child, or go to the opposite extreme and overprotect him.

About 1930 parents of retarded children began to organize to help each other. They realized that mental retardation occurred in every kind of family—whether the parents were highly educated or illiterate, wealthy or poor, "good" citizens or "bad" citizens. Those that lived in communities in which there were special classes or schools formed parents' organizations, to find help and guidance through talks with the school staff and with parents of other retarded children.

Local organizations merged into state organizations, and in 1950 the National Association for Retarded Children was organized. The membership includes parents, professional workers, and interested citizens. It consists of more than 150,000 persons from more than a thousand state and local units in the 50 states. There are now more than 150 clinics in 50 states, the District of Columbia, and Puerto Rico that are devoted exclusively to working with the mentally retarded.[2]

In 1905 the first law in the United States allowing sterilization of the mentally retarded was passed by the Pennsylvania legislature. By

---

2. For families who live in areas in which special schools are not available, excellent material for guidance and training may be obtained from The National Association for Retarded Children, 420 Lexington Avenue, New York, New York 10017.

1960 practically every state had a sterilization law in effect. However, because of public feeling that such a compulsory act infringes upon the rights of the individual, compulsory sterilization is infrequent.

The prospects for the future development of care and education for the mentally retarded are greatly dependent on the early recognition of retardation and on improved services for the mentally retarded. These services would include provision for day schools and day care centers in order to give the child educational independence and a happier and busier life.

The present trend is toward keeping mentally retarded children in their own homes and wherever possible integrating their activities into community programs. This trend has focused attention on long-term planning.

In October, 1962, after a year of study, a distinguished group of 28 experts (physicians, lawyers, social scientists and lay citizens, appointed by the Department of Health, Education, and Welfare, at the request of President Kennedy) presented to the President a report on the problems of mental retardation in this nation. The panel's report included more than 90 recommendations affecting some 5,400,000 children and adults, and involving between 15,000,000 and 20,000,000 family members in this country.

The panel estimated that the cost of care for these affected was approximately $550,000,000 per year, and that the loss to the nation was several billion dollars of economic output because of the lack of training, education and preparation of mentally retarded for jobs.

It recommended a broad attack on specific causes of this loss, and also on problems in the social, economic and cultural environment that nourish specific causes. Also they recommended that the program of maternal and infant care be greatly strengthened, and that social, economic, educational, and health opportunities be improved in slums and deprived areas.

Safeguarding and promoting the welfare of the mentally retarded child in case of parents' death, disability, or inadequacy, is a weighty responsibility. In general, if a child lives in an institution (about 4.0 percent of the mentally retarded population do), the superintendent of the institution has legal custody. However, legal rights of all children vary from state to state. The National Association for Retarded Children, and its state and local affiliates are actively interested in planning for and obtaining uniform legal rights of mentally retarded persons.

Children unable to work in competitive society and to manage their own affairs are now legally called permanently disabled, and they are entitled to the full social security payments that are allotted to the totally dependent as long as they live.

Mentally Superior Children

We know much less about the mental, physical, and emotional traits of mentally superior children than we do about feeble-minded children. We were much slower to learn that the gifted child needs special attention, than to recognize needs of other special groups. Formerly, gifted children, if they conformed to routine school procedures, were not viewed as needing any special methods of training. The gifted child was referred to as a "bright child" but special thought was given him only when he presented a "problem." It was the problem, not the child, on which attention was centered.

If the mentally superior child drifted along in school at the pace set by the capacities of the "normal" child, his abilities were never challenged. He was duly promoted and perhaps "skipped" a grade now and then; he received excellent marks with little or no effort and developed habits of idleness, daydreaming, or indifference. If, on the other hand, he reacted against his boredom and effortless existence by trying active and, to him, interesting experiments, he was liable to be judged "emotionally unstable," "high strung," or "nervous." It was popularly supposed that such traits were inherent in intellectually superior children, but this conception has been shown to be groundless. Scientific study has proved that gifted children are as emotionally stable as normal children and may in fact be more so. Any apparent instability probably results from the way these children are handled at home or in school.

When, in an effort to meet the needs of a mentally superior child, the school would move him up several grades to give him interesting intellectual competition, that child would find himself unable to fit into the group socially or physically. A child nine years old, with average nine-year physical size and emotional maturity, has real problems in a class where the chronological ages of other children are 12 to 14. The gifted child may be vitally interested in class parties, games, and sports, and he may engage in them as much as possible, but his interest and participation with others in the class are checked by age, immaturity, and tradition.

He may try to solve his problems by turning for companionship to children of his own chronological age, but he enjoys more complicated and highly competitive games than they do. He is also able to engage in longer, more complicated games which lead to remote goals. His vocabulary is larger than theirs. He thus often finds it difficult to locate other children of his own age with whom he is congenial, and therefore he may be labeled as a child who cannot "get along" with other children.

Since he cannot wholly participate in physical activities of older classmates, his play tends to become sedentary and he may invent solitary games, compile lists, make collections, draw elaborate designs, or develop laborious mathematical calculations. He may develop particular skill in a sport that does not depend on group participation, such as swimming or skating.

The difficulties mentioned do not exhaust the list of problems created by the difference in mental power between the gifted child and the average child of the same age. There are also conflicts within the superior child himself, produced by the combination of emotional immaturity and intellectual superiority.

Problems of home discipline arise when the child, young in years but mature in intelligence, has a parent of only average intelligence. Then the parent-child relationship may suffer. The child may lose respect for the parent's opinions, and the parent may resent the superior intelligence of the child and penalize him by rejection or by severe and unwarranted punishment.

It is difficult for mentally superior children to learn self-government and conformity to procedures unless they see sound reasons for required behavior. Unless intelligent adults recognize and make proper provision for them, the potentiality of these children for competent leadership in our society is lessened. Unwise handling of the gifted child at home or in school is a detriment to his character formation and satisfactory adjustment in adult life.

Comparatively few school systems in our smaller communities make adequate provision for the mentally superior child. Experiments in education are being tried in attempts to work out solutions. A moderate degree of acceleration combined with enriched curriculum is one method. In areas having large populations, special classes formed entirely of gifted children are also used advantageously.

CHILDREN WITH PHYSICAL HANDICAPS

In this section, we will briefly discuss selected physical handicaps found among children. Although in recent years science has made significant advances in the prevention and treatment of disorders in hearing, vision, and speech, a significant proportion of children in the United States as well as throughout the world have handicaps in one or more of these areas.

Deaf and Hard-of-Hearing Children

Before we can understand the whole problem of deafness and partial loss of hearing, and the possible effects of a program of prevention and treatment, we must know some of the types and causes of hearing defects.

The deaf person is totally lacking in ability to hear; but the person who is merely hard of hearing has some ability, the amount varying greatly with different persons.

There are two kinds of deafness: the first is congenital, which is the result of either the development of an imperfect embryo or the transmission of hereditary tendencies leading to deafness; the second is acquired deafness, which occurs after birth as a result of disease or injury. It is not easy to determine, in examining a baby, whether he was born deaf or became so within his first few months, since it is difficult to ascertain whether or not an infant hears a sound.

Deaf-mutism has been a term used throughout the years to include every form of deafness coupled with the absence of speech. The expression has often given the erroneous impression that mutism is a simultaneous occurrence—that a person born deaf is also born with vocal chords that don't function. But congenital deafness and congenital mutism are rare. If a deaf person is unable to speak, it is only because he was unable to hear sound and thus could not imitate sounds to produce speech. The words "mutism" and "dumb" should be discarded, for they are but an added stigma.

The National Health Survey of 1959–1961, found that there were about 6,250,000 persons with impaired hearing in the United States—a ratio of 35.3 per 100,000. In 1963 there were in the United States approximately 45,594 deaf and hard-of-hearing children in school, of whom 28,551 were in public school classes and 17,043 were in public or private residential schools.

Attitudes toward the deaf and the hard of hearing have gradually improved, but even today there is much misunderstanding. In very early times, people destroyed the deaf as well as the blind, or kept them locked up as they did the mentally ill. In fact, they were considered mentally ill. A deaf person was considered a disgrace to his family.

Later, the deaf were treated somewhat better, but still harshly. The deaf often had no more legal rights than infants or insane. Under Roman law, people born deaf could have no civil rights. In Hindu law, the deaf were unable to inherit worldly goods. Naturally, in early times there was little or no attempt to educate deaf children, since it was believed they would never be able to carry out the duties of citizenship.

Even today, our laws reflect old attitudes toward the deaf. In law books, there may be nothing on their legal status, or else they may be grouped with the insane. If a person charged with a crime is found to be deaf, he is at once presumed to lack a sound mind and he goes through the same test as that for an insanity plea. In New York, civil service regulations classify the deaf with the seriously handicapped and the insane, as people to be barred from examinations. Since they do not hear, they misinterpret things and people infer they are mentally unsound. The characteristic attitude, then, is one of coldness and indifference.

Knowing they are set apart and considered different, and not being included in many activities, they tend to associate with others who are also deaf. There is great strain on their nervous system and their eyes, for they have to use their other senses more, especially that of sight. They are often sensitive to certain sounds through vibration, and for this reason many enjoy dancing.

The hard of hearing, also, suffer from misunderstanding. It is often thought they could hear better if they tried harder, but that is not so. Most of them exert much greater effort than the person of normal hearing. They are subjected to numerous embarrassing situations in trying to make themselves understood. It is no wonder they have a feeling of inferiority.

In considering the emotional effects of deafness, it is important to know when and how the deafness occurred. If it is congenital, or was acquired very early, the effects would be different from those of deafness acquired later in life. The reactions to acquired deafness depend also upon the personality before deafness.

Since even total deafness, as well as partial deafness, is difficult to recognize in a very young child, parents may believe the child to be stupid. Even if the deafness is recognized, parents may assume a hostile feeling toward the child. Although these feelings may be unconscious, the child senses them and feels rejected. Since the whole learning process is so much more complicated for the deaf child, it becomes a frightening experience. Thus there may be an emotional blocking toward it.

Joseph C. Solomon of Mt. Zion Hospital, San Francisco, California, states that this feeling of bodily impairment may be so distasteful that the child will tend to repress his feelings about it. This may show itself in deceitfulness. Since the child feels isolated, he builds phantasies of himself. Thus he is more likely to suffer emotional disturbances. As he grows older, he may believe that only those who can hear are happy, and therefore he may feel depressed and inclined to isolate himself from social contacts. The deaf are usually quite suspicious. Doctor Solomon says the person of normal hearing knows that most of what is said around him isn't worth hearing anyhow, but the deaf person always thinks he is missing something.

Until the early 1920s, little attention was paid to the hard of hearing as a special group. In fact, until recently, they were grouped with the deaf. But they are different from the deaf, both in their defect and in their educational needs. In a study of the intelligence, achievements, and personalities of the hard of hearing at Columbia University in 1931, it was found there is no relation between auditory loss and intelligence; the hard of hearing should be educated with the normal rather than the deaf; the intelligence of the hard of hearing is of the same quality as that of the normal; and hard of hearing do not have a language handicap as do the deaf. Whereas the deaf do not hear and respond intelligently to spoken language, the hard of hearing retain actual hearing and can respond intelligently to language, as long as the sound is near enough.

One of the greatest problems in dealing with defective hearing among children remains that of detection. Detection in a very young child is still most difficult, although easier than in the past. A child is usually not said to be deaf before the age of two, for it is not until he reaches the age at which he should be responding normally to speech, but does not, that one can be sure he is deaf.

The American Society for the Hard of Hearing, founded in 1919, stimulated research for methods of testing the hearing of large groups. The result was the group audiometer. Once this technique was employed, people began for the first time to realize that a large number of school children had deficiencies in hearing.

A thorough testing program in the schools is essential to detect all those with even a slight hearing deficiency. If this were done, special remedial materials could be prepared for those who needed them, and considerable expense to the schools and society in general could be eliminated.

In a program of conservation of hearing for the hard of hearing, the teachers, nurses, and parents each have a part. Certain types of behavior in a child may be indicative of a hearing loss. Such behavior might be continuous inattention, a bewildered expression when directions are given, a habitual turning of the head to bring the better ear near the speaker, incorrect pronunciation of common words, excessive restlessness, or withdrawal from the group. If moisture is noticed from the ear canal or if the child complains of pain or noises in his ear, he should be examined. All children returning to school after having had any contagious diseases should have hearing tests immediately and at frequent intervals thereafter for the next few years.

Much could be done to help prevent hearing disorders. A health program is all-important, because many childhood illnesses have serious effects on the ears. Earlier attention should be given to ears, nose, sinuses, and throat during acute childhood illnesses. There should be early removal of infected tonsils and adenoids. Some authorities believe that, if hearing disorders are to be prevented, child welfare agencies should offer parents a general and special health education program, including instruction on general home sanitation for improved health.

Parents and teachers should also realize that medical attention is necessary for the undernourished child, the child with frequent colds or defective teeth, the mouth breather, or the child who complains that his ears feel "closed up," or that he has head noises. It is particularly important that the after effects of diseases be under careful observation.

Besides this program of prevention and detection, much can be done for the child who already has a hearing loss. This treatment will include medical, emotional, and educational care. Early medical treatment can arrest the development of the defect, and even correct the impairment. Much can be done in the school to help the hard-of-hearing child make a sound emotional adjustment. Since he is usually shy and withdrawn, he must be encouraged to take part in school activities—in clubs, in games on the playground, and in recitation. He should not be made to feel that he is different, but should be helped to accept his handicap and develop compensations. His fears would be eased greatly if teachers made special efforts to be sure that he understood all directions.

Parents' attitudes will often determine the feelings of the child and, if parents are sensitive about his lack of hearing, he will be sensitive too. Parents need to incite him to do all things that other children do so he will gain self-confidence. A child in his social development has difficulty enough without finding he has been set apart as queer and different. The normal tendency of parents is to give a handicapped child attention; this attention may spoil him if it is not directed toward helping him carry on normally.

Educating the deaf is obviously a problem quite different from educating the hard of hearing: whereas most hard-of-hearing children have been able to hear enough to have acquired speech, the deaf child may not have a memory pattern of words he has already heard, and so must learn speech and language by another method.

As a result of the rise in population and the accompanying increase in the numbers of deaf children, particularly in the larger cities, day schools for the deaf have been provided as a part of regular public school systems. These schools seem to be better than special boarding schools for the deaf because they keep the handicapped children in the natural environment of their own homes and a public school, and do not stigmatize them as utterly different.

The National Research Council, in its second conference on Problems of Deaf and Hard of Hearing, in 1929, and the White House Conference on Child Health and Protection, in 1930, both promoted research in the education of the deaf and hard of hearing. This research included the following: surveys of teaching personnel, of teacher-training courses, and of laws concerning hearing tests; development of adequate tests for educational and psychological examination of the two groups; studies of curricula, and of personality and vocational problems; surveys of the cost of programs in conservation of hearing; medical research; investigation of the use of hearing aids and other amplified devices.

Blindness and Defective Vision

The term *blindness* is a general one designating any distinct lack of power to respond to the stimuli which give rise to vision. It may be total or partial, and may be due to injuries or deficiencies in any part of the optical mechanism, either in those organs accessory to the retina, or in the retina itself, or in the connections between them. Most state and federal administrators define blindness as visual acuity of 20/200 or less in the stronger eye, with correcting glasses. A person may have normal vision, but his field of vision might be so restricted that he sees only a very limited area at a time.

Children that are able to see partially are usually categorized into three divisions for purposes of special education: (1) children having a visual acuity between 20/70 and 20/200 in the better eye after all possible medical and optical help has been provided; (2) children with serious, progressive eye difficulties; (3) children suffering from diseases of the eye and of diseases of the body that seriously affect vision.

The means of detecting defective vision in children varies. It may be found early by a doctor making a routine physical checkup for alert, methodical parents; or it may not be discovered until the child is examined upon his entering school. Danger signs to watch for in children, as in adults, are inflammation in or about the eyes, abnormal growth, opacities, headaches or pain in seeing, flashes or spots before the eyes, nearsightedness or farsightedness, the viewing of objects from odd angles, and optical defects that are obvious in the structure and appearance of the eye.

Special sight-saving classes for partially seeing children have accomplished much in recent years. Placement in these classes depends in large part on the resources available in the community, the opthalmologist's report and recommendation (there is not complete professional agreement on the treatment of all defects) and, if possible, a psychologist's report on the personality needs of the child.

Parental consent is imperative for placing children in special classes. Furthermore, if possible, the parents should be invited to visit the schoolroom in which such classes are conducted, so that they can see that their child is not being discriminated against because of his defect, but rather that he is being provided with special educational facilities. The reaction of the parent will in turn influence the pupil's attitude toward his position in a special class.

Numerous problems of administration arise in program planning, especially for the small and rural communities. In some states, however, various special arrangements have been made for the partially seeing child in such communities. In some areas, special educational facilities are available for the partially seeing child in his own rural school; in another, there may be a class for various types of handicapped children. Special classes for the partially seeing may be incorporated in consolidated schools, which are more likely to have better facilities and advantages for children than are the small, one-room, general schools. In some communities, special classes have been established in connection with the practice-teaching programs of teachers' colleges. Also, partially seeing children might be placed in special classes in the nearest city.

Wherever the child goes to school, he must not be made to be fearful of the reaction of others to his defect nor should he feel that his handicap is an extra burden on his family—either social or financial.

The teacher of the partially seeing must be aware of the influences affecting the child from within and without. Many children have built up a defense mechanism as an excuse for inability to accomplish certain aims. The teacher must be able to point this out as a faulty excuse and direct the child to overcoming his inferiority. She must be able to consider the personality of the child in relation to his handicap. Some states train teachers especially for teaching the sight-saving classes. In others, a school may select the most likely person from its staff and prepare her specially for the task of teaching the sight-saving class.

In most sight-saving classes in regular public schools, the child attends the special class only for study and preparation of the assignments, but goes into the regular classes for recitation and class participation.

One of the most important functions of a teacher in this type of class is vocational guidance; this cannot be separated from educational guidance, since the final goal of most education programs is the preparation of the child for work. The nature of the guidance in a sight-saving class is determined by the types of special problems presented by the children in the class; consequently the teacher must be extremely discerning.

In 1963 there were some 21,531 blind or partially blind children in this country. Of these, 13,962 were in public school classes, and 7,569 were in public or private residential schools.[3] The trends in sight conservation that have been developing since 1963 seem fairly obvious. It is a widely accepted concept that techniques by which a visually handicapped child can receive the maximum education for his own capacity must be implemented. The social adjustments of such a child depend to a large extent on the security and freedom his family and teachers permit him, and on his own capacity to enjoy vicariously what his sighted friends can see.

Children with Speech Defects

It is estimated that approximately 6 percent of all children between the ages of two and 16 years have some speech defect. This handicap may be associated with another physical handicap, such as deafness, cerebral palsy, cleft palate, or malocclusion of teeth; or it may be an emotional reaction to inner conflicts.

A child first learns to use words for highly subjective reasons. Words enable him to get what he wants and to understand what is occurring in his immediate environment. He learns that language is a way of conveying what is expected of him and what is approved and disapproved.

---

3. Standards Division, U.S. Children's Bureau. Department of Health, Education and Welfare. Washington, D.C., 1968.

Each child learns to speak in his own way, and they learn at different ages. Some children speak one- or two-syllable words at nine months. Usually before the end of the second year, children learn to speak a sequence of two or three words and then rudimentary sentences. By the third year children usually speak short sentences correctly.

If a child is abnormally slow in learning to talk, or if he has a speech difficulty, such as stuttering, parents should get professional help in diagnosing and treating the difficulty.

Trouble in articulation and sound reproduction may be due entirely to teeth irregularities or reverse swallowing. Such conditions can usually be cleared up by medical or dental care and speech therapy.

When a child's speech difficulty is due to an emotional conflict, parents have a primary responsibility to consider carefully their own mental and emotional attitudes toward each other and toward the child. Is there open dissension between them on ways of caring for the child or means of disciplining him? Are they placing too much emphasis on the child's achievements in various areas of his life? Are they comparing him to other children in a competitive way? Do they permit him to express his own wishes and feelings, or do they repress his natural expression? Are they praising his small accomplishments?

In all speech disorders the functional and emotional cause of the defect must be known in order to plan treatment. Parents, teachers, and others closely associated with the child must understand the reasons for the child's handicap and work intelligently with the child to help him overcome a condition over which he may have no control.

GUARDIANSHIP

The special service of guardianship has been employed for many children in the following categories: (1) children who have been found defective; (2) children who have been declared dependent, neglected, or delinquent; (3) children of divorced or separated parents; (4) children who have lost either one or both parents. Guardianship is for the welfare of the child and it is usually considered to be the legal substitute for a parent.

Guardianship is an ancient institution. It was used by the family before the time of Christ. Under Roman law, every child had a guardian. The father was natural guardian and had great authority—the power of life and death over his children. Upon his death, the child was required to have a guardian: this guardian would be a tutor if the child was a boy under 14 years of age or a girl under 12; he might be a curator if the child was older.

The History of Guardianship

The history of guardianship in England can be divided into two parts—before 1660 and after. Before 1660, guardianship was largely feudal or borough (town) guardianship; after 1660 guardianship was designated largely by statute. English law in regard to guardianship was concerned almost exclusively with the guardianship of infant heirs.

Soon after the Norman Conquest, when land holdings became hereditary, the lord of an estate had the wardship of the person and property of his tenants' heirs and the right to arrange their marriages to his advantage (if the heirs were under 21). All male tenants were required to give military service when called upon by their lord. In return, the lord owed them protection of their persons, heirs, and land holdings.

English law did not state that all children must have guardians. The court itself made the decisions on whether or not it should appoint a guardian for a particular child.

In the United States, the 13 original states made early provisions for orphans and their estates. Guardianship of the person and management of his property, personal and real, were under the jurisdiction of various courts. Special courts were created to handle guardianship matters. The suggestion of assigning probate and equity cases to a spiritual or ecclesiastical court was rejected, and common law courts handled them at first. Subsequently, as a result of the growth in population, special probate courts were established. By the nineteenth century, most states had brought their various statutes concerning guardianship (including those on probate and equity) together in one law. In general, such a law provides for (1) guardianship under the jurisdiction of special courts, (2) testamentary guardianship, (3) administrative details. The only important changes in the twentieth century have been restriction of the father's power of testamentary appointment, and removal of the disabilities that women suffered in guardianship matters.

Current Laws on Guardianship

Every state has laws governing guardianship, but from times past, and even today, those children with estates form the majority protected by such laws. Far too much emphasis has been placed on the preservation of the estate rather than on the protection and guidance of the child. The elements of guardianship which contribute to the well-being of the child are the presence of an adult who is responsible for his welfare and the existence of property rights which protect him from dependency.

There is no law saying that every child must have a guardian. Usually, the protection of a legal guardian is not accorded children in the following categories: the orphaned child who does not have an estate of a size that necessitates legal guardianship; the child without property who is abandoned or neglected, or is without proper care owing to the absence or inadequacy of parents; the child who has come to the attention of the court for some other reason. Unfortunately, there are no definite means of determining the number of children in need of guardianship, or of determining the conditions of these children under existing circumstances.

Not only should there be concern about the number of children without the protection of guardianship, but there should also be concern about the quality of protection given to those children that do have guardians. Are the laws that govern the guardian and the ward adequate to promote the welfare of the child? Are the administrative procedures and facilities adequate to insure the child's protection? Are the persons directing and carrying out the administration cognizant of the needs of children and of the best methods currently available for meeting those needs? What should we do to give all children without parents the best possible protection and care? These are the questions of importance to the child welfare worker and to the community.

By definition, a guardian is "a person to whom the law has entrusted the custody and control of the person or estate, or both, of an infant, whose youth, inexperience, and mental weakness disqualify him from acting for himself in the ordinary affairs of life." He is responsible to the court that appointed him for the person of his ward and/or for his ward's estate, and must observe the laws and regulations governing his office, which is one of trust.

There is no uniformity of state laws covering guardianship. The majority of the states adopted English law and have based their laws upon principles incorporated in it, making modifications in them from time to time as the need arose. Louisiana is an exception; its laws of "tutorship" stem from the Code Napoleon.

The relationship of the guardian and ward is quite similar to that of parent and child. In fact, it is the legal substitute for that relationship. It differs in that the guardian is not liable for the support of the child, or entitled to the labor of the child. The needs of the child are supplied from the child's estate. The material needs aside, the personal and social responsibility of the guardian to his ward, which the state requires him to perform, correspond to that of the parent. This relationship between guardian and ward ends when the ward reaches his majority, or when he marries if this takes place sooner; but, whether the relationship is ended or not, guardianship of the estate continues until the ward is 21.

Natural Guardians

Parents are the natural guardians of their children. Natural guardianship does not devolve upon other relatives. However, this type of guardianship is for the person of the child and gives the parent no power over his real or personal property. It is necessary for the parent to be appointed guardian of the estate by the court in order to assume control of the child's property.

The mother's position as guardian of her children has not always been a favorable one. Statutes giving her "equal" rights or "joint guardianship" with the father are relatively recent. By 1930, 39 states had passed such laws. Under English common law, the father was the sole guardian of his children during his lifetime and could by deed or will place them under the guardianship of whomever he pleased without regard for the wishes or consent of the mother. With her assumption of guardianship rights, the mother also assumes obligation to support her children, a responsibility that was not legally hers under common law.

It is appropriate to mention here the position of the mother of an illegitimate child. In the United States and England today, the mother is sole guardian of her illegitimate child.

According to the doctrine of *parens patriae* the state has the authority to determine the proper custody of the child. Although social forces are marshalled to keep the child in his own home and to strengthen the family, it is sometimes necessary to remove the child from the custody of his parents for his welfare. In cases of dependency, neglect, or delinquency the juvenile court is usually delegated the authority to award custody of the children to persons or agencies or institutions as it deems fit. Statutes of the several states say that a parent who knowingly or willfully abandons or refuses to support his child forfeits parental rights.

The states also modify the authority of natural guardians as *parens patriae* by laws requiring compulsory school attendance and regulating child labor. These modifications govern the authority of appointed guardians as well.

Testamentary Guardian

Testamentary guardianship, as created in England in 1660, provided that the father might deed, will, or dispose of the custody of his minor children, and that such disposition superseded all other claims. This form of guardianship is supported in general by all of the United States, but there have been modifications to restrict the power of the father, to give the mother testamentary rights, and to bring testamentary guardians under the supervision and authority of the courts. The guardianship may be of the person, the estate, or both. The authority for it lies with the testator, the person making the will. The office of testamentary guardian is one of trust and cannot be delegated or willed to another. In most states, testamentary guardians may be appointed by the surviving parent, or by either parent if the other has abandoned the home or is incompetent.

There are some authorities who hold that the testamentary guardian derives his authority from the will of the parent and that there is no necessity for confirmation or supervision by the court. The view that the testamentary guardian should be under the supervision of the court for the protection of the child would seem the better. In authorizing the guardian to assume responsibility for both the person of the child and the estate, the parent delegates more power to the guardian than he himself possessed, since he could not assume control of the child's estate except by appointment of the court; it is therefore desirable that the guardian be held accountable in the exercise of his great authority. The welfare of the child is the concern of the state, and unless the state can supervise, it can have no assurance that the child's well-being will be maintained.

Guardians by Judicial Appointment

Statute or common law in each state designates which kind of state court shall have jurisdiction over guardianship. This function may be assigned to the probate, county, orphans', or surrogate's courts. The probate court has jurisdiction in the largest number of states; the county court in the second largest number. It is up to the discretion of the court, in each case, whether to appoint a guardian.

In the appointment of the guardian, the court may be guided by statutory provisions specifying the order of the right to guardianship. In California, for example, this order is as follows: (1) the parent,

(2) the testamentary guardian, (3) one who already stands in the position of a trustee of a fund to be applied to the child's support, (4) a relative, and (5) the probation officer of the court if the child is a ward of the juvenile court.

Other specifications about the qualifications necessary for guardianship are included in the statutes of some of the other states. A number of laws require that the guardian be "suitable," a "reputable citizen" or other similarly vague characteristics; such terms are no assurance that the guardian will indeed be qualified to protect the child.

Investigation of Guardian Fitness

All states permit courts to investigate the qualifications of guardians before appointment, but not all require the court to do so. Whether it is required or not, the court should always make such an investigation and satisfy itself that the candidate is fit to meet the needs of the ward. This verification is of paramount importance. To appoint without certifying that the guardian will meet all requirements that the situation demands is to make a farce of protection of the child. Needless to say, an investigation is of no value unless it is made by a person or persons qualified to determine the particular needs of the ward and the particular fitness of the guardian to meet those needs.

It is accepted policy that, if the child is old enough, he should be consulted in the appointment of a guardian. Under common law, when a child reached the age of 14, he assumed full responsibility for any criminal act, and the old forms of guardianship—nurture and socage—were terminated. The age of 14 is significant now too, inasmuch as the minor at that age may, in most states, petition and nominate his own guardian, who must then be appointed by the court if he is found suitable. In 22 of these states, the child of 14 has the right to nominate a new guardian to replace the one the court has previously appointed.

A California decision declares that, under the code of that state[4] "a minor on arriving at the age of fourteen years has an absolute right to nominate a nontestamentary guardian to displace the one already placed, even though the displaced guardian may be one of his parents, the question of the nominee's suitability alone coming under the discretion of the court." The advisability of such a provision as this one is questionable. Certainly the child should be consulted on his preference,

---

4. California. *Code of Civil Procedure,* secs. 1748, 1750.

but to allow the discretion of the court to be limited to such an extent by the selection of an inexperienced adolescent is debatable.

Guardians ad Litem

This type of guardianship is temporary. Such a guardian is frequently appointed for a specific purpose in the absence of a permanent guardian. The powers and duties are limited to the particular purpose for which appointment is made. These powers may include consent to adoption, to medical care, to entrance into the armed forces, or to marriage; furthermore the guardian may be making these kinds of decisions for a child whom he has never seen before his appointment by the court. In addition, such guardians may be appointed to represent children in court. They may also be appointed, even though there is a permanent guardian, to aid in the final settlement of an estate, the sale of real property, or the mortgaging of real estate. Because guardians *ad litem* have the power to make decisions vitally affecting the life of the minor, a careless appointment is fraught with danger for the minor. However, if they are carefully selected, they do serve useful purposes in the settlement and handling of estates.

Public Guardians

The office of public guardian exists in most of the 50 states to meet needs which the laws on guardian and ward do not cover. He is a county official who serves as guardian temporarily or when no one is able or willing to qualify. There are no uniform methods for appointing this officer, but all states require him to take oath and give bond in varying amounts. Under the statutes, the public guardians are governed by the same statutes, have the same powers and duties, are subject to the same liabilities, and receive the same compensation as other court-appointed guardians, and they may be removed for the same causes. Often banks and trust companies serve as guardians, usually of the estate. They invest the funds and manage the estates of their wards and collect fees as guardians. Since 1933, estates of less than $5,000 that are deposited in banking institutions have been protected by federal legislation.

As the office now operates, it is not a satisfactory arrangement. However, some such office within the state department of welfare might be developed to serve children satisfactorily.

Guardianship of the Estate

The duties of the guardian to the ward in the guardianship of the person are not of such a nature that they can be easily specified in the law. However, his duties and powers in the guardianship of the estate are such that they may be and are set down quite specifically.

The guardian is bonded to insure the estate against loss through his handling. In some states, he may be bonded by a bonding company; in others he may register personal sureties with the court as bond. It is vital to the protection of the child that the bond be adequate to cover the amount of the estate and that the court make sure that it remains adequate by requiring from the guardian a periodic accounting and inventory. Such safeguards act as a deterrent to the guardian who might be tempted to break his trust and to speculate with the ward's estate or appropriate it to his own uses.

It is the practice for the court to approve the expenditure made for the ward out of the income of the estate after such expenditure has been made. No provision is made for supervised planning in advance of the expenditure. Such planning, although it might provide for flexibility to take care of unforeseen needs, could be misused by an unscrupulous guardian.

Guardian Compensation

Compensation to the guardian is usually in proportion to the income of the estate. It is sometimes fixed by statute as a percentage, but more often it is left to the discretion of the court. The fixed percentage clearly stated in the statute is considered to offer more protection to the ward than does the discretionary amount fixed by the court.

Termination of Guardianship

Although guardianship usually continues until the ward reaches his majority, most states provide that the tenure of a particular guardian may be terminated for good reason upon substantiated complaint. California statutes provide that the guardian may be suspended for abuse of trust, waste or mismanagement of the state, failure to file inventory or render accounting within the time allowed, failure to perform duty, incapacity, gross immorality, interests that are adverse to faithful performance of duties, departure from the state, insolvency of the estate, and termination of the need for the guardianship.

The court that fails to supervise the guardian adequately and depends on the filing of a complaint and proof by an interested person to disclose the incompetence of guardians, gives the child a bare minimum of protection. Many persons who know of abuses by guardians hesitate to bring complaint in behalf of the wards because they fear the possibility of involvement in suits.

At the termination of guardianship, the whole period of guardianship should be reviewed by the judge immediately, so that any loss can be recovered by the ward before jurisdiction leaves the court. Review by the judge is advisable because the ward himself may not be able to understand his affairs despite his attainment of majority. The judge should see to it that the guardian, in addition to turning over the estate, explains to the ward, in his presence, the condition of the estate and any advice regarding it.

It is the consensus among writers on the subject that the laws and administrative procedures pertaining to guardianship need a general strengthening and revising so that they provide more adequate protection for all child wards, whether or not an estate is involved. Enactment of uniform laws of guardianship, and clarification on which courts have jurisdiction are plainly required.

The revised laws should state intelligently and clearly the qualifications for guardians and their powers. If the ward has an estate, there should be provision for prompt inventory, adequate bond, annual supported accounting, supervised planning before the fact of expenditure, and protection against unwise investment or other mismanagement. The compensation of guardians should be specifically stated, and provisions for the time and terms of final settlement should also be incorporated in the law. It is desirable that some degree of mobility may be effected with safety by a provision for the prompt transfer of records from one jurisdiction to another so that the costly and lengthy initial procedure of appointment need not be repeated.

The ward should not be left unprotected for long periods after the probate of the will, as many wards now are. A temporary arrangement could be authorized by law, pending the appointment of a nominee. Some means of notifying the court of the death of the surviving parent should be prescribed by law so that action in the appointment of a guardian may be taken promptly.

To enforce such legislation there must be, of course, adequate facilities and personnel for successful supervision and investigation. Although this might not be feasible in rural areas, where the volume of guardianship cases would not warrant the employment of full-time personnel for supervision, other resources in the community might be employed. Facilities and personnel for the critical examination of guardians' accounts and reports on the estates of their wards are also essential to better guardianship.

The guardianship laws that are currently in effect were written many years ago and need review. If we are to safeguard the children now under guardianship and those who will be, these laws will have to be reexamined. Often, however, it is the administration of the law that permits abuse. The need for a change in guardianship law and administration is obvious. The only important change that has occurred in the past one hundred years is the extension of certain rights to mothers.

The numerous differences in the laws of guardianship from state to state have little justification. Lack of uniformity does not mean that any one state has a superior system of guardianship. The differences are historical, having developed either by chance or as a result of pressure from special interests. The laws of every state are inadequate to meet the needs of present-day conditions.

It is generally conceded that a uniform law on guardianship, to be effective, should specify the following:

1. the requirement of a guardian for every child;
2. a clear designation of the court of jurisdiction and the court of appeals;
3. a definition of the rights, duties, and functions of the various guardians;
4. a requirement of bond from all guardians, the amount to be determined after inventory of the estate;
5. specific directions for annual accounting;
6. a requirement that the court proceedings be published at the time of the final settlement;
7. the rate of compensation for the guardian;
8. explicit directions for removal of the guardian;
9. the requirement that reliable information be provided the court for selection and continued supervision of the guardian;
10. a uniform social service program.

Other suggested improvements of guardianship are these: all courts having jurisdiction over guardianship should be equipped with social and administrative services; guardianship procedures should be prompt and comprehensive.

Testamentary guardians should be subject to the same requirements and liabilities as other guardians. They should be required to qualify and meet the court approval immediately after the death of the surviving parent, instead of waiting three to six months for the will to be probated.

Supplementary services to the probate court should include social services performed by qualified children's workers, and property service performed by salaried lawyers and auditors.

PROTECTIVE SERVICES

If a court decides that a child is neglected, it may transfer the guardianship of that child to an agency that has been selected for supervision of neglected children. Children who are designated as juvenile delinquents may also be assigned to agencies, authorities, or institutions outside of their homes. However, many protective services are rendered to children in their own homes, thus allowing parents to retain guardianship of their children.

Protective work, strictly speaking, is the work that provides security for the child who is abused, abandoned, or neglected by his parents or guardians. Sometimes neglect is not willful but due to ignorance or misfortune. When a parent can provide the support, education required by law, and the medical and other care necessary to the child's welfare, but refuses or neglects to do so, or when a child is abandoned by its parents, the protective function of law enforcement officials may be necessary.

Protecting the child not only from neglect, but also abuse and exploitation, is a problem for the citizens of a whole community. Many agencies and organizations have an interest in such children, as do child welfare agencies, the court, and law enforcement officials.

Child welfare workers and probation officers attempt to protect children from neglect and abuse through social casework and the use of selected social services in dealing with parents. The primary objective of their work is to keep the child in the home if at all possible. When these efforts fail, placement of the child in a foster home or an institution may be suggested by the worker, if not demanded by the appropriate court.

The family is the fundamental unit in our society that has the responsibility for developing healthy children. It is expected to care, love, nuture, train, guide, and protect its children. The community, too, is responsible for providing certain services for its children and protecting their rights. In a very broad sense, the neglect of children is traceable to the failure by the parents, by the community, or by both to carry out their responsibilities in meeting the needs of their young.

Any community has the responsibility of preventing and correcting neglect that has resulted from parental failures. This can be done by providing services to promote the parents' strengths and desires to assume their complete role as parents. The community has the obligation to provide good family and child care by means of child welfare services designed to motivate and strengthen parental desires and capacities, when found wanting, for assuming a healthy obligation for the rearing of their children.

In the past several years there has been concern in medical circles as well as among protective service workers for the plight of the abused or battered child. In 1962 the Children's Bureau convened two conferences on the subject, and the results were a statement of principles and a suggested model for state legislatures for the reporting of cases of child abuse. All 50 states, as well as Guam, Washington, D.C., and the Virgin Islands, have encouraged legislation making it necessary for physicians to report injuries of children to law enforcement agencies if they believe the injuries have been inflicted by adults.

The removal of children from their own home without the knowledge or consent of parents is a law enforcement function. Some child protective agencies have been given this power, but prefer to use law enforcement personnel when it is necessary to remove children from their own home. Petitions must be filed in court immediately, or as soon as possible, in order to detain a child outside of his home. In serious cases of neglect, the court may take guardianship of the child from the parents and transfer it to an agency that will supervise a child in an institution or in a community foster home.

It has been found to be much more effective if a specific agency in the community has the responsibility for receiving complaints of child neglect. In other words, the responsibility should not be divided or multiplied because inevitably it does not become anyone's explicit responsibility. When child welfare services are provided by a community, the protective duties of the agency include at least an implied, if not official, obligation to do something about child neglect.

Community agencies dealing with child neglect have as an objective some form of environmental manipulation or modification in order to promote the welfare of neglected children. This modification of the social-psychological environment may necessitate changing the attitudes of one or both parents, or, in extreme cases of neglect, removing the child from the home to another and more desirable physical, social, and psychological environment.

An agency that is charged with the responsibility of bringing about change on behalf of neglected children generally has access to authority, directly or indirectly, in dealing with its clients. However, the professional worker is likely to have better results if she uses authority implicitly rather than explicitly, and if she treats a proposed goal as a concern of the community rather than a demand of the agency. This approach has contributed to the successful treatment of many families with problems of child neglect.

It has been reported that much of the neglect of children on the part of parents is associated with such factors as marriage at an early age, divorce, separation, desertion, illegitimacy, high mobility of the family, and economic, physical, and emotional pressures on the parents.

In financially poor homes, neglect is often physical. It is manifested by lack of food, clothing, medical care, and sanitary surroundings. A preponderance of an agency's cases on neglect is concerned with children suffering from physical neglect. Physical neglect is obviously easier to detect and to prove than psychological rejection or neglect. Families in the higher socioeconomic levels are more apt to have emotionally neglected children. Overprotection by a neurotic parent may be found in these families, as well as underprotection by parents too busy to spend a normal amount of time with their family.

Approximately 90 percent of child neglect cases are handled successfully by an agency without resort to court action. In other words, the legal definition of neglect becomes significant only if court action is felt to be necessary for the interests and welfare of a child. An agency, then, is able to treat most of its cases of child neglect, physical or emotional, without using the court.

Child protective services are administered by public and voluntary agencies in the community. Ideally these agencies should be divorced from the judicial function of a court for two reasons: first, social casework should never be associated with force or with a penalty leveling agency; second, an agency that is completely separate from a court is in a better position to present evidence that can be reviewed objectively by the judiciary. Early responsibility for these protective services was undertaken by voluntary agencies, such as societies for the prevention of cruelty to children, children's aid societies, and humane societies. The New York Society for the Prevention of Cruelty to Children was established in 1875 and is generally considered to be the first child protective agency in the world. East of the Mississippi

River, the voluntary agencies continue to carry on their child protective function. However, since the enactment of the Social Security Act (Title V, part 3) by the United States Congress, the trend has been for public agencies to enter into the child protection field.

Supplementary Readings

Allan, A., and Morton, A. *This is Your Child: The Story of the National Society for the Prevention of Cruelty to Children*. Routledge and Kegan Paul, London, 1961.

Bacon, Margaret, and Jones, Mary Brush. *Teen-Age Drinking*. Crowell, New York, 1968.

Beauen, Paul, M.D. "The Adoption of Retarded Children." *Child Welfare*. April, 1956.

Bell, Winifred. *Aid to Dependent Children*. Columbia University Press, New York, 1965.

Berlin, Irving N. "The Emotional and Learning Problems of the Socially and Culturally Deprived Child." *Mental Hygiene*. July, 1966.

Blos, Peter. *On Adolescence*. Free Press, New York, 1962.

Chesser, E. *Cruelty to Children*. New York Philosophical Library, 1952.

Child Welfare League of America. *Standards for Child Protective Service*. Child Welfare League of America, New York, 1960.

Coles, Robert. *Uprooted Children*. University of Pittsburg Press, Pittsburg, 1970.

Creak, M., and Ini, S. "Families of Psychotic Children." *Journal of Child Psychology and Psychiatry*. No. 1, 1960.

de Francis, Vincent. *Protective Services and Community Expectations*. The American Humane Society, Denver, 1961.

Dunn, Lloyd, et al. *Exceptional Children in School*. Holt, Rinehart, and Winston, New York, 1963.

Egg, Maria. *Educating the Child Who Is Different*. John Day, New York, 1968.

Feldman, Francis L., and Scherz, Frances H. *Family Social Welfare: Helping Troubled Families*. Atherton Press, New York, 1967.

Flammang, C. *The Police and the Underprotected Child*. Charles C. Thomas, Springfield, Ill., 1970.

Fontana, Vincent J. *The Maltreated Child*. Charles C. Thomas, Springfield, Ill., 1964.

Friedenberg, Edgar Z. *The Vanishing Adolescent*. Dell, New York, 1970.

Garrett, Beatrice L. "Foster Family Services for Mentally Retarded Children." *Children*. November–December, 1970, Vol. 17, No. 6.

Glazer, Nona, and Creedon, Carol, Eds. *Children and Poverty*. Rand McNally, Chicago, 1968.

Gould, Jonathan, Ed. *The Prevention of Damaging Stress in Children*. Churchill, London, 1968. (Report of the U. K. Study Group No. 1 to the World Federation for Mental Health. Presented August 6, 1968 at the Seventh International Congress on Mental Health.)

Gyorgy, Paul, and Burgess, Anne, Eds. *Protecting the Pre-School Child*. Lippincott, Philadelphia, 1965.

Heyder, D. W., and Hughes, Blanche. "A Contribution to the Training of Brain-Injured Children." *Mental Hygiene*. October, 1967.

Hornecker, Alice. "Adoption Opportunities for the Severely Handicapped." *Children*. July–August, 1962.

Kvaraceus, William C., and Hayes, Nelson E. *If Your Child Is Handicapped*. Porter Sargent, Boston, 1969.

Levinson, Abraham. *The Mentally Retarded Child*. John Day, New York, 1965.

Lorand, Sandor, M.D., and Schneer, Henry I., M.D. *Adolescents*. Dell, New York, 1961.

Mamula, Richard A. "The Use of Developmental Plans for Mentally Retarded Children in Foster Home Care." *Children*. March–April, 1971. Vol. 18, No. 1.

Martinez, Edgar E. *The Child with a Handicap*. Charles C. Thomas, Springfield, Ill., 1959.

Rickard, Geraldine, and Cohen, Hasket. "Assessing the Emotional Development of Children." *Mental Hygiene*. October, 1966.

Schreiber, Mayer, Ed. *Social Work and Mental Retardation*. John Day, New York, 1970.

Seidman, Jerome Martin. *Educating for Mental Health*. Crowell, New York, 1963.

Simmons, Harold Ernest. *Protective Services for Children: A Public Social Welfare Responsibility*. California State Department of Welfare, Sacramento, 1968.

Simons, Savilla Millia. *Services to Uprooted and Unsettled Families*. Columbia University Press, New York, 1962.

Strang, Ruth. *Understanding and Helping the Retarded Reader*. University of Arizona Press, Tucson, 1965.

Young, Leontine. *Wednesday's Child*. McGraw-Hill, New York, 1964.

Zuk, G. H. "The Religious Factors and the Role of Guilt in the Parental Acceptance of the Retarded Child." *American Journal of Mental Deficiency*. 1959. Vol. 64.

[Photo by Cary Osfeld.]

7

Unmarried Parenthood

The child born out of wedlock and his unmarried parents present special problems in any area where society discriminates against them because of illegitimacy itself.

Children have been born out of wedlock ever since there has been any form of marriage, but earliest records show that the attitude toward illegitimacy depended on the traditions of the particular culture. In some primitive tribes, then as now, a young woman who had borne a child was considered a more eligible spouse. Among other primitive peoples, the man who committed adultery or fornication was killed, or flogged, or punished by having his head shaved, or disfigured in some other way. A woman found guilty of either of these crimes was beaten, killed, or disfigured.

When children have been born out of wedlock in more complex monogamous societies, always the mother and child have suffered.

Harsh punishment for the mother and denial of legal rights to her child have been the general rule.

The illegitimate child generally arrives in the world as an unwanted child. He does not belong to a family group which gives him care, affection, and individual attention, and, instead, he has only the impersonal body of law to defend his welfare. The mother may pass him on to someone else, so that he is deprived of normal home life and parental care and support. The infant mortality, dependency, and delinquency rates are higher among illegitimate than legitimate children.

The future of the illegitimate child is more irrevocably determined by society's laws than is that of the legitimate child who has the family to intercede for him in life.

The terminology used in referring to the child born out of wedlock has varied considerably. During the periods when his status has been less favorable, the terms "bastard" or "filius nullus" (nobody's son) have been used; in periods when he has been treated with more consideration, the terms "illegitimate child," "love child," "child born out of wedlock," or "natural child" seem to have been more common.

We find the Biblical injunction: "A bastard shall not enter into the congregation of the Lord. . . ."[1] Again, in early Athens there is an account of how Pericles picked out five thousand bastards, as defined by Athenian law, and sold them into slavery. It is interesting to note that, subsequently, Pericles had a son by Aspasia who was not his lawful wife. But in this case, he set the law aside and granted all citizenship rights to his own son.

In the Middle Ages in Europe, the children born out of wedlock were literally "nobody's children," having no legal claim on mother or father. They were usually kept in the class of serfs. It was during this time that foundling asylums were established by religious organizations on the continent of Europe to prevent infanticide, which was common.

The first foundling asylums were established in Italy in the sixth century and in the course of time they were to be seen in all the large cities of western Europe. At the end of the twelfth century, Pope Innocent III introduced in a Roman hospital the first "tours" or turn boxes, a sort of crude cradle, one side of which was left open to the street to receive an infant. If any mother wished to leave a baby, she

---

1. Deut. 23:3.

placed it in the box, rang a bell, and slipped away undiscovered; the child was received into the home. Spain and Portugal soon adopted this practice. Turn boxes were introduced into France and Belgium in 1811, and later into other countries. They are still used in some places.

In England, the first foundling hospital was established in London in 1739 with public funds. At that time, unmarried mothers, when found with their children, were forced to do penance in a public church before the entire congregation, or were punished severely by other methods of torture. To avoid such treatment, many of them murdered their infants and the hospital was founded as a place where they might leave them instead.

LEGISLATION

The cruelty of the common law in England in the sixteenth and seventeenth centuries was such that there resulted a great increase in the number of illegitimate infants that were reported dead at birth. This situation led to the enactment of an English statute in 1623, which made infanticide a capital offense punishable by death, unless the unwed mother had reported her pregnant condition and had at least one witness who could testify that the child was stillborn.

In France, although bastards were serfs in the Middle Ages, by 1789 they were not outcasts, although they were still treated as inferior to legitimate children. In 1793, the new law was enacted. It stated that the rights of the illegitimate child should be the same as those of other children. "There will be no more bastards in France," declared the proponents of this law. Illegitimate children in the French Republic were granted, in 1896, what amounted to equal inheritance rights. By 1912, the establishment of paternity, if requested by the mother or child, was a legal responsibility of the state.

Between 1892 and 1915, organized labor in Norway was in support of the movement to increase the rights of illegitimate children. Some of the resolutions were introduced into the government conventions by Representative Johan Castberg, and, because of his activity in the matter, a bill that was passed in 1915 bears his name.

The Castberg Law, still effective, placed the responsibility of establishing paternity on the state, and required the mother to report the facts about paternity to the local authorities who then followed through on the legal establishment of paternity. Contributions for the child's maintenance, in accordance with the standards of living of whichever parent was in the better circumstances, were to be made until the child was 16 years old. Then, if either parent was so situated that he or she might reasonably be expected to make contributions to allow the child to continue his education beyond the age of 16, that parent could be ordered to do so. If the question of paternity remained undetermined because of the involvement of more than one man, each man was to contribute a certain amount.

The father was responsible for the cost of the mother's medical care and for her maintenance during those periods before and after confinement, when she was unable to work. The state took the responsibility for collecting the maintenance.

The child inherited from the parents as if he were legitimate. However, if there was only the presumption of paternity, he would not inherit from the possible father but would only receive maintenance. Legitimation of a child by the subsequent marriage of his parents was made possible by this law.

In early England, the illegitimate child was the responsibility of the parish and was treated like any other vagrant or poor person. In order to protect the taxpayer and relieve the burden on the parish, the Elizabethan Law of 1576 made the father and mother responsible for the support of the illegitimate child. In 1609, a subsequent law declared, "Every lewd woman which shall have any bastard which may be chargeable to the parish shall be committed to the house of correction, punished and set to work for one year." In 1662, the parish was authorized to seize the property of a mother or father who ran away, leaving an illegitimate child dependent on the parish. An act was passed in 1744 to make the laws relating to rogues, vagabonds, idle, and disorderly persons more effective. According to its provisions, a woman who left her own parish, gave birth to a bastard child in a parish to which she did not belong, and became dependent was to be publicly whipped (naked above the waist until she became bloody) and committed for six months to the house of correction.

The nineteenth century saw a change in attitude. An act of 1844 gave the primary claim for support to the mother instead of to the poor-law authorities and emphasized the liability of the father rather than the mother. Thus the father now became primarily responsible for the support of the illegitimate child, just as he was for the legitimate child of the legal family.

In England, before the Middle Ages, legitimation after birth was possible if the parents had been free to marry at the time of the child's conception. The Statutes of Merton in 1236 ended this, however, except in cases in which Parliament granted individual permission. There was a gap of about six centuries before the Legitimacy Act of 1926 permitted legitimation after birth, without parliamentary intercession, in cases in which the parents had been free to marry at the time of birth.

Denmark has an interesting solution to the problem of supporting illegitimate children: the liability for support is apportioned among all of the "possible" fathers. In Russia, no legal distinction is drawn between legitimate and illegitimate children.

American legislation on illegitimacy is patterned after the English law, and was introduced into the colonies as early as 1609. The mother of a child born out of wedlock was referred to as a "lewd" woman and her child was known as a "bastard." The stern religious code of the Puritan settlers often required the mother to confess her sin before the church congregation. She might be placed in stocks, publicly whipped, imprisoned, or, like Hester in Hawthorne's *The Scarlet Letter*, be sentenced to the lifelong wearing in public of a scarlet letter *A* for "adulteress."

Although one of the reasons for the cruel treatment of the unmarried mother and child was the desire to protect public funds, the father of the child actually faced little inconvenience. His responsibility was hard to prove, and burden of support was placed on the mother. If she could not carry it, the child was exposed to whatever methods the community had of caring for dependent children.

Some of the most significant and effective provisions that have been made by the laws of different states, or that could and should be made, are the following:

1. that the terms "bastard," "bastardy," and "illegitimacy" be eliminated from all laws relating to the child born out of wedlock;
2. that court action be initiated only by the mother or a welfare agency, and at any necessary time regardless of the age of the child;
3. that paternity proceedings be heard in a court that handles either children's cases or domestic relations, and that is equipped to make a social investigation before the hearing and to provide casework services;

4. that some method be devised so that cases can be settled out of court entirely, or by civil action, without involving criminal or quasi-criminal procedure;
5. that support orders and their supervision and enforcement be changed or modified, and that adequate supervision be provided with approval by the court.

Social agencies and social workers have written a great deal on the subject of whether it is advisable to initiate paternity proceedings; they have tried to view the question from the standpoints of the child, the mother, the father, and the community.

In recent years there has been a strong tendency in several states to protect the child. The more progressive and enlightened courts in this country now hold that the chief purpose of a paternity proceeding is to secure the health, welfare, and happiness of the child.

Most of the states have provided that, upon the marriage of the parents, the child becomes legitimized. There is, however, some variation. In Louisiana, only the child of parents who might legally have married at the time of the child's conception may be legitimized by the marriage of his parents.

The child's rights of inheritance are now allowed to some extent in all states. Most states permit an illegitimate child to inherit from his mother a share that is equal to those of her legitimate children, though there are many exceptions and limitations. The statutes of a number of states provide that an illegitimate child cannot inherit from his father unless the father acknowledges the child in the presence of witnesses. Some states, such as Arizona and North Dakota, on the other hand, have attempted by law to wipe out all distinction between illegitimate and legitimate children.

The definition of a dependent child in the Social Security Act makes grants to the unmarried mother possible under the Aid to Families with Dependent Children program. In the Old Age and Survivors' Insurance program, the illegitimate child is entitled to benefits "if the father was supporting the child or had the legal obligation to do so."

The fact that an unwed, teen-age mother is a minor makes many legal principles generally applicable to minors also applicable to her.

The ambivalence of the public attitudes toward the unmarried mother, the father, and the child born out of wedlock, is partly responsible for the unreasonableness and inconsistency of laws pertaining to illegitimacy. The most striking feature of many existing laws is the large number that are wholly unadapted to modern social conditions. Legislation pertaining to the unmarried mother and the child born out of wedlock is more humane in the Scandinavian countries than in the United States.

Most agencies and social workers recognize the serious social and emotional factors the mother is faced with during court proceedings, and they believe that she should be fully acquainted with these factors before she makes her decision. Casework treatment should help her understand her attitude toward the father, and her feelings about her child.

In some states, court action to determine paternity must be taken before an unwed mother may receive aid; if the mother resides in one of these states, it is important for the social worker to discuss the implications of this type of action with her. It should be mentioned here that the Social Security law makes no distinction between legitimate and illegitimate children in aid to dependent children. Many agencies have recommended that the statutes be amended to specify that the hearings in a court action to determine paternity be closed, thus providing more humane treatment for the mother.

There are many arguments against legal proceedings. The present emphasis on criminal or quasi-criminal procedure would not seem justified in view of the social and emotional factors at stake. If the father obtains his first knowledge of fatherhood through a notice to appear at an agency or a court, or through arrest, it may, understandably, be difficult, if not impossible, to obtain his cooperation later. If paternity could be acknowledged by the father in an agency interview and later in closed chambers, thus saving the mother, father, and families involved from the distastefulness of a public court proceeding, a great step would be taken in the improvement of existing laws. State laws should be liberalized to make this possible.

Present legal procedures in collecting support money are futile, even when judgment is rendered. It has been found that a large portion of the men forced to pay are in arrears within two years after the court proceeding; 73 percent, within five to seven years after. There is no machinery in our laws for enforcing these orders except to put the fathers in jail. This procedure would not benefit the father, mother, or child. The idea of punishing the father of the child born out of wedlock still dominates many of the state laws.

The ambivalence of the public attitudes toward the unmarried father and mother is partly responsible for the unreasonableness and inconsistency of laws on the establishment of paternity. The laws are both punitive and protective. The most striking feature of a large number of existing paternity laws is the total lack of adaptation to modern social conditions.

THE PHILOSOPHY OF THE SOCIAL AGENCY

As private agencies and public relief agencies developed in America, social workers recognized that the conduct of the unmarried mother was not the result of inborn depravity, mental retardation, or both, but that social and economic conditions could be contributing factors. The insight that social workers gained through casework gave them a heightened awareness of the need for more basic knowledge and understanding of the personality structure of both unmarried parents.

Then in 1920 psychiatry began to influence the philosophy of social workers, and consequently the work of social agencies, public and private. The fields of psychology, biology, sociology, and anthropology made contributions to studies of personality structure, human behavior, and the dynamics of everyday living. As a result of research and study in all of these scientific disciplines, there emerged an understanding of the effects of social, cultural, psychological, and emotional factors on women who bear children out of wedlock.

The U.S. Children's Bureau in 1920 organized regional conferences in Chicago and New York to study problems of illegitimacy. These conferences, which utilized much of the scientific research mentioned above, drew the attention of the public to the social and financial costs which result from the neglect of unmarried parents and their children.

One of the results of these conferences was the general public recognition that illegitimacy did not occur only among the economically or socially deprived, or the dull and uneducated. Also people began to realize that unmarried mothers did not present one integrated, unified, traditional behavior pattern. Rather, the behavior pattern is the result of the conflict between one of a number of different subcultures and the psychological and emotional life of an individual. These cultural and individual differences are what create differences in the way unmarried mothers feel about their pregnancy and planning for the future of the child.

Gradually, social workers saw that new methods in casework with unmarried mothers were necessary if the workers were to increase their usefulness to the unwed mother, the father, and to the child. So instead of putting major emphasis on the mother's psychological motives and internal dynamics, they began to think that the real need was to determine the worth and dignity of the individual as related to the well-being and dignity of the group.

Now the unmarried pregnant girl is seen, by social workers, as a person affected by the whole social heritage in which she lives, and by the social values of a society to which she is exposed.

For many years the father of a child born out of wedlock was thought of primarily as the villain who should be punished. Then social workers began to realize that the unmarried teen-age father faced almost as many problems as did the unmarried teen-age mother, and that he too needed an opportunity and help in resolving such issues as these: his relationship with the girl, her family, and his own parents; continuation of his schooling; child support; marriage; employment. His thinking on all of these questions is likely to be accompanied by guilt, confusion, and conflict. In brief, unmarried fathers cannot be grouped as a single type any more than unmarried mothers can.

Decisions on the future of the child become the key problem to be faced by both unwed parents. Most young people, especially teen-agers, who go steady and engage in sexual relationships do not wish to have a child—and do not even anticipate such a situation—so that it is usually a shock for them to discover that they are expectant parents.

Because of shock and fear, the teen-age couple usually first consider panic solutions, such as abortion. In only 15 states are abortions legalized, and then only in specified situations. Consequently, teen-agers think of illicit abortion; or they plan some other way to escape from the reality facing them. Most do not know of sources they might go to for help and advice. The school nurse, if she has a good relationship with the students, has a major function in referral of the girl to proper agencies. A school social worker or counselor has the opportunity to identify in school the girl whose behavior indicates that she is troubled. This person can also make a follow-up of all school drop-outs to learn the reason for leaving school.

When both the unwed pregnant girl and the boy are willing to work with a social agency equipped to give services to them, they find that working out a plan together, for the future of the child, gives them a better understanding of factors and responsibilities involved in illegitimate pregnancies. This effort also helps them to reach a decision on their future relationship to each other or the termination of it. It should clarify for both their own readiness for marriage and the meaning of the responsibilities it entails.

If the child is placed for adoption, there must be enough information available about him so that he will not have to resort to fantasy about his own parents or his adoptive parents, and enough security in his adoptive home so that he will face the reality of being an adopted child. Parents who adopt must recognize that adopted children need more affection, approval, and sense of belonging than their own children would.

The AFDC program has been sharply criticized for "contributing to and encouraging illegitimacy," and yet state public welfare directors point out that of the entire national AFDC case load, only a small percentage (13 percent) are children born out of wedlock.

According to some reports a substantial number of all legitimate first children (approximately 20 percent) are conceived before marriage. These are not children of forced marriages—their parents simply did not wait for a legalized marriage. Limited studies of highschool marriages, in which the girl and possibly the boy have not finished high school, show premarital pregnancy rates that range from 33 percent to 87 percent.

Statistics on the number and proportion of unwed mothers in the United States vary. They differ from year to year, and from place to place. However, the following general statistics are representative: Twenty-five percent are youngsters from ten to 14 years old, and approximately 75 percent are between 15 and 24 years old. Of this second group 45 percent are between 15 and 19, 27.9 percent are between 20 and 24 years of age. Thirty-three percent are white, 67 percent, nonwhite. About 49 percent live in small towns and rural areas. That a slightly higher percentage is in the cities is partly due to the fact that unmarried pregnant girls often escape to urban centers to hide their condition.

What is the unmarried mother like, and why did she become an unmarried mother? The answer to this question is a complicated one. Most of the studies of unmarried mothers indicate some common elements in their backgrounds. Few of them have happy, secure relationships with both of their parents. The family situation has been in some way distorted. There are conflicting feelings of love and hate. For some girls, pregnancy is an act of defiance of her family. She not only punishes her family, but at the same time punishes herself for having these aggressive feelings toward her family. Later, she may punish her baby by rejecting him. Some of these girls have difficulty in their relationships with both men and women. Some are able to carry on superficial contacts with casual acquaintances and friends but are not able to enter into a close and lasting relationship with anyone. A girl whose feelings of loneliness are increased by lack of tenderness in her home environment is prone to misinterpret a mutual sexual desire as mutual tenderness.

In talks with agency workers, many unwed expectant mothers show a similar behavior pattern. They want to get money, attention, interest, and love for themselves—as though they were still in the midst of the strife and conflict of adolescence. They cannot accept responsibility, but must project it on the agency, the worker, the parents, or the father of the child.

Possibly it will help us to visualize the position of the unmarried expectant mother if we compare her with the married woman who has the sanction of our culture and society. In contrast to the happily married woman who has desired pregnancy and a child, and who may be surrounded by love and acceptance, the unmarried pregnant girl cuts herself off from every source of love and friendliness she has ever known. She may be overwhelmed by fear and guilt, and for the duration of her pregnancy she has several months of disillusionment and lovelessness ahead of her. Under the circumstances, she fails to build up a reserve of real love to invest in the baby.

If the unmarried mother has had a dominating mother, there is a striking similarity between the girl's relationship to her own father and her relationship to the father of her baby. She may take the baby into the home of her mother and place upon her the responsibility for his care. If she cannot do this she may show little conflict about placing the baby for adoption.

The girls who are most immature, as well as the girls who have been raised in the impersonal atmosphere of an institution, often fight to keep their children. Theirs is a desire for possession. By keeping their babies, they often try to satisfy their need for human contact. This feeling is not one of the best ingredients of good motherhood.

More frequently than not, the unmarried girl wishes to conceal her pregnancy from the father of the child. Usually there are two motives for this concealment: denial of a positive emotional relation to the father, and narcissistic fear of being rejected and condemned by him.

What are the unmarried mother's needs? First of all, she needs to know, as does any expectant mother, where she can go for medical care by a qualified physician. She is usually bewildered, ashamed, full of anxiety, and very much alone. She has feelings of guilt and fear and discouragement. Where will she be treated as a person in need of medical attention and advice, and not as a public offender?

Those agencies within a community that provide medical and casework services to unmarried mothers should be known to those to whom the girl is most likely to go first for help: physicians, lawyers, nurses, ministers, teachers, and personnel supervisors in factories, offices, and stores. In fact, all agencies, public and private, providing social service to an unmarried mother should make their services a part of common knowledge. Newspapers and women's magazines, including the "love story" variety, are excellent advertising media for this purpose.

Frequently, it is to a doctor that the pregnant girl turns first. What, then, is his responsibility? Essentially, it is the same responsibility he has toward any obstetrical case—to give the best medical care before, during, and after delivery—plus the additional responsibility of referring the girl to the proper community agency for casework service when she first comes to him for help.

If there is a nurse, it is her responsibility, like the doctor's, to maintain the same high standard of service to the unwed mother that prevails in other obstetric cases. If the doctor has not referred the patient to the proper community agency, the nurse should do so.

Neither the doctor nor the nurse should assume the responsibility of being a child-placing agency. That many do so is an established fact. Many of these independent placers are not heartless traders in human beings, but are essentially compassionate, kindly persons who have no conception of the dangers involved. Many doctors, feeling sorry for the panic-stricken unmarried mother, will, upon her request, find a couple wishing to adopt a baby and arrange for them to pay the girl's complete medical expenses in return for the baby.

Generally, the scarcity of babies gives unscrupulous individuals ample opportunity to "place" babies at a considerable profit to themselves. Hence, at the baby's birth, a time when she should not have to make such an important decision, the natural mother is often subjected to considerable pressure to relinquish the child.

Regardless of the motives of the independent placer, the inherent dangers in placement done by someone other than a recognized social agency are the same—dangers to the child, the adoptive parents, and the natural parents.

The child's happiness is at stake. If a separation from his natural parents assures him his best chance for happiness, certainly his adoptive parents should be carefully chosen by people professionally trained in this work.

The unmarried mother has both a medical and social need and it is the responsibility of the hospital which gives confinement care to meet this complex need. If it is to be done adequately, a carefully individualized service and a special type of skill are required. This skill is not a part of the training which the doctor or nurse receives, but it does belong to the medical social worker. Her responsibilities are to interpret medical social problems to the patient, the physician, and the worker in the child welfare or family agency, and to coordinate medical service with community and home resources. Interpretation and reinforcement of the doctor's plan for medical care can be very important if the mother is disregarding medical advice as an expression of resentment toward her situation.

The casework skills used with unmarried mothers are the same as those employed with anyone else. The girl should have the services of a skilled social worker as early in her pregnancy as possible. Some expectant mothers may wish to remain in their own homes until the time of birth; the nonresident mother who needs immediate placement away from home will probably use the maternity home if one is available.

MATERNITY HOMES

A maternity home should be well managed by a competent staff, it should have a flexible policy, and it should be homelike. Its impersonal atmosphere may be especially useful for the young, rebellious girl who has rejected or has been rejected by her family, and it may also serve the need of the frightened girl. The distinguishing feature of the maternity home is that it provides care for the mother and child after confinement. It may have its own hospital unit or it may rely on community hospital service. Increasing numbers of maternity homes are affiliated with social agencies, as are the Salvation Army homes. Other well known maternity homes are the Florence Crittenton Homes, established in 1893 by a New York businessman, Charles N. Crittenton, in memory of his daughter Florence. The maternity home is needed by only a small number of unmarried mothers. Hospital and foster home care for the mother and child may meet the need better than group care.

Maternity homes should be carefully regulated by the states. Specifications for their operation should be clearly stated in statutes, and their licenses should be revoked if at any time these specifications are violated or ignored. The authority for licensing should be vested in the department of public or social welfare.

The value of maternity homes lies in what they can offer to further the girl's development and understanding of herself and her relationship to her child.

Her stay in the maternity home should be as short as is consistent with good casework. Therefore, the home should not undertake an extended program of education or vocational training or retraining. It should adapt its program to each individual. No particular time for the girl's admission or discharge should be prescribed. Advice to the mother on whether to give up or keep her baby should not be offered.

A maternity home for unmarried mothers should offer medical care at standards equal to those of the general hospital, since one of its objectives is to reduce the mortality rate of mothers and illegitimate children. Inspectors should keep this objective in mind when, before licensing a home, they check it's location, building construction, equipment, personnel, and system of reports and records.

In regulating maternity homes for unmarried mothers, laws should particularly emphasize the fact that the license to operate a maternity home does not include the right to place children. The general public often thinks of a maternity home as a direct source of supply for people who want to adopt a baby, and it would be difficult for the home's superintendent to resist the pressure of prospective adoptive parents and their lawyers if the true function of the home were not limited and made clear by law.

Every girl in the maternity home has an intense problem. To be an unmarried mother in a society such as ours is not considered an acceptable role. The unmarried mother has to make some sort of adjustment to the community and to herself, which will include consideration for the welfare of the child. A good maternity home, then, should meet the physical and emotional needs of the unmarried mother in accordance with today's highest standards. Therefore, if the maternity home does not have a social worker, a psychiatrist, and a psychologist on its staff, it must have the services of all three readily available to it.

Perhaps the environment that is most conducive to the mother's adjustment is a foster home, if she cannot remain in her own home. Life in a happy, normal home in which there are other children and an understanding foster mother may give the unmarried mother who has never known satisfying relationships a sense of belonging for the first time.

There is also a need, and a great one, for more trained caseworkers; no worker should have to carry a case load of more than 35 unmarried mothers.

As a result of the knowledge gained in conference discussions, and in studies of the problems confronting the unmarried parents and child born out of wedlock, several agencies throughout the years have developed services for unmarried mothers and fathers in a number of communities throughout the United States.

Among the services offered to the unwed pregnant girl are programs of education, health, and welfare assistance for those girls who leave or are excluded from school. These programs offer the girls an opportunity for continuation of education, as well as health care, prenatal and postpartum care, group and individual counseling, adoptive placement, vocational training, homemaking and child care training, and continuing health care and welfare services.

Programs are financed in different ways: by city or county health and welfare departments, or by some combination of these sources; by private funds; by contributions of Federal Agencies (the U.S. Children's Bureau; the Office of Education; and the Office of Economic Opportunity); from miscellaneous sources, such as the Y.W.C.A., various religious organizations, universities, and others.

Most of these programs are free to the girls. The programs are located in foster homes, the girl's own home, health centers, community centers, public libraries, special public schools, agency homes for unwed mothers, and other available locations. They are directed by social workers, educators, physicians, psychiatrists, or nurses, and they employ additional personnel such as recreation leaders, nutritionists, dietitians, teachers, and health nurses.

Many programs have some requirements for admission. The age preference is between 13 and 19 years of age. Some specify recent school attendance. Others accept only girls in their first pregnancies. Most will not accept a girl past the fifth month of pregnancy, though some will take a girl up to the eighth month.

Requirements for all programs are parental consent, attendance at a specific hospital or clinic, and registration for prenatal care. Many of these programs serve married as well as unmarried teen-age mothers. In a number of these programs, individual counseling services are provided to the unmarried fathers.

Most of the school systems allow the girls in these programs to return to the school she attended before her pregnancy.

Because the unmarried pregnant girl usually lacks the benefits of a mother and father working together in her behalf, some agencies, in an effort to overcome past traumatic family situations and provide for the girl's psychological needs, now assign both a male and a female worker as part of the plan to help the girl with her problems. Generally the female worker first concerns herself with the immediate material needs of the girl: she must help arrange for living quarters for her during the remainder of her pregnancy, as well as for prenatal care, delivery, postnatal care for mother and child, and so on. The male worker is a counselor and advisor, thus becoming more a father figure for the girl. At times during the planning, both male and female workers will see the girl together and plans will be worked out among the three of them.

Constructive involvement of the unmarried father begins as soon as the unwed mother has received satisfactory answers to her questions about her own physical care and is able to discuss with the worker the experience that brought her to the agency.

Generally the unmarried mother is not interested in punitive action against the father. Once she has been assured that this is not the interest of the worker or the agency, and the value of the father's participation in working out problems has been explained to her, she is usually willing to give the name of the father and agrees to allow the agency to contact him. If, for some reason, she does not agree, the agency is guided by her wishes.

THE FUTURE OF THE CHILD

After the worker has helped the mother to decide where she will go to have her baby, casework with the mother should focus on future plans for the child. In her contacts with the mother, the worker should be sure to acquaint her with the realities to which she and her child must adjust, the purpose being not to moralize but to equip the mother to meet future needs.

In the discussions, the worker discovers how the mother feels about establishing paternity of the child. It is now believed that paternity should not be established for support alone, but that the relationship of the mother to the father is the important consideration. This should be explored with the mother, and with the father, if possible. Perhaps the feelings in the relationship can be worked through, and paternity established; for some couples, if it seems wise, marriage may result.

If the mother is one who was deprived of love and affection in childhood and is resentful of her mother, she may decide to keep her baby at all costs; but in her relationship with the worker, she may be able to release these feelings and come to a decision about the baby which is based on the welfare of the child and not on her own earlier deprivations.

Studies have shown that if the mother's parents, no matter how inadequate they had been in the past, could be uncondemning and genuinely concerned in this crisis, the unmarried mother usually chose to give up the baby for adoption, believing this to be the most realistic solution. If she kept the baby, it was not because she needed to defy her parents, but because she had decided that procedure was best for the child.

Experiences of social workers in child guidance clinics and child placement agencies indicate that an unwed mother's decision to keep her baby, no matter how carefully deliberated, creates numerous problems for her in living arrangements, education, employment, future relationships to her own parents and to the father of the child, social life, dating, and marriage. The role of the social worker is that of helping the girl to gain a balanced perspective before the birth of the baby. If she keeps the child, she may place it with a foster mother because the strain of working and maintaining a child becomes too great. She often loses interest, fails to pay board, or becomes jealous of the child's relationship to the foster mother. Then she either deserts the child or causes him to be placed elsewhere; the child may be neglected in an inferior home where she has placed him, or he may become a behavior problem as a result of insecurity and a series of placements in different homes. Ultimately these children come to the attention of the agency, perhaps for the first time.

If she attempts to keep her child's illegitimate birth secret, she lives in perpetual fear of discovery. This results in constant insecurity for both mother and child.

In the course of groping for solutions, social workers have shifted from one philosophy to another. Many workers feel that separation of the mother and child immediately after birth is bound to be a traumatic experience, leaving its mark upon both. There was a time when interested persons urged the enactment of a law requiring the unmarried mother to nurse her child for a period of three months; the hope was that she would become so attached to it that she would be unwilling to give it up. Consequently, some of the children whose mothers did not give them up, but rejected them nevertheless, were unhappy and maladjusted.

The mother should be given every opportunity to decide whether to retain her child or give it up for adoption. The worker must guide her to a decision, not by urging her in any one direction but by making sure the mother is aware of the advantages and disadvantages of either plan. If the advisability of adoption is indicated early in the contact, much of the casework should be done before the birth of the baby so that the mother is prepared socially and psychologically to give up the baby shortly after birth.

The caseworker needs to examine her own feelings: has she a need to have a client decide a particular way? This self-examination should leave her free to enlighten the client about the various alternatives and then to handle the casework relationship with a clear understanding of the client's needs. Also workers need to remind themselves constantly that the unmarried mother has been confronted by disapproving, hostile, and sometimes cruel attitudes before she comes to a social agency.

PATERNAL RESPONSIBILITIES

Until recently, the prevailing attitude toward the unwed father was so dominated by the support element that other factors were obscured. Today, an awareness of the father as a person rather than just as a means of support has caused us to emphasize different procedures in casework with him.

Agencies that have undertaken to offer social services to the fathers have found that, on the whole, the men have been most cooperative and that the contact has proved helpful and worthwhile in working out a plan for mother and child.

Generally, society is either protective or punitive toward the father of the child born out of wedlock; no moderate attitudes seem to be held except by workers in a few agencies. The fathers are usually regarded as having responsibility but no rights. A worker in a social agency must be free of moral judgments if she is to make any progress with the father. We must remember that, if his first reaction is hostility toward the worker and society at large, it is because of society's demand that he support the child regardless of whether he gets any of the satisfactions associated with usual fatherhood. Many fathers might wish to legitimize the relationship and might even favor marriage, but very often the mother's immature decisions prevent it. Perhaps the father is no more able to support the child than is the mother; should he bear the entire support of a child, a burden that may prevent his marrying someone he cares for later on? The punitive attitude expressed through legislation to enforce financial responsibility has produced retaliatory devices that can be used by a supposed father. He may call in witnesses to cast doubt upon his parenthood by swearing that they, too, had relations with the mother. If the father does not voluntarily acknowledge paternity or agree to support the child, legal procedures are futile. More desirable and lasting results are obtained by a casework approach to the father than by court action.

If paternity proceedings could be placed under the jurisdiction of a Juvenile or Domestic Relations court, rather than a criminal court, particularly if the parents are juveniles, we might come nearer to a satisfactory solution. If the father and mother could be enabled to establish paternity, it would be desirable whether the child was adopted or whether his mother kept him; the child, then, would have his father's name and the worker would have information about the father for use in planning if the child should be adopted.

In adoption, it is quite as important to know the heredity of the father as it is to know the mother's. The adopting parents usually want accurate knowledge of the background of the father; and the child, as he grows up, will want to know about him and should be told as much as is known. If we were considering the child only, justice might require that paternity be established in each case. However, a paternity case is concerned with three individuals, and the purpose should be to make each one an effective personality with as little damage to his integrity as possible.

There is certainly a need to articulate and interpret the experience social workers have had in working with fathers, so that the community's attitudes of confusion and ambivalence might be reduced. Any preventive measures against illegitimacy would necessarily, it seems, have to be based on such a reduction and ultimate change.

Now what of the child? He is here, as material evidence of his parents' deviation from our cultural pattern. What are his needs?

First of all, he has needs which are closely connected with his mother's early needs. He is in need of prenatal and postnatal care. Every child has a right to protection from unnecessary hazards at birth. Whether he receives such protection depends on whether there are social and medical services available in the community, whether these are sufficiently financed by public or private funds to accommodate unwed mothers, and whether the mother goes to the agency giving the services. The shifting of unmarried mothers' applications from agency to agency (and such shifting is known to exist) only prolongs the day when the social cost must be met—at inflation prices.

The child's next great need is to have his mother and father and the social worker meet to discuss his future life. If his mother decides to keep him and his parents do not marry, then he is handicapped by the lack of normal home life. His mother probably must work to support herself and him. She may marry later, but chances are great that by this time the child will have experienced a succession of foster homes or institutions and his feelings of insecurity will be mounting.

If the mother marries, hoping thus to solve her problems, the child is a constant reminder to the husband of the mother's earlier conduct. When she becomes aware of this, she may reject the child or she may become overly solicitous. Also, jealousies may arise between this child and her legitimate children.

If the child and the mother are living in a foster home and the mother is at work all day, division of responsibility and authority is difficult. The child is usually under abnormal pressure to "be good," and feelings of insecurity develop. Is it any wonder that another generation of bewildered, dependent, and emotionally deprived children reach adulthood with the same emotional handicaps as their forebears?

Much debate has occurred the past few years on the value or disadvantage of removing the item relating to legitimacy from the birth record. The Children's Bureau has maintained that it is desirable to keep this item on the record if the information is properly safeguarded. It is thought to be of definite value to have the most accurate and complete information possible on the social status of every child, in a properly safeguarded state file, and also to have statistical data on birth out of wedlock that will assist in social planning for unmarried mothers and their children.

The major argument for elimination is that an entry of illegitimacy on the birth record stigmatizes the child. This argument fails to distinguish between the information recorded on the birth certificate and that which is issued from the state birth records for various purposes.

Even when the item on legitimacy is omitted, the status of the child is subject to question if the father's name is not given on the birth certificate. The same situation occurs when a certificate of age for school entrance, for work permits, and for other purposes is blank in the space allotted for the name of the father. Consequently, there is a growing belief among authorities in many states that illegitimacy should be noted on a birth record form that would be held confidential except for use in research and statistics. A short form, which would not contain the information on legitimacy, would be issued for school or other purposes.

In 1920, California and Massachusetts omitted the item on legitimacy from their birth-record forms. Subsequently, five other states were authorized to omit this item: (1) New York in 1936 and Utah in 1939, by statutory provision; (2) Maryland, Nebraska, and New Hampshire by ruling of their state departments or boards of health. In Texas, a law was passed in 1937 to authorize omission of the item, but this provision was repealed in 1939. Massachusetts, after many years of experience with the lack of safeguards provided by the omission of the legitimacy item, now specifies that only the following may examine records of children of illegimate birth, or may receive certified copies of those records: a person requesting information about his own birth; the person's parents or representatives; a person whose official business entitles him to this information; someone possessing a court order.

The Bureau of Census has been engaged for some time on a revision of the proposed Uniform Vital Statistics Act. Under the provisions of this proposed uniform birth-registration law, the birth records of the state are to include accurate information on each child, including his social status, but such records are not to be available for public inspection. The act further provides that the content of certified information from official state records shall be limited to those items which are of particular value to the person requesting such information, and that no data shall be issued from the state records unless the purpose for which they are to be used clearly justifies that use. Under this plan, certificates required for school attendance or work permits will give only the name of the child and the date and place of his birth.

If laws would be enacted in every state to provide safeguards for all birth records, such as those required by the New York law and by the proposed Uniform Vital Statistics Act, the result would be complete protection of birth records of children born out of wedlock, and the need for special clauses for these children would be obviated.

The number of children born out of wedlock is increasing; between 1940 and 1960, illegitimate births increased more than 250 percent. In 1969 the number of illegitimate births to girls under 20 years of age was estimated to be one out of 14 live births. What happens to numbers of children who are born out of wedlock and who are not adopted is statistically unknown, and the fate of these offers a field for intensive research.

As better economic and social resources (such as economic security, health care, recreational and educational facilities, and psychiatric and psychological clinics) become available to all people, problems of sexual adjustment and problems of illegitimacy should decrease.

It goes without saying that illegitimacy could be prevented by abstention from illicit sex relationships. But such abstention is, in to-day's society, counter to the permissive indulgence, the excitations, and the various other social and psychological forces that encourage sexual freedom.

Whether contraceptive control should be included in sex education has raised sharp controversy in American communities. Opposition has been based on racial, religious, moral, political, and economic grounds.

The Planned Parenthood Federation of America, a voluntary or-ganization which under medical direction carries on a program of in-terpretation to the public, has set up teen-age clinics in many cities to extend help to unmarried teen-agers, whether they are parents or not.

We know that if illegitimate births are to be prevented, or even reduced, society must focus its attention on many troublesome issues. Certainly, it is easier and more pleasant to ignore these issues, or to place full blame on the victims rather than to accept any personal re-sponsibility for public social policy.

Since our greatest number of illegitimate births are first births to girls of younger age groups, we know that these girls and boys are not yet ready for marriage, and in fact are usually very unsophisticated about sex. Their knowledge of contraceptives is limited; and because these boys and girls are ashamed to admit this lack of knowledge and experience, also because they lack money to purchase birth control devices, they are reluctant to discuss or employ contraceptives. Also the romance that is attached to the unpremeditated sexual relationship prevents use of birth control devices. Consequently, sex education is of primary importance, if for no other reason than the increase of venereal disease among teen-agers. It is imperative to replace ignorance with knowledge, and to replace community apathy with intelligent action.

Supplementary Readings

Berg, Renee. "Utilizing the Strengths of Unwed Mothers in One AFDC Program." *Social Work*. July, 1964.

Child Welfare League of America. *Standards for Services to Unmar-ried Parents*. Child Welfare League of America, New York, 1960.

Clark, Vincent. "Illegitimacy in the Next Decade: Trends and Im-plications." *Child Welfare*. December, 1964.

Holt, Simma. *Sex and the Teen-Age Revolution.* McClelland and Stewart, Toronto, 1967.

Kriesberg, Louis. *Mothers in Poverty: A Study of Fatherless Families.* Aldine, Chicago, Ill., 1970.

Middleman, Ruth C. "A Service Pattern for Helping Unmarried Pregnant Teenagers." *Children.* May–June, 1970. Vol. 17., No. 3.

Miller, Diane S., Danforth, Joyce, Day, Anne L., Steiner, George J. "Group Services for Unmarried Mothers: An Interdisciplinary Approach." *Children.* March–April, 1970. Vol. 18., No. 2.

National Conference on Social Welfare. *Brief and Intensive Casework with Unmarried Mothers.* Child Welfare League of America, New York, 1963.

Osofsky, Howard. *The Pregnant Teen-ager: A Medical, Educational and Social Analysis.* Charles C. Thomas, Springfield, Ill., 1968.

Pochin, Jean. *Without a Wedding-Ring: Casework with Unmarried Parents.* Schockon Books, New York, 1969.

Roberts, Robert W., Ed. *The Unwed Mother.* Harper & Row, New York, 1966.

Schiller, Alice. *The Unmarried Mother.* Public Affairs Committee. New York. 1969.

Schmideberg, Melitta. "Psychiatric-Social Factors in Young Unmarried Mothers." *Social Casework.* January, 1951.

Shlakman, Vera, and Furie, Sidney. "Birth Control and the Lower-class Unmarried Mother." *Social Work.* January, 1966.

Vincent, Clark E. *Unmarried Mothers.* Free Press, New York, 1961.

Wynn, Margaret. *Fatherless Families.* Michael Joseph Ltd., London, 1964.

[*Photo by Christy Butterfield.*]

8

Children Who Become Delinquent

The term "juvenile delinquency" means many things to many people. There is no generally accepted definition. In the legal sense it means any act or conduct that brings a child within the jurisdiction of the juvenile court. Most juvenile court laws in their definition of delinquency include violation of a state law or local ordinance, and acts or conduct likely to endanger the morals or health of the child himself or others; examples are running away from home, exceeding the control of parents or guardians, frequenting questionable places, or associating with immoral persons. Sometimes that which constitutes delinquency in the juvenile court in one state is included in the definition of neglect in the juvenile court in another state.

We know that the acts for which children are brought into juvenile courts range from mere mischievousness to the most serious offenses that can be committed by either child or adult. We know, too, that many social agencies and child guidance clinics deal every day with children whose problems are as serious as those of children who come before the juvenile court. Chance, the economic resources of the family, and the social resources of the community often determine whether or not a child gets in juvenile court.

It will give more meaning to our discussion if, instead of thinking of "juvenile delinquents," we think more specifically of young people: of boys who steal automobiles, who enter homes or stores to steal, who pilfer from dime stores; of boys who organize in gangs to steal, destroy property, or terrorize neighborhoods; of boys who do things that may endanger their own lives or those of others, such as playing with fire and tampering with railroad equipment; girls who run away from home to seek excitement, or to get jobs that will give them "a lot of money," or to follow and be near boy friends who have moved; of girls who steal to get pretty clothes; of girls who become sex delinquents and sometimes prostitutes; of boys and girls who rebel against parental authority to an extent far beyond what is normal to the adolescent youth; and of boys and girls who seek adventure and excitement in unwholesome ways such as drinking, using drugs, and frequenting questionable places of entertainment. All of these are classified by some as "juvenile delinquents"; actually, some of them are emotionally maladjusted individuals who need help.

Just as it is hard to define, juvenile delinquency is difficult to measure. We have no nationwide statistics. No count is available of the children whose acts might be classed as juvenile delinquency, but who are dealt with by their parents, schools, or social agencies so that they never come to the attention of the police or juvenile court. Also, there are no accurate figures available to show how many come to the attention of the police. The Federal Bureau of Investigation collects and publishes statistics of arrests from fingerprint records. But since laws in many places prohibit the fingerprinting of juveniles, these statistics do not include many children who come to the attention of the police. In the main, moreover, the FBI's figures are related to the upper teenage group and individuals above the ages of juvenile court jurisdiction.

In 1953 the United States Children's Bureau issued a report on the number of delinquency cases handled by juvenile courts. This report states that although the population of children from 10 to 17 years of age increased only 10 percent between 1948 and 1953, juvenile court cases during that period rose 45 percent. During 1953 about 435,000 children came to the attention of the juvenile courts because of alleged delinquency. This number exceeded the number of juvenile cases recorded during World War II, which at that time was the highest number in the nation's history. An estimated 1,250,000 children came to the attention of the police between 1948 and 1953.

In 1967 the President's Commission on Law Enforcement and Administration of Justice estimated that in any given year 2 percent of the children between ten and 18 years of age make an appearance in juvenile court. It estimated that the proportion of all persons who reach their eighteenth birthday with at least one appearance in juvenile court is approximately 10 percent for both sexes and 17 percent for boys. One in six boys thus makes an appearance in juvenile court during his adolescence. In urban delinquency areas, the estimate is as high as 50 percent. Most children who engage in delinquency do not become adult criminals, although many criminal careers have their start in delinquency.

SOCIETY AND JUVENILE DELINQUENCY

Traditional rural American society, culture, and behavior patterns served as an insulation or a control against delinquency and crime. There is considerable evidence that many forms of deviant behavior are less frequent, though not absent, in rural areas. The extent of crime and delinquency in the United States outside of metropolitan centers tends to assume the same spatial pattern as large population areas—rising as one approaches large urban centers.

Although many rural and small town social controls have been lost, not all rural areas in America have experienced losses in control due to the influences of urbanization. The isolation of many large areas from direct urban contacts has protected those rural areas from delinquency. Delinquency rates tend to be higher in rural counties with industrial development than in nonindustrialized counties.

The direct relationship between the growth of industrialization, urbanization, and juvenile delinquency has been noted by observers and reported in the literature for a number of years. Spatial urban studies, moreover, indicate a relationship between juvenile delinquency and several indices of social disorganization which cluster around slum or inner city living. The highest concentrations of official rates of juvenile delinquency occur in zones surrounding the industrialized, or inner, city and progressively decrease as one approaches the periphery of urban areas. Several authorities have pointed out that any significant reduction of juvenile delinquency in our urbanized society will not occur unless the deeply rooted economic and social problems of our slums are greatly improved.

Juvenile delinquency is by no means a new social problem for the people of the United States. It has been with us for decades and has appeared in various forms and magnitude. Other nations have had similar experiences, particularly those with industrialized societies.

The form that juvenile delinquency may assume in a given society is related to the values of the social system. If individual rights are considered more important than group rights, then a society will have difficulty controlling individual behavior. Likewise, if upward social mobility is encouraged, and material success is valued, social restraints are pushed aside by the ambitious. Because American society has such a highly interrelated social system, the public is not going to demand fundamental value changes in order to control juvenile delinquency or crime in the foreseeable future. In other words, we should be prepared to tolerate a high amount of nonconformity among our youth. This does not mean that we cannot reduce or control a significant portion of delinquency, but it does mean that we are not going to eradicate the problem dramatically with any particular program within a given period of time.

The President's Committee on Juvenile Delinquency and Youth Crime feels that delinquency is a symptom that emerges from a society's failure to provide the conditions, services, and experiences that would make it possible for youth and their families to participate adequately in our society. The inner areas of our large cities that have been brought to our attention through empirical findings are prime examples of the committee's position. In these areas, children and youth bear the brunt of society's failure to be as concerned with their plight as it is with that of other children in the nation.

It is recognized that juvenile delinquency is not limited to youth living in our inner cities, since it is found in every social class, but the interest in it as a problem of inner city areas suggests the possibility that delinquency is a subculture. The subject of these areas and the families of the poor as sources of delinquency has been given considerable attention in the literature and in prevention programs.

Individually, there is a distinct group of delinquents that have been recognized as "aggressive" offenders. These individuals tend to display traits associated with psychopathy. They tend to be bullies, they show little concern for others, and they are guilty of assaultive behavior. They are more egocentric and less group oriented than the usual juvenile delinquent. As a type they are not numerous among delinquents.

They tend to be unresponsive to treatment and carry their behavior patterns into adulthood. As adults, they have been referred to as potential murder victims, owing to their aggression.

Another special type of juvenile delinquency is found among our middle classes. Delinquency among suburban middle-class population is less than is found in the inner city, as indicated by official statistics. Although "hidden delinquency" may be a middle-class phenomenon, the types of offenses committed by middle class youth are nevertheless different from those committed by the inner city delinquent. These delinquents commit more frequent assaults, thefts, and breaking and entering offenses than do the suburban middle-class youths.

"Middle-class delinquency" and delinquency found in a middle-class residential area are not necessarily the same. Many blue collar families with high wages, but with lower-class behavior patterns, have moved into middle-class suburban communities in increasing numbers since 1945. Their children still have lower-class behavior patterns and commit delinquent acts that are erroneously attributed to the middle classes in general, owing to the delinquent's place of residence. Such children have been credited as contributing as much as two-thirds of the delinquent acts reported for middle-class areas. When middle-class youth commit delinquent acts, the offenses take the form of automobile theft, sexual experiments, and the use of alcohol and drugs.

Delinquent behavior is influenced only in part by problems rooted in the psyche or social structure. It is also an individual response to evaluated social situations and relative opportunities. An expanded theory, the I-theory, incorporating this point of view is included in the appendices. The psychosocial explanations of juvenile delinquency are based on the assumption that delinquent behavior is traceable to deep-seated personality problems or anomalies in the social structure. To be sure, many cases may reasonably be explained by either the I-theory or a psychosocial theory. However, what is very often overlooked is that a youth may commit a delinquent act without being in the throes of a personality conflict: he may be behaving quite blindly, merely carrying out some of the values of his peer group. A boy may commit a juvenile act, or an adult a crime, without being deeply dedicated to crime or without being emotionally involved in the act. Deeply rooted behavior patterns do not disappear with the onset of adulthood, whereas many of the delinquencies of children and youth do. Thus, much juvenile delinquency can be better explained on the basis of introspection and situational opportunities. Juvenile delinquency is a response to certain social situations for many delinquents.

A disproportionate number of juvenile delinquents come from the slums. Of these, a large number are between the ages of 15 and 16 years, and the chance is high that the individual delinquent comes from a female-centered home and commits his unlawful acts in the company of companions. It is estimated that between 60 and 90 percent of all delinquent acts are group-linked.

A good proportion of children and youth who are behavior problems at home and at school seek recognition, response, and security among peer groups, and it is only incidental if the group is delinquent-oriented. It is in the slums that violent gangs develop. Unsupervised minor and playful pursuits among children of the inner city often develop into serious delinquent behavior.

Although not as much has been written on middle-class delinquency as on the delinquencies of the lower-class child, several positions summarizing middle-class delinquency are found in the literature. Among them are statements attributing delinquency to the following causes: (1) the middle-class adolescent's problem of sex identification; (2) the diffusion of working-class values and behavior patterns to middle-class youth; (3) the weakening of the deferred gratification pattern of the middle-class family; (4) the increasing difficulty sons have in trying to maintain or equate the upward social mobility of their fathers; (5) the lack of social and community services in suburban communities.

THE FAMILY AND DELINQUENCY

If we are to consider intelligently the reasons for the behavior of a child who is labeled a juvenile delinquent, we must examine closely the needs that must be met by a child's own home and parents. Has he had two present, understanding, and affectionate parents; a home in which he could receive good physical care? Could he admire and build ideals around his parents? What of the spiritual values of his home? Has he had the security of familiar surroundings and a constant family circle? Long periods of absence of one or both parents from the home, or long periods of living in a school or with relatives during early life tend to have an unsettling effect on a growing child and to discourage the formation of solid habits of self-discipline. Inconsistent or overstrict discipline deters the child's formation of any code of right behavior. Bickering, groundless complaints, nagging—all of these symptoms of parental rejection contribute to rebellion of the child and to his desire to escape from unpleasantness and look for acceptance and affection outside his home. The delinquent is not the child, but the adult who has failed in the early life of the child to give him that combination of love, security, and discipline that is needed to help him grow up to wholesome adulthood.

Does poverty in the home contribute to delinquency? It can, but usually through circuitous rather than direct means. In various ways economic hardship may promote and encourage theft. If the income is so low that extreme frugality is necessary, and a child does not fully comprehend the reason for deprivation, he may resort to dishonesty and deceit to satisfy natural desires. The accompaniments of poverty most conducive to juvenile delinquency are probably overcrowded living quarters and lack of space for wholesome play. The total lack of privacy in the home results not only in physical discomfort but in emotional irritations and tension. The lack of decent recreation space means that streets and alleys are the only areas where children can play, or the older boys and girls can meet.

If there are enough positive elements in the environment of a child to give him emotional stability, he can face even the knowledge that his father is serving a prison sentence or that his mother is a prostitute without going to pieces.

The present-day attitude toward the juvenile delinquent is becoming more constructive; the delinquent child is coming to be regarded as a child in need of help. He has failed to secure in his life so far the satisfactions and recognition necessary for his adjustment to standards of the community. The more deprived and unsatisfactory his life experiences are, the harder he must struggle to make up for them. His behavior is an effort to solve his own emotional needs.

The first opportunities he has for this adjustment are in his own home, and these are controlled primarily by the mother. In his early months he must learn what he can and cannot do, when, where, and to whom. These restrictions he can accept if, at the same time, he feels assured of the love and security of his parents. If the child in his early growth period does not have this parental acceptance, if he feels unloved or unwanted, then he can respond only by securing for himself certain substitute pleasures in an effort to compensate for a lack of parental warmth. Because he is insecure in his own family, he may be unable to love and relate himself to any person sufficiently to make a personal adjustment to social standards. This early pattern of family relationship has some effect on his contacts with school, church, and community.

Many adventures or situations are welcomed if they offer him an escape from the hurt of lack of love and loss of pride; several substitutes will compensate lack of affection if they offer thrills, excitement, and feelings of adequacy. His behavior may well be an expression of protest against the lacks in his own life.

This maladjustment within himself or between himself and his environment explains why one child in a family may indulge in delinquent behavior when his brothers or sisters do not. Children born to the same parents never experience identical family situations: the ages of the parents, financial condition, order of birth, family responsibilities, and many other factors contribute to difference. Although a child may have all the material things money can buy, his temperamental values may lead him into asocial behavior.

It is often loosely said that juvenile delinquency can be blamed on poor health, poor housing, poverty, and poor neighborhoods. Studies show that the stresses and strains occurring in a child's emotional life are more important than any of these factors for the internalization of social values. Although material conditions can be causal factors, it is the neglected, unloved, emotionally deprived child who is least able to resist destructive influences and who is most susceptible to opportunities for delinquency.

The role of familial relationships in juvenile delinquency has been strongly emphasized by such authorities as Cyril Burt in England and Harry Shulman, William Healy, Sheldon and Eleanor Glueck, and C. Ray and Ina Jeffery in the United States. This is a segmental approach, which immediately gives rise to the question whether the role of familial relationships can be isolated from other factors in the development of juvenile delinquency. Of course, the answer is in the negative (as we cannot do so any more than we could isolate any other one factor). Groups and their social systems, which are the foundations of social behavior, are extensively interrelated. Familial relationships are inextricably bound up with many other social systems. The separation of the family from other groups in society is entirely arbitrary and academic, and it can be done only for the purposes of analysis and ease of presentation. However, the removal of one social system from a web of social relationships and a minute examination of it are scientifically permissible only if we keep it clearly in mind that the system with which we are dealing is a functional part of the composite larger system. As long as the importance assigned to the familial system is relative to that of the other social systems affecting the socialization of the child and his emerging modes of conduct, such a procedure is permissible.

This type of analysis is in accord with the principle that social systems in a society are interrelated.

In any discussion of the role of familial relationships in promoting juvenile delinquency, it is either implicitly or explicitly hypothesized that where conventionality, intelligence, emotional stability, understanding, sympathy, and security exist in the home, the inducement to this type of behavior is reduced to zero. A corollary to this position and the principle of the interrelationship of social systems is that such conventional homes exert some positive influence on detrimental influences outside of the home. If these assumptions have any validity at all it would appear that the home should be a very important starting point from which to launch one type of program for the prevention of juvenile delinquency.

The family is said to form the basis of the child's value system and to develop in the child permanent life patterns, which, if they coincide with those of the larger society, prepare him for conventional social living. The family is purported to be the most effective transmitter of attitudes and values. Discipline, precept, and example are prominent in the transmission of familial attitudes and values. Ideally the child should learn to internalize the values of the larger society within the family.

Through the process of socialization, society attempts to internalize in its individual members certain group norms and ideals. Socialization is a term which denotes the process the individual undergoes in acquiring patterns of behavior, habits, attitudes, and ideas of the society into which he is born. The problem of maintaining order in society is one of conditioning the individual so that his values will be in harmony with the basic values or norms of society. The family is potentially the most effective agency of social control. It has almost exclusive contact with the child during the period of greatest plasticity, and it has continued primary contacts for a period of several years. However, the problem of control within the family varies greatly.

Many American parents fail in home discipline, not because of design or malignance, but because of neglect, indifference, ignorance, and unwillingness to accept the social responsibility for directing their children. In our society of constant social change, parental values often prove inadequate because many parents have no definite standards; their discipline is inadequate and, most important, inconsistent; some parents fail to keep pace with societal change while others have interests that are not concerned with the rearing of children. The basic problem of initiating a delinquency prevention program in the home is essentially one of educating and directing parents, and impressing upon them the importance of their continued responsibility for the socialization of their children according to the norms of the larger society.

Defective discipline and vicious examples of antisocial behavior within the family have been found to be more significant in promoting juvenile delinquency than have broken homes and poverty. Such conditions within the family do not promote the internalization of larger social values. The emotional tone of the home, the behavior and attitude of parents toward the child, the presence of love and affection for the child—in short, the kinds of familial relationships within the family—determine the effectiveness of socialization and internalization of social values for the child.

Several studies have revealed the importance of parental attitudes in influencing the behavior of children. For example, it has been reported that parental attitudes are more influential than the physical environment of the home; that maladjustment in children tends to be associated with harmful attitudes of parents; that children's attitudes toward right and wrong are influenced more by their parents than by other groups outside the home; that families in which one or both parents are regular members of a church positively affect the religious behavior of children in later life.

Parents' attitudes toward their children, and children's conceptions of their parents differ significantly among delinquents and nondelinquents. One study reports that the majority of a group of delinquents felt that their fathers were indifferent or hostile toward them, whereas only a small minority of the individuals in a control group made up of nondelinquents had this feeling. Eighty percent of the delinquents also felt that their mothers were not deeply concerned about their welfare, whereas only 30 percent of the nondelinquents had the same feeling. Seventy percent of the mothers of delinquents were found not to be giving their sons suitable supervision, whereas this failing was found in only 10 percent of the mothers of nondelinquents.

The investigation of the effects of familial relationships upon a child becomes more complicated as soon as it is understood that the social system of the family will subtly affect one child in the family differently from another. This variation has been brought out clearly in a study by Healy and Bronner, whose research was an attempt to reach down into the family life of recidivists in juvenile delinquency. Cases selected for the study were those for which nondelinquent siblings could act as a control. A comparative study of the emotional life and the behavior of the delinquent and of the nondelinquent siblings convinced the investigators that delinquency per se must be considered as a way of expressing oneself when accepted ways of doing so have been blocked by unsatisfying familial relationships.

Burt in 1925 made an intensive study of 200 cases of juvenile delinquents. He compared these offenders with a control group of 400 nondelinquent children, holding such factors as age, social class, school attended, and area of residence constant. After making many detailed comparisons of the two groups, one of the conclusions he drew from the study was that the most common and the most disastrous conditions for the delinquent child center on family life.

It has been pointed out in preceding paragraphs that the child who becomes a delinquent is more likely to come from a home in which he is neglected, rejected, or subjected to harsh and unjust punishment. In a large proportion of cases one parent is missing. When both parents are in the home, it has frequently been found that the delinquent has parents who are constantly bickering or who are openly hostile to each other.

It is true that a child may grow up to be a socially integrated adult even in a home in which siblings have been shown preference and in which he may have been deprived of parental love. It is known that children who are brutally abused or punished unjustly may mature into socially integrated personalities. However, it may also be argued that children reared in apparently ideal homes may also develop into juvenile delinquents. Such observations do not minimize the importance of the home and familial relationships in the development of delinquency, but only illustrate the principle that social behavior is interrelated with various social systems, and cannot be adequately explained on the basis of one social system, such as the family. Familial relationships and the internalization of social values cannot in reality be considered without reference to the impact of other social systems on the behavior of the individual.

It has come to be assumed in our society that the parents' greatest contribution in rearing socially integrated children centers on the methods that may be used by them in socializing the children. Two polar methods of family control can be readily identified in our society. One method is based on issuing commands and punishing disobedience. Under this method no attempt is made by the parents to give the child an understanding of why rules are established or why punishment is used for their violation. When punishment is harsh the child may develop fear of the parent as well as resentment. Under such a method the parent sets himself above the child and establishes formal dictatorial familial relationships. This kind of relationship precludes communication of a truly confidential nature between the parent and child, and hinders the establishment of rapport. If the child is to accept and internalize the values of the parents, rapport must first be established. In other words, such a method attempts to control social behavior by coercion and authority. This type of system is effective only in those social situations in which the chances of evasion of the norm are eliminated, because it does not promote the internalization of the parental values.

The second method of child control is more flexible and democratic. Under this method the parent explains to the youngster why certain types of behavior are expected. Punishment may be inflicted for violation of rules, but it is not necessarily warranted every time a rule is violated. Ideally, under this method the child is so thoroughly assimilated into the family's social system that rapport and sympathetic understanding between the members of the system are sufficient to promote the internalization of the desired values, thus, making punishment unnecessary. In other words, the method of control that is effective is the one which the child internalizes, and it thus becomes his own system of motivation. Under this type of family system the child is close enough to the parent to understand what the parent wants, and at the same time he is free to choose within given limits of activity what his parents have outlined as proper conduct.

Within the framework of the above assumptions it may be hypothesized that satisfying familial relationships are associated with family social systems embodying the following postulates among others.

1. Children are never punished for behavior that merely annoys or disturbs a parent. Punishment is used only when it is necessary to help the child to internalize a fundamental social value.

2. Parents do not use false information or give misinterpretations to children in order to control them. Incredulous parental explanations and other immature devices of control, when recognized as such by the child, lessen his confidence in the parent and weaken the intimacy of their social relationships.

3. Parents do not make promises to children that are lightly conceived or that they have no intentions of carrying out. Children have good memories, especially for anticipated rewards, and do not easily forget parental promises. A series of such unfulfilled promises can easily destroy the confidential social relationships between child and parent.

4. The social relationships between parents and their children are relatively constant. In other words, parents are consistent in their behavior toward their children and do not alternate radically between extremes, either in rates of originating communication or social interaction.

5. Parents do not violate the confidence of their children, react emotionally to such confidential information, or base the punishment of children upon that information.

6. Parents do not continually make their children feel inferior as a means of controlling them or keeping them in a subordinate role. Children are encouraged by their parents to build up confidence in their social relationships and gradually to assume mature roles.

7. Parents allow their children to discuss plans, problems, or pleasures with them. At these times the child is permitted to explain his problem or past behavior and is encouraged to accept responsibilities and to face realities and truth. Parents do not think they are too busy to listen to such little confidences and plans. Intimate communication is often lost between parents and offspring owing to the parent's lack of interest in the child's topic of conversation. If parents do lose rapport with their children, they also lose some ability to control, guide, and advise in that they may not know what their children are doing or experiencing outside the home.

8. Parents agree on a constructive plan of discipline. They are consistent in implementing such a plan and, in the presence of the children, they do not disagree or interfere with each other's attempts to maintain these social relationships.

9. Parents are not more concerned with the physical conditions of the home than with the enjoyment their children may derive from having playmates in the home. Children are allowed to play and romp in the home, the primary restriction being that they are not to destroy or dismantle its furnishings. If the familial relationships are satisfying, home becomes a pleasant place for children to go, and they are not driven away from it by the incessant nagging and forbidding techniques of parents.

10. Parents build up a child's respect for government, the police, the courts, the school, and the church by not being overcritical of these institutions and agencies in the presence of the child.

In addition, we may point out that self-restraint and social responsibility cannot be taught to children without discipline, tempered with understanding and love. Parents are in the best possible position to do the teaching, if we assume that most of them are interested in helping their children to internalize the values of the larger society. Undoubtedly, very few parents consciously and deliberately allow their children to become juvenile delinquents; yet many appear to be doing just that. Many parents show little interest in their children and spend little time with them or on them. Where parental interest and love for the child is present, we have perhaps one of the best family bulwarks against the development of juvenile delinquency.

The differences in child rearing that exist among families in our society are due to differential family systems. There are demoralized families, families that reject their children, families that overprotect their children, families that are in a state of constant tension, friction, and frustration. Such social relationships within a family militate against the internalization of socially acceptable attitudes and values in the individual, even if we assume that all parents are aware of and interested in such values.

Strict supervision of children is said to be a middle-class pattern. Middle-class children are protected against early pleasure behavior, are subjected to close and consistent discipline, and are constantly reminded of the value of education. The value of education and society's ideal values concerning sexual behavior are accepted to such a degree by middle-class children that, by the time of late adolescence, behavior in these areas can be projected for early adult life.

In comparison, lower-class children for the most part are given less supervision and greater freedom of activity than middle- and upper-class children. The lower-class children have more freedom in the choice of companions, recreation, the distance they are allowed to go from home, and sexual and educational behavior; in brief, they are not strictly supervised by their parents. On the basis of these limited findings we may entertain the hypothesis that the primary reason lower-class children are over-represented in official delinquency statistics (the differential implementation of justice notwithstanding) is the fact that they are more apt to be reared under family and community systems that do not promote the internalization of the larger society's social norms.

Even if the individual does not learn to internalize social values and norms in the family, it does not necessarily follow that his behavior outside the home will be delinquent. Part of the social life with which an individual comes in contact within the community may be conventional, and part of it may be unconventional, depending on the community or neighborhood systems in which the individual lives. Several studies have revealed the existence of a differential spacial distribution of delinquency in various communities. The individual with few internalized social values is less likely to become delinquent, if he interacts with conventional neighborhood systems. The individual with internalized positive values will tend to avoid unconventional social systems, because they do not provide satisfying experiences in light of his value system. Thus the individual who is in the process of internalizing positive values, whether he lives in the slums or in a middle-class neighborhood, may be helped in the process if he is permitted only to interact with conventional systems in the community or neighborhood.

The most fruitful and far reaching point at which society might attempt to control delinquency, although perhaps the most difficult, would be that of the interpersonal conditions of family systems. The emotional tone of the home, the behavior and attitudes of parents toward the child, the presence of love and affection for the child—in short the kinds of personal relationships within the family—determine the effectiveness of socialization and the internalization of social values for the child. As long as we continue to have families that fail to completely socialize the child, we will continue to have the seeds of delinquency in our society.

Everything that happens on a group oriented basis outside of the home constitutes a possible unconventional social situation in the experience and socialization of the individual. Personal contact and participation in neighborhood systems have more significance for the individual than do the more indirect contacts of the larger community systems. Attitudes and values are effectively transmitted through the personal relationships of neighborhood groups, especially when the individual emotionally identifies with such groups. In areas having high rates of official delinquency, the number of unconventional systems for the individual to come in contact with is greater than the number of conventional systems. However, unconventional systems may appear in areas having low rates of official delinquency if enough families in the area fail to internalize in their children conventional values.

It has been pointed out that the way to control delinquency in unconventional groups is to make conventional behavior more attractive than unconventional behavior through indigenous leadership and the pull of group selected activities. The effectiveness of such a program depends on the rigidity of the value system of the delinquents involved and the degree of internalization of the values in question. However, an individual's membership in a particular system does not control his behavior in all social situations, owing to differential valence systems. The best society can do is to attempt to control certain obvious social situations and, thus, make it more difficult for the individual with temperamental values to act in an unconventional manner. Society cannot control every possible social situation, and, furthermore, individuals with temperamental values can always find social systems that give vent to their values.

THE SCHOOL AND DELINQUENCY

In past years, many scholars have asked the question, "Is there anything in our school system that could be a causative factor in delinquency?" It has been pointed out that failure of some of our schools to take into account and make adequate provision for individual differences is one of the main errors. Public school classes are rigidly set up by chronological age; because the varying abilities of different children are disregarded, some are thus placed at a disadvantage. Although almost every child has had considerable contact with other children before entering school, it is usually in the school that, for the first time, he must learn to adjust his individual wants to the desires of a definitely organized system. In the school, moreover, the child usually meets types of competition that for the first time may add up to a serious threat to him.

The school gives the child a greater exposure to class consciousness. Sooner or later, he must answer his own questions on who he is, where he lives, what he possesses, and what he can do. In some cases, unless he can answer in a way to meet his own emotional need for status, compensatory behavior of a negative nature may develop.

A teacher who is in daily contact with a child may do much to help him to adjust, and thus perhaps prevent future trouble, if she is trained to recognize signs of behavior difficulties in their early stages and to refer the child to the appropriate place for help. The classroom is a splendid place for spotting children with problems so that they may be helped before their maladjustment can lead them into court.

The relationship between the public school system and its pupils varies from one school district to another. To the extent that school districts approximately correspond to social classes, the problems children bring to school tend to be determined by social class.

The school is generally considered to be the leading public institution for the support and development of the social norms and values of our society. The methods and practices of some schools make it difficult to realize these objectives, especially with children from the poorer neighborhoods. Poor teaching methods of instructors can lower a child's motivation to learn or to accept authority and in some cases they can cause hostility and alienation.

When children enter a school system, they have been socialized to a considerable degree by their family, community, and social class. The lower-class child, upon entering public school, is essentially coming up against a middle-class social system. The system has not only middle-class ideals, but also middle-class teachers, speaking a middle-class language. From the start, public school may not be a very comfortable or rewarding experience for the lower-class child. In comparison, the middle-class child finds most of his values, attitudes, drives, and skills reinforced and rewarded by the middle-class school system.

Needless to say, the methodology a school staff uses in responding to the educational and adjustment problems a child brings and faces in an educational system is of great importance to the child. The staff should recognize these problems and not allow structured methods to guarantee school failure for poor children having problems that are linked with social class.

Several recent studies have found that schools in poorer districts have the most outdated buildings, the least experienced teachers, the most crowded classrooms, and the poorest counseling services of all.

When a school is not adequately equipped to meet the learning and adjustment problems a pupil brings with him to class, a failure process may be set in motion. As the child is promoted from grade to grade, the proportion of his underachievement in successive classes become progressive and his failure may become conspicuous. When the failing child reaches this point, he cannot admit that education is important and he begins to flaunt its standards and goals. He may begin to commit truancy, and finally he drops out of school. A student who fails in his school work tends to be shunned and excluded by other students and by some individual teachers. A failing student's own evaluation of himself and his future tends to deteriorate. His school experience becomes frustrating and bitter. He tends to turn to and associate with other students who have failed. He may accept negative standards of conduct that are more easily attained than those of the school system.

Educational failure in general, regardless of social, ethnic, or racial background, often begins early, accumulates, and at times leads to delinquency. There is considerable evidence that school failure and delinquency are related. Boys from white-collar homes and boys from blue-collar homes who do failing work in school have approximately a five- to sevenfold greater chance of becoming delinquent than boys who have the same background but who are not doing failing work.

One explanation for poor school achievement among children with lower-class backgrounds is that the subsystems of which they are a product do not prepare many of them with the proper vocabulary, interests, and attitudes for school. A high proportion of them appear to have poor auditory and visual discrimination; some are unfamiliar with books and writing material; some are unable to sustain attention; others lack internal controls over personal behavior, or experience in formal situations like the classroom.

However, the school, as well as the student's family and community, contributes to scholastic failure. A number of studies show that not only do children with lower socioeconomic background begin at low levels of performance in school, but their achievement shows progressive deterioration the longer they remain in school. Schools in general provide no opportunity for these children to overcome this deficiency. It has been felt by many that the school not only fails to offset the initial handicaps of children from the lower socioeconomic classes, but actually contributes to their school failure. If this is true, the school is an important factor in promoting juvenile delinquency, since delinquency is associated with school failure.

CHILD LABOR AND DELINQUENCY

In several studies made at various times since 1955, it has been reported that working children contribute more than their share of problems to the juvenile courts. This is notably true of children working in street trades and in domestic service; a higher percentage of these children come before the courts than do children employed in other occupations. However, there are dangers in all forms of child labor, not the least of which are the enervating and detrimental effects of employment that lead to cumulative fatigue and overstrain. As discussed in Chapter 5, the conditions accompanying migratory labor create special problems for the child: the frequent change of abode may affect adversely the child, and lead to nonattendance in school and a feeling of impermanence. Truancy itself is a type of delinquency.

Local officials should be constantly on the alert to protect working children from exploitation and from employment in occupations that threaten them with moral hazards. Any violations should be reported to state enforcement officials.

Unemployment and the age at which youth enters the labor market may help to explain partially the age distribution of juvenile delinquency. Sixteen is the age at which delinquency rates appear to be highest in most jurisdictions. It is the age limit for compulsory school laws in many states, and it is also the age at which most youngsters drop out of school. Because he has time on his hands, and needs money, an unemployed youth may readily turn to delinquency.

The President's Commission on Law Enforcement and Administration of Justice recommends, among other plans, the following programs as means to offset the contribution of economic conditions and unemployment among youth to juvenile delinquency.

1. The executive branches of state and local governments should enlist the cooperation of the business community for publicly financed programs in order to provide jobs for unemployed youth.

2. Programs for on-the-job training of youth should be increased and expanded. On-the-job training is superior to training before employment, especially for positions requiring few or no skills. If these programs are to be expanded, they must be subsidized.

3. The public should commend the efforts of private corporations who have voluntarily added unemployed youth to their payrolls. These young people have been trained as a public service. If America's largest corporations engaged in similar programs, an untold number of potentially delinquent and unemployed youth might very well be reached.

4. Training programs that are publicly financed and privately administered should not only train youth but also guarantee them employment after graduation from the program. This might help counteract the strong emphasis employers put on experience in selecting applicants for positions. In other words, these youths need not only training, but also work experience if they are to compete successfully in our labor market today.

5. There are a number of faults in America's public education that should be corrected. Urban segregation, failures in reading and other academic work, and truancy and dropping out all contribute to the delinquency syndrome, and they present problems, sparing either that should be remedied without time or money.

6. Vocational education should be related to reality and the practical needs of youth.

7. Provisions should be made for the employed youths to obtain leaves of absence from school in order to improve their work skills and to experience upward mobility.

8. The theory and administration of public welfare need to be radically revised. Adequate payments should be made to the victims of unemployment. Work programs for families on public welfare without unrealistic cuts in benefits should be introduced into the public welfare system. Provisions should be made for low income families in the area of child health services. Proper school clothing is needed for many poor children and youths.

9. Mild criminal records should not be put on a public record or held against an offender who is seeking employment. Changes in the criminal justice system are needed to remedy this situation.

10. Job vacancy studies need to be implemented with a recording and reporting system. We need to fit the supply of labor to the demand in more specific ways than has previously been done.

RECREATION AND DELINQUENCY

Although some types of juvenile delinquency may be looked upon by the offender as fun, recreation, or a leisure time pursuit, one cannot conclude that recreational programs prevent delinquency.

In past years a number of studies have been carried out in an attempt to show a relationship between the two broad categories of delinquency and recreation. These studies reveal the following: (1) recreation does not prevent delinquency; (2) nondelinquent children are more likely than delinquents to be involved in organized recreation; (3) organized recreation and delinquent behavior are not mutually exclusive; (4) neighborhood recreational facilities do offer delinquent and nondelinquent children a way of spending their time that is at least some alternative to delinquent activities.

Another aspect of recreation and delinquency that has recurring popularity in different sections of our society is the possible relationship between delinquency and such passive activities as attending immoral movies, viewing violent television programs, and reading comic books on crime. A few studies have been attempted with the objective of revealing the possible effects of these types of communication on behavior. The studies have been premised on the popular belief that crime as portrayed in various media produces delinquent behavior in the viewer, particularly in children and youths. Methodologically this is a very difficult problem to program for any valid and realistic results.

In spite of the difficulties, studies in the field have revealed the following: (1) delinquents read comic books more than nondelinquents; (2) delinquents are more interested than nondelinquents in comics that have themes of crime and violence; (3) in a study made in 1933, Blumer and Hauser found that half the truant and problem boys in their sample felt that motion pictures on crime promoted their own interest in crime; (4) high school boys and girls became more sympathetic to criminals after viewing crime pictures; (5) inmates in a prison attributed certain unacceptable behavior to motion pictures.

A study made in England in 1958 revealed that violence depicted on television did not turn nondelinquents into delinquents. It was concluded, as it was in American studies, that youngsters had to be already predisposed toward delinquency before television could incite them to such activity.

Those who deny that recreation is an aid in maintaining law-abiding behavior have pointed out that organized recreation is essentially oriented toward the middle class and thus does not include lower-class children, who make up a disproportionate number of delinquents. In response to this criticism, several demonstration experiments and programs of a recreational nature for youth have been instituted in selected urban ghettos. Leadership for these programs was drawn from the population in the immediate neighborhood. The results of these projects indicated that a delinquent youth gains in self-esteem through community participation and constructive social action.

The use of leisure-time activities for the purpose of preventing delinquency is illustrated by programs from the field of aggressive casework. Aggressive casework, or the detached worker program, is more closely related to group dynamics or group work than to the type of activity that is generally referred to as recreation. Nevertheless, it is a leisure-time pursuit, and since the late 1940's the approach has been used in several cities in an effort to reduce delinquency among neighborhood gangs.

In practice, the worker does not wait for youth to come to his group work agency. He seeks out groups of youth or gangs in a neighborhood and attempts to establish a relationship with them. Once he has been accepted by a gang and has attained rapport with them, he attempts to channel their energies into more conventional activities. It is generally agreed that aggressive casework is an effective means through which the larger community can reach hostile and destructive groups. It has been found that projects which start out with an aggressive casework approach tend to move from a street corner framework to one offering a broader range of interests and activities, such as adolescent service centers.

An innovative group work project, now in the planning stage, that may have significance for those interested in delinquency control is the introduction of social group work methods and leaders into public school systems. Under this plan the social group worker would direct students in ungraded classrooms. These children would be assigned to the group worker after their regular classroom behavior was judged intolerable. The objective of this new project would be to use games and other techniques to give these problem students the feeling of accomplishment and success as learners. An attempt would also be made to furnish the setting of this special class with objects to arouse the interests of the students. It is hoped that the sensate and intellectual experiences of these problem children can be merged into a meaningful and relevant educational process.

The Task Force on Juvenile Delinquency, a section of the President's Commission on Law Enforcement and Administration of Justice, has cited in a report some of the above studies as well as several others that deal with the value of student participation in high school activities. These studies indicate the following: (1) students who participate in extracurricular activities receive higher grades and drop out of school less often than those who do not participate; this substantiates earlier findings; (2) athletes receive slightly higher grades, drop out of school less often, and go on to college more often than nonathletes; (3) delinquent youths participate less in organized activities than do nondelinquent students. The report points out that if youths who might otherwise be exposed to delinquent behavior could be involved in constructive activities, this could be an important step toward promoting positive social behavior.

DELINQUENCY IN NONMETROPOLITAN AREAS

Poverty and crime are not centered exclusively in the ghettos of our large metropolitan cities. The President's Task Force on Juvenile Delinquency points out that over two-thirds of the poor live outside our major metropolitan centers.

Approximately one-third of the population in the United States was living in cities in 1890. By 1960 approximately two-thirds resided in urban areas. An urban area contains 2,500 or more persons; a small city contains between 2,500 and 50,000 persons. When the proportion of residents who live in small cities (33.7 percent) is added to the 30.1 percent living in rural areas, the total number of persons living in areas other than large cities is considerable. Although crime rates are higher in metropolitan areas, in 1965 more than a million offenses were reported by the police in rural areas and in small cities. Many smaller cities may be satellites of larger cities, but the delinquency patterns of these areas differ from those found in the slums of our large cities.

For a number of years, rural areas have been reporting a lower incidence of crime and juvenile delinquency than urban areas. In 1963 the rate of juvenile delinquency was 10.3 per 1,000 children in rural areas, 22.6 in semirural areas, and 31.8 in urban areas.

The President's Task Force reports that in nonmetropolitan communities one in five children is a delinquent at least once before he reaches adulthood. Large numbers of children do engage in delinquent behavior in nonmetropolitan areas in this country.

The offenses committed by nonmetropolitan delinquents differ from those committed by urban delinquents. The behavior of rural youth is less serious, in general, and less sophisticated than that of urban delinquents. A great majority of the rural and small town delinquents, both male and female, comes from the lower socioeconomic classes. Large numbers of them are those individuals who have dropped out of school before graduation. They not only do poor academic work, but are less likely to participate in school activities and look upon themselves as being outside of the school system.

In general the juvenile delinquency observed in nonmetropolitan communities is closely, if not functionally, related to a system of excluding the youthful delinquent from participation in lawful and meaningful community behavior. In other words, more alternatives should be offered to youth than the two extremes of success in a structured system or adjustment to low status in the system if not successful. This recommendation is more easily hypothesized than implemented. Nevertheless, some good suggestions have been made for formalizing such a project.

One suggestion points out that little formal training is needed to carry out the occupational requirements of many positions, such as teachers' aides, recreational aides, research assistants, and nurses' aides.

These positions in turn may be used as entry points into fields that would offer upward occupational mobility to the person who was willing to put in additional time to gain further experience and training. This new concept of career opportunities has to be implemented by community action. The proponents of this concept feel that, if it is indeed implemented, delinquency will then be curtailed in nonmetropolitan and rural areas.

The new career program for rural youth is important because it would provide skills and help to develop personal dignity not only for those individuals who will remain in the rural area but also for the many others who will migrate to urban areas in the future. These migrants will thus be provided with skills that may be marketable in metropolitan areas.

RELIGION AND DELINQUENCY

In any lengthy discussion of juvenile delinquency, sooner or later the subject of religion is raised. Many individuals feel that religion is an effective factor in the development of the personality of the youth, and thus a preventer of delinquency. In correctional institutional procedures, in the parole process, and in probation reports, religion is often referred to as an important factor in rehabilitation. However, many students of the field point out that, contrary to the common belief in the effectiveness of religion as a treatment agent, there is in reality no clear scientific evidence to support the belief that it has any effect on curbing delinquent behavior.

The President's Task Force on Juvenile Delinquency concludes that the relationship of religion to juvenile delinquency is obscure and that religion is a highly varied personal experience. In most individuals, it may be totally unrelated to delinquency, but in some cases it may be instrumental in preventing it. There are also a few examples in which religion or the use of religion has driven young people into juvenile delinquency.

When religion is used as an element of social control, its role can become ambiguous. Interest groups may use it for their own ends. However, we know of social action programs for the underprivileged that have been effective, at least partly because of the rapport and identification of the participants with the sponsoring religious authorities.

In recent years a number of programs that are associated in some way with religious organizations, have been established in various cities in an attempt to prevent and control delinquency. One such program is the East Harlem Protestant Parish. This project has been in existence for a number of years. No completely reliable method has so far been developed to evaluate its work. It is situated in an area marked by high crime, delinquency, mortality, morbidity, and poverty rates. The leaders of the project are convinced of its effectiveness as a positive influence in the neighborhood.

Another example is Our Lady's Youth Center in El Paso, Texas. It was started in 1958 in a Mexican-American slum marked by a high degree of violence and group tensions. The program had three major goals: (1) the development of a sense of identity and solidarity of the people in the area as citizens of the larger community; (2) the promotion of youth activities in a youth center; a leadership training program allowed the young people themselves to plan activities and administer the programs; (3) a program in Christian living, called "Cursillo de Cristiandad." All three aspects of the El Paso program have been judged successful; and, in addition, it has created a social environment in which delinquency rates have diminished.

Finally, there is also the program of the Damascus Pentecostal Christian Church. It was founded in 1958, and consists of a drug addict center in the Bronx, New York. The addicts may stay at the center or in a center-operated camp outside of the city. The complete program approach to addiction is through religion. The addict is considered a sinner; he must accept this judgment and recognize his need of God's help in order to be cured. Medical help is provided when necessary. It is estimated that 250 to 300 addicts have been rehabilitated by the director, the Reverend Leoncia Rosado, since the inception of the program.

In planning juvenile delinquency prevention and control programs, it is worth remembering that religious identification can play an important role in helping a minority community to develop a sense of identity. The strength of a community is related to a sense of identity among people when they belong to a group in which they mean something. Religion can create a focus of identity for minority groups, and it has done so throughout history. Programs associated in some way with religion, which have been developed for the control and prevention of juvenile delinquency, have created a focus of identity for the economic, ethnic, racial, and religious minorities. Whereas religious faith and practice are not essential for programs dealing with problems of delinquency, they can be integrating influences for social action.

THE USE OF DRUGS AND DELINQUENCY

Juvenile delinquency is not a clinical entity. It consists of many forms of behavior that are considered to be unlawful. One of these forms is the possession of illegal drugs as defined by the law.

While long known to our society, the use of drugs by an increasing proportion of our population has accelerated with a phenomenal growth since the early 1950's. Whereas drug use may not be classified as the leading type of juvenile delinquency found among official cases, it is certainly an important one. It has been considered a social problem for a number of years by sociologists.

As an individual and social problem, drug use is a complicated phenomenon with numerous facets and causes, types, theories, and methods of control. Richard Brotman and Frederick Suffet give an excellent summary of the dimensions of the drug problem among youth in the introduction to their study on *Youthful Drug Use*.[1] Among the characteristics they mention are the following:

1. Drugs are used for many purposes: to combat disease, reduce pain, induce relaxation or sleep, increase energy or wakefulness, aid sociability, create pleasure or euphoria, and deepen self-understanding. Drugs used for medical or functional purposes are legally permitted, whereas drugs used for recreation, with certain traditional exceptions, are legally prohibited. The drugs taken for recreation include marijuana, hallucinogens (hashish, mescaline, LSD), amphetamines, barbiturates, heroin and other opiates, and ethereals which can be sniffed (glue, gasoline, cleaning fluid).

2. Research on drug use by youth has included studies of school populations. The studies indicate that the primary choice of illicit drugs among young people is marijuana. On various college and high school campuses surveyed, the proportion of students who have tried marijuana ranges from 6 percent to 74 percent.

3. The use of a particular drug, the frequency of use, and the amount used at a particular time may be classified. On these founda-

---

1. Richard Brotman and Frederick Suffet, *Youthful Drug Use*. U.S. Department of Health, Education, and Welfare. Washington, D.C. 1970. pp. 1–7.

tions, classifications have been developed to designate a user as either an "experimenter," an "occasional user," or a "heavy user." There are degrees of involvement with a drug and there are terms for persons who are heavy users of certain drugs: pot head (marijuana), acid head (LSD), speed freak (amphetamines), and junkie (heroin). Research has revealed that, among school populations at least, the proportion of drug users (mainly of marijuana) who are experimenters or occasional users is much greater than the proportion of heavy users.

4. Just as there is no single type of drug use, there is no single type of drug user. Since drug use cuts across all types of economic, ethnic, and social classes, it is evident that many types of people come under the heading of drug user.

5. In the 1920's and the 1930's marijuana users were found mostly among merchant seamen, jazz musicians, and ghetto dwellers. By the 1960's the drug had spread to the youth of the middle and upper classes. It is used by students in high schools and colleges across the country, by conventional young adults in urban centers, and by persons, such as hippies, who are experimenting with unconventional life styles. Brotman and Suffet point out that some recent research on student populations has shown that marijuana users, compared to nonusers, tend to be more interested in the arts, more liberal in political attitude and more involved in political activities, somewhat alienated from their parents' generation, and less involved in religious activities.

6. Likewise, the use of LSD and other strong hallucinogens seems to be concentrated among students, hippies, and urban young adults. Publicity given to pharmacological research linking LSD to chromosome breakage appears to have caused a reduction in LSD use.

7. Heroin addiction has been mainly a problem of ghetto males in large urban population centers. Most addiction may still be attributed to this group, although there is some evidence that heroin use may be increasing among middle class and suburban youths, as well as among younger age groups in general.

8. It has been found that amphetamines are used so widely that it is difficult to characterize the user. They are used by truck drivers to stay awake on the road, by students to study for examinations, by housewives to lose weight, and by athletes to increase energy. When they are used simply to produce a "high," they are employed mainly by persons participating in a drug subculture.

9. The sniffing of glue or other ethereals appears to be one of the least researched areas of drug use. The little information available in the literature indicates that it is carried on mainly by urban male

juveniles from minority groups, but there has been some recent indication that it is spreading to the suburbs.

10. The most widespread unintended physical consequence of drug use is addiction, which may occur if the drug produces both tolerance and withdrawal symptoms. Both opiates and barbiturates have these properties. At times specific physical ailments are associated with a drug. Heroin addicts may develop hepatitis (from using unsterile needles) or malnutrition (since the drug suppresses the appetite). The most severe physical consequence is death, which may result from an overdose of heroin or barbiturates.

11. The psychological consequences range from simple habituation, which results in short-term uneasiness or irritability if use is terminated, to actual psychotic episodes. Although apparently rare, cases of psychosis (or at least panic reactions), precipitated by the taking of marijuana or LSD, have been reported.

12. It has been claimed that heavy use of marijuana may lead an individual to become a social "drop out." It is not known, however, how often this phenomenon occurs, nor is it clear whether it is attributable to the action of the drug or to the fact that a heavy user may become involved in a subculture which opposes the values of the conventional world.

13. The law regulates the manufacture of drugs used for medical purposes, in order to ensure the purity of the product. It also requires that potent medicines (such as amphetamines and barbiturates) be dispensed only on the prescription of a physician, whereas others (such as aspirin), which presumably are less likely to be dangerous if they are not used in exact doses, can be bought without a prescription.

14. The use of drugs other than alcohol and tobacco for pleasure or social purposes is generally prohibited. Under Federal and state law the possession or sale of marijuana, heroin, LSD, and other narcotics are criminal offenses, punishable by imprisonment.

15. The medical control of illicit drug use is promoted through treatment and rehabilitation. Medical attention is generally required for persons who have taken overdoses of amphetamines or barbiturates, or who have experienced a panic reaction to a strong hallucinogen. Medical techniques have been devised for safely withdrawing persons from addicting drugs.

16. Treatment is often applied to users whose drug use is defined as a sign of disturbance in his social environment or personality. Various techniques are used to uncover the underlying problem of which drug use is seen as a symptom. These techniques may include individual

or group therapy, family therapy, and social case work. The practitioners of these techniques may be psychiatrists, psychologists, social workers, school guidance counselors, and former drug users.

17. Education is one method employed for the prevention of drug abuse. The premise which underlies preventive education is that the dissemination of information about drugs will lead people to avoid modes of drug use which may produce negative consequences. The major locus of education is, of course, the school. Most high schools incorporate material on drugs into health education curricula, and many have undertaken special drug education programs. Some educational campaigns are aimed at broader audiences.

18. Selection of the form of drug control—which might be punitive sanctions, rehabilitation, or education—depends on many factors, including value judgments, social considerations, and the institutional or professional realm in which control is located.

264

Supplementary Readings

Bandura, Albert, and Walters, Richard H. *Adolescent Aggression.* Ronald Press, New York, 1959.

Blumer, Herbert, and Hauser, Phillip M. *The Movies, Delinquency, and Crime.* Macmillan, New York, 1933.

Bordua, David. *Sociological Theories and Their Implications for Juvenile Delinquency.* U.S. Government Printing Office, Washington, D.C., 1960.

Boszormenyi-Nagy, Ivan, and Framo, James L., Eds. *Intensive Family Therapy: Theoretical and Practical Aspects.* Hoeber Medical Division, Harper and Row, New York, 1965.

Burt, Cyril. *The Young Delinquent.* University of London Press, London, 1925.

Clinard, Marshall B., Ed. *Anomie and Deviant Behavior.* Free Press, New York, 1964.

Clinard, Marshall B. *Sociology of Deviant Behavior.* Holt, Rinehart, and Winston, New York, 1963.

Cloward, Richard A., and Ohlin, Lloyd E. *Delinquency and Opportunity.* Free Press, New York, 1960.

Cohen, Albert K. *Delinquent Boys.* Free Press, New York, 1955.

Drake, St. Clair, and Cayton, Horace R. *Black Metropolis.* Harper & Row, New York, 1962.

Fleisher, B. *The Economics of Delinquency.* Quadrangle Books, Chicago, 1966.

Glueck, Sheldon, and Glueck, Eleanor. *Predicting Delinquency and Crime.* Harvard University Press, Cambridge, 1960.

Gold, Martin. *Status Forces in Delinquent Boys.* University of Michigan Press, Ann Arbor, 1963.

Matza, David. *Delinquency and Drift.* Wiley, New York, 1964.

Merton, Robert K. *Social Theory and Social Structure.* Free Press, New York, 1957.

Nye, F. Ivan. *Family Relationships and Delinquent Behavior,* Wiley, New York, 1958.

O'Dea, Thomas F. *The Sociology of Religion.* Prentice-Hall, Englewood Cliffs, N.J., 1966.

President's Commission on Law Enforcement and the Administration of Justice. *Task Force Report: Juvenile Delinquency and Youth Crime.* U.S. Government Printing Office, Washington, D.C., 1967.

Roberts, Joan I. *School Children in the Urban Slum.* Free Press, New York, 1967.

Rogers, Everett M., *Social Change in Rural Society.* Appleton-Century-Crofts, New York, 1960.

Shaw, Clifford, and McKay, Henry O., Eds. *Juvenile Delinquency and Urban Areas*. University of Chicago Press, Chicago, 1942.

Short, James F., Jr., and Strodtbeck, Fred L. *Group Process and Gang Delinquency*. University of Chicago Press, Chicago, 1965.

Stinchcombe, Arthur L. *Rebellion in a High School*. Quadrangle Books, Chicago, 1964.

Tait, C. Downing, Jr., and Hodges, Emory F., Jr. *Delinquents, Their Families, and the Community*. Charles C. Thomas, Springfield, Ill., 1962.

[*Photo by Christy Butterfield.*]

9

The Treatment of Delinquent Children

The failure of criminal procedure to protect delinquent children adequately was obvious, and it was apparent that a new humane approach to juvenile delinquency was necessary. This may be best expressed by one of the points of the Children's Charter endorsed by the White House Conference on Child Health and Protection in 1930, which emphasized that every child in conflict with society has the right to be dealt with intelligently as society's charge, not society's outcast.

The instituting of the juvenile court represented a child-centered and intelligent approach in dealing with the juvenile delinquent. Many authorities in the field of juvenile delinquency disagree on the meaning of "juvenile court." The term is simply one of description, not derivation. It is axiomatic that the juvenile court is not a court of equity or a common-law court, but rather a statutory court. A juvenile court may be broadly defined as a court having special jurisdiction of a parental nature over delinquent, dependent, and neglected children.

THE JUVENILE COURT

The juvenile court is an American product, but the legal principles manifested by it may be traced centuries back to the English system of common law and equity. The responsibility for and care of all minors and their estates were vested in the king who, in turn, designated the chancery to act for him. As guardian, the king earned the title *parens patriae*, father of his country.

In America, when the colonies attained independence, each state took the place of the crown as the *parens patriae* of all minors.

Of significance is the controversy on whether the juvenile court is wholly of chancery origin or of criminal origin. Some authorities argue that it is of criminal origin, since crime and delinquency are based upon intent. Yet this would not seem to be wholly accurate, since delinquency, as one classification, and neglect or dependency, as the second, both come within the categorical periphery of the juvenile court.

In theory, the basic philosophy of the juvenile court has been that of rendering aid, protection, and care to dependent and delinquent children. Only when the punitive factor has been submerged are the courts able to deal with children constructively.

The History of the Juvenile Court

The advent of the juvenile court was not spontaneous. It was an outgrowth of, and inextricably tied to, legislation of the past. For example, English laws for the reform of juvenile offenders were enacted as early as the tenth century. Nine hundred years later, Britain's Juvenile Offenders' Act of 1847 was enacted to govern the trials of all children under 14 years of age. Legislation to curtail publicity against children involved in court cases was adopted in Switzerland during the first half of the nineteenth century. In South Australia, the chief secretary in 1889 approved the granting of probation and the holding of separate hearings for children under 18.

The various steps which led in America to the creation of the juvenile court began in the early decades of the nineteenth century. One by one there appeared, in statutes, certain specific features of a juvenile court, such as that of separate confinement, separate hearings, and probation. A reform movement against confinement of juvenile offenders with adult criminals resulted in the establishment in 1825 of the House of Refuge in New York. As early as 1869, a Massachusetts law was passed to provide for the presence of the visiting agent or an officer of the state board of charity at the trial of juvenile cases.

The plan of restoring young offenders to good citizenship under supervision of the court, without confinement in an institution, first took statutory form in Massachusetts in 1878. Similar in many respects to this 1878 law for probation, though more limited, was a municipal law of 1861 authorizing the mayor of Chicago to appoint a commission before which boys between the ages of six and 17 could be heard on charges of petty offenses. About that time Michigan organized a state agency for the care of juvenile offenders, and New York enacted a law which allowed the courts discretionary power to place juvenile offenders in the charge of suitable persons or institutions willing to receive them.

As a result of a movement initiated by the Federation of Women's Clubs in Illinois, the legislature of that state enacted the first juvenile court law in April 1899. It was officially styled "An Act To Regulate the Treatment and Control of Dependent, Neglected and Delinquent Children." The act did not create any new or special courts; it simply indicated that in counties whose populations exceeded 500,000, the circuit court judges should designate one or more of their members to hear all juvenile cases. It also provided for a separate juvenile court room and separate records. The title "juvenile court" was given for the purposes of convenience only.

On September 12, 1899, the legislature of Colorado passed the famous "School Law" which, though in reality a truancy law, contained some of the features of the current juvenile court laws. It was mainly due to the indefatigable efforts of Judge Ben B. Lindsey, author of this law, that the Colorado Juvenile Court Law was adopted some four years later.

The history of the juvenile court movement includes the struggles of numerous great men, such as Judge Lindsey in Colorado, who have unselfishly aspired toward reforms for the purpose of saving children rather than punishing them.

Now all states, as well as the federal government, the District of Columbia, and Puerto Rico, have juvenile courts. In the United States there are approximately 2,700 juvenile courts, no two of which are exactly alike. In most states the unit of jurisdiction is the county. In some states it is the town, the city, the borough, or the judicial district.

The county system was sometimes thought to be the most desirable because it conformed to the established governmental structure. It seemed also to offer the best guarantee of serving rural as well as urban areas. There were, however, some disadvantages. Many counties lack adequate juvenile detention facilities, and detain children in unsuitable places, usually jails that are used for adult offenders as well. Most counties cannot afford specially trained judges or trained juvenile court personnel. Therefore certain states have set up state-administered and state-financed juvenile court systems which operate on a larger jurisdictional scale. The state system makes it possible to assign specially appointed judges to a circuit system for juvenile court hearings and to employ qualified court personnel.

The great majority of juvenile courts are distinct from the ordinary court system only in that they have separate hearings. Their judges are engaged in criminal, civil, equity, probate, or other legal business most of the time. Separate juvenile courts, which are either entirely autonomous or part of a domestic relations court system, are operated in a small number of counties in about 30 states and the District of Columbia. Another type of juvenile court is one that is coordinated with another special court set up to handle cases that present social problems, such as the court of domestic relations or the family court. This kind of juvenile court may be a subdivision or a coordinate branch of the special court. The legal status of all three types of juvenile courts is uniformly recognized; that is, each is considered "a court of superior jurisdiction and a court of record."

Delinquency is not the only kind of case dealt with in juvenile courts. Of the children who appear in juvenile courts, about 13 percent are there for other reasons. Many appear for reasons of neglect or dependency. Also, in a number of states, the juvenile courts have jurisdiction over cases of feeble-minded children. In addition, some courts rule in cases of guardianship, custody, adoption, illegitimacy, and physical handicap, and some even concern themselves with permitting and annulling marriages of minors.

The Federal Juvenile Delinquency Act of 1938 has established juvenile court procedures for youths under 18 charged with violating federal law, but under this law it is possible, as it has been since 1932, to transfer all federal offenders under the age of 21 to state authorities willing to receive them.

In addition to its jurisdiction over the delinquent child, the juvenile court in most states has certain jurisdiction over adults (primarily parents or guardians) charged with contributing to the delinquency, neglect, or dependency of a child, and it may order the parent or other legally responsible person to contribute to a child's support.

The fundamental principle that the juvenile court has exclusive jurisdiction over children in need of aid, protection, and guidance is not always assured. A number of states exclude children who have committed certain offenses, such as rape, manslaughter, murder, and other felonies, from juvenile court jurisdiction. Certain states, or counties within a state, apply this only to children above a specified age. In at least 40 states the juvenile court has concurrent jurisdiction with other courts. Therefore, in these states, the case of the delinquent child may be heard in either juvenile or criminal court; the decision on this point may be left to the judge, the district attorney, or sometimes the child himself.

Taking the juvenile to a criminal court, as such, is inconsistent with the basic principle of the juvenile court. We know that some people, who have never accepted the proposal to bring all children's offenses before a juvenile court, still demand that any child who has committed a serious offense should be tried in public in a criminal court. However, belief in the noncriminal nature of juvenile delinquency has become so general that the jurisdiction of the juvenile courts has continued to encompass increasingly more types of offenses.

Methods of selecting juvenile judges vary in different states. In only a few juvenile courts is the judge chosen solely because of qualifications for this special work. Often the appointment is made according to seniority or in regular rotation.

The so-called "Missouri Plan," in force in Missouri since 1941, has won the endorsement of the American Bar Association. Under it the governor appoints the juvenile judge from a list of three names submitted by a selective commission or panel. This judge then serves a one-year "trial period," after which he runs for election for a full term by popular vote.

The Standard Juvenile Court Act proposes that for a county having a population of 100,000 or more, the governor shall appoint a judge of the juvenile court from a list of names that has been submitted by a panel of seven persons. Panel members are the presiding judge of the court of general jurisdiction, two members designated by the county bar association, two from the county welfare department, and two from the county board of education. In states in which state juvenile courts exist, the panel will consist of nine members, the additional two being from the Department of Health and Mental Hygiene. In small counties, the act itself recommends that a majority vote of the population determine whether this same method shall be used.

In 1949 in California a Commission on Juvenile Justice recommended that the judge of a county juvenile court be selected by a panel consisting of the presiding judge of the superior court and four persons appointed by the county supervisors, including one representative each of public education, public welfare, and the law.

The tenure of office of the juvenile judge also varies in different states as does the formal background of each. These variations are evident in the results of a survey that was sponsored by the National Council of Juvenile Court Judges in 1963. The council sent questionnaires to all those judges exercising juvenile court jurisdiction, and 1,564 of them responded for a 70 percent return. Among the respondents the following characteristics were found: (1) 71 percent had law degrees; (2) 95 percent of those serving in jurisdictions of 1,000,000 or more had law degrees; (3) 48 percent were without undergraduate degrees; (4) the average age was 53 years; (5) 75 percent had been elected to office; (6) 62 percent had previously been elected to another public office; (7) of the full-time judges in the group, 72 percent spent a quarter or less of their time on juvenile matters; (8) a third of the full-time judges reported that no probation officers were available to their court.

Before any juvenile courts existed, private child protecting societies had carried on much of the work with juvenile delinquents. This included investigation, detention, and probation. Then, while juvenile courts were first developing, there was a growth of administrative child welfare agencies, so that a great number of different kinds of services and assistances were available for children. This somewhat parallel development of juvenile courts and child welfare agencies presented many questions; there arose considerable confusion on which functions should be those of the court, and which belonged to the social welfare agency. Some thought the function of the juvenile court should be wholly judicial and that welfare agencies should assume complete responsibility for all juvenile casework. These persons believed that the court, no matter how socialized its procedure, still remained a court with its own structure and function, and should not be placed in the position of having to serve as a social agency.

An opposing school believed that all cases on neglect and dependency, as well as those on delinquency of a child, should come before the juvenile court, since it is often difficult to determine at what point neglect and dependency are separate from the end result—delinquency. Factors causing all three are often identical. Also, the absence of available social welfare services in many areas made it necessary for the court to assume responsibility for any care and treatment necessary to the child's rehabilitation.

Juvenile judges themselves have decided views of their functions.

Some juvenile courts try to limit their intake to cases in which only judicial action is required. They feel that cases of dependency and neglect need not be brought into court unless problems of custody or willful neglect are involved. In short, they do not think the court should become an all-inclusive child welfare agency.

Most judges wish to refer child welfare problems that require detailed and long-term treatment to a good social agency that offers such services. Often services to a child and his family are so closely related to the functions of both court and social agency that a decision on who takes responsibility must depend on the specific factors in the case.

The Procedures of the Juvenile Court

Official cases in a juvenile court are usually handled in the following manner. Filing of a formal petition starts the proceedings. Any citizen may file a petition if he has knowledge of a situation that is detrimental to the welfare, health, or education of a child who comes within the jurisdiction of the juvenile court. In some states certain requirements, such as swearing out affidavits, having an investigation made before filing a petition, or verifying the petition, must be fulfilled before formal jurisdiction of the case is assumed. In certain states informal complaints are sufficient. The judge or probation officer may investigate complaints to determine whether a petition should be filed. If a complaint has been made by a private person, an agency, a parent, or another relative, a summons may be issued to bring the child in, or, if deemed necessary, a warrant for his arrest may be issued. Those most often filing petitions are the local or state police, the railroad police, the FBI, school authorities, social agencies, probation officers, parents, relatives, or neighbors.

When the police apprehend a juvenile, the place to which they take him depends on the nature and seriousness of the case, the age of the child, and the degree of cooperation between the police and the juvenile courts. They may take him to the police station for a brief period, to the office of the juvenile court, or to a detention home or other facility where he can be kept during investigation.

When a child is taken into custody for an offense, the parent, guardian, or custodian is notified as soon as possible. Unless the court has ordered otherwise, the child is released to the custody of the parent, upon the parent's written promise to bring the child to court at such time as the court may direct. However, it may be unwise to return some children to their own homes, such as those who are beyond the control of parents or guardians, or those whose appearance in court cannot be assured if they are returned to the parents' custody. These children may be placed in detention, in either an institution or a foster home, or, if the location is a small county in which facilities for detention are not available, the child may reside in the probation officer's own home pending court hearing.

If the child is at court under arrest he will ordinarily be arraigned. Usually the arraignment consists of a statement to the child of the charge made against him, of the section of the statute he has violated, and of his rights and privileges. This is done very simply and carefully so the child will understand the procedure. A hearing date may be set.

Before the court hearing the probation officer makes a social investigation of the child's background, family conditions, neighborhood, and school situation. (If probation facilities are not available this investigation may be conducted by a social agency.) The probation officer studies the various aspects of the information he has obtained in the social investigation: circumstances of the offense; record of former behavior difficulties; home conditions, including employment, housing, health, and moral conditions; and the findings of psychological and psychiatric examinations, if these services are available. On the basis of all this information, he prepares his recommendations to the court, with the purpose of giving the child the best possible opportunity to become a good citizen. If the case is to go before the court at a hearing, this hearing should be scheduled as soon as possible after it has been studied, because detention should not be extended any longer than necessary.

The juvenile court hearing is an important part of the procedure for the handling of juveniles referred to the court. In some juvenile courts the judge selects a referee, who holds the hearing and by this means expedites the business of the court. A hearing before a referee follows the same rules as a hearing before a judge. The findings and disposition made by a referee, however, must be reviewed by the judge, since action is not taken without his approval. The hearing may be, and usually is, the only occasion in which the judge is seen by the child and his parents. In court they may realize for the first time the state's interest and responsibility for the welfare of all children, and learn the conditions under which the state may intervene in the parents' upbringing of a child.

The room in which juvenile court is held should be small, and the hearing should be informal but dignified. Privacy is a fundamental feature of juvenile court procedure. The presence of spectators in a juvenile court hearing imparts the atmosphere of a criminal court procedure. Also, unfortunately for the child, it makes him the center of attraction and it may keep him and his parents from speaking as freely as they should.

Privacy was established in juvenile court hearings to avoid publicity. Generally speaking, newsmen are excluded from the hearings, and the names of offenders under a given age are kept out of the papers —usually by agreement of the editors. There are several schools of thought about publishing names of juvenile offenders. Some believe that the names of those who are 18 or older, and of repeaters who are even younger, and of any who have committed felonies or other atrocious offenses, should be published as a deterrent to delinquency. Other persons are vehemently opposed to publication of the name of anyone coming within the juvenile court jurisdiction, maintaining that such action unfairly casts a shadow over that child for the rest of his life. As a rule, whenever the judge and probation officers wish to avoid press publicity, they will find that a truthful explanation to the newsmen will win their full compliance.

On the basis of the findings uncovered before the hearing, and the facts brought out during the hearing, the judge makes his decision about future plans for the child. His decision is subject to a rehearing when warranted, and to modification or change whenever such change seems beneficial for the child. The Standard Juvenile Court Act (Section 18) lists possible dispositions the judge can make. Most of the existing juvenile court laws have similar provisions.

In many courts the probation officer is obliged to be present at the hearing of each of his cases in order to supplement verbally his written report, or to answer questions the judge may have.

Whether the child is placed on probation (a status that can be established only by a specific court order) and allowed to remain in his own home under protective supervision, or whether it is decided that his welfare would be most adequately served by commitment to an institution, foster home, or hospital, the probation officer continues to supervise him as a helping service. He helps the child to make adjustments in his personal and emotional life as well as in environmental situations. Another task of the probation officer is to interpret to the public the functions of the juvenile court and his own activities, and to focus community resources on effective prevention of juvenile delinquency.

Certain juvenile cases are disposed of informally—that is, without filing a formal petition, preparing an official court record, or holding a court hearing. The probation officer may adjust the situation without resort to court action. He may work in cooperation with juvenile police or other agencies that may be of assistance. This procedure varies throughout the country, and there is considerable difference of opinion in regard to the practice itself. The juvenile courts have begun to recognize the value of well qualified intake supervisors, who determine whether a case should be handled formally or informally, and whether it could be handled more effectively by a social agency that is equipped to deal with the particular situation.

The first agency to come in contact with the delinquent child is most often the police. For this reason, it is important to obtain full co-operation from the police in any program concerned with juvenile delinquency, either in methods of handling children who are in difficulty, or in the prevention and control of conditions that contribute to delinquency. In many localities, special training in handling juveniles is now being given to police officers as a part of their basic training course. In urban centers many police departments contain a special unit whose major responsibility is work with juveniles, and in small communities a special officer is often assigned to deal with juveniles.

The Gault Decision

Important procedural changes in our juvenile courts were brought about by a decision of the United States Supreme Court on May 15, 1967. The case was that of a juvenile named Gerald F. Gault. It was an appeal from a judgment of the Supreme Court of Arizona, which had dismissed a petition for a writ of habeas corpus. The petition sought the release of Gerald, who had been committed as a juvenile delinquent to the State Industrial School by the Juvenile Court of Gila County, Arizona. Briefly, the case developed in the following way.

On Monday, June 8, 1964, at about 10 A.M., Gerald Francis Gault and a friend, Ronald Lewis, were taken into custody by the sheriff of Gila County. Gerald was then still subject to a six-month probation order, which had been entered on February 25, 1964, as a result of his having been in the company of another boy who had stolen a wallet from a lady's purse. The police action on June 8 was in response to a verbal complaint by a neighbor of the boys, Mrs. Cook, about a telephone call she had received in which the caller or callers had made lewd or indecent remarks.

At the time Gerald was picked up, his mother and father were both at work. No notice that Gerald was being taken into custody was left at the home. No other steps were taken to advise them that their son had, in effect, been arrested. Gerald was taken to the county detention home for children. When his mother arrived home at about 6 o'clock, Gerald was not there. Gerald's older brother was sent to look for him at the trailer home of the Lewis family. He apparently learned then that Gerald was in custody. He so informed his mother. The two of them went to the detention home. The deputy probation officer, Charles D. Flagg, who was also superintendent of the detention home, told Mrs. Gault why Gerald was there and said that a hearing would be held in juvenile court at 3 o'clock the following day, June 9.

Officer Flagg filed a petition with the court on the day of the hearing, June 9, 1964. It was not served on the Gaults. None of them saw this petition until the habeas corpus hearing on August 17, 1964. The petition was entirely formal. It made no reference to any factual basis for the judicial action which it initiated. It stated only that "said minor is under the age of 18 years and in need of the protection of this Honorable Court and that said minor is a delinquent minor." It requested a hearing and an order regarding "the care and custody of said minor." Officer Flagg executed a formal affidavit in support of the petition.

On June 9, Gerald, his mother, his older brother, and Probation Officers Flagg and Henderson appeared before the juvenile judge in chambers. Gerald's father was not there. He was at work out of the city. Mrs. Cook, the complainant, was not there. No one was sworn at this hearing. No transcript or recording was made. No memorandum or record of the substance of the proceedings was prepared. Information about the proceedings and the subsequent hearing on June 15 derives entirely from the testimony of the juvenile court judge, Mr. and Mrs. Gault, and Officer Flagg at the habeas corpus proceeding conducted two months later. From this, it appears that at the July 9 hearing Gerald was questioned by the judge about the telephone call. There was disagreement on what he said. His mother recalled that Gerald had said he only dialed Mrs. Cook's number and handed the telephone to his friend, Ronald. Officer Flagg recalled that Gerald had admitted making the lewd remarks. Judge McGhee testified that Gerald had "admitted making one of these (lewd) statements." At the conclusion of the hearing, the judge said he would "think about it." Gerald was taken back to the detention home. He was not sent to his own home with his parents. On June 11 or 12, after having been detained since June 8, Gerald was released and driven home. In the record, there is no explanation of why he was kept in the detention home or why he was released. At 5 P.M. on the day of Gerald's release, Mrs. Gault received a note signed by Officer Flagg. It was on plain paper, not letterhead. Its entire text was as follows:

Mrs. Gault:
Judge McGhee has set Monday, June 15, 1964, at 11:00 A.M. as the date and time for further Hearings on Gerald's delinquency.
s/Flagg

At the appointed time on Monday, June 15, Gerald, his father and mother, Ronald Lewis, his father, and Officers Flagg and Henderson were present before Judge McGhee. Witnesses at the subsequent habeas corpus proceeding of August 17 differed in their recollections of Gerald's testimony at the June 15 hearing. Mr. and Mrs. Gault recalled that Gerald had again testified that he had only dialed the number and that the other boy had made the remarks. Officer Flagg agreed that at this hearing Gerald had not admitted making the lewd remarks; however, Judge McGhee claimed that he had. Again, the complainant, Mrs. Cook, was not present. Mrs. Gault asked that Mrs. Cook be present "so she could see which boy had done the talking, the dirty talking over the phone." The juvenile judge said that she didn't have to be present at that hearing. The judge did not speak to Mrs. Cook or communicate with her at any time. Officer Flagg had talked to her once—by telephone on June 9.

At this June 15 hearing a referral report made by the probation officers was filed with the court, although this move was not disclosed to Gerald or his parents. It listed the charge as "Lewd Phone Calls." At the conclusion of the hearing, the judge committed Gerald as a juvenile delinquent to the State Industrial School for the period of his minority (that is until 21), unless sooner discharged by due process of law.

No appeal is permitted by Arizona law in juvenile cases. On August 3, 1964, a petition for writ of habeas corpus was filed with the Arizona Supreme Court, which referred it to the superior court for a hearing. The superior court dismissed the writ, and appellants sought review in the Arizona Supreme Court. The Arizona Supreme Court handed down an opinion affirming dismissal of the writ and stating its conclusions on the issues raised by appellants and other aspects of the juvenile process.

The Gault family then appealed the state supreme court's decision to the United States Supreme Court. In their appeal they pointed out that the Juvenile Code of Arizona, at least as it had been applied to their case, was invalid because, contrary to the due process clause of the Fourteenth Amendment, juveniles were taken from the custody of their parents and committed to a state institution pursuant to proceedings in which the juvenile court had virtually unlimited discretion, and in which the following basic rights were denied: (1) notice of the charges; (2) right to counsel; (3) right to confrontation and cross-examination; (4) right to a transcript of the proceedings; (5) privilege against self-incrimination; (6) right to appellate review.

The United States Supreme Court held that the Juvenile Code of Arizona deprived children charged with delinquency of the procedural safeguards guaranteed by the due process clause of the Fourteenth Amendment. The Court also held that due process guarantees apply to all children alleged to be delinquent. These guarantees include the following: the right to adequate notice of charges; the right to representation by a lawyer, either retained or appointed by the court; the right to confrontation and cross-examination of witnesses; and the right to be advised of the privilege against self-incrimination. The United States Supreme Court has set these minimum standards for all juvenile courts in the country. The Court did not rule on the right of appeal from a juvenile court order or the right to a transcript.

Legislative Changes

The laws pertaining to delinquency and delinquents are important, not only because they define the range of possible kinds of treatment but also because they express in a sense the general public point of view on the child deviate and nonconformist in a given state. These laws manifest two presently conflicting objectives of the state: to protect its property and its social groups, and to insure protection and treatment for children who have broken the law.

The states have enacted their delinquency laws at different times in the course of a span of seventy years. Consequently, it is natural to find wide variation. Some states have thoroughly revised early laws in the conviction that the group's best interests, that is, "protection of the state," lie in a well ordered program aimed at the reform or rehabilitation of the individual. Essentially the once prevalent objectives of penology have been subordinated to reformation of the individual.

The laws of the 50 states differ on age limits, the type of court having jurisdiction, the nature of proceedings, the scope of jurisdiction, the provision for social treatment of children who have committed serious offenses against persons, and the administration of probation. In the hope of clarifying these points in state delinquency laws and encouraging future legislation based upon modern principles of reform, a model law was drafted in 1921. A subsequent conference, held in 1923, endorsed the model law, and it was later adopted by the National Probation and Parole Association (now the Council on Crime and Delinquency) and the United States Children's Bureau. This model law was entitled the Standard Juvenile Court Act. It was adopted in 1925 and revised in 1949 and 1959. It has been used extensively by legislative bodies, juvenile code commissions, and other organizations in preparing and amending juvenile court laws. A number of states have incorporated part or practically all of this model act into their statutes.

In 1953, after intensive work on the development of new standards, the Children's Bureau, the National Probation and Parole Association, and the National Council of Juvenile Judges issued a new publication entitled *Standards for Specialized Courts Dealing with Children.* Its material is intended as a guide to aid judges, probation officers, social workers, legislators, and citizen groups in strengthening and improving juvenile court work in their communities.

More recently, in 1968, the Joint Commission on Correctional Manpower and Training issued a paper entitled *The Future of the Juvenile Court* by Ted Rubin and Jack F. Smith of the Denver Juvenile Court. The authors analyze changes taking place in the juvenile court.

Selected laws pertaining to the treatment of young offenders have been instigated by the American Law Institute. The American Law Institute, an unofficial body, met in Washington, D.C., in 1940. A model act, called the Youth Correction Authority Act, was drafted by that body in the form of a proposed bill which could, with local modification, be introduced into state legislatures. The work that went into the preparation of this model act was a significant advancement in the treatment of a group of youthful offenders under 21 years of age.

This model act proposed that these youths, when convicted in a criminal proceeding, be committed to a state agency, or authority, which takes full charge of their correctional treatment. The authority must establish its own diagnostic clinics and approve or create detention homes or other facilities for correctional care. The basic philosophy of the members of the American Law Institute was that rehabilitation must be substituted for punitive treatment.

This act provides for an indeterminate period of treatment measured by the social danger of the offender to the community. Its aim is to restore the offender as quickly as practicable to society.

In 1941, California adopted the act in a limited form. Subsequent amendments broadened its area of concern to include the whole subject of delinquency prevention and research, and the word "correction" was dropped from the title of the state act and of the agency it established.

A few other states have assumed centralized responsibility for the treatment and prevention of juvenile delinquency. In 1947 the Youth Conservation Commission was created in Minnesota, and in the same year Wisconsin established, under the Department of Public Welfare, a Youth Service Commission. In Massachusetts, the Youth Service Board was set up to deal with juvenile offenders. In 1949, Texas formed a State Youth Development Council to conduct research and administer state institutions for delinquent children. In a few additional states, the act drafted by the American Law Institute has indirectly affected the modification of court procedure for dealing with youthful offenders.

Detention

Detention is usually presumed to be the care of children outside the home pending disposition by the court. It may also be employed for runaway, lost, or homeless children pending final plans for their welfare, or for children awaiting admission to other institutions.

Detention is one of the facilities that a juvenile court must provide for the children who come before it, and the laws that set up the court generally state that a suitable place for detention of its wards shall be provided and maintained at county expense. Children should not be held in jails or in police lockups, but they may need to be held in secure custody until final action has been taken. These children should be held in detention homes or institutions especially designed to meet their needs.

Suitable facilities for detention of children are generally lacking. City and county jails are still used for this purpose in many places. Many jails do not provide for segregation of adult and juvenile offenders. An effort has been made in a number of areas to use, for detention care, foster homes that have been carefully selected to meet a delinquent child's needs.

Detention care should not be used as a method of punishment, but as an opportunity for treatment of the child. All children in detention should receive good physical care (medical care if needed), planned and enjoyable recreation, and, if they stay more than a couple of days, educational instruction. There should be someone on the staff who will observe the child's behavior and be able to help him with any emotional difficulties. There should also be a program of activities to keep the child occupied.

When a child is placed in detention care, there is a crisis in his life. To him, detention generally means the denial of his rights and needs, a denial that seems much more severe than his behavior has warranted. He may interpret detention as a further rejection by his parents and the community. Detention, as it now exists, generally increases hostility, anxiety, and defensiveness, and it may result in more serious behavior disorders.

Careful planning can change all this. It can transform detention into a resource which will decrease unhealthy repressions and substitutions that could lead to further complications in his personality development. Temporary care can be used to provide an auspicious setting for the study of the child and his problems.

Although the practice of using the common jails and lockups for the detention of children is prohibited by statute in most states, surveys made by the National Council on Crime and Delinquency in 1965 show that more than 100,000 children and youths of juvenile court age are held in jails or comparable places of detention every year. Most of these jails are rated unfit for adult offenders by the Federal Bureau of Prisons Inspection Service. Many of these children do not need to be detained in the first place. Detention should be used only for children who have committed delinquent acts and who, in addition, are considered dangerous to the community and unlikely to remain available for court or other jurisdictional matters.

Children who do not require secure custody should not be detained merely for police investigation or for a social study by the probation department. Children whose only deviant act is truancy should not be placed in detention.

Juvenile Probation

What is juvenile probation? It is difficult to define exactly: in general, it has been defined as a type of treatment, by means of which the child remains in the community under the supervision of a probation officer.

The term "probation" is derived from the Latin word *probare*, which means "to prove." Today probation still implies this meaning, for it affords the individual offender a chance to prove himself. Society recognizes that many offenders, given the opportunity, can mend their ways without the need of severe disciplinary measures, and it gives them that opportunity through probation.

Probation permits the juvenile to stay in the community, at his own home or the home of a relative or foster parent, under the supervision of a probation officer, instead of going to a correctional school. Community resources can be used for his rehabilitation, and, from an economic point of view, probation is less expensive than institutional care.

Unfortunately, probation has been allowed to take on negative aspects in some rural areas or small towns. For example, in some places a child is sent home from the court hearing without any definite plan having been made for his improved care; in others, the child checks in once a month and answers a few standardized questions on whether he has been good since his last visit, and the probation officer never really knows what has been happening to the child. This kind of probation becomes a type of systematized leniency. Actually, to put someone on probation should be viewed as the granting of a treatment period, not as an act of leniency: it should be explained as such to the child, his parents, and the community.

Probation supervision is primarily a counseling relationship between the probation officer and the child—not a series of threats and warnings. The probation officer may enlist the aid of the family, the school, the church, other community agencies, and individuals to help him instill in the youth a feeling of self-confidence and self-respect. The officer also tries to help the child acquire socially acceptable habits, attitudes, and social values; to give him some understanding of the motives underlying his behavior; and to help him understand that he, as an individual, must accept certain socially imposed responsibilities and restraints.

In order to help the child make a satisfactory adjustment during his probationary period, the probation officer must find out first just what is needed, then establish a relationship of trust with the child and his parents, and finally aid the child to see the real source of his problem and achieve a solution mainly by himself. In order to understand the motivations, feelings, and attitudes of the child, the probation officer must learn about the child's home, school, friends, religion, and neighborhood. The officer must be able to use the element of authority wisely in his work with the child and to employ casework methods and groupwork techniques.

There has been considerable discussion on whether casework principles can be used successfully within the authoritarian framework of the juvenile court and probation. There is no conflict between authority and casework when the authority is constructive. All casework help is actually directed toward providing an opportunity for an individual to see his problem more clearly, face it, and determine what he wants to do about it. The wise parent uses constructive supportive authority. The wise agency recognizes when this type of help is needed.

Well directed authority has positive values for the child who has never had to conform to a standard of behavior or accomplishment that has been set up under definite and consistent training. At first, he may not be able to clarify his thoughts about his responsibility in self-control and self-direction, but, with the support of the kindly, constructive authority of the well qualified probation officer, he may find the strength he needs to attain his goals. Parents, too, may need supportive authority and guidance from the probation officer, especially if they at first resist outside help with their family problems, because of fear, guilt, or feelings of inadequacy.

The effectiveness of probation in rehabilitation of the child and his family rests to a large extent on the careful selection of the children recommended for probation and on the quality of personnel on the probation staff. The standards for education and experience of probation officers are becoming progressively higher throughout the country. Many people hope that soon minimum qualifications everywhere will be at least college graduation with one year's experience in a casework agency under competent supervision.

Some additional factors must be considered here in reviewing the success of probation. In many places, present case loads carried by the probation worker make constructive work with an individual child practically impossible. Time-consuming reports, record-writing, staff meetings, and case conferences absorb too much time and energy of workers. The National Probation and Parole Association recommends for each probation officer a maximum case load of 25 probationers under supervision, plus five prehearing investigations per month. If an officer has fewer than five investigations to pursue, an assignment of supervising five probationers can be substituted for each investigation not undertaken.

Probation officers now frequently have case loads of 50, 75, or 100, in addition to ten or 15 prehearing investigations per month. Salaries are too low to keep many of the best probation officers from leaving for other fields in which the salary is more closely proportionate to the skill and training required.

Probably the first concrete example of probation as we understand it today was practiced by John Augustus, a Boston shoemaker.

John Augustus may well be called the first probation officer. As an unpaid voluntary worker, he undertook to save from degradation individuals whom he found in the Boston courts; this he did from 1841 until his death in 1859. John Augustus started by seeking probation for common drunkards, but later extended his services to individuals guilty of other crimes. In 1843, he entered the field of juvenile probation by taking juvenile delinquents under his unique and pioneering probation system.

The success of John Augustus with juveniles laid the foundation for the development of special services to juvenile offenders. From 1861 to 1867, Chicago had a commissioner to hear cases of delinquency in boys; this commissioner had the authority to place the boys on probation. The Massachusetts Acts of 1869 and 1870 provided for the supervision of juvenile delinquents by agents from the Board of State Charities.

In 1878, the first official law in the country to make probation an official service was passed. This law empowered the mayor of Boston to appoint a probation officer in Suffolk County. In 1891, statewide probation was attained in Massachusetts when it became mandatory that each municipal, district, and police court appoint a probation officer. Maryland became the second state to pass a probation law, in 1894. Vermont followed in 1898.

The year 1899 was a momentous one in juvenile probation development. Rhode Island passed a general statewide probation law. Minnesota passed legislation to provide probation for juvenile offenders, making no provision for adult probation at the time. However, the most significant event occurred in the state of Illinois, where the first juvenile court in the country was established. Since then, probation for juvenile delinquents has been provided in all states, the District of Columbia, the territories, and the federal judiciary system.

Case History of a Probationer

The following case summary shows how a well qualified and intelligent probation officer helped a boy acquire socially acceptable attitudes and social values:

John Jones, a slim boy of 16—neat, well groomed, and polite—came before the juvenile court for violation of the curfew and possession of a dangerous knife. Previously, it was learned, he had played truant from school and had once taken his stepfather's car without permission and damaged it.

Severe conflict between his parents had often focused on him. His stepfather was very critical of him, and the boy was hostile in return. The mother was overprotective of the boy and extremely critical of the stepfather. To complete the family picture, a younger brother accepted the stepfather's supervision. In speaking of his family, John said, "We don't do anything for recreation."

John's school report showed habitual tardiness and a tendency to waste time in class. In his autobiography he wrote, "Some classes are too hard and some of the teachers are too mean." His school counselor couldn't recall ever having seen John smile. His polished facade tended not only to minimize criticism of his behavior but also to shield him from close ties with adults. His contact with peers was apparently good.

At court, John's case was continued for six months, during which time the boy would be under supervision of the probation office. The probation officer decided to direct his attention almost exclusively to the boy, rather than to the parents; the parental conflict seemed clearly to derive from deeply rooted emotional problems of many years' duration, and to offer little promise of response to such contact as he could provide.

The probation officer began by referring John to the guidance clinic for diagnostic evaluation. This report disclosed no extraordinary pathology but said that he showed "a kind of passive-aggressive resistance" to authority and perceived parental figures as "impersonal monsters."

The boy was returned to his home. There the probation officer saw him frequently, although John at first resisted contact by forgetting appointments. John was still showing some resistance by the end of the six-month period; and supervision was extended for another six months. The granting of this extension had a marked effect. John seemed to realize now that the probation officer was actually concerned about his interests rather than simply performing a required routine on a case referred by the police. The contacts from then on became more fruitful.

Although John was still reticent about his inner feelings, he did begin to talk about experiences within the family and about some of his thoughts pertaining to them. Gradually there developed a most remarkable change in his personality, from a withdrawn and unhappy appearance to a rather cheerful and outgoing attitude. He became interested in his own welfare—in the possibility of getting a job, or even of setting up his own radio shop, an area in which he had considerable knowledge and skill. His school reports reflected the new attitude, and he, on his own initiative, conferred with the counselor about junior college requirements.

When the case was closed, one year after it came before the court, the probation office felt that John was well on his way to a successful adjustment. The boy continued to call on the probation officer from time to time, entirely of his own volition, for preventive services.

PROTECTIVE, INSTITUTIONAL, AND PREVENTIVE SERVICES

Protective work is defined as the work that provides security for the child who has been abused, abandoned, or neglected by his parents or guardians. Sometimes neglect is not willful, but is due to ignorance or misfortune. When a parent can provide the support—the education required by law and the medical and other care necessary to the child's welfare—but refuses or neglects to do so, or when a child is abandoned by its parents, the protective function of the juvenile court is exercised.

Protective work began in 1875, under private auspices, with the organization of the New York Society for the Prevention of Cruelty to Children. Later family welfare societies, humane societies, juvenile protective societies, and many others devoted much attention to the protection of children, both through private efforts and through the promotion of legislation.

For many years, protective services for children were confined primarily to urban areas. Then, after the enactment of the Social Security Act in 1935, help was given to rural areas to develop services for children. Whether public or private, urban or rural, there can be no doubt about the economy of protective services, both in human resources and in money.

Protective services are usually initiated by someone outside the family who has complained that children are being mistreated. The protective agency may therefore start its work in the capacity of legal authority, with a responsibility to obtain proper care for the child, whether or not the parent or guardian wants its services.

If a neglected child can be allowed to remain in his own home because it is felt that his parents can be helped through the protective supervision of the probation officer or by a caseworker in an agency, the child is not removed until the parents have been given a fair chance to show they can adequately care for him. In other cases, a child must be removed at once and placed in a foster home or an institution for a temporary period until permanent plans can be made for his best interests.

Occasionally a child comes to the court or agency to make a complaint against his parents or his home. The situation calls for special objectivity by the probation officer or agency worker, for it is realized that the rights of parents cannot be ignored before a careful investigation has been made of the child's story, even though the inclination may be to accept the child's appeal as fact without hesitation.

Most correctional institutions for juveniles have generalized programs of mass treatment for their charges. Some, unfortunately, still offer little more than custodial care. As long as a state permits its correctional institutions to be a dumping ground for every delinquent child, regardless of his mental or emotional capacity, the administrator or institutional staff will find it extremely difficult to set up a program that will offer a correctional plan for the individual child.

Size is another problem: most correctional institutions are too large. More than one-third of them are designed to house more than 200 children; experts believe 150 is a desirable maximum. Then, too, there are physical shortcomings—run-down buildings, worn-out heating systems, inadequate sanitary equipment. Another major problem is the lack of sufficient salary funds to attract and hold a well trained staff of adequate size.

Until the man in the street sees the need for change in these conditions there is slight prospect that much lasting reform treatment can be accomplished in the majority of correctional institutions throughout the country. Nevertheless, correctional institutions in some states show significant progress in their work for rehabilitation of the socially unadjusted children committed to their care. The best results are in those states in which the defective delinquents and those children with serious emotional disorders have been singled out and sent to institutions especially designed for them.

In those institutions that have been the most successful, the delinquent is regarded as an individual who has conflicts which he has aggressively expressed against the community. The period of time in the institution is used for intensive treatment and training that direct the child toward creating new social attitudes, establishing vocational competence, developing legitimate leisure-time interests, and restoring and maintaining physical health.

Casework is an integral part of the total institutional plan, and, for the best results, it should be conducted with the child's family at the same time. Within an institution, more than anywhere else, the caseworker has an opportunity for direct and consistent work with the child, since he is always observable by some member of the staff. Casework here becomes a teamwork process, with the caseworker as the coordinator. All members of the staff who have contacts with the child are included in the plan for his rehabilitation. This includes the cook and the gardener, as well as the psychiatrist and the cottage parents.

Casework with the child's family may be carried on by the probation officer or by a worker from a social agency who has access to the family. A cooperative plan is worked out between the worker at the correctional institution and the worker who sees the child's family.

The use of a foster home instead of an institution has a distinct advantage for some children, particularly for the child who needs the normal and informal social environment of a family home. There will always be some children who cannot adjust to group living and at the same time make the necessary adjustment to return to their own family.

Frequent evaluations of the child's progress and the progress of his family are essential in judging how satisfactorily the present program is working toward the final release of the child. Many times an institution keeps a child longer than it should because it has not carefully evaluated his ability to succeed in the community, or because work has not been done outside to reestablish his family or, that proving impossible, to prepare a substitute family to accept the child.

It is of utmost importance that work with the child and family not be ended as soon as the child is released from the institution. The period of readjustment into the home and community is a particularly difficult time for both the child and his family. There must be an understanding and well qualified person who will keep in touch with and give help when needed to the child and to members of his family during the rehabilitation period. Such a person may be the parole officer, a worker from a child or family agency, or, as has been suggested by some authorities, a worker from a statewide agency that has been set up for the exclusive purpose of handling the readjustment of released children and adolescents.

We know that since the early 1960's there has been an increase in juvenile delinquency, and authorities are convinced that certain influences can contribute to delinquency. But there are areas of uncertainty. We cannot say that one specific condition or even any given set of factors will inevitably produce delinquent behavior. Such behavior may appear when certain personal and social factors are brought together in a particular situation; but may not occur a second time when the same combination is present, with all its factors seemingly identical.

We cannot predict that delinquency will occur in every child because of a broken home, poverty, slum life, unhealthy family or neighborhood influences, physical or mental handicap or abnormality, emotional instability, bad companions, lack of education or recreation, or overstimulation by press, radio, television, motion pictures, or comic books. Although we can say that these conditions, or combinations of several of them, provide a more fertile ground for the development of delinquency than would a wholesome environment with emotionally mature parents, economic security, and education and recreation facilities, we must also recognize that they do not always produce delinquent behavior and that the more "normal" situations may not prevent delinquency.

Local, state, and federal agencies, private agencies, and many individuals recognize the need to learn more about the causes, and combinations of causes, of delinquency, and about ways for treating these causes in order to prevent and control delinquent behavior.

The desire to learn more about causes has led many groups into research and study. To attain really effective prevention and control, we must take the following measures: coordinate the findings of these groups; determine what needs have not been met; set aside sufficient funds to train people to work intensively with families and children when pathology is first recognized; establish small institutions for study and treatment of children who show early symptoms of behavior difficulties; set up courses in mental hygiene for all teachers; interest and educate parents so that they will be able to recognize actual danger signals in a child's behavior, and be willing to seek help in evaluating his needs and to sustain a long-term constructive program to meet those needs.

Prevention of delinquency is the responsibility of everyone. After the home, the probation officer and the police are the first bulwark in prevention. Because of their constituted power, they are in strategic positions to furnish enough information to parents, social agencies, church organizations, and community leaders to help in plans for protecting juveniles and preventing delinquent behavior.

The school can contribute by planning a curriculum to meet the educational needs of each child, whether of superior, normal, or limited mental ability, and by giving other types of assistance that are known to be of value. Many schools furnish counseling and guidance services to locate and deal with behavior problems in their early stages, and to help the young person prepare for a job that appeals to him and that is suitable to his capacity. In the modern school, the school social worker and school counselor are considered necessary adjuncts. Many high schools give thoughtfully planned courses that help children to prepare for marriage and family relations, and to develop sound and healthy attitudes toward sex.

Many churches, like many homes, assume responsibility for keeping children out of trouble by providing activity programs for leisure time, and by offering sex education courses to prepare them for family life.

Social agencies have advanced in the problem of juvenile delinquency control too. Since the development of social group work, many agencies have used this valuable method to aid children in personality and social adjustment through participation in group activities. By heightening the status of the child or adolescent, group work often helps divert predelinquent tendencies to socially acceptable behavior.

Agencies of communication—the press, radio, television, the stage, and movies—often encourage efforts for prevention and control of delinquency by arousing interest in the problem and awareness of its scope. Other forms of communication are lectures, exhibits, and pamphlets that interpret existing conditions and outline methods for prevention and control. Many constructive research studies are under way.

Within the Children's Bureau is a Division of Delinquency Service. Its major function is to give technical aid and consultation to states in these areas: coordination and planning of community services to prevent delinquency; treatment and rehabilitation of delinquent youths; training of personnel for services to delinquents.

The National Council on Crime and Delinquency, and the Delinquency Division of the Children's Bureau have been the two most prominent organizations for establishing standards in the field of delinquency control. These organizations conduct studies on various aspects of juvenile delinquency in different types of communities, and on state and local correctional systems.

The President's Task Force on Juvenile Delinquency, in its 1967 report, summarizes some of the difficulties encountered in attempting to prevent and control juvenile delinquency. Among the themes mentioned in the report are found the following.

1. Delinquency is an integrated feature of our society. It is not likely to be removed by crash programs.

2. Broad changes in community structure have to be made, and specific immediate causes of delinquency removed.

3. Delinquent behavior is caused not only by problems of a socio-psychological nature, but also by responses to immediate situations and opportunities.

4. The school system remains an important place for the development of delinquent attitudes and behavior patterns.

5. The solution of youth employment problems is an important objective in any prevention program.

6. The official labeling of juveniles as delinquents may well create more problems than it solves.

7. The police have a critical role in delinquency control.

8. There is a large gap between theory and practice in the juvenile court.

9. A graded series of alternatives to the traditional dispositions of probation or institutionalization should be devised. Stronger communication should be established between correctional programs and the local community.

10. At present we know little or nothing of the effectiveness of potential solutions to juvenile delinquency problems. We need systematic research in this area.

11. The various disparate federal programs in the field of juvenile delinquency need to be integrated and provided with better administrative leadership.

12. The correctional process—its present classification of tasks, and the level of skill needed by personnel to perform their rehabilitative duties—should be evaluated.

CHILD GUIDANCE CLINICS

Too often a child whose overt behavior is indicative of emotional difficulty is left untreated, and he later becomes the child we term "a juvenile delinquent." Children do not ask for help and protection except through their symptomatic behavior.

The child guidance clinic has been established in an attempt to mobilize the resources of the community in behalf of children who are seriously at odds with their environment, or in distress because of unsatisfied inner needs, and whose difficulties are revealed in unhealthful traits, unacceptable behavior, or inability to meet social and scholastic expectations. It renders service by studying and treating selected children, and also by focusing the attention of physicians, teachers, social workers, and parents on the mental hygiene approach to problems of child behavior. The essence of this approach is that behavior is studied objectively, without bias or prejudice, to discover the causes—usually multiple—which produce it, and an effort is made to modify it by eliminating or alleviating harmful causes.

In the title "child guidance clinic," a restricted meaning has been given to a term that has had wide application, because parents, schools, courts, and medical and social agencies of various types have long been engaged in guiding children. Child guidance clinics have attempted to provide guidance whenever the services of these agencies have not been sufficient to meet the child's need. The clinics offer a synthesis of techniques which are more effective in combination than they could be singly. But they can put their combined resources at the service of only a handful of children. Their only hope of wider accomplishment is in strengthening the capacity of other elements of the community to carry day-to-day responsibility for child guidance in its broader sense.

Before 1922, there were only a very few mental hygiene clinics devoting much time to children. In 1909, Dr. William Healy founded the first psychiatric clinic planned specifically for children, the Juvenile Psychopathic Institute of Chicago. This clinic was connected with the Juvenile Court of Chicago, and was the first clinic for children in which the psychiatric, psychological, and social approaches were combined.

Dr. Healy was interested in searching out the causes of delinquency and in finding ways of preventing children from developing into adult criminals. Each offender coming to the clinic was studied from the medical, psychological, and social points of view. Dr. Healy served as physician-psychiatrist and was assisted by psychologists who gave mental tests and probation officers who obtained social histories. The child was regarded as the product of the forces which had been reacting on and within him, and the findings of the Institute showed the close relationship between the child's emotional life and his delinquency.

The clinic was financed for the first five years (1909 through 1913) by private funds, and from 1914 to 1920 by Cook County. In 1920, it was renamed the Institute for Juvenile Research and was taken over by the state of Illinois; its services were extended to cover a wider field of child guidance.

Judge Harvey H. Baker of Boston, who had trained at the clinic as a student, urged the establishment of a similar clinic to serve the Boston Juvenile Court. When he died his friends established the Judge Baker Foundation Clinic in 1917. Dr. Healy and Dr. Augusta Bronner, his assistant, left the Chicago clinic in care of Dr. Herman Adler, who had come from the Boston Psychopathic Hospital, and went to direct the Judge Baker Foundation Clinic, later renamed the Judge Baker Guidance Center.

Two other centers in which the foundations of child guidance were being laid down were the Boston Psychopathic Hospital, which established a clinic for children in 1912, and the Henry Phipps Psychiatric Clinic, established at the Johns Hopkins Hospital in Baltimore in 1913. These two clinics included psychiatric social workers on their staffs, thus setting the precedent for the team approach of the clinic. They also set the pattern for serving the whole community rather than just the juvenile court.

In 1915, a clinic was opened by the Allentown State Hospital in Allentown, Pennsylvania. One of its original purposes was to serve the public schools as a clearinghouse for all children suspected of being in the exceptional class, securing for those children diagnosis and prognosis, and advising school authorities on what environment and course of action would serve the interest of each individual child.

The Ohio Bureau of Juvenile Research was established in 1915 as a division of the State Department of Public Welfare, and set a precedent for direct state responsibility in the care of psychiatric problems of children. Its original purpose was to study delinquency, its causes and motives, and to work for their eradication or correction.

Dr. George F. Inch of the Kalamazoo State Hospital in 1916 persuaded the judge of the Grand Rapids Probate Court and the county commissioners to pay the expenses of a traveling clinic that would examine children on referral from the court. Not much beyond diagnostic service was offered.

While the foundations of scientific child guidance were being established in those various centers, related developments were taking place elsewhere in the psychiatric field. Young physicians were receiving training in the newer dynamic concepts of mental disorder; they were acquiring a broader understanding of their patients, and were learning to take an interest in family, school, and community settings as conditioning factors.

This growth was accelerated by the establishment in 1909 of the National Committee for Mental Hygiene, whose program included efforts for better care of the insane and education of the public in the nature of mental disorders and the need for preventive measures. The committee's work included surveys of the care and treatment of the mentally deficient and mentally disordered, and studies in delinquency and neuroses.

The beginning, in 1918–1919, of formal training in psychiatric social work at Smith College and the New York School of Social Work was impelled by the necessities of World War I.

The development of child guidance clinics was accelerated and strongly influenced by demonstration clinics conducted by the National Committee for Mental Hygiene, through the Division of Delinquency, which had received the financing from the Commonwealth Fund, a private foundation established in 1918.

In 1920, the Fund had asked Professor Henry W. Thurston, of the New York School of Social Work, to formulate a plan for work in child welfare. A temporary advisory committee, including representatives from the fields of psychiatry, psychology, education, social work, as well as representatives from the juvenile court, was formed. The recommendations of·this committee and of Mr. Thurston were considered by the director of the Fund, and a program to deal with methods for the prevention of delinquency was formulated. This program, designed to cover a five-year period, was adopted in November 1921 and initiated early in 1922. Its major purposes were the following: (1) to conduct psychiatric study of difficult and delinquent children, and develop sound methods of treatment based on such study; (2) to develop the work of the visiting teacher; (3) to provide courses of training for those qualified to work in the child guidance field; (4) to extend the knowledge and use of these three methods.

To carry into effect the first three of its purposes, the Fund provided grants to three agencies recognized as leaders in their respective fields: First, the New York School of Social Work was enabled to offer additional courses for psychiatric social workers and visiting teachers, to provide fellowships in psychiatric social work, and to establish a psychiatric clinic known as the Bureau of Child Guidance for the study and treatment of children presenting special problems and for the field training of students. Second, the National Committee for Mental Hygiene was enabled to establish a Division on the Prevention of Delinquency, through which demonstrations of "psychiatric work in the diagnosis and treatment of children coming from the juvenile court" were to be given. Finally, the Public Education Association of New York was enabled to set up an organization known as the National Committee on Visiting Teachers, equipped to conduct demonstrations of visiting-teacher work in a number of cities.

In order to carry out the fourth purpose, the Fund established its own agency, called the Joint Committee on Methods of Preventing Delinquency, which was to coordinate the program as a whole and publish interpretations of the work that had been accomplished in articles or special studies.

In the program as formulated by the Commonwealth Fund, the juvenile court was considered a good starting point for a psychiatric approach on delinquency. In 1922, the Fund's Joint Committee sent announcements, which explained the program, its aims, the scientific basis of the work, and its expectations, to 225 juvenile courts, and published these announcements in appropriate periodicals. The committee offered a demonstration service which would examine and treat problem children, demonstrate methods and values, and help with organization of permanent clinics to follow. This offer was contingent upon a certain degree of interest and upon promise of permanent local support for the work. Replies came from 34 courts, 13 requesting the service, and five stating that such a service was not needed.

Demonstration clinics were established in St. Louis, Norfolk, Dallas, Monmouth County in New Jersey, Minneapolis, Los Angeles, Cleveland, and Philadelphia.

During the five-year demonstration period, child guidance clinic service in the United States had increased, partly as a result of that program, about fourfold. In the eight clinics permanently established as a direct result, the pattern of child guidance had been clarified. The focus of professional attention had shifted from delinquency and the court to the more subtle evidences of maladjustment in the home and the school. Means of linking the clinic with the community had been learned. The mutual responsibility of clinic and social agencies had been revealed and effective methods worked out. Financial policies had been shaped by failures and successes. Channels for educational opportunities had been formulated.

In 1927, at the end of the demonstration program, the Commonwealth Fund decided to continue advisory service to cities which sought aid in establishing child guidance work. The Joint Committee changed its name from the Joint Committee on Methods of Preventing Delinquency to the Division on Community Clinics.

Its task was to help communities to realize their programs in the soundest and quickest way, and to aid in the maintenance of high standards by discouraging inferior endeavors posing as child guidance.

Today's clinic functions as an agency for helping children adjust to their immediate environment, with special emphasis on their emotional and social relationships, so they will be able to develop, to the utmost of their capacities, into well balanced, mature human beings. This task is performed in two ways: (1) the direct study and treatment (by a synthesis of psychiatric treatment, psychological social work, and some pediatric techniques) of children whose lack of adjustment has become evident to some or all of the adults concerned with their welfare; (2) the circulation of those concepts and attitudes, which are grouped for convenience under the heading "mental hygiene," throughout the agencies responsible for child care—the home, the school, the social agencies, and the courts. The clinic teaches by serving some children, and, by teaching, serves all children.

For its financial support, it looks to the sources commonly used by social agencies—the United Community Fund or private donors. Its staff includes a full-time psychiatrist who acts as executive head, a full-time psychologist, two or three full-time psychiatric social workers, and two or three clerks. With this staff, a clinic may be able to accept slightly more than 300 new cases a year.

The clinic selects for study and treatment children of normal intelligence, whose difficulties are traceable to emotional imbalance, whether in the child or parent; or to a lag between the child's capacity and the demands made upon him, of which educational maladjustment is an example; or to destructive influences in the social environment. Children are brought to the clinic for one or more of these reasons: unacceptable behavior, such as disobedience, stealing, lying, temper tantrums, and truancy; personality problems, such as nervousness, inattention, shyness; school difficulties, such as poor work, retardation, or indifference; some crisis in the child's life—such as transfer from a broken home—that makes an analysis of his capacities and qualities desirable as a guide for constructive action. Clinic cases include an unusually high proportion of children with I.Q.'s both above and below the "normal range."

Since the child's problem is usually due to an emotionally disturbed family situation, coordinated treatment of child and parent is essential for best results. Children are referred to the clinic chiefly by social agencies, schools, courts, parents, and relatives.

The interchange of experience and technique between the child guidance clinic and other social agencies takes place through the medium of the cooperative case; the agency refers a problem to the clinic; the agency worker takes part in the initial conference and usually administers most of the treatment processes agreed upon.

In addition to this intensive teamwork, provision is usually made for briefer contact between the clinic staff and the social personnel of the community through observation visits to the clinic and through short courses given by the clinic staff for agency workers. The clinic influences public opinion chiefly through the schools, social agencies, and physicians with whom it cooperates on cases, and to some extent by lectures and courses of instruction for parent-teacher associations and child study groups.

Several states are still without adequate child guidance or psychiatric services, and in many small towns and rural areas such services are available only on an itinerant basis.

Nevertheless, throughout the years the juvenile courts have co-operated closely with mental health services if they were available in a locality. The services have come from four different sources.

1. They may be provided within the juvenile court system. Many courts have psychologists, either part-time or full-time. In addition, a psychiatrist may be available to provide diagnoses and some treatment to the juvenile delinquents.

2. They may be provided by a child guidance clinic or a university department in the community.

3. They may be provided by private practitioners. The cost of private services limits the clientele to upper- and middle-class juvenile delinquents. The great majority of people who petition juvenile courts for help in controlling their children are from the lower class. In addition, public officials refer their children to the juvenile courts. On the other hand upper-class families are more apt to detect deviant behavior in their children early and to use private services for their rehabilitation than are members of the lower class.

4. They may be provided by community health clinics. Since 1960 a number of community health clinics have been established and, in some areas they have replaced the child guidance clinics in services to delinquent youths.

Supplementary Readings

Abrahamsen, David. *The Psychology of Crime*. Columbia University Press, New York, 1960.

Allen, Francis A. *The Borderland of Criminal Justice*. University of Chicago Press, Chicago, 1964.

Bennett, Ivy. *Delinquent and Neurotic Children: A Comparative Study*. Basic Books, New York, 1959.

Bernstein, Saul. *Youth on the Streets: Work with Alienated Youth Groups*. Association Press, New York, 1964.

Burchinal, Lee G., Ed. *Rural Youth in Crisis: Facts, Myths, and Social Change*. U.S. Department of Health, Education, and Welfare, Washington, D.C., 1965.

Caplan, Gerald. *An Approach to Community Mental Health*. Grune and Stratton, New York, 1961.

Caplan, Gerald, Ed. *Prevention of Mental Disorders in Children*. Holt, Rinehart, and Winston, New York, 1961.

Children's Bureau. *Juvenile Court Statistics*. U.S. Department of Health, Education, and Welfare, Washington, D.C., 1964–65.

Eissler, K. R., Ed. *Searchlights on Delinquency*. International Universities Press, New York, 1949.

Fleisher, Belton. The Economics of Delinquency. Quadrangle Books, Chicago, 1966.

Gibbons, Don C. *Changing the Lawbreaker*. Prentice-Hall, Englewood Cliffs, New Jersey, 1965.

Havighurst, Robert J., et al. *Growing Up in River City*. Wiley, New York, 1962.

Martin, J. M., and Fitzpatrick, J. P. *Delinquent Behavior, A Redefinition of the Problem*. Random House, New York, 1965.

Matza, David. *Delinquency and Drift*. Wiley, New York, 1964.

McCorkle, L. W., Elias, A., and Bixby, F. L. *The Highfields Story: A Unique Experiment in the Treatment of Juvenile Delinquency*. Holt, Rinehart, and Winston, New York, 1958.

Nelson, E. K. *Community Approaches to the Prevention of Crime and Delinquency*. University of Southern California, Los Angeles, 1961.

President's Commission on Law Enforcement and the Administration of Justice. *Task Force Report: Juvenile Delinquency and Youth Crime*. U.S. Government Printing Office, Washington, D.C., 1967.

Rosenheim, Margaret K. *Justice for the Child*. Free Press, New York, 1962.

Rubin, Ted, and Smith, Jack F. *The Future of the Juvenile Court: Implications for Correctional Manpower and Training*. Joint Commission on Correctional Manpower and Training, Washington, D.C., 1968.

Sheridan, William H. *Delinquent Children in Penal Institutions*. U.S. Department of Health, Education, and Welfare, Washington, D.C., 1964.

Sheridan, William H. *Standards for Juvenile and Family Courts*. U.S. Department of Health, Education, and Welfare, Washington, D.C., 1966.

Spergel, Irving. *Street Gang Work: Theory and Practice*. Addison-Wesley, Reading, Mass., 1966.

Srole, Leo, et al. *Mental Health in the Metropolis*. McGraw-Hill, New York, 1962.

Wheeler, Stanton, Ed. *Controlling Delinquents*. Wiley, New York, 1967.

Wolfgang, Marvin E., Savitz, Leonard, and Johnson, Norman, Eds. *The Sociology of Crime and Delinquency*. Wiley, New York, 1962.

10

Children in Foster Homes

In the field of child welfare, when children live away from their own homes their place of abode is in either a foster home, an institution, or an adoptive home. The foster home, the institution, and the adoptive home have a definite place in an overall child care program.

Until about 1917, orphanages were recommended for any youngsters who presented problems to society. In that year, a shift from the use of the institution to the use of the foster home for substitute parental care began, and it steadily gained momentum in the following three decades. This change was due to an increased knowledge of the needs of children and a consequent reaction against institutional care, which in the main did not seem to meet these needs. In fact, the reaction became so extreme that, at one period, institutions were tolerated only when no foster home was available.

Foster homes, however, also prove to have their serious weaknesses. It therefore became necessary to reconsider both the role of the institution and the role of the foster home. The pendulum has started to swing back toward a middle position on the arc between the two extreme attitudes. We now realize that the question is not one of institution versus foster home, but rather one on what kind of substitute care is best for the growth and development of each particular child. Institutions exist because there are children who need the type of care offered in group living. Foster home care provides something that is more similar to the "own home" situation, in which the majority of children feel more secure and thus free to grow and develop physically, emotionally, and socially.

Although the needs of the child should guide us in any placement decision, we often find that the type of resource immediately available is the determining factor. It is well, therefore, to review the two types of substitute care that exist for the child who requires it. The first is the foster home. The problem of securing the proper type of home for an individual, as well as the shortage of homes and the high rate of turnover in homes, all make it difficult to give a child the security that is the objective in every placement. A great deal must be done to inform the public about foster home programs; and the types of problems that can be lessened by foster home placement must be more clearly differentiated from those which will be only intensified by this type of placement. The second is the institution. There is no shortage of these, but a surplus—in fact, the problem is that there are too many of them, but too few that are professionally oriented.

Most foster care, whether in institutions or foster homes, has been seriously inadequate. The low board rates paid foster parents and the meager salaries paid institution workers are not commensurate with the services expected, and this fact often has prevented the selection of the kind of substitute parent a child needed. Those engaged in providing foster care for children have a grave responsibility in making sure that the basic and special needs of each child are met and that he is placed in the setting most capable of meeting these needs. To perform this duty best, the child welfare worker, in addition to being familiar with the child, his problems, and his background, must have a knowledge of both foster home and institutional facilities.

THE PLACEMENT SETTING

In this section we will outline certain general principles to answer the question, when do we make an institutional placement and when a foster home placement? However, the appropriate placement for each child must be decided after skilled casework has determined the needs of the individual child. Among the factors which should determine where a child's welfare can best be achieved are the nature of the child's relationships to his own family, the strength and permanence of the emotional ties which bind him to them, as well as his age, physical and mental condition, temperament, and habits.

We know that some parent-child relationships cannot be adjusted to a natural home, and that some cannot be adjusted to any placement situation. We know that substitute care is not good for every child, but yet we cannot believe compulsively in the family at all costs.

There seems to be fairly complete agreement on the fact that "young children" need the anchorage and affection that can be secured only by the experience of belonging to one person. The "young child," therefore, should not be placed in an institution. There is some difference of opinion on the age limit below which a child should be classified as a "young child": Some would classify a young child as one below three or four years of age; others would include all preschool children in this category; some feel that all children under seven or eight years of age fall into this group; still others believe that the term "young children" refers to all children in their preadolescent years. However, there is a general consensus that institutional living is too complex for the child under six, since it tends to be a continuous group experience for him.

In general, family life in a foster home is to be chosen for nearly every child capable of forming new family relationships. It is desirable for all children under six, and has been found to be practically a "must" for infants.

In contrast to the very young child, children between the ages of approximately six and 12 may have something to gain from an institution. During these years, adults become diminishingly important, and competition and cooperative relationships with other children grow. The adult influence never quite disappears, however. The most important phenomena to observe in children who are at this intermediate stage are the behavior patterns that they are developing.

Generally institutions can best serve the following groups:

1. The child who, because of illness or accident involving the parents, must be temporarily out of his home but who has such an emotional tie with his parents that it is difficult for him or them to accept foster parents. This child responds better in the impersonal atmosphere of an institution.

2. The adolescent who is going through the period of breaking away from his own home and finds a foster home so repressive he cannot take root in it; or the adolescent who has been disappointed in adults whom he loves, and dares not relate to other adults. The adolescent coming from one of these situations will be determined to prove the foster home is bad and foster parents intolerable. Institutions are advisable for these children.

3. The child with behavior problems that are not understood and with whom the average foster parent cannot cope. For this child, the institution may be used as a study home where, in an objective, sympathetic situation, his temperament, desires, habits, and ideas may be observed in order that treatment and a permanent beneficial plan can be worked out. An institution thus used must be equipped to give skilled services and relate these to the day-to-day life of the child.

4. The child whose health needs and care have to be attended to on a strict schedule that his own parents cannot be trusted to keep. Many parents feel their own status less threatened by institutions because they believe that the change in environment is the important factor, and thus that the need for placement is not their fault.

In addition to the groups of children mentioned, the three following groups are considered to progress favorably in institutions:

1. The physically handicapped child (blind, deaf, epileptic, crippled). Partly because it is difficult to find foster parents willing and equipped to take handicapped children, and partly because special training is necessary for teaching the handicapped, it is recognized that institutional care is valuable for this group. A program planned and operated for the specific needs of the crippled, blind, epileptic, and deaf supplies special training to broaden the capabilities of those afflicted.

2. The low-grade feeble-minded. High-grade subnormals, however, must be treated individually, and only a small percentage need be in institutions.

3. The advanced delinquent who has become a menace to himself and to the community. The institution can be used for study, observation, and treatment of those children for whom a greater degree of skill than the placing agency is able to find in a foster home is necessary for carrying out treatment.

Foster home placement is a constructive alternative to a child's own home under certain conditions, as the following:

1. There is obvious need for a foster home because the mother is ill and has no available resources, or because the parents have died, or because the parents are feebleminded or alcoholics.

2. A parent projects her own emotional problems onto a child and cannot be helped to see her part in the child's problem.

3. A parent and child, despite the understanding of what separation means, find that they must endure it because they cannot work out their problems in a family unit.

4. A parent requires separation from the child to work out alone what she feels she must do.

5. A parent's sense of inadequacy is due to an identification with her own inadequate parents, and is too deeply rooted to yield to casework treatment.

6. A parent's untreatable immaturity precludes the minimum of security necessary for her child.

7. Parents' unconscious motivations dominate their relationship to the child. An illustration of this kind of motivation is the unresolved resentment against having to share the spouse with the child as in childhood they had to share one parent with the other parent.

Whatever the reason for it, placement in a foster home is presumed to be for a limited period of time. The foster parents accept the temporary nature of their task and the child, too, is made to realize that this home is not permanent.

It is equally important to know when not to place. A mother who will prevent any satisfactory placement is the mother who insists on immediate placement because her ambivalence makes her fearful that she may not carry out her decision if she were to have time to think it over. Also, the parent who feels guilty because she has rejected her child vacillates between lavishing affection and showing outright rejection; she cannot tolerate affection between herself and the child, and at the same time she prevents the child from relating to a foster mother. A placement in such a case is likely to result in failure. The worker, then, is confronted with an ominous array of stipulations on when to place, and where and how. Consequently, it takes courage to "play God" in the light of our present-day understanding, and to participate actively in separating a child from his home and determining the best method of substitute care for each individual child.

Neither the institution nor the foster home should be regarded as the only form of care. Changes in the child's needs or his situation may necessitate interchangeable use of both forms. The primary objective, for the duration of every case, must be that of serving most adequately a child who is under the care of the agency.

Foster care is provided in various ways: at one extreme, the parents themselves find foster parents with whom they make informal private arrangements; at the other, placement results from court action and the state retains permanent custody of the child.

TYPES OF FOSTER HOME CARE

At the present time, there are five possible types of foster homes. There is the *free home*, where the foster parents are not paid for keeping the children. In this type, often the foster parents accept affection and complete responsibility for the child as compensation. This home is of limited usefulness today. Previously it was the main type employed, and the workers used the home in a humble and self-apologetic manner, weighted down by the need to be grateful.

Another type of home is the *work home*. Here the children receive board and lodging in return for their services. This home is of very limited use today, suitable only for certain older children.

The *wage home* is the same as a work home except that wages are paid to the foster child in addition to his board and lodging.

The *adoptive home* provides a child with free care, with the understanding that if the placement is satisfactory, the child may be adopted.

The home most useful today is the *boarding home*, and this is the type with which we shall be concerned in this chapter. The foster parents receive remuneration for their care of the children in the form of board rates. This type of home is suitable for the majority of children requiring foster family care.

From past and more recent statistics we may draw the following significant indications: that there is a trend from institutional to foster family placement of children; that there is a marked increase in foster family care for children under public auspices; that under private auspices there is a smaller decrease in foster family care for children than there was in institutional care; that more extensive use is made of the boarding home than of the other types of homes. These trends can be attributed to our modern philosophy and practice in regard to substitute care. The fact that foster home care has increased is a result of the concept that for most children a family life is preferable.

The increasingly prominent role played by public funds is an indication of the greater responsibility assumed by the federal government.

State agencies have been stimulated by public interest to provide better services for children, and they have received federal funds to aid them in doing so. These developments have encouraged use of foster family care.

The increased use of the boarding home reflects concern for the real welfare of the child. The principle of making children work for their living has been discarded. Moreover, monetary payment to foster parents is considered preferable to some other kind of payment that is actually at the expense of the emotions of the child.

THE SELECTION OF A FOSTER HOME

In foster home care, the most vital need is to place the child in a home in which he has some chance for happiness. To guarantee that chance, great care must be exercised in home-finding.

Let us define the term "home-finding": It is a process by which prospective foster homes are first *found* and listed, then *evaluated*, and then *selected* for use by the social agency.

It is a grave task, which carries great responsibility. Finding the right kind of foster home is basic to the success of foster family care.

Home-finding is not to be viewed as a high-powered process that automatically turns out a specified number of homes in record time. It entails much more than just finding any home; it requires the use of the most skillful casework methods and should be undertaken only by well trained, qualified workers. Too often, this important task has been put into the hands of new, inexperienced workers. Child placing differs from other casework in the degree of responsibility that falls upon the worker. Without suitable homes and (once these are found) the correct matching of the child to a home, the value of foster family care may be lost.

Home-finding has gone through various stages. At first, a moralistic approach was used. The foster home was considered either good or bad, and it was the job of the home-finder to measure the goodness and the badness. The worker would suddenly descend upon the unsuspecting foster parent, catching her off guard, in order to see if there were any signs of liquor in the house or dirt under the rugs, or if the yard was well kept. If the superficial evidence pointed to cleanliness and respectability, the home was considered good.

Along with this philosophy went the belief that the home selected was always right and that if the foster child failed in the home it was not because of any demerits of the home but because of something within the child.

As home-finding developed, there came into use the "invaluable" outline. Every home was evaluated according to a strict, complete, minute outline. In this way, the worker felt she could know the home. But in reality the outline gave only a very static picture of superficial values and served to mask any doubt the worker might feel on whether she really understood the forces operating within the home.

Since the advent of psychiatric influence in social casework, home-finding has benefited greatly as a result of the recognition of the importance of emotional forces in the home. The home-finder now realizes it is necessary to study the home in order to gain some insight into the motivations of the foster parents and into the intrafamilial relationships. Thus she finds that the determination of a proper home does not rest on a measuring of goodness or badness, but depends on an understanding of what motivates certain behavior and how this will affect the foster child. The home is now looked at primarily in terms of its interactive potentialities. Thus home-finding has become a living, dynamic part of casework—a most essential part of a foster home program.

Even though today the physical attributes of the home are not the main consideration, they are still important. The child's physical needs must be met and the home study must determine whether or not the home can do so. Often the physical environment has important emotional value for the child, and may act as a constructive or destructive catalyst on the emotional forces operating in the home.

THE WORKER'S ROLE IN EVALUATION OF FOSTER PARENTS

The motivations leading foster parents to request a child are many and varied. Some are unconscious, others conscious. They range from the desire to utilize vacant space to the complex need for narcissistic gratifications. Whatever these needs may be, it is not the task of the home-finder to label them either good or bad. Rather it is her job to understand the motivations and to determine whether they are so neurotic that the needs of foster children will be sacrificed to them.

It is the task of the worker to determine whether or not it will be possible to match the needs of the foster parents with the needs of certain foster children and in that way make a suitable placement.

Equally important, and complexly tied in with the motivations of

the foster parents in seeking a child, are the familial relationships existing among the members of the foster family group—the basic emotional
relationships of one individual in the family to another. The foster home
worker cannot expect to find a home with absolutely no problems and
no faults. However, it is generally accepted that the foster parents who
are normally gratified in their own lives, especially in areas of love and
achievement, will be the most satisfactory foster parents. Only harm
can come from placing a child in a home in which the family's emotional needs have an excessive and unreasonable quality.

It is essential that a child not be placed in a home as a means to a
foster parent's end—for instance, to help the spoiled child in the home,
or to bring the husband and wife closer together, or to fill the neurotic
craving for a child just lost. This kind of motivation would only work
to the detriment of the foster child, who would be merely a tool in the
pattern of relationships within the family.

Because negative aspects are to be expected in every home, what is
important is to sense and understand them. If they are not too bad, they
can often be handled by the skillful worker, and even neutralized by
the placement of a child who will fit into that particular setting.

Taking all these factors into mind—the motives of the foster parents in asking for a child, the interrelationships among the members of
the foster family, and the physical standards of the foster home—the
child welfare worker must determine whether or not a home can offer
to the foster child the tolerance, affection, flexibility, and security that
he needs.

QUALIFICATIONS OF FOSTER PARENTS

The outstanding contribution of a good foster home is that it satisfies
the child's needs for security and recognition; to fulfill those needs, the
foster parents must have certain qualifications.

It is important that the foster parents have a settled philosophy of
life. They should have sound moral and ethical standards, and an appreciation of spiritual values. In attempting to meet a child's needs, foster
parents must be sensitive and understanding enough to adapt themselves
to whatever effects that child's emotional deprivations may have on his
own personality.

The foster parents must be able to treat the child on his own level.
They should compare his achievements with his own previous record,
rather than with those of a group, and give him praise whenever it is

deserved. Every child who must leave his own home and live away from his own family suffers a profound social and emotional disturbance never altogether compensated. The mere fact that he must be cared for away from his own parents carries implications that may affect his response to foster care; he may even have been "threatened" with foster home placement. If a child could talk out his problems it would be easier to help him; but because children are inarticulate, they express their difficulties by their behavior.

It is essential that the foster parents be willing to work with the agency, and be able to accept and use the agency's assistance in dealing with behavior and personality deviations outside their previous experience.

Perhaps one of the most difficult things for foster parents to do is to maintain pleasant, constructive relations with a child's own parents if they visit the children in the foster home. In any communication with the parents, there must be close cooperation betwen the foster parents and the agency. It often requires great tact and resourcefulness, when children are being cared for in a foster home, to keep the real parents from being resentful and jealous of the foster parents and fearful that their children are being won away from them. Yet for the children's sake, especially if it is planned that they may eventually be returned to their own homes, such reactions by parents must be avoided, and the children should be encouraged to keep up contacts with their own families.

The child should never be told that he will be sent away from the foster home if he doesn't behave. He should at all times be assured that the foster parents want him in their home and that they consider him a part of it—that he is important for his own sake.

The child should not be permitted to shirk his reasonable responsibilities; if he undertakes an obligation that is within his power to meet, he should be expected to fulfill it. The foster parents should be interested in his activities and progress, and should be ready with help and support where needed. The child should be encouraged to develop any natural talents and abilities he may have.

The foster family will naturally have a place in the social and recreational life of the community, and the child is entitled to participate as a full member of the family in those activities that are suitable for his age group. There should be plenty of opportunity and facilities for recreation and companionship. Except in work homes, where a work pattern is prescribed, children should not be required to do work other than simple home duties which do not interfere with school, health, and necessary recreation. A child who is required to perform certain tasks in the home, suitable to his own capacities, tends to develop a feeling of security and importance, since the tasks assure him of a responsible place in the home and afford an opportunity for accomplishment. Children in work homes may be employed only as permitted under the school and labor codes.

All children must attend school as specified under state law, and they should be encouraged to obtain the maximum amount of education possible in keeping with their ability and in view of possible future occupations. Arrangements for vocational or special training may be worked out with the agency. Most agencies have some provision for a personal allowance for the child. This gives the child an opportunity to learn how to spend money, plus a feeling of independence.

THE PROCEDURE IN FOSTER HOME PLACEMENT

An office visit by prospective foster parents has a value that is generally accepted, and it is being required more and more. First of all, it is thought useful to place some responsibility on the applicants. Their visit to the office is often indicative of their interest and purposefulness, and it immediately gives them an active part in the enterprise.

This first interview with the applicant is the start of the casework process which eventually results in acceptance or rejection of the home. The majority of first interviews will yield sufficient information to determine whether further study should follow. However, basing a rejection on the first interview alone is not wise, for it places too much responsibility on the skill of the worker.

In the office interview, the worker presents the application blank, which the applicant may sign at that time or at some later date. In home-finding today, it is believed wise for the worker to use the application blank freely as an opening for interpreting to the applicant just what is involved in being a foster parent.

This is a main function of the office interview—to give the applicants a realistic idea of the experience of foster parenthood. The worker helps the prospective foster parents to understand what is involved in the process and what their responsibility will be to the child, to the agency, and to the child's parents. She also attempts to help them comprehend the function of the agency and the child in the total placement process.

The worker must see the applicants as they are, and not as the agency would like them to be. Instead of looking for an ideal, the worker must see the actual persons plus their potentialities and capabilities—their willingness and capacity to change and learn with new experiences, their tolerance and basic understanding of children.

The child welfare worker doing home-finding is limited by three important considerations. One is that the prospective foster parent comes to the agency not as a client seeking help, but as a giver of help who is offering the agency needed assistance. Another is the time element with which the worker must deal. She cannot, as she might be able to in most other types of cases, take a long time to understand her client. She must achieve her objectives within one or two office interviews and a few home visits. Third, the worker is faced by a person who most likely is looking upon this experience as either an acceptance or rejection. A rejection of the home is invariably interpreted by the applicant as a rejection of her. Thus, for the applicant the period preceding decision by the agency will be marked by fear and anxiety.

These considerations must all be incorporated into the casework skills utilized by the home-finder. She must be able to accept the foster parents' offer of help and, without losing their cooperation, explain the need for an adequate investigation. Within a limited period of time, she must learn enough about the home to arrive at a conclusion on its suitability for use. If she must reject the home, she must do it in such a way that she does not reject the foster home applicants themselves.

The office interview furnishes the worker with a means of observing the applicants, which is an important aid in understanding them. Not only are the things the applicants say important, but when and how they say them. Are they tense and nervous, or natural and relaxed? Do they tenaciously cling to a vision of an ideal foster child of a certain sex and age, and are they unwilling or unable to change? Do they set up rigid demands which make their real desire for foster parenthood questionable? How do they speak of their own family—are they independent beings or merely images of their parents? Do they show resistance to any part of the plan? How do they appear to accept the limitations that the agency would impose upon them?

It is hoped that, in this initial interview, it will be possible for the worker and the applicants to decide together whether or not they wish to continue with the application. The applicant should feel free to discontinue or continue, and he should feel that he had his just share in the decision.

During the office interview, it is customary to explain to the applicants that it will be necessary to make home visits and to obtain their cooperation in this procedure. This is not as easy as it sounds, for the applicant may have difficulty in accepting the fact of investigation.

The home visit is a continuation of the casework process already begun, and it serves to clarify further the worker's understanding of the prospective foster parents. It is a means of seeing the home as it is and also of observing how the occupants behave within its setting.

Careful observation is needed to gain insight into the emotional forces operating within the home. Much can be learned from the emotional tones and movements displayed by the family members. In seeing the family together, the worker can glean some feeling about the relationships. It may be possible to observe who plays the dominant role in the family, and how that domination is accepted; the kind of participation, if any, displayed by the children in the family life; how various members of the family, and the servants if there are any, feel about having a foster child come into the home. All these considerations must be taken into account by the worker in her attempt to understand the family. Thus the home visits become an invaluable part of the home-finding process.

The worker needs to know something about the early experiences and background of the prospective foster parents. But these factors in themselves are not as meaningful as is an understanding of the way the foster parents felt about them in the past, how they dealt with them, and how they regard them now.

The use of outside references in learning about the foster family was formerly a universal practice. Today there is no set policy; different agencies make use of them in varying degrees, if at all. The trend is away from reliance on this type of information, especially when the worker has gained security in her professional skills and experience.

Most references can at best give a picture of the family's standing and acceptance in the community. It has been found that people who supply references generally tend to praise, apparently endorsing the philosophy that people who would open their home to a child must be good and kind and worthwhile. One outside reference still used to a great extent is that of the family physician. However, it is used as mainly a medical reference rather than a social one. Agencies also use the school references to some extent to verify the adjustment of the children in the prospective foster family.

Throughout the home-finding process, the worker constantly weighs and evaluates, and finally she is in the position of denying or gratifying the important wish of someone who has offered something to her. It is in this decision that she feels the culmination of her responsibility.

There may be many reasons for rejection of a foster home. It may be that the home is not within the placing area of the agency, or that it is not located in a satisfactory neighborhood offering the minimum advantages to the child, such as adequate medical care, schooling, and recreational facilities. Perhaps the physical health of the prospective foster parents is not good enough to care for foster children.

Perhaps the rejections are based on the motivation of the foster parents and on familial relationships. The home would be rejected if the need of the applicants to have a child was so neurotic that it would be detrimental to any child placed there. A rejection could be made if one or both of the applicants were deemed unable to accept the responsibility of another child without destructive disruption in their present family life.

A home would be questioned if it were offered for use merely to obtain financial remuneration when the parents were insecure and had no real interest in children. The home would be questioned if a child was desired merely as a tool to achieve a change in the family's own child or in their marital relationship. Workers may find it difficult to reject a home if they have identified it with their own home and so seem to be rejecting their own home.

It can be seen that there are no fixed answers to a question of rejection. The worker has an unevadable responsibility in this task, which requires a great deal of insight and understanding.

Applicants should be told why they cannot take children for foster care. They have a right to know. It is very important, of course, to handle the rejection in such a way that it does not leave lasting unpleasant effects upon the applicant or upon the community.

There are various methods of refusal, and the one used depends on the individual situation. The desired objective is for both the applicant and the worker to make the rejection a joint result. However, this is more easily said than done.

One method that is generally recognized to be bad practice is to make the reason for the rejection vague and evasive. This only increases the applicant's anxiety and hostility. She does not know just why she was refused and she may not be sure whether she was refused permanently; therefore she is continually hoping and trying.

Also, prolonging an investigation after a decision of refusal has been reached is very unwise unless it is necessary to do so in order to obtain some reason for refusal that will not be destructive to the applicant. The prolongation only increases the applicant's frustration and makes the refusal more difficult to accept. Generally speaking, the applicant should be informed of the decision as soon as possible.

Once she has approved a home, the home-finder's job is finished unless her duties also require her to supervise the child in the home. If she does this, she can go on with diagnosis and evaluation.

CENTRALIZATION AND DECENTRALIZATION

Whether the home-finder has the dual task of finding the home and then supervising the child within the home, or whether she is through once she has approved the home depends on how the home-finding process is organized within the agency. It may be either centralized or decentralized.

The centralized plan operates usually in the following manner. The agency has a special department in which the workers do nothing except home-finding. In this department, in addition to the home-finders, there are usually one or two staff members who work in liaison with those in the agency who are in need of homes in which to place children.

Under the centralized system, the worker is not under the urgent pressure of finding a home immediately for a certain child so she can spend adequate time in studying the home.

In situations in which the home has been in use for some time, the worker as a result of constant contacts with foster parents, may lose her professional objectivity in her opinions about them, the manner in which they operate the home, and the way they deal with the child. A home-finder in the centralized system can go into that home and evaluate it objectively, taking into account the worker's experience with the home; thus the home may be preserved for use with other children for whom it might be desirable.

If the centralized home-finding process is to function effectively, it is important for the worker who is supervising the child in the home to evaluate this home critically from time to time. Only in this way can the department be aware of the continuing suitability of the home. The home-finder merely begins the process of examining and evaluating.

Under the centralized system, the home-finder carries out the entire home-finding process and withdraws after approval or rejection of the home. If a home, after a period of use, needs a reevaluation, the home-finder again provides her services.

The centralized system is used in an agency in which case loads are high and there is a need for the full-time services of home-finders. In small agencies, it is not a necessary or practical plan, since case loads are not high and each worker has time for home-finding.

Criticism of the centralized system has been that there is a lack of understanding and cooperation between the home-finding and the supervisory departments. The home-finder, it is said, tends to identify so much with the foster parents that she loses a feel for the child, whereas the children's worker tends to identify with the child to such an extent that she often does not understand the foster parents and hence makes a request for a home without having much realization of the difficulties and factors involved in its selection. An advantage claimed for the centralized plan is that the home-finder has more time to devote to the home-finding process and therefore can investigate more homes and do a more intensive job with each. In studying the home, the worker can look at it objectively in terms of its value as a foster home for general use.

The decentralized system is used in an agency in which there is not a special home-finding department but in which everyone, at least in the foster home department, does home-finding. One advantage that has been cited for this system is that one worker contacts the home and continues to work with it throughout the child's stay there. In this way, it is possible for one worker to build up a good relationship with the foster family for the duration of placement. Another asset mentioned is that the decentralized home-finding process is more informal. Further there is a clarification of the agency's function as a child-placing agency whose main purpose is to serve the children; if this main purpose is established, the foster parents are important only as they serve the needs of the child.

THE NEED FOR FOSTER HOMES

With the development of urbanization and higher standards in the foster home placement field, there has been a corresponding lack of foster homes. This deficiency was particularly noticeable during the war years. At that time many homes were broken up by the draft; mothers needed to work for financial reasons and many felt a patriotic duty to do so. This necessitated placement of their children. Day care was provided for many children, but there were still a great many others needing regular full-time foster family care.

While the need for child-placing facilities increased, the number of available homes decreased. Many foster families were broken up by the war and could not continue their foster home activities; many foster mothers found outside jobs which enabled them to make more money than they could as foster mothers, in addition to giving them the status of performing a patriotic duty. There was too little emphasis during the war years on foster parenthood as a patriotic occupation.

In addition to the loss of old homes, there was, of course, great difficulty in finding new ones. During this time also there was a lack of skilled child welfare workers, which complicated the placement problem.

The housing shortage was an important factor contributing to the increase in children needing placement and to the insufficient number of homes.

There is no doubt that the deficit of homes has resulted in the selection of many which would not have been used if homes were plentiful. In weighing the positive and negative factors, the worker has tended to accept the home if the positive slightly outweighed the negative. Many foster homes have been crammed with more children than they should have and this has had detrimental effects on both the foster parents and the children.

One beneficial aspect resulting from this acute home shortage has been a reevaluation of standards carried out by many child placing agencies. These agencies faced the fact that they would not be able to find nearly the number of homes they needed if they kept their prewar standards. It was almost impossible not to lower them. The important thing was to do the lowering with the least harm to the child. Thus many agencies in the field recognized a need for an evaluation of their current standards to see what could be eliminated without resultant damage to the foster child.

It was seen that there was a need for a more realistic basis for the selection of foster homes from previously rejected parents that had been grouped under such labels as "too old," "widowed," "too young," or "no experience with children."

In reevaluating standards, we need to recognize what is essential to the needs of the child and what can be dispensed with in most cases. Many physical standards can be modified, when necessary, as long as the child receives the basic love and affection and opportunity for emotional growth that he requires.

It has become increasingly recognized and appreciated that the board rate paid the foster parent may well have an important effect on the number of suitable foster home applications. During the growth of social work, there was always an image of the lady bountiful who should not be paid for her services. This feeling is still reflected today in the salaries of social workers. Foster parenthood, too, has had such a heavy veil of altruism attached to it that foster parents have been considered good people who did not need to be paid.

There is an increasing awareness today of the importance of paying the foster parents adequately for the job they perform. Social agencies and children demand a great deal from foster parents. We depend on their services for desirable placement for most children. Certainly they should be paid according to the value of their services.

Adequate remuneration for the job of foster parenthood would contribute to a feeling of responsibility and pride on the part of foster parents. There would be incentive to be a foster parent and to do a competent job. Working on this assumption, the Connecticut Children's Aid Society at one time raised its board rates for babies. It secured 22 more homes than it had in the previous year. There was also an improvement in the quality of the applications and the homes obtained.

The need is to provide board rates high enough to attract families of average income who would be interested in becoming foster parents and who would take an interest in the child, but not so high that the rates would attract persons for financial reasons alone. Board rates vary throughout the country, depending on age and physical condition of the child.

RECRUITING FOSTER HOMES

In order to secure an adequate number of foster homes, applications must continually be stimulated. In general, practicing foster parents have been the best recruiters of new foster homes that meet the standards for acceptance. This recruitment source increases in proportion to the satisfaction of the foster parent. If foster parents are dissatisfied with the agency and their job, they do not make very good publicity agents.

A number of foster home applications are secured through ads in the newspapers. However, the percentage acceptable out of the number that applies in answer to an advertisement is very meager, and the elimination of the unsuitable homes is time-consuming. Also, the many homes refused must be handled carefully in order not to incur their ill will, which could be harmful to the agency in the community. People have a hard time understanding why their homes are refused when the agency still asks for more. The trouble with an ad in the newspaper is that the information it gives is too scant for interpretation of requirements and standards.

Often better results are obtained through direct personal contact with various clubs and groups throughout the community. This personal contact, in the form of formal addresses, plus general contacts, provide a fair source of homes. Radio is also a useful publicity medium, and more use should be made of it.

What this task of seeking sufficient homes really amounts to is one of skillful community organization. We need to reach the general public to let it know what the needs are and how we attempt to meet these needs. The job is one requiring more than casework skills alone; it calls for good community organization techniques and the use of downright plain publicity. For their publicity, social agencies could make good use of publicity experts, a type of service they have made too little use of in the past.

The publicity might be accompanied by a skillful interpretation of just what foster parenthood means and requires. Not only must the needs of the child be presented, but the role of foster parenthood must receive the respect and distinction it deserves.

LICENSING FOSTER HOMES

The laws of practically all states now provide for licensing of boarding homes or boarding houses caring for children, and in many states the licensing of any family home receiving children for care and accepting compensation for this care is authorized.

It is usual for the states to allow the placement of a child in the home of relatives without requiring inspection or licensing. Such a plan is unwise. The biological fact of relationship does not mean that the home will be suited to the child.

There is wide variation between states in the character of legislation and in the method of delegating authority to licensing agencies.

The state department of welfare should be charged with the legal responsibilities for licensing foster homes and child placing agencies, for determining the standards under which they must operate, and for seeing that these standards are maintained. It should be empowered to delegate to any authorized child placing agency the responsibility for investigating foster homes used by that agency and recommending them for licenses. It should delegate to the county welfare unit the task of investigating and licensing homes that are used by parents for direct or so-called "independent" placement of their children. If there is a question on the sanitary condition of the home, the local health department may be asked to cooperate by making an inspection.

The state department, if it is to maintain satisfactory standards, must furnish an adequate service of supervision and consultation to child placing agencies and to its accredited licensing agency.

Logically, any agency qualified to become an authorized child placing agency should also be empowered to recommend, for licensing, the foster homes it uses. Delegation of the licensing function to another agency is only duplication of effort and acts as a countercheck on the work of the placing agency. In effect it is an illogical qualification of a trust. Can we decide that an agency is trustworthy in the complicated process of placing a child but that it is not qualified to recommend a license for the homes it uses?

It is common practice to issue a license for one year to one location, with the provision that the license may be revoked for cause before expiration. Such revocation may be initiated for various reasons which lie within the general area of nonconformance to standards. Many states provide specifically that the license may be revoked if any boarders are taken into the home without prior approval of the placing agency. They also require reinspection of the home at the time the license is renewed, since home conditions may have changed radically in the one-year period.

Since licensing is inextricably bound up with standards, it appears that uniformity of standards must come before uniformity of licensing practices. Today there are wide differences in the standards set up by the various states that the home, the foster family, and the child must meet in order to qualify for participation in the placement process. In general, state standards tend to emphasize physical environmental factors more than emotional, cultural, or spiritual aspects.

The Child Welfare League and the United States Children's Bureau have both published carefully constructed sets of desirable standards. It is generally recognized that standards for foster care in a given community must be modified to meet the standards of care for all children in the community.

The most vital factor in the selection of satisfactory foster homes is the skill of the worker in evaluating the assets of the home. Perhaps the elaborate standards devised by some states were thought to be necessary because of the inexperienced workers doing placement. When skilled workers with sound casework training are engaged in child placing, the ideal in establishing standards would appear to be to delineate desirable features without fixing rigid boundaries within which the foster home must be compressed.

INDEPENDENT PLACEMENTS IN FOSTER HOMES

There are always some parents who wish to place their children independently. The home they use may have been chosen by them or suggested to them by a relative or friend. It is probably unlicensed and unknown to any agency. It may have been accepted because of the pressure of circumstances, the main concern of the parent being to find a place where the child could be left rather than to insure the type of care the child needed. The conditions and relationships within this independent home are unknown to the parent; sometimes there is exploitation of the child. In some homes, exorbitant fees are charged.

The parent may not know of the requirement that children must be placed in licensed homes, or she may wish to avoid supervision and feel antagonistic to any suggestion of services which she would consider interference with parental rights.

The problems created by the unlicensed independent home might be lessened by interpreting to the community the difficulties inherent in placing children in one and by publicizing the information that a list of licensed homes was available at a local private or public child placing agency.

The county welfare department should undertake supervision of the independent home, because it is nearer the home than the state administration. The state should issue the license upon recommendation by the county and should act in a consultative capacity.

When the independent home has been brought under control and regulated by means of a license, there still remains the problem of obliging it to meet higher standards of care.

Many of the evils of the independent home can be eliminated by a system of licensing, although probably there will always be independent homes that will manage to operate without licenses. Some states do locate and license independent homes and have set up special divisions to handle investigations.

PREPARATION FOR PLACEMENT IN THE FOSTER HOME

Where does the preparation for placement begin? Some caseworkers contend that a child cannot really be prepared for placement; the separation from his parents must be experienced. No child can face separation without trepidation and anxiety. But the separation may entail less agony if a child welfare worker helps the children to face some of their feelings toward their own home before they are removed.

We know that physical removal of a child from a home does not remove the impress of the emotional experiences he has had in that home, although if the damage has been mild new opportunities and stimuli may prove entirely favorable to his development. The child about to be placed has already experienced faulty relationships in his own home. He has met rejection if only in the form of having his parents separate themselves from him by death. The mores of our culture make us want to belong to someone, and they condition us to regard as desirable certain attachments and loyalties; this conditioning leads the child to think that his departure provides positive proof of his unpopularity with his parents, or that it will be testimony to his inner fear that his parents haven't measured up. The extent of the trauma and the amount of damage done will be determined by many factors—the personality of the child (whether he encounters much or slight pain in living), the kinds of people with whom he has lived, the extent of his deprivation by them, and the number of his unassimilated and unsolved problems.

The needs of a child in a foster home are basically the same as the needs of other children. However, they are intensified and distorted and harder to meet because of the child's past experiences and the limitations of his present environment.

The placement worker's first meeting with the child should be carefully planned; first impressions are important. The situations should be developed to relieve the child as far as possible of feelings of shyness, awkwardness, and constraint. Any arrangement that will break the ice is worth trying, for the placement worker will be closely associated with every phase of the child's life from the first meeting until his return home and afterwards, and will thus exert an extensive influence.

Children, even when very young, are particularly sensitive to sincerity in the people with whom they are thrown. They detect at once a condescending attitude. Their defense is to assume a pose of attention, when in reality their thoughts are traveling in more interesting fields. A straightforward, friendly approach is more likely to reach a child. The placement worker should be direct and scrupulously truthful and make sure that others are so in their dealings with the child. She must be quick to receive impressions and confidences.

The worker knows so definitely what she intends to do, or is carried along so swiftly by the flow of circumstances, that she may forget to explain the situation to the child, step by step, a procedure necessary if he is to acquiesce in the plan. Before making any move with a child, it is best to be certain that he has some idea of it and of the plan in which he is to play the principal part so that he does not think, and will not later think, that the facts have been misrepresented to him.

In the rush of a day's work, there is a temptation to hurry a child through an interview or medical or psychological examination, to give little or no heed to his natural confusion and fears at the time, or to make a new arrangement for him and give him only a scant or unsatisfactory reason for it.

Often, because of pressure from work and because of her desire to expedite the placing, the placement worker may forget entirely to consider what may be going on in the child's mind. Nothing is so important from beginning to end as the child's point of view. More than likely he is dazed and puzzled by being taken from place to place, examined by physicians, and introduced to strange people. (A new outfit of clothing may form the only bright spot in the day.) A description of the home to which he is going and the people among whom he is to live will help, just as a description of the child helps the foster family. He should know whether he is to be in the city or in the country, and what he may expect to find in the way of good companions and good times. The experience will nearly always be entirely new to him, and the worker can make it appear interesting—an adventure, in fact—instead of an ordeal to be dreaded. She must ask for his cooperation. He must feel that he has a part in the making of plans. Whether the placement will be successful is determined by whether the child can actually accept placement.

Throughout the placing, the child's attitude toward his own parents will demand consideration. It is deep seated, going back to memories of early childhood. There are children who retain a staunch loyalty to parents in spite of neglect. Although they clearly remember ill treatment or parental behavior that has led to disruption of the home, they defend parents fiercely, making excuses for them and fixing the blame upon others. Another child may have feelings that are just the reverse. He wonders why his parents let this happen to him and thus denied him a basis of equality with other children. He feels deep resentment toward them; he is ashamed of his parents, and of himself because he is ashamed of them. An older child who leaves his home, with direct knowledge that the change in his life has been caused by the unacceptable behavior of his parents, suffers acute feelings of inferiority. It is only if the worker and the foster family understand this sensitivity and respect it, that they can help him make any headway in reaching a wholesome adjustment to his problem and thereby decrease for him an emotional strain which, if unrelieved, may become unendurable in later years.

Adults often think that the best way to assist emotional adjustment is to keep the attention of a child focused on his present environment and to help him forget as rapidly as possible everything that has gone before. This is not difficult for children to do, and if it seems to be what is expected, they lend themselves willingly to the forgetting program. But humans achieve stability and emotional comfort by retaining a definite thread of continuity of experience and memory. Consequently, a conscious effort by the foster parents to help a child forget all that has preceded his arrival at their home is one of the most certain causes of emotional strain and confusion.

One of the most difficult things about placement is its total quality. It is more total, more final in feeling than almost any change children ordinarily experience. Any change in the average family is experienced by both parents and child, and takes place within a structure that remains constant; the mere physical stability provides partial insulation against fear. A normally satisfied child in his own home looks forward to adventure and change. A foster child is more apt to dread and resent it, until he is made to feel that change may bring him a happy experience.

THE WORKER AS A SYMBOL OF SECURITY

The worker is the one constant factor in what may be a situation that is constantly changing. She must be the anchorage to give the child some security. When everyone else seems to have failed him, she will be a friend to help him out of his troubles. She must overcome any personal prejudices to prevent their hampering her work. The worker's unconscious attitudes toward parents and children, stemming from her own life experiences, are a subtle but important personal factor and are crucial in her work with children. Child placing affords fertile ground for overidentification with parents and children, which can be a serious block to good child welfare work. An awareness of one's own tendencies is a safeguard. After all, taking a child from a home has a peculiar wrenching quality not only to parent and child but to the worker. There is always some discomfort in child placing. The deed the worker does in order to help brings some pain. This is inherent in the service.

The feelings of the child should always be considered, and for this reason it is thought unwise to allow him to be seen by the foster parents before he goes to their home. A request to see the child first sounds reasonable, but it should be made plain to the prospective foster parents that the experience of being inspected would be extremely painful for the child, especially if they reject him, and a long series of difficulties might ensue. There is the added danger of giving the child the sense of being a pawn in the care of the organization. He is only too ready anyway to believe that no one cares particularly for him and that he is different from other children.

The actual introduction of the child to the foster parent varies in each case; in general, however, it is advisable for the worker to leave as soon as the situation allows, since two people make a warmer and freer contact when unobserved. Because the worker is not a member of the household, the foster mother and child should begin mutual understanding as soon as possible.

A worker should never allow a child to get the impression that she is in a hurry. The child may know there are other children under her care but he must feel he is as important as any of them. If an emergency arises that would prevent the worker from accompanying the child to his new home, it is better to postpone the placement than to bring an outsider (a substitute worker) into the situation.

If there is a wide divergence of standards between the natural home of the child and his foster home, the adjustment will be smoother if the worker counsels the foster parents not to expect to change him too quickly; she should give a circumstantial account of the conditions in his natural home. As pointed out before, the adjustment the child must make to the different standards is a source of emotional strain. Bewilderment and confusion can follow a sudden change, especially if the child feels that conformity is necessary to receive food and shelter.

CHANGE OF FOSTER HOMES

Sometimes it is necessary to move a child from one foster home to another. The reason for this type of change may be one of several. The move may be necessary because of some change in the foster family it-self which makes it impossible for the family to continue cooperative and adequate care. It may be due to faulty preparation for the first placement. The child may have outgrown the home; or he may need a different school or community, or more recreational facilities. It may be that the child's own family lives so near that there is a constant deleteri-ous interference. Perhaps the foster home is too far from the agency for adequate supervision. Finally, there may be a change of plan, so that adoption is decided upon or a free or wage home is desired.

There is little difference between the handling of a placement and that of a replacement, except that preparation for the replacement is a longer and more difficult process. The worker should evaluate the real situation in the foster home in the light of the child's present and past experiences and try to decide if replacement is necessary. If she thinks that it is, she must work as if the child were in his own home and give him insight into the reasons for the replacement. The new foster mother must be prepared in the same way as the first foster mother.

In replacements, the worker has more knowledge of the child's capacities and characteristics than was possible in the first placement, and that asset often makes replacements more successful. When the worker has had a chance to observe the child in one home, she can judge better how he will behave in another type of home, whether he will adapt himself to family life, and what sort of foster mother and father he most needs.

This advantage, however, is offset by one important disadvantage. The child's own attitude will not be propitious. If he has been happy in the first foster home, he will not wish to be moved. If he has had an un-happy experience in one home, he will dread going to another. If he had to leave the first home through some fault of his own, he is likely to be either self-distrustful because of his failure or defiant and careless of the effect he makes. Neither of these moods promises well for his be-havior in the next adjustment he will have to make. A child who has proved too much for his first foster parents is likely to go to a second home with a determination to get the better of the parents there as well. To deal with these attitudes, the worker should consult the child's own feelings and preferences as much as is practicable.

The worker should avoid interrupting the school year or half year. Because many causes for replacement are more chronic than acute, it is better to postpone the move until the child has been promoted.

The use of a temporary study home often helps to divide into small steps the separation of a child from his own home, and, in addition, a less consequential change might actually be in accord with the child's own impulse for growth. A temporary study home is a home in which the caseworker places a child temporarily in order to observe his behavior and attitudes so that she can evaluate him for a more permanent placement. The initial period in the temporary home gives the child an opportunity to try out, with the caseworker's help, many aspects of the new way of living. The worker will be available if the child reacts with struggle, pain, fear, bad temper, or misbehavior to the day-to-day experiences of study home, clinic, and agency procedures.

A temporary home may help a child to move to a new, more permanent situation. Some children reach out directly and with little confusion for what they need. They are resilient, not too damaged by painful experience, and ready, if given a little time and opportunity, to find in a new situation what is helpful to them. The success in placement rests ultimately with the child, but the caseworker must provide the means to it.

Placement in the temporary study home may also help the parent with the difficult decision on whether to place the child in a permanent foster home. The parent often has conflicting desires, and must battle his guilt and fears in resolving them. When the parent comes to the agency to ask for placement, something has already happened to the family solidarity. Emotional separation has already begun, and the parent has given up a certain amount of responsibility. Placement has real meaning for parents, and those who seek it have a definite purpose in doing so. It enables them to carry out certain plans. These plans may have developed as the result of pressures of illness, job difficulties or unpleasant family or marital conditions. Whatever the causes, the background and total life experiences of each applicant are different, and so the meaning of placement is different for each applicant.

Unless the worker is sensitive to the underlying purpose, and not the overt explanation alone, she misses the real points on which her future work with the case should be based. The worker must try to help the applicant decide whether placement of the child is the realistic answer to her problem. If the client decides that placement is not what she wants, it is the duty of the worker to refer the client to the place where she can get the kind of service she needs. If placement is desirable, can the worker's own agency supply the service and the foster home most suitable for the child involved? Would institutional placement be more satisfactory in this case?

The worker sustains a three-way relationship—with the parent, the child, and the foster home. This relationship varies according to the

needs of the three other participants. The child is an unwilling partici-
pant. It is often a function of the worker to assure the parent that she
does retain legal responsibility for her child; the agency simply assumes
the responsibility for the care of the child.

Effort, time, and expense can be saved for client and agency by a
thoughtful and painstaking intake service. This protects the child placing function of the agency: it helps prevent hopeless placements; it
helps parent and agency determine whether placement is desirable,
what type of placement seems advisable, and where this service can be
most satisfactorily obtained.

THE CHILD WITH BEHAVIOR PROBLEMS

Children legally defined as delinquent are usually children who have
lacked security and a stable home situation. The deprivation may have
been economic or emotional. Whatever the cause, the child has felt rejected, insecure, or inferior, and in his frustration has struck out against
authority. This reaction has identified him with destructive influences
and eventually brought him into conflict with the law.

Formerly a child like this was considered an institutional problem,
but as our understanding of the underlying causes of behavior grew,
we began to see that what he needed was a normal home life that would
give him a sense of personal security and adequacy as well as opportunities for physical care, recreation, and education. Foster home care was
found to be most useful in helping him to overcome conflicts and disturbances so that he was no longer a "problem."

The child welfare worker has to select with special care foster parents who will have patience, who will be able to accept the child as he
is, and who will share the concepts of behavior and the theories of
treatment held by the agency. Foster parents may find that a child is
unable to accept or give love because he is unable to face painful realities of his own life. They may find that change in a child's behavior
may come slowly—that there may be frequent regression to unacceptable behavior. Foster parents must understand these occurrences and be
willing to bear disappointments and still persist in the effort to help a
child move toward a goal of success.

Casework service for the foster parents, once the home has been
approved, is a subject for much consideration. Many agencies regard
their foster parents as part of the professional staff and treat them accordingly. There is some indication, however, of a trend toward con-

sidering foster parents as clients with certain needs who should be helped, if possible, by casework to enable them to achieve satisfying relationships and thus become better foster parents.

Agencies have sponsored group meetings of foster parents to supplement the agency program of individual supervision. These meetings have augmented the foster mother's understanding of the child and his problems as well as the role of the foster parent in the child's development. One method of carrying out this objective has been formal courses under the auspices of universities; another has been informal talks followed by a discussion period. In both of these programs, emphasis has been on the prevailing ideas regarding child care and development and on the specific problems of children in foster homes.

These foster parent meetings for group education have also generated some good collateral results. They have helped the agency to find more foster homes, to improve agency policies by comparing the ideas of workers and foster parents, and to make the needs of children in the community known.

THE PHYSICALLY HANDICAPPED CHILD

Foster home care of the physically handicapped child, especially the child with rheumatic fever or orthopedic conditions, has been demonstrated as one satisfactory resource in treatment. It has also been used effectively for children in postoperative conditions and for those who have anemia, asthma, malnutrition, and other illnesses for which the prognosis is favorable and nursing care, but not intensive medical supervision, is necessary.

Care in the selection of foster homes for these children is imperative. Such a home must meet standards for physical care—such as conveniences, space, heating facilities, ventilation, and fire prevention—and also be able to keep up the morale of the ill child.

The foster mother must be free to devote whatever time is necessary to the child. She must understand the importance of keeping accurate medical records and be willing to accept and intelligently carry out instructions. She must be patient and understanding in regard to the vagaries of behavior a child develops because of illness.

The children's worker is responsible for securing a suitable home for children who have been selected and referred by the hospital medical social worker for foster home care. The children's worker does the actual placement, describes to the child's own parents the foster home and the care the child will receive there, and, in cooperation with the medical social worker, works with the child to help him accept foster home care. By working with the child before his actual placement, the children's worker makes herself known to the child and forms a needed link for him between known and unknown experience. She continues her supervision of the foster home and her relationship with the child's own parents until his eventual return. The interpretation of the nature of the child's disease and of the type of medical care necessary is the responsibility of the medical social worker, if medical social service is available.

The foster home must guard against overemphasis of physical care, which can produce attitudes of self-interest that may become neurotic.

When the child returns home, the follow-up may be done by the children's worker or the medical social worker, depending on the individual situation.

THE MENTALLY DEFICIENT CHILD

The care of the mentally deficient in foster homes, now referred to as Family Care, was first introduced into Belgium approximately 400 years ago.

In 1892, various institutions in France formed a cooperative arrangement for experimenting in foster home care. Choosing the small city of Dun, they sent to family homes there both insane and mentally deficient persons. Boarding these patients in private homes seemed from every standpoint—emotional, physical, and financial—to be successful.

One of the consequences was that foster home care began to be used as a treatment method in the United States. In this country, however, entire communities have not combined to board or house a group of mentally deficient, as in Dun, but foster homes scattered throughout the various states are caring for individuals.

In choosing a foster home, the selection of the proper foster parent is of the greatest importance. It requires real skill to understand the simple functioning of the defective's mind. It is of utmost importance that the foster parent understand the limitations and vagaries of the mentally deficient, and have unlimited patience.

Like all other people, the mentally defective child needs a home and emotional security. He suffers from the lack of close family ties. Frequently he is rejected by his family, and usually by the community, and consequently it is especially necessary to secure foster parents who accept him and are interested in him.

The child welfare worker will need to see the defective child and the foster parents frequently to give support and interpretation, if the foster home placement is to be successful.

A PLACEMENT CASE

The following case is of interest because of the variety of placement responsibilities the worker was obliged to deal with in one family situation.

It concerns an American Indian family living on a reservation in a western state. Six children were involved. The father, aged 40, was an alcoholic World War II veteran, who worked sporadically at seasonal labor. He spent a great deal of time in jail on charges of drunkenness and cohabitation. He seldom went home and assumed no responsibility for the support of his wife and six children. When approached by the worker, he blamed his wife for his drinking. He said she was "no good." He asked how he was expected to be sure that all the children were his and how he was expected to be sure that his wife had not lived with many men.

The mother, Susie, aged 34, was healthy and attractive, and spoke English well. She had attended an Indian boarding school for about six years. She was a good worker and could have supported herself as a permanent domestic in a good home near the reservation. When questioned, she told the worker she wanted her husband to support her and the children; if he would not, she did not intend to work and support the family. She went to live with a young Indian man in his twenties. This was her only known extramarital affair.

There were two older daughters, Lisa, 16, and Emma, 14. The oldest son, Ransom, was 12. The three younger children were Charles, eight, Jim, six, and Harry, four. The mother said she did not want the older girls. She seemed to love the 12-year-old son but would not take any responsibility for him. Of the older children, she told the worker she thought the "best plan is to place all three of them in a boarding school off the reservation." The authorities approved her application and these three children entered boarding school.

While the worker was attempting to reestablish a home for the younger children, the tribal court took them away from their mother because of her behavior and awarded them to the paternal grandmother.

(The tribal court has jurisdiction over members of its own tribe.) The paternal grandmother was a reliable woman and loved the children; but three months later she became very ill and had to be hospitalized.

In the meantime the worker had interested the maternal grand-mother in an effort to supervise the mother, Susie, and to help reestab-lish a home for the mother and small children. The maternal grand-mother had taken Susie into her home and was trying to help the social worker convince her to assume some responsibility in the situation. The maternal grandmother said that Susie could bring the youngest boy, Harry, to her home, but that she would not have the other two, Charles and Jim. The worker agreed to let the mother take the youngest child and see how the plan worked out. Because no temporary foster home was available, it was necessary to place the two boys—ages six and eight—in a small institution that accepted children of all races and na-tionalities. The children who lived in this institution attended public school, and received medical and dental care. The housemother, though not professionally trained, was a warm, accepting person with an inter-est in these two little boys.

The worker carefully explained to the boys that this placement was only for a little while, until their paternal grandmother was well again. At first they were uneasy and worried, but with the help of the institution staff and the worker they made a happy adjustment to many new conditions they had to meet in this completely unfamiliar situation. Later, when they were again home with their grandmother, they talked with enthusiasm about the good times they had enjoyed in the institu-tion.

The paternal grandmother was at first very worried about the three children. The medical social worker in the hospital explained that the placement was only temporary; that the children had not been taken away from her, and when she was at home again and well the children would be returned. At the end of six weeks the grandmother was able to return to her own home, and two weeks later the two boys came home to her. In the meantime the maternal grandmother told the worker that the mother, Susie, did not care for the youngest boy; so he too was returned to the home of the paternal grandmother.

The three older children at first showed their fears, frustration, and hostility toward their situation by aggression and defiance of all regula-tions of the boarding school. The worker visited the school, and, be-cause she understood that their feelings were the result of rejection and desertion by their own parents, she was able to explain their point of view to the school staff. After the worker's visit, the children benefited from the staff's improved understanding of their problems, and as a result they made a slow but satisfactory adjustment.

The worker continued to work with the mother, and the home was eventually reestablished, and the children reunited. The Indian community has, to some extent, overcome its fear that a social worker will remove children from their own relatives permanently. This is an important step in an agency's endeavor to win the people's trust and confidence in the social work being done on the reservation.

Supplementary Readings

Boehm, Bernice. *Deterrents to Adoption of Children in Foster Care.* Child Welfare League of America, New York, 1958.

Brieland, Donald. *An Experimental Study of the Selection of Adoptive Parents at Intake.* Child Welfare League of America, New York, 1959.

Child Welfare League of America. *The Need for Foster Care.* Child Welfare League of America, New York, 1969.

Child Welfare League of America. *Today's Child and Foster Care.* Child Welfare League of America, New York, 1963.

Costin, Lela B. *Licensing of Family Homes in Child Welfare.* Wayne State University Press, Detroit, 1965.

Dinnage, Rosemary. *Foster Home Care, Facts and Fallacies.* Longmans, London, 1967.

Fanshel, David. *Foster Parenthood: A Role Analysis.* University of Minnesota Press, Minneapolis, 1966.

Haitch, Richard. *Orphan's of the Living.* Public Affairs Committee, New York, 1968.

Hylton, Lydia F. *The Residential Treatment Center: Children, Programs, and Costs.* Child Welfare League of America, New York, 1964.

Jenkins, Shirley, and Sauber, Mignon. *Paths to Child Placement.* New York City Department of Welfare, New York, 1966.

Maas, Henry S. and Engler, Richard E. *Children in Need of Parents.* Columbia University Press, New York, 1959.

Parfit, Jessie, Ed. *The Community's Children.* Longmans in association with the National Bureau for Coöperation in Child Care, London, 1967.

Schaffer, H. Rudolph. *Child Care and the Family.* Bell, London, 1968.

Stone, Helen D. *Reflections on Foster Care.* Child Welfare League of America, New York, 1969.

Weinstein, Eugene A. *The Self-Image of the Foster Child.* Russell Sage Foundation, New York, 1960.

Werner, Ruth Margaret. *Public Financing of Voluntary Agency Foster Care.* Child Welfare League of America, New York, 1961.

Wolins, Martin. *Selecting Foster Parents: The Ideal and the Reality.* Columbia University Press, New York, 1963.

Wolins, Martin, and Piliavin, Irving. *Institution or Foster Family Care: A Century of Debate.* Child Welfare League of America, New York, 1964.

[*Photo by Christy Butterfield.*]

11

Institutional and Adoptive Home Care

In Chapter 10, we discussed placement of children in various types of foster homes. The foster home is one type of substitute care for children who must, for one reason or another, live away from their homes. Another type of substitute care is the institution. In this chapter, we will discuss placement in institutions as well as a more permanent kind of placement—that in the adoptive home.

THE INSTITUTION

Let us assume that we have a child whose characteristics and circumstances indicate institutional care. When are we to decide that placement shall be in an institution? More than a study of the child is necessary. A knowledge of the institution is essential to the critical decision of placement. We should not make such a placement unless available institutional services are of such superior quality that they can meet this child's needs better than other available services can. First let us look at a few of the principles involved in good administration of an institution for children or youth.

Administration and the Institution

The administration of a children's institution may be looked upon as a double activity. One is the managerial activity, which includes all of the basic processes that are necessary to make it function efficiently as an organization. The other activity comprises the services that are rendered to the children in the institution, that is, the product of all the institution's managerial processes. In most large organizations these two functions are carried on by separate sets of personnel. Training for one function does not necessarily qualify a person to perform in both areas, although traditionally the skilled professional has tended to move from the role of rendering a service in a given organization's program to a position of administrative, supervisory, managerial, or executive leadership. For example, the professional child welfare worker may become the director of a large children's agency; or the successful probation officer, the chief of a large adult or juvenile probation system. To be sure, a good knowledge of what constitutes professional training and a professional service are invaluable assets for an administrator to have, and he should have them, but the skills associated with a service are not sufficient for producing an efficient administrator of an organization. He needs some knowledge of the managerial side of administration. Likewise the skilled technician, even in his role as a technician, needs some knowledge of these same managerial principles if the organization, the administrative directives, and his particular role in the system are to become more meaningful to him.

Aside from the variations in complexity of organization, class of personnel, and types of service, institutions also differ in the degree of skills required to render those organizational services considered necessary to maintain an optimum level of efficiency.

In general terms, it may be said that the best organizational structure for an institution is that one which most facilitates the accomplishment of all of the objectives of the program. Ideally, an institution's organization should aim to promote the following ends: (1) the maximum returns from the personnel available; (2) the development and improvement of personnel; (3) a professional climate of competence, sincerity, industriousness, high morale, and an absence of emotional tensions; (4) an attitudinal awareness, oriented to meet emergency situations with the least possible difficulty and damage to the institution's program; (5) facile two-way lines of communication, vertically through the chain of command, and horizontally through the departmental levels of the organization (the maintenance of communications within an organization is important to the children served as well as to the system's personnel; the organizational structure should provide for some means of communication from the management through the personnel to the children, and vice-versa); (6) a continuous professional service for its children that is in keeping with the raison d'etre of the institution.

Much of the tone and climate of an institution for children and youth is a reflection of the leadership by its administrator. It is important that he be a man of some training and education, not only in the general field of administration but at least in one specialized service provided by his institution. There are few managerial positions in the administrative field in which knowledge, experience, insight, and sensitivity to special situations are as important as they are to the head of a children's institution. No social system that does not anticipate the appointment of most of its institution heads, either by promoting from within or by seeking better qualified and more experienced persons from similar systems, can possibly be built on a sound foundation.

There is a trend in some fields toward a constant increase in the proportion of an institution's personnel having highly specialized professional training. This is generally considered a desirable development, but it has some drawbacks which an institutional administrator should be aware of. Specialists are usually recruited at a relatively high rate of pay and, unless the institution provides for it, there is the distinct possibility that they will find themselves in jobs with very limited opportunities for advancement. In addition, specialized employees very often lack an interest in the total picture of the administration and workings of an institution, and in time they become disgruntled. This has sometimes been met with some success by requiring all new employees to work for a period of from 30 to 90 days as rank and file personnel before undertaking their specific duties. During this time, they would also be required to participate in the organized in-service training program for new employees.

Administration of an institution for children or youth should be based on a clear-cut, logical, and consistent statement of policy, agreed upon by the head of the institution and its governing board. Policy should be consistent with the law and the ideals of the professional aegis under which the institution functions.

The rules and regulations, issued by an institution's administration, should be detailed enough to leave no doubt in the minds of his personnel of the basic objectives and specific limitations of the procedures. Regulations should be broad enough to permit some degree of discretion on the part of responsible subordinates throughout the hierarchy of the organization. Rules and regulations are, fundamentally, a means of limiting the authority of subordinates and, at the same time, a means of delegating authority to them. The balance between the limitations and extent of delegated authority depends on the system and personalities involved.

Personnel problems are constantly present for any administrator. They originate on every organizational level with infinite variety and fluctuation. Although they may be separated into many categories, two common categories that have been used are (1) those dealing with recruitment and retention of personnel, and (2) those which concern the individual worker and his adjustment. The complexity of an institution determines to some extent the types of personnel problems that will arise, and influences the methods used in processing them.

The need for personnel in most institutions is great, and the recruitment of staff is an important and constantly ongoing task. This is especially true for certain types of children's institutions which attract poorly trained and rejected manpower. The rate of turnover in an institution's personnel varies with the type and location of the institution. For example, the rate of turnover may be greater in institutions for juvenile delinquents or in institutions for dependent children that are located in isolated rural settings, less in suburban institutions, and almost nonexistent in an institution located in a larger city. No matter what the difference in rates of turnover may be, it is clear that the survival of any institution depends on the relative stability of its personnel. The tasks of recruitment and retainment are simply more difficult for certain types of institutions than they are for others. In any organization, a method must be devised not only to attract personnel, but also to retain them. Like public relations, the recruitment problem is not an isolated activity for the administration of an institution. The behavior of the administration and staff, professionally, publicly, and socially, has some effect on their professional and public image and, thus, on recruitment. Recruitment cannot be abstracted from an organizational system because, in reality, all aspects of the system affect its potential attractiveness to various levels of personnel.

Another important administrative variable is finance. Good fiscal management is essential to the successful administration of any institution or system. Fiscal management is basically a tool of top management, and it should be adapted to the requirements of the administration. The purpose of fiscal management and control is to provide the head of an institution with the financial information he needs to direct the work of his organization. This information is necessary for making many administrative and policy decisions.

Also essential of course is the absolute integrity and reliability of all personnel. Administrators of institutions have at their disposal a vast reservoir of manpower and supplies, and are generally isolated spatially and administratively from the controls of the central system of which they may be a part. Management of a children's institution in accordance with central office decisions and intent is ethically and professionally essential, if the dictates of central control are not to be usurped.

The administration of institutions for children or youth, when carried on professionally and efficiently, results in an end product or service of the highest quality, if all other supporting factors are equal. Poor administration results in a poor product, economic loss, low morale among personnel and children, and eventual termination of the institution·and its program, if left to run its course.

The Contribution of Modern Institutions

The well run institution has both general assets and liabilities for children. The advantages of institutional life include primarily an opportunity for group living through which respect for the rights and abilities of others may be recognized; regularity of personal habits; regularity of meals and well balanced diets; impersonal and objective adult supervision; consistent disciplines; and, if handled constructively, wholesome group competition. Group interests may enable children to attain greater social acceptability. On occasion, training a child in acceptable social behavior through the pressure of the contemporary group is sound, if an objective adult sets the spirit. The child, for example, puts away his toys because other children in the group say, "Here we all put away our toys."

Certain disadvantages are also prevalent in many institutions. Some of these are overly routinized life, lack of personal freedom and initiative, restriction of friendships and social life primarily to institution population, limited opportunity for economic experience, and insufficient outlets for emotional needs. Many of the disadvantages can be minimized in a good institution. For those children who, as a temporary experience, need organized routine and impersonal life, this method of care may be effective. However, when a child cannot achieve security in this impersonal and organized environment, then the placement is defective and other arrangements should be made.

Placement of a child in an institution is not a simple maneuver. It is a complex and sensitive procedure. The person or agency responsible for determining that a child should go to an institution must know whether this particular child will profit from the services the institution is equipped to give.

To determine whether institutional placement offers the best form of therapy for the child, a child welfare worker must use casework procedures that give her an understanding of the life experiences and emotional attitudes to which the child has been subjected. She should also have firsthand acquaintance with the child in order to learn and understand his feelings about his present situation. Placement in many cases is the climax to a period of family and home disintegration experienced by the child. Many children in the adolescent period are breaking away from the parental ties and may adjust better in a group setting.

Institutions need to define their intake policies carefully. A child should not be admitted merely because there is space for him, nor should there be inflexible regulations, relying upon tradition, to determine which child shall and which shall not receive care. Intake should be based upon broad and flexible principles allowing an institution to accept those children who, it is convinced, will profit by its program.

It cannot be emphasized too strongly that institutional placements should be regarded as temporary—for limited periods only. Regardless of how fine its program is, an institution will tend to overprotect, overentertain, and overwhelm the child in the course of a long period of time. The continual programming in an institution cannot prepare a child for the future when he will be alone and entirely dependent on his own resources for finding friends.

Standards to which children's institutions should conform are outlined by the Child Welfare League of America. These standards are not beyond the attainment of any good institution for children, but it is generally felt that a large proportion of today's institutions do not approach these standards.

An institution's contribution to the children in its care depends on three factors: (1) the staff and its philosophy, (2) the efficacy of the services, and (3) the place the institution occupies within the total child welfare program of the community.

The Importance of a Suitable Staff

The first and most important element in an institutional program is the administrator and his staff. They determine to a large degree whether the institution is going to move, and whether backward or forward.

The director of the institution sets its tone. He must be competent. The morale of the staff depends largely on whether they have confidence in his knowledge and skills of performance. He must be fair, honest, and impartial. He must be considerate. He must be sensitive to the feelings of staff and children. He must be available to the staff for individual conferences. He must allow them to feel free to make suggestions for changes they consider important. He must create comfortable living and working conditions for the staff, recognizing the need for time off and for occasional opportunity for a long weekend or a night away from the institution.

The size, composition, duties, and qualifications of a staff should depend on the purpose and function of the institution.

In selection of maintenance staff, consideration must be given to their physical, mental and moral health and also to their attitudes toward children, since they, as well as professional staff, will frequently be in direct contact with the children.

In the selection of professional staff, it is most essential to consider the underlying motive of the person seeking an institutional job, since salary will not usually be a major inducement. Ideally, the professional staff should consist of social worker, registered nurse, recreation leader, house parents, physician, dentist, psychiatrist, and psychologist.

The social worker is the person who helps the child relate his institutional life to his past and future life; it is she who works with the natural or foster parents, the child, and the community for the child's return. She is in the case from beginning to end because she is the link that connects the child, his family, and the institution.

If it is possible to have a complete professional staff, there should be a resident physician, but, if it is not, a registered nurse can supplement the services of a doctor employed for part time. Both doctor and nurse should have special training and experience with children. Their duties will include regular physical examinations of staff and children, use of preventive medicine, observation aimed to detect illness, the operation of clinics, and leadership in health education.

A good recreation leader will not demand play, but will stimulate it through a lively program of games and athletics offering release for physical and emotional energies. Swimming, ice skating, and roller skating should be encouraged by frequent use of facilities in the community. Hikes, visits to museums, and passive recreation such as dramatics, table games, hobbies, and movies can be vital experiences if there is a recreational leader with the time and training to provide and direct these activities.

The skills and knowledge we ask of house parents are important enough to require specific training for the job. Salaries provided for house parents, however, are usually too small to repay an investment by them in preparatory training. Unless higher salaries are made available, the institution cannot rely on getting couples who are adequately trained and qualified to make real contributions to the life of the deprived child with whom they must deal. With the salaries as they are, the best that can be expected is to hire house parents with personalities pleasing to children, and with genuine affection for them. In-service training will have to do the rest.

There should not be too great a difference in age between house parents and children. In any case, the house parents must have a youthful point of view and a keenly developed sense of humor. It is good practice to secure a married couple, provided both the man and woman are well adjusted in their marriage and both are qualified to work with children. If the house father is employed outside the institution during the day, as much should be known of his occupation, personality, and attitudes as is known of the traits of the house mother.

The house mother and father naturally see the children more frequently than do other members of the staff. Therefore, their behavior and even their little mannerisms are an important factor in training. Their stability of character, cultural interests, speech, and personal habits all set an example for children. Of course, they will have to be more than a good example; they will have to be able and willing to share the interests and ambitions of each child under their care. They have the greatest opportunity and the greatest responsibility for fulfilling the children's needs for security and affection. They can supply these essentials when the children have respect and warmth of feeling for them.

Institutional staff members should have personal interests and avocations outside their work which give them relief from their duties, broaden their points of view, and enrich their own lives and the lives of the children.

The part-time services of dentist, psychiatrist, and psychologist can be used satisfactorily when coordinated with the whole treatment program; staff members should be advised to make observations and take them to these specialists. It is certain that any institution could give better service if it had complete full-time professional staffs, but this is not always possible or practical.

The services of a psychologist are most helpful to the institution in making a satisfactory placement in school and in planning a program for the child at the beginning of his institutional stay. Tests of intelligence, achievement, performance, and attitude should be given.

Participation in social service conferences and staff meetings can do much to enrich the knowledge of all staff members. There is a wealth of literature on child care, and this should be available to the staff. Certainly no member should be ignorant of the three fundamental needs of children—security and affection, self-esteem, and thrill and adventure.

Institutional staffs should have training in child welfare in order to carry out a vital and intelligently planned program. The philosophy of the staff members is an integral part of the success of the institution. The staff must really want to help the child become an independent, self-sufficient individual so that he may return to a satisfying life in the community. To be most effective, staff members must enjoy living with children and gain satisfaction from watching and helping children grow and develop.

Services and Program

The services and program of an institution should be such that they make allowance for the difficulties of a child, help him to overcome them, and enable him to develop into an independent individual capable of adjusting to his own home or to a substitute home when he is transferred there.

Large institutions may have either centralized, congregate housing or a decentralized cottage plan. The cottage plan institution, in turn, varies in the number of children per cottage. The Child Welfare League standards set 12 as the maximum number to be desired, but in many institutions the number of children per cottage ranges from 12 to 30. Whatever the number of children in the cottage, the organization is one of group living, and not, as it is sometimes euphemistically called, "a family." This does not mean that the purpose of a large institution is not sometimes better served by this type of plan.

Small institutions, when administered by alert and intelligent people dedicated to advancing thinking in the field of child welfare, make an important contribution to the children they serve and to our knowledge in the field of institutional care. Certain small institutions are leading the way in attempts to study and treat children on a truly individual basis with a highly trained staff, and they are sharing the knowledge they have gained. Some of these institutions have been described in current child welfare literature; among them are the following: Hillside Children's Center, Rochester, New York; Sheltering Arms, New York City; Rice Study Home, Cambridge, Massachusetts; Children's Community Center, New Haven, Connecticut; Ryther Child Center, Seattle, Washington; Hawthorne-Cedar Knolls, New York. As we continue to move toward a time when most of our children's institutions will be small ones committed to special treatment objectives, much depends on the ability of staff members of various institutions to carry out in practice those special services that their institutions may be able to contribute to the general field of child care.

The Development of the Child as an Individual

Individualization within the group is important. The program must be aimed toward helping each child to develop as an individual. Each member of the staff must know as much about each child under his care as possible. Every staff member should know why the child behaves as he does, in order to help with the child's adjustment. Every child in the group must feel that he is important to staff members in the institution. Individual dress to suit the child's needs, individual hair arrangements or hair cuts are simple ways of forwarding self-esteem. A program allowing for some degree of privacy and some place (a bunk, a locker, or dresser) where personal possessions may be kept is very important. Frequent and regular visits of relatives should be encouraged to enhance the child's sense of belonging and to generate his interest during his institutional stay. Another measure of the success of an institution's program is the extent to which children's relatives participate. It is through the worker that the parents are advised of illnesses, helped to understand behavior problems, and offered interpretation of general progress in education and adjustment. Without interpretation and guidance, parents may become unsympathetic or afraid to show interest in the child. At the same time, the child needs the interpretation of casework to give him an understanding of family situations; he needs to know that his parents are interested in his school achievement. The child's visits to his home, and the parents' visits to him should be very frequent if they help the child. The worker who has the child's confidence can determine whether they do or not.

Contact with the family is paramount in deciding when the child may return home. It must be remembered that an institutional placement is always temporary, and so indications of the advisability of termination should be constantly watched for. The child should always be aware of the probable duration of his stay and of what factors will be responsible for ending his placement. When it is time to return home, the family and the child must be reconciled to the changes that have occurred during placement.

After the child returns home from the institution, there is still a vital need for supervision from the institution's field staff. If contact with family has been frequent, and if preparation for return has included interpretation for both child and family, and if institutional supervision continues after return, adjustment should not be too difficult.

Perhaps the worst feature of the old institution was its regimented, custodial life which suppressed individuality, initiative, and independence. There is necessarily more routine in group living than in family living, but constant striving for flexibility can lessen the ill effect of routine. There should be as few sets of rules as possible. Like intake policy, group living should have guides, with a minimum of rules.

There should be flexible programs of schooling, vocational training, recreation, health, religion, and social education to meet the needs of all types of children. The training program should provide facilities to promote individuality; the child who has had little schooling will need private tutoring from a staff member; the child with talent or skill should be encouraged to develop that skill whether it is in athletics, music, or handicraft. A great variety of work and play opportunities should be available so that the child may enter the activity that most interests him.

The Relation of the Institution to the Community

Unless the children of an institution participate in community life, they will be unprepared to accept normal living outside of the institution. Therefore, the circle of opportunities for play, study, work, and worship with the outside world must be constantly widening. Organizations, such as the band, Camp Fire Girls, and athletic teams, within larger institutions can join in contests with similar groups in the community. Members of smaller institutions can join groups outside.

It is better for the children to attend schools off the institutional premises with boys and girls of the community. In regard to worship, church activities in the community should be available for those who wish, or whose parents wish, special denominational philosophies.

The question of money warrants special attention. If children under institutional care are denied community contacts, they fail to learn how to earn and spend money. Experience with money can be most important in the process of guiding children to independence. Real money in the form of an allowance should be given on a varying scale that is based on age. Within the institution, there should be jobs with pay. Older children should have the privilege of taking outside jobs, such as mowing lawns and washing cars. Freedom of choice in expenditure will build up judgment and a sense of values.

In addition to encouraging normal and creative lives for the children, contacts with the community help to generate community interest in the institution. The community is not often utilized as a resource for voluntary contributions of time and funds to the institution, but, when it is, a friendly atmosphere between children and locality should prevail.

Institutions for children are valuable only as an integral part of a total community child welfare plan. This statement can be verified by a study of the history of the National Child Welfare Division of the American Legion. After World War I, there were some zealous Legionnaires who hoped to found a large number of orphanages, but after consultation with welfare leaders, such a plan was shown to be inadequate and superficial. The Legion, upon serious thought, raised a large national endowment fund and with the earnings of this fund sought to strengthen and help establish child welfare facilities and help existing local agencies to meet the needs of veterans' children.

This Legion Child Welfare Program has three major objectives: (1) education on children's needs, and creation of resources for meeting those needs; (2) support of sound legislation and more adequate government appropriations for child welfare needs; (3) direct financial aid and service to children of veterans in their own homes, or in any other child welfare facility through which the child can receive the kind of care and treatment best suited to his needs; this financial aid can be used as temporary support during waiting periods in which local aid is not immediately available or it can supplement inadequate local resources. In these ways, then, the Legion in child welfare makes itself a part of the total national child welfare program.

When the nature of the child and the circumstances of his removal from his natural home are examined and found to indicate the need of group care, that is the time to consider temporary care in an institution, but only if good institutions are available.

It is desirable that the institution have its own trained child welfare worker, so that her work may become an integral part of the program and so that it can permeate the thinking of the staff and the board members. If the institution is too small to employ a child welfare worker, it should seek the services from a cooperating agency. Since many of the institutions are receiving public wards, it seems logical that the county departments of public welfare, who, for the most part, have the guardianship of these children and are responsible for their care and support, should also provide the casework services of a child welfare worker. If the work is done by a cooperating agency, then the doors of the institution should be open to the child welfare worker from that agency at all times. If she is to have the responsibility of casework with the child's family, she should have the benefit of the institution's knowledge of the child while he remains in the institution. Visits to the institution by the child welfare worker should be welcomed, records should be open to her, and joint conferences with the staff of the institution should be a recognized part of the program.

ADOPTION

To adults, adoption means the taking of another's child as one's own by legal process. To the adopted child, adoption means the acquisition of a parental equivalent and a parent-child relationship.

There seems to be no time in the history of man when adoption did not exist. In the earliest known society, the rites of adoption included weird and grotesque simulations of birth. The Babylonian Code of Hammurabi (compiled during his reign from 1792 to 1750 B.C.) shows the existence of adoption more than 4,000 years ago. Specific laws set forth in this Code make it appear that the Babylonians were particularly interested in protecting the property rights of citizens who had adopted children and insuring that an orphan child would be provided for, that formal acknowledgment would be made of his adoption, and that he could not be cut off from the inheritance of property without legal process.

One of the recorded instances of adoption among the Hebrew people was Abram's assumption of the responsibility for Lot, son of Abram's (later Abraham) deceased brother Haran. The Bible refers to other adoptions, such as that of Moses by Pharaoh's daughter, and that of Esther by Mordecai.

The ancient Romans practiced adoption as part of their civil law, the principal motive being to acquire heirs. Emperor Germanicus received his crown through his adoption by Tiberius, which had been ordered by Augustus Caesar.

Adoption was also included in early Spanish law and was incorporated in the Code of Napoleon. In the "Great Code" of Alfonso V of Castile, provision was made for investigation to show whether adoption was good for the child.

Adoption was known in the Anglo-Saxon tribes but, possibly owing to the peculiarities of feudal tenure, disappeared in England. The first law legalizing adoption in England was passed as late as 1926.

Because the colonists brought with them the principles of the English common law, adoption as such was not known in American legal procedure until about the middle of the nineteenth century. Before that time, adoption by a deed that had been certified and filed, as in a transfer of property, was permitted in a number of southern states. The first state to pass a specific adoption law was Massachusetts in 1851. By 1867, three additional states, Pennsylvania, Wisconsin, and Illinois, had done so. Today there are adoption statutes in all of the states.

Each state has developed its own procedures, and there are no two states with identical laws. No one state can be said to have a model adoption law, but some states approximate an ideal more closely than do others.

The adoption laws in the United States are quite different from those of older nations. They place more emphasis on the rights and welfare of the child as an individual and less on the property and privilege of the adoptive parent.

Early adoption laws in this country tended to provide a simple procedure whereby the person wishing to adopt a child merely had to petition the county court in the county where he resided, and the state that had custody of the child. If the parents were living, their consent was required. If the court was satisfied, the adoption was granted. Subsequent laws and amendments were more detailed: in some, state residence requirements for a petitioner have been specified; in other statutes, joint petition by husband and wife, is necessary, as well as the consent of the child, if he has reached a certain age, that age varying in different states; the legal effects of adoption on all parties concerned have been set forth; whoever has legal guardianship of the child must give consent if the parents are dead; provisions have been added for the adoption of a spouse's child by a former marriage, or of a spouse's illegitimate child.

In general, the legislation on adoption in the various states has been concerned with the following: the parties to the adoption; the court having jurisdiction; the content of the petition; the age and residence of the petitioner; consent and notice; investigation and supervision, and the agency responsible for these tasks; the hearing; probationary residence period; the decree and the closing of the records; inheritance rights; new birth certificates; annulment; and appeal. In some of these matters, there is considerable variation from one state to another, and not all states have made provisions for every one of them.

The parties to the adoption are, of course, the adopting parents, the child, and either the natural parents or the person or agency having guardianship of the child.

Depending on the state law, the court that has jurisdiction may be a juvenile or domestic relations court, a court acting in separate sessions as a juvenile court, or a court having no juvenile jurisdiction. In some states, there may be concurrent jurisdiction by two or more courts. Some laws require that the petition be filed in the county in which the petitioner resides; some, that it be filed in the county of the child's residence; some state that it may be filed in either county; and some, that it may be filed also in the county containing the institution in which a destitute child has received care.

In general, the petition to adopt a child consists of a form stating the name and residence of the petitioner, the name and age of the child, the address of the parents or guardians, the address of the child, and the name by which the child is to be known if the decree is granted. It may also state the occupation and age of the petitioner and possibly his reason for wishing to adopt the child. When the petition is filed, the court will appoint the time and place for the hearing.

In the majority of the states, any adult person may file a petition and, if the petitioner is married, the spouse must join in the petition. A number of states require that the petitioner be a resident. In some states, the petitioner must be ten years older than the child; in others, 15 years older; but in one state, any person older than 20 years of age may adopt a child under 17. Certain states prohibit the adoption of a child who has in him the blood of any race other than that of the adopter.

In some states, upon the filing of the petition, the clerk of the court must immediately notify the state department of welfare in writing. Thereafter, in all cases in which a licensed organization is not a party to the adoption (except if adoption is by a stepparent and the natural parent retains custody and control) the state department of welfare must conduct investigation to determine whether the child is a fit subject for adoption and whether the proposed home is suitable for the child. This must be done before the natural parents' consent to adoption by the foster parents can be accepted.

Provision is made in approximately one-third of the states for an annulment of adoptions under certain specified circumstances. The circumstance most frequently cited is development by the child of insanity, feeble-mindedness, epilepsy, or venereal disease within five years after adoption.

An important section of all state statutes concerned with adoption is that on the subject of inheritance. Under common law, an adopted child does not inherit from or through adoptive parents except as the state statute provides.

Recent changes in state legislation reflect a trend toward making adoption laws and procedures consistent with sound principles of child protection. More than 40 states have made provision for a social study of proposed adoptive placements, and for recommendations to the court regarding the suitability of the placement before final action is taken on the petition for adoption.

Great advances have been made in most of the states since the 1960's toward better safeguarding of the rights and welfare of children in adoption, both by legislation and by improved standards of child placing agencies. However, much remains to be done before the maximum amount of protection can be assured to all concerned. Every state law should contain a provision that children may be placed for adoption only by qualified agencies that have been either licensed by the state department of social welfare, or investigated by a representative of that department.

The proceedings should be held before a court accustomed to handling children's cases in the locality in which the petitioner is known or resides. The court hearings should be closed to the public and the records should be confidential and available for examination only by the persons intimately concerned or on a court order.

The Children's Bureau recommends the following adoption procedures:[1]

---

1. *Essentials of Adoption Laws and Procedures.* U.S. Children's Bureau, Washington, D.C., January, 1949.

1. The consent of the natural parents should be obtained, or, if their rights have been relinquished or terminated by a judicial decree, the consent of a person or agency having legal responsibility for the child.

2. A probationary period of residence, preferably of a year, with the home under supervision by the state department of social welfare, should be required, to determine whether the adoption is suitable. If it is not suitable, provision should be made for the removal of the child from the home.

Laws are needed to cope with the adoption of children in one state by persons residing in another. New birth certificates should be issued in adoption cases to all children born in any state, regardless of where the adoption takes place.

Good adoption laws alone, however, cannot accomplish their purpose unless there are adequate safeguards in related laws—such as those affecting the relinquishment and termination of parental rights, regulation of child placing agencies, and determination of guardianship and custody—to assure the welfare of the child and the rights and obligations of the parents. No transfer of parental rights should be valid without judicial sanction.

Types of Adoption

In the field of adoption, as in all other phases of child welfare, the child and his needs are the focus on which the intricate machinery that has been developed to meet these needs centers. This complex structure has evolved through the years as a result of experience and increased knowledge, and it should continue to change to conform to changing needs.

There are four types of adoption: (1) independent adoptions, (2) stepparent adoptions, (3) agency adoptions, and (4) the adoption of the illegitimate child by its father.

Independent adoptions are those in which the natural parents choose a home and place their child there for adoption, or relinquish their child to a person who will place it for the parent.

In the stepparent adoptions, one natural or adoptive parent retains his custody and control of the child, but the stepparent petitions to adopt the child. The usual reason for this type of adoption is to insure that the stepchild will have the legal rights and privileges of a natural child. The stepparent may also want to be assured that no one else will have a claim on the child in the event of the natural parent's death. Stepparent adoptions prevent the interference of the other natural parent in plans for the child.

In an agency adoption, the parents relinquish their child to an agency licensed by the state to find homes for children and place children for adoption. The agency may also include foundlings and abandoned children in its adoptive placements.

The procedure for the adoption of an illegitimate child by its natural father varies in the states. In some states it is possible for the natural father to adopt the child by publicly announcing it as his own, receiving it in his home, and treating it as his own.

Those Who May Be Adopted

Before a child is considered for adoption, it should be made certain that the child cannot possibly be cared for by his own family. Often a study of the situation reveals that the difficulty is only temporary and that the child can remain with his parents or be placed for a period in a boarding home and later returned to his parents. Adoption should never be planned in haste or decided upon in an emergency. Ample time for consideration should be allowed the child's family, and every possible assistance should be offered to enable them to rear him before he is placed for adoption.

If a child's own parents have forfeited their natural rights to consent to adoption, the agency must exercise great care in placing that child for adoption. If parents do not wish to give up their children and there is any possibility that with the assistance of the agency they can provide a suitable home, action toward adoption should be delayed. Improvement of the home situation so that a child can be returned to his natural parents is always the first objective.

Agencies in the past have set up rather arbitrary requirements for the children they regard as adoptable and the prospective parents they will consider. It may be that many more children are adoptable than are given for adoption. As a result, many children, particularly older ones, in need of homes are never placed, and many persons who would like to adopt children and could provide good homes for them are not allowed to do so. Instead of trying to place the "apparently ideal" child in the "apparently ideal" home, the agency should provide longer and more thorough periods of preparation and follow-up. This would insure a higher percentage of success even in those placements which, although acceptable, do not meet all the high standards commonly thought to be desirable. It is naturally more difficult to place an older child than an infant, but even a child handicapped by being crippled or deaf may be placed successfully under special conditions.

However, the requirements today are less arbitrary than they used to be. Agencies are alert to the need for research in all aspects of adoption and for identifying conditions to predict the success of adoptions. Workers are not as inclined to seek the perfect adoption by matching superficial factors of the child with those of the prospective parents, nor do they pay as much attention to external appearances, such as neatness of the adoptive home. They now assume the more difficult task of seeking the emotionally mature couples who can accept a child wholeheartedly, and who are able to change, take risks, and grow into parenthood.

Public attitudes have changed, too. Couples who have adopted a child are apt to be proud of the fact and not secretive about it. There is a more accepting attitude toward children born out of wedlock. Adoption of children over six years old and children of minority groups still presents a problem. Specialized help is needed in this field.

To facilitate placement of the "hard-to-place" child, such as the older child, the handicapped, the child with emotional problems, and children of minority groups, there is a growing practice among agencies of sharing information on such children who, because of one of the above reasons, have remained in boarding homes or institutions long beyond the time at which placement for adoption was indicated. State-wide clearing services for the purpose of finding homes for these children have been established in several states and localities; and plans for extending this service on a nationwide basis, with the help of the Child Welfare League of America and the United States Children's Bureau, are under consideration. Mr. Michael Shapiro, director of the National Adoption Project of the Child Welfare League, has been active in the establishment of such clearing houses.

In finding a home for a "less desirable child," it may be necessary to place the child in a home which, according to the most exacting standard, is less desirable. Adoptive parents who are older than is commonly thought desirable may, nevertheless, provide a home that is greatly superior to the foster home or institution in which the child would have to stay if not adopted. Even a single person may, in some cases, provide a home superior to anything else the child could expect.

It has been said that "every placement is a special problem," because each child has some special need or hereditary factor which requires a specially chosen and adopted home.

In 1953 about 90,000 adoptive petitions were filed in the United States, according to estimates by the Children's Bureau; this is 80 percent more than were filed in 1944, the date of the Bureau's first national estimate. Slightly more than 50 percent of the 1953 petitions were filed by persons unrelated to the child. Of the children adopted by nonrelatives, 45 percent were placed in adoptive homes without the aid of a recognized child placing agency. These estimates were based on reports from 29 states.

Other statistics of a broader nature indicate that as of March, 1962, 583,100 children were served by public juvenile and private child welfare programs. Thirty-nine percent of these children were with their own families, 10 percent were living in adoptive homes, 30 percent in foster homes, 18 percent in institutions, and the remainder, three percent, in a variety of living arrangements.

Those Who May Adopt

In choosing the foster home, the worker must determine whether the child can reasonably be assured of the following: economic security —not wealth, but sufficient income so that he will not need to feel himself a burden to his adoptive parents, and so that he will be able to complete his education in accordance with his capacities; good physical conditions, such as a clean, safe room, and opportunity for outdoor play every day; and, most important of all, real family life—warm affection, acceptance of him as a person, understanding, and sympathy.

It is best to place a child in a home in which his mental capacities, temperament, and personality are somewhat similar to those of his adoptive parents and their close friends. Otherwise, he may be forced to struggle too hard to keep up with standards that are too high for his level of attainment, or, if his abilities greatly surpass those of his family and associates, he may not develop his fullest capacities. Racial and religious backgrounds should also be matched where practicable.

Ideally, constitutional types, racial antecedents, appearance, and temperaments would be identical. In practice, general similarity of these factors is important. The ultimate selection of a home is a weighty decision for the caseworker, and it is influenced by her sensitivity.

Minimum criteria for a good home should not be regarded as complete and absolute by the person selecting an adoptive home for a child, but should be thought of only as a guide in evaluating and selecting a home. A home may fulfill all the requirements of a so-called standard list, and yet may lack so many other desirable features that it should be classified as an unsatisfactory home. Sometimes unlisted influences in a home are of much greater importance than those enumerated in the standard lists.

Protection of the Child in Adoption

Before a child is placed for adoption, a social investigation is necessary for the protection of all concerned. In the event the child's natural parents are living, an inquiry into their reasons for wishing to surrender him may reveal a situation which can be dealt with in some other way so that the family can be kept together.

The worker's primary interest is the child, but in addition she must be prepared to extend her services to the parents who seek to adopt the child. Their entry into the case naturally complicates the casework.

The applicant to an adoption agency usually believes she has arrived at her decision after very careful consideration. She has, perhaps, consulted relatives, friends, her clergyman, and a lawyer, who may concur in and substantiate her desire for a child. But the worker must probe more deeply, and determine the motives in applying for a child.

Although popular literature and public sentiment may lead one to conclude that motives for adoption spring from a bountiful altruism, that is not always so. It is equally misguided to assume that adoptive parents have no needs to be met and no satisfactions to be gained from adopting a child. It is the worker's task to recognize the real reasons that lie behind the request for a child, in order to place the child in a home in which his satisfactions and those of the parents do not conflict, but rather work to their mutual benefit.

Most parents want to adopt a child because they have not had one of their own. In many situations this is because of biological inability to produce a child, which inevitably results in feelings of anxiety and insecurity. The worker should be informed on current concepts concerning the causes of sterility. Sterility may have multiple causes. Reasons for sterility are hard to evaluate and many apparently true physical causes have turned out to be psychogenic. If there is a feeling of guilt on the part of either husband or wife because of sterility, how does this affect their relationship to each other? Is the sterility the sole reason for adoption? Are the parents able to accept the reality of this condition and develop constructive compensations so that they can comfortably assume nonbiological parenthood? If sterility has not been definitely established, what is the attitude of the applicants toward further medical study? If exploration of this question shows a great unwillingness on the part of either the man or woman to have additional diagnosis and treatment when such has been recommended, is this indicative of an unconscious wish to have the agency refuse their request for a child? If applicants set up a detailed list of specifications which the child must fit, this may be an indication of their anxiety about adoption and of an ambivalent feeling about having a child.

The worker should give thoughtful attention to the pattern of dependence and protectiveness that has evolved between the man and woman. Is it such that a child will inject a rivalry situation causing irritations and tensions so great that a harmonious, emotionally stable family life cannot be worked out? If the applicants are middle aged, the worker will want to know whether they can be flexible in meeting the needs of a child. Some applicants may insist on the utmost secrecy in regard to their application. This attitude may denote conflict or anxiety concerning adoption.

Applicants who wish to bolster a tottering marriage, solve problems of instability, alcoholism or infidelity, replace the ideal of an own child who died, provide a pet or plaything for an own child, or obtain an object toward whom a woman can direct all of her emotional satisfaction all offer situations that would be obviously detrimental to an adopted child.

In trying to estimate the parental motive for adopting a child, the worker must try to be aware of all possible factors. She should try to discern whether the parents, in addition to bestowing love on the child, will be able to see him as an individual with qualities for growth and not merely as a satisfaction of their own needs. They should be able to accept the child's limitations and, through their love and understanding, help him to achieve maturity. The child should not be an object on whom they can project their own thwarted ambitions.

The Responsibility of the Worker

Adoption is not a temporary placement of a child. It is a permanent placement and will affect the child for the rest of his life. It is not a normal condition for children to have substitute parents, or for families to have adopted children. For these reasons, the child welfare worker has an enormous responsibility in evaluating and selecting the "adoptable" child and the "acceptable" home.

As in other phases of casework, the first requisite, perhaps, is that the worker strive for self-awareness and self-understanding. It is only by scrutinizing herself that she may achieve the delicate balance of objectivity and warm understanding with which she may best serve the child. Her goal is to fulfill the needs of the child, and yet the needs which she herself brings to her work are an important factor. It is of the utmost importance that she be able to recognize in her clients— the child, the natural parents, and the adoptive parents—not only their motives and needs as exemplified in their behavior, but also the bases and causes of this behavior. The degree to which she achieves this recognition is, in large part, determined by the degree of her own self-awareness.

During the first interview, the worker should ask herself if the applicants seem to be able to fulfill the needs which the agency has found to be the child's. She should try to gauge the applicant's readiness for the steps in adoption. She must not allow herself to become too involved in problems which may seem to be present in the prospective adoptive parents. The applicant has come with a request for a child, and the worker must focus on that.

She begins by clarifying and explaining agency policies and procedures, and their purpose and necessity in the light of the child's welfare. If the role of the agency is presented skillfully, it will do much to establish a relationship which will help the worker to a better understanding of the foster parents.

The worker may present the application form at the first interview, if it is agency policy to do so. It may be either a brief form asking for information on questions of immediate concern to the agency, or a more complete type of questionnaire. The manner in which the worker presents and interprets the form is very important and can have a profound influence on the general attitudes of the applicants. Members of the Child Welfare League of America have pointed out the importance of this initial application.

A vital part of the worker's services to the adoptive parents is discussion of the question on what they are to tell the child about his status. She should acquaint them early with the necessity of telling him of his adoption, but this subject cannot be properly confined to any specific period in her relationship with the parents. The adoptive parents should anticipate that, at some point, it will be natural for the child to ask questions about his own parents. This type of question should be explained and discussed with the adoptive parents so that they will be able to handle it with ease and lack of tension. The child's questions should be met with honesty, but tempered by a timing of what and how much may be discussed with the child at a given stage of psychological development.

The services to the child begin the moment the worker and the child meet. This is particularly true for the older child, more than for the infant. The worker should recognize that the child may be anxious and fearful, and should convey to him her protective interest. It is possible that early in the work with the child, the worker may be able to form a tentative estimate of his capacity for an adoptive relationship. Her realization of the significant influence of the adoptive process on the child will aid her in her subsequent study of him. In working with the child, she gains insight into his individuality as much from his behavior as from what he says. In noticing his use of toys, for instance, and his reactions to examinations, to other children, and to adults, she may see indications of the degree of his readiness for the new experience.

Although the child must feel sure that the worker is interested in him, she must not become so protective that she negates opportunities for his growth. The fact that the child is a growing, developing being aids in his capacity for adjustment to the adoptive situation.

The worker must realize that, although the interests and needs of the child are paramount, she must achieve the understanding to meet as adequately as possible the myriad conscious and unconscious needs of the natural and adoptive parents and she must constantly bear in mind her responsibility to them. As a member of a professional adoption agency, she must recognize the agency's ultimate responsibility to the community whose primary interest is the welfare of the individual child.

She should recognize at all times her responsibility for conforming to the legal requirements of adoption, which have been set up primarily as safeguards for the child but which also serve as protective measures for the adoptive parents. She has a very real responsibility to strive for better adoptive legislation, because present laws should indeed be improved to meet the changes within the whole framework surrounding adoptions. She should be aware of the great need for interpreting to her clients the validity of legalized adoption in order to mitigate the wrongs attendant on private and nonprofessional placements.

If she is able to gain the support of the community for the best type of adoption program, she will strive to insure community cooperation in her work, and to lessen the prevalence of undesirable adoption procedures.

The Responsibility of the Agency

Although the worker may take an active part in improving adoption programs, the kind of participation is largely determined by her agency's policies and views. The agency must keep its policies in conformity with the adoption statute under which it operates, but the practical and emotional complications that cannot be written into even the most comprehensive law are also properly the agency's concern. Even the most competent agencies have not as yet been able to achieve ideal procedures for dealing with the complex emotions that attend the adoptive process. Widespread public concern has arisen, and it is not entirely unjustified.

Agencies cannot dismiss such criticism as entirely illogical or uninformed, for they must gain the rapport with the community that is essential to the whole program. By paying careful attention to complaints, recognizing their valid aspects, and making a sincere attempt to explain some of the difficulties encountered, the agency can do much to improve its own program and gain the support of the community to which it is responsible.

Careful interpretation of the adoption program to the public is vital. If this type of public relations is effective, it may reach prospective adoptive parents and parents considering relinquishment, and these people will, in turn, bring to the process of adoption a comprehension and grasp of the implications which will be of appreciable aid to the child welfare worker. It is such reciprocal interest and understanding between the agency and the public that will prove efficacious in reaching the goal.

The agency and the worker are powerful determinants in the future welfare and happiness of the child and should never lose sight of the importance of their task. By constantly examining and evaluating their procedures and by utilizing the contributions of research findings and new practices, they may work toward an increasing competency and skill in function.

Since, in the light of present knowledge, adoption appears to offer the greatest protection to the dependent child, the worker and the agency should expend their concerted efforts toward expanding the adoption program and improving adoption techniques.

These improved techniques are then furthered and applied through the tools of casework techniques, skills in interviewing, and a working knowledge of the principles of child welfare. With the assets of training, a conscious philosophy, and experience, the worker is able to serve her client as effectively as possible.

Placement of the Child

Opinions on the best age at which a child should be placed for adoption differ. Some believe that the earlier the adoptive parent-child relationship is established, the better are the chances for the development of an emotionally healthy child. Others contend that it is wiser to wait until the child is from a year to 18 months old, since by that time it is possible to determine more accurately his physical and mental development.

The meaning of "early placement" in adoption is almost as varied as the number of agencies using the term. Some adoption agencies have regarded any age less than six months as an example of an early placement, whereas the current use seems to designate placements of babies under three months old as early.

Adoption agencies are demonstrating that the protections their services offer to natural parents, children, and adoptive parents do not preclude the early placement of a baby. Casework services to natural parents, legal safeguards, careful selection of adopting parents, and the study of social and medical history need not be sacrificed. Agencies have learned that adoptive parents are eager to take risks that caseworkers formerly hesitated to impose. The unrealistic expectation that an agency can "guarantee" a baby is no longer endorsed either by agencies or by adoptive parents. Long-term observation of every infant's development is no longer considered a necessary part of an adoptive placement.

The psychological values to be derived from promoting these early parent-child attachments are readily apparent, and not only in the child and adoptive parents: caseworkers have reported the favorable responses with which natural parents have greeted the knowledge that their children had been placed, and the resolution of many conflicts as a result of the reassurance that a good plan had been made and carried out. The following cases will illustrate some actual "early placements."

When Mr. and Mrs. F. first indicated their interest in adopting a child, Mr. F. was 29 and Mrs. F. a year younger. They had been married for four years and had known since shortly after their marriage that no children would be born to them because Mrs. F. did not ovulate. Although this was a great disappointment to them, they said, in the interview, that they then began to think in terms of adoption, since life to them would not be complete without a child or children. During the early years of their marriage both young people worked; they bought a pleasant suburban home which they enjoyed renovating to their own taste, and built up enough of a financial reserve that they felt they were ready for parenthood.

The intake interview and subsequent home study revealed that the F.'s were attractive people with extremely pleasant, warm personalities. They had both been reared in families wherein they had much in the way of security, although Mr. F.'s father was a rather severe disciplinarian. Both Mr. and Mrs. F. were college graduates; they met while attending college. They had interests in common as well as many other bonds, and their marriage was a particularly good one for each. Mr. F. had a job as advertising and circulation manager for a small but old and well established technical book concern. He was enthusiastic about his work; and his employer, in the course of the home study, indicated that Mr. F. could be expected to go far in the business world. Their religion stressed positive values and was really a manifestation of the golden rule, and the F.'s endeavored to practice this precept.

The couple put a good deal of thought and consideration into the kind of child they hoped to get from the agency. They had no prejudices toward any nationalities, nor did they have any preferences in the coloring of a child, because all variations of coloring and complexion were represented in their families, but they did want a child of the Caucasian race. They hoped to get a child whose intelligence could be expected to be within the range of normal, but they realized that there was no accurate way of predicting intelligence; in short, they were prepared to meet the needs of just a baby and to enjoy doing so. Mrs. F. wanted a young baby; what she had in mind, apparently, was a child under three months old. They would like to be considered for a child who might have a minor or correctible handicap.

The couple indicated their ability to handle the questions of a child's adoptive status with sensitivity, intelligence, warmth, and imagination, and their application was accepted for the placement of a child.

Meanwhile, Anne J., an 18-year-old girl from a different part of the state, was referred to the agency by a maternity home. Anne, who was unmarried, was expecting to become a mother and was interested in arranging for the placement of the child for adoption. Since the maternity home provided casework service for all its girls, the responsibility of helping Anne formulate a plan was undertaken jointly between the adoption agency and the maternity home.

Anne was a petite, pretty girl who had graduated from high school the previous June and who had been expecting to go on to a university, a plan she had been forced to change because of her illegitimate pregnancy. Her mother, who was a former school teacher, was active in several women's clubs; her father was a moderately successful business man.

Anne's mother took her daughter's pregnancy particularly hard and was most fearful that anyone in the community should find out about it, and some of this anxiety was communicated to Anne. Anne decided to plan on the baby's placement for adoption. She did not want to marry the 18-year-old youth who had fathered the child. When Anne told the baby's father of her pregnancy, he in turn confided in his family, and his father telephoned Anne's father and said the boy would do whatever Anne wanted him to do. Anne and her family took this offer under advisement and decided they would prefer to handle the matter themselves. Anne planned to write to the father and tell him the outcome after the baby was born and placed, but she had not seen or heard from the young man since early in her pregnancy, and she did not wish him drawn into the matter personally.

From the time of Anne's first visit by the worker until the day she gave birth to a son, most of the interviews centered on Anne's testing out of the worker and the agency to see if in her opinion they could be trusted to do well by her child, and on her resolution of her own internal conflicts over her intention to place him for adoption. She finally decided that her plan was sound, and after the baby was born and ready to leave the hospital the child came under care of the agency and was placed in a foster boarding home. He weighed 6 pounds and ½ ounce at birth. He was five days old when admitted to care, and the pediatrician declared him healthy and normal. Anne came into the office and signed relinquishments 12 days later. She wanted the relinquishment to be early, because she wanted her son to be established in his adoptive home as soon as possible.

The baby's record indicates that Anne stressed the importance of her child being placed in a home in which the adoptive parents would be educated, well adjusted, happily married people who had religious values, and who would give her son educational opportunities.

When the baby was relinquished, the agency had considerable

knowledge of his background, which seemed generally favorable; he was in good health and was developing very well, and was now legally free for adoptive placement. The agency had a wide selection of homes for him but decided on the F. home as the most suitable.

When the F.'s saw the baby he was less than three weeks old; they were delighted with him, accepting and understanding the reasons he was available to them in adoption. The period following placement was uneventful. The F.'s have given the baby much in the way of security, and he has brought them much happiness.

The second case concerns a baby who was placed for adoption when he was 14 days old. The adoptive parents were eager for as young a baby as possible. They both believed that a baby needs and thrives on security, and they felt that the sooner the baby was permanently placed the better off he would be emotionally. In addition, although fully conscious that by adopting they were accepting their inability to have children, they felt it was desirable to have a baby "almost as young as if we'd had our own." The period following placement revealed no problems, and legal adoption was completed shortly after expiration of the six-month period which their state required.

In evaluating the experience, as they applied for a second baby, the couple analyzed their preference for a very young infant. They felt it was best for the parents and the baby in that it gave them all the opportunity to "grow together" from the baby's earliest age. The adoptive mother said, "In fact, it is terrific for the parents," and expanded this by saying she felt it was a much fuller experience than it would have been to have had an older baby placed with them. She indicated she had found out "lots happen between two weeks and six weeks in a baby's development," and she "wouldn't have missed it for anything." The adoptive father recalled his awe and the spiritual feeling he had when he held his own son: "so small I could hold him in one of my hands."

The only possible disadvantage to this situation that they could think of would be if the child had some kind of serious medical problem at birth which did not "show up" until one or two months of age. They felt that this might be quite difficult for some adoptive parents, but actually they would still want the baby as young as possible, even if it meant taking care of a medical problem.

In a third case, the adoptive parents consistently requested a tiny infant. They had adopted a first child independently, and therefore had the baby in their home when he was three days old. They did not wish to take the risks that would be involved in another independent adoption, but they hoped the agency would place as young a baby as possible in their home. The adoptive mother said, "But I want to have to get up at night and do all the things I would if I had my own baby."

They did not wish to miss a minute of the baby's development. They wanted their three-year-old son to have the experience of a very young sister. To them, it seemed the way to start a very normal family life for all of them.

This placement was made 17 days after the baby's birth. When the baby was about four months old it became evident that she had a turned-in foot, and consequently she had to wear a cast two or three months. The parents accepted this comfortably, and their attitude was, "If we had our own, she might have developed a medical problem, too."

The final case involved twins who were placed at the age of five weeks. Examinations by the agency's pediatrician found them physically normal in every respect. The adopting parents had consistently requested twins and it was felt they were appropriate prospective parents for the additional demands which twins impose. They had an ideal physical environment, sufficient income to meet emergencies, insight into the special problems of twins, energy, and an abounding love for all children. They, too, had emphasized, "the tinier, the better."

In looking back a year later, these parents said they would have felt deprived if they had been denied one day of those early weeks. They pointed out that their babies were alert, and that they watched everything, "taking things in" from the first—seeing, feeling, and relating to the parents and the environment. They asked, "Do people think a baby is just a thing for two months?" All the fatigue, the necessity of getting up a number of times during the night, the almost constant feeding, diapering, and bathing occasioned by having twins was nothing compared to the joy of having the young infants.

In each of these cases the adoptive parents had requested a tiny infant and had indicated that the lack of developmental testing was of no importance to them. They all expressed the belief that the baby stands on its own merits and they were therefore unimpressed by tests or lengthy histories on natural parents. They also felt that an adopted baby need not come with a "gold certificate of guarantee" and said that if the child developed medical problems they would react exactly as they would for a child of their own: they would simply seek medical attention.

The natural mothers in these cases were girls whose babies were delivered in maternity hospitals where patients were seen regularly by a caseworker. They were all girls who had never shown any indecision in their plans for adoptive placement of their children. Furthermore, all of them had requested early placement of their babies because they wished them to be in their permanent homes "with both parents" as soon as possible. They had all had regular medical care and examinations and had been found to be in excellent health. There had appeared to be no known evidence of serious hereditary problems. Each natural mother was told of the placement soon afterwards, and the reaction of each was the same—a sigh of relief accompanied by a statement such as, "Now, I can close the book with a happy ending and look to the future."

It is agreed that the most successful placements are generally made before the child is five years old, since a younger child fits more readily into a home without having established ties and behavior habits that are difficult to break.

At placement, the worker should reemphasize to the adoptive parents that perfectly smooth initial adjustments are rare, and prepare the family for deviations from the "they all lived happily ever after" formula. If this preparation is carefully done, the parents may be able to appreciate the satisfactions that lie in differences as well as similarities. The parents should also gain from the worker a realization that the agency's continuing responsibility and supervision throughout the probation period will be a means of both protecting the child and insuring a satisfactory familial adjustment.

All reputable adoption agencies keep records of each child, which include whatever they have been able to learn of the previous life history and ancestry of the child, the results of physical and mental tests, as well as the steps in the agency's own care of the child.

Some adoptive parents may prefer to know nothing at all of the child's own parents. This preference may be due to their inability to accept the fact of nonbiological parenthood or to their desire to use ignorance as a protection when the child will be ready to ask questions about his own background. Other parents will demand all available information about the child. For the protection of the adoptive parents, it is generally conceded that they should receive the family health history of the child when this is known, especially if there should be a history of epilepsy or functional psychosis. The medical history of the child should be available, along with information on his general mental level, but not a specific intelligence quotient rating. Usually, the names of the real parents are not given unless the adoptive parents expressly ask for them. Agency policies vary on this point because, in some instances, the possession of the knowledge may have unfortunate consequences.

The child himself, when he grows up, will have a natural curiosity concerning his parentage, about which he has a right to learn. If he has received a proper sense of security in his adoptive home he can accept whatever facts are available.

The factors which may operate when the child wants to know about his own parents should be clearly impressed on the adoptive parents by the agency, so that they may be able to provide the understanding and support the child will need.

Placement of the Child Born Out of Wedlock

In working with an unmarried mother who wishes to relinquish her child, the worker should be careful that her own feelings about illegitimacy do not cause her to adopt too passive a role as the mother struggles to reach a decision. Too active a role by the worker may constitute an equally formidable barrier to the successful resolution of this crucial crisis in the mother's life. Although these feelings may not be easily discernible or even present in every case, the worker's intellectual awareness of their possibilities is a beginning step in her self-understanding. Their complexity defies any sort of precise definition and, in most people, such feelings could not possibly be isolated from the total personality. The understanding of these subconscious attitudes toward illegitimacy is a continuously developing process, a knowledge of the dynamics of human behavior.

Many unmarried mothers surrender their children for adoption for economic reasons; others do so because they are afraid of social stigma, or of ruining future chances for marriage by keeping the child; still others submit to pressure from family and friends, usually at a time when they are under great emotional stress and incapable of rationally considering their own real desires in the matter, and later bitterly regret the decision. Since more than half of the children surrendered for adoption are born of unwed mothers, illegitimacy constitutes one of the greatest problems of the worker. The problem is heightened during war years, not only by the increase in number of illegitimate births, but also by the fact that many married women, in the absence of their husbands, give birth to babies by other men. In these cases, the legitimacy of the child depends on whether or not the state law provides that a child born to a married woman is presumed to be the child of her husband and therefore legitimate, and that court action is required to prove the contrary.

The first step in working with the unmarried mother should be the evaluation of her total situation—economic and social factors, as well as her attitude toward the child and her wishes in regard to keeping it or surrendering it for adoption. Sufficient time should be allowed to elapse after the birth of the child so that she can view the situation realistically and make a wise decision. It is desirable, if possible, to establish the paternity of the child, both for economic reasons and for the later information on the child, as well as for determination of the family history prior to adoption. Where no paternal history is available, it is necessary to have the most complete and detailed information obtainable about the mother and her family, and a slightly longer period may be needed to observe the child.

Some of the reasons that people choose to participate in independent adoptions are the following: (1) a long waiting period elapses before one can secure a child through the licensed adoption agencies; (2) those participating in these adoptions are either unaware of, or unconcerned about, the dangers involved; (3) the licensed agencies have established rigid criteria of adoptability; (4) in the desire for secrecy, frequently a mother wishes to place her own child; (5) financial inducements may be offered to the natural parents; (6) agencies may not be equipped to handle adoptions quickly, owing to shortage of personnel; (7) the lay public is generally uninformed about sound adoption practices, as is evidenced by the apathy toward proposed protective legislation.

In many areas of the country, there flourish undesirable maternity homes: some are operated by well-meaning but uninformed women; others are strictly commercial enterprises, practically like a black market in nature. Both types are apt to be attractive to the unmarried mother, since they offer secrecy and prompt disposal of the baby, conveniences that are often just what she is looking for. However, most of the well-intentioned women that operate the first type of home lack judgment in placing babies. The second type of establishment may even advertise maternal care before and after birth of the child and promise to dispose of the baby, though, in some states, advertising of this nature is forbidden by law. The main reasons for the success of these maternity homes are the scarcity of babies for adoption, the stigma of illegitimacy, and the fact that unmarried mothers do not know of the aid they can receive from the social services.

It has been suggested that social workers have not developed skills and techniques for working with the "overprivileged client," the person who has led a self-directing life and has economic security and cultural advantages. This type of client is one who tends to make arrangements for independent adoption. In dealing with persons of this type, the worker may feel socially insecure and hence be either too timid to ask pertinent questions or too aggressive and critical in areas of unimportance.

Administration of Adoption Laws

To safeguard the interests of the child, the natural parents, and the adoptive parents, it is not enough that a good adoption law be on the statute book. A good law that is poorly administered can be subjected to many abuses.

To secure good administration of a law requires public support. If the people are not interested and do not support the law, that particular law loses much of its effectiveness. Much of today's activity in child placement by unethical persons and organizations exists because of inadequate laws; but a "model adoption law," though it may cover up inadequacies, will not in itself cure all of the evils.

What is needed in addition to the law is an enlightened public that has been made keenly aware of its responsibility for ascertaining that the welfare of all the parties to an adoption are protected. This objective is not easily attainable. It will have to be accomplished by an educative method, in which the normal channels of disseminating information are utilized. Articles in the press and magazines, talks on radio and television, and addresses before clubs and organizations, are some of the means of communication that can be used to draw public attention to the facts.

A good adoption law backed by a good administration could still be hampered in effectiveness and direction of purpose if related laws on the statute books were inadequate. Laws dealing with such questions as determination of guardianship and custody of a child, the relinquishment of parental rights, and the regulation of child placing services must all provide for the welfare of the child, and for the clarification of the rights and obligations of the parents.

If the United States as a whole is to have a good adoption procedure as well as related child welfare laws, some uniformity in standards must exist among the states. Otherwise, a state with adequate child welfare laws, properly administered, might discover that its own high standards were being circumvented because a neighboring state has inferior laws and administration. The phenomenon of migration to do "business" in the state with lax laws has many precedents, and could occur in adoption. A state with inadequate child welfare laws and poor administration could prove a haven for "traders in children." For example, because the demand for children greatly exceeds the number available for adoption, unethical maternity homes could find it profitable to establish themselves in the lax state, pay the cost of an unwed mother's transportation from her home state, and simply add this to the fee charged to the adoptive parents.

The best insurance against allowing this kind of transaction to occur would be for all the states to have good, well administered child welfare laws. In order to eliminate independent placements, it is necessary to educate the public on what is involved when children are placed for life; to enact good legislation to provide and finance sound placement procedures; and to adjust the programs of social agencies to meet the task of changing the conditions—that is, of informing the public of the need for standard, legalized adoption procedures conducted by qualified licensed agencies.

Supplementary Readings

Beedell, Christopher. *Residential Life with Children*. Humanities Press, New York, 1970.

Broten, Alton M. *Houseparents in Children's Institutions*. University of North Carolina Press, Chapel Hill, 1962.

Buck, Pearl. *Children for Adoption*. Random House, New York, 1964.

Burmeister, Eva Elizabeth. *The Professional Houseparent*. Columbia University Press, New York, 1960.

Child Welfare League of America. *Standards for Services of Child Welfare Institutions*. Child Welfare League of America, New York, 1964.

Dinnage, Rosemary. *Residential Child Care, Facts and Fallacies*. Longmans, London, 1967.

Dittmann, Laura L. *Early Child Care*. Atherton, New York, 1968.

Farmer, Robert Allen. *How to Adopt a Child*. Arco, New York, 1967.

Flint, Betty Margaret. *The Child and the Institution*. University of Toronto Press, Toronto, 1966.

Humphrey, Michael. *The Hostage Seekers*. Humanities Press, New York, 1969.

Isaac, Rael Jean. *Adopting a Child Today*. Harper and Row, New York, 1965.

Kornitzer, Margaret. *Adoption*. Putnam, London, 1967.

Kornitzer, Margaret. *Adoption and Family Life*. Putnam, London, 1968.

Leary, Morton L. *The Law of Adoption*. Oceana Publications, New York, 1954.

Patten, Jack. *The Children's Institution*. McCutchan Publishing Corporation, Berkeley, California, 1968.

Pringle, Mia Lilly. *Adoption Facts and Fallacies*. Longmans, London, 1967.

Randell, Florence. *The Adopted Family*. Crown, New York, 1965.

Rosner, Gertrude. *Crisis of Self-Doubt*. Child Welfare League of America, New York, 1961.

Rowe, Jane. *Yours by Choice*. Routledge and Kegan Paul, Ltd., London, 1969.

Smith, I. Evelyn, Ed. *Readings in Adoption.* Philosophical Library, New York, 1963.

Society for Research in Child Development. *Perspectives on Adoption Research.* Child Welfare League of America, New York, 1965.

Weinstein, Eugene A. *The Self-Image of the Foster Child.* Russell Sage Foundation, New York, 1960.

Witner, Helen Leland. *Independent Adoptions.* Russell Sage Foundation, New York, 1963.

[*Photo by Cary Osfeld.*]

12

The Future of
Child Welfare

The field of child welfare embraces many services, agencies and social institutions not only in the United States but throughout the world. Considering the wide scope of the field, predicting what the future holds for child welfare would be tenuous at best. To complicate such an endeavor, the United States and the rest of the world have been experiencing rapid change socially, economically, technologically, and politically. Although these fluid conditions prevent us from discussing large-scale developments in child welfare with any precision, we can analyze, with some degree of confidence, certain trends and future needs.

STRUCTURED PROGRAMS

The common goals of all programs in the field of human welfare appear to be two: to make the world a better place to live in, and to help people find satisfaction and achievement in the society in which they function.

Large numbers of organizations, having different philosophies, work side by side for a better world and society. They are all doing different things in different ways. All are driven by powerful and conflicting inner motivations and by terrific external pressure of time and circumstances. Many of them are without clear pictures of specific individual goals and ideas of the means to reach desired ends. However, we must remember that social movements are relatively slow and complicated phenomena.

We must remember, also, that in the emergency period immediately following the Great Depression of 1929, the government was able to move from a program of seclusion and security—one serving a limited number of clients who were set apart from the great body of citizens—to one attempting to serve a cross section of society. Although probably far from an ideal program, it was a step in the right direction. Today, the federal government operates in a more enlightened public interest and with more knowledge, serving people who had never before been considered for public welfare benefits. Indeed, it is beginning to take the responsibility for the fulfillment of the universal minimum needs of our entire population.

To carry into effect the general principles underlying programs for the welfare of children, certain machinery at the state level is necessary. No one structure of operation can be specified for all states, and the exact gearing of the machinery has to vary with existing situations. However, there are certain constants in all social systems.

For instance, it is nationally recognized that in every state department of public or social welfare there should be a children's division. It is also recognized that this division should have a segregated budget so that money will not be withdrawn from work with children when there are other pressures, and that it should have a child welfare staff skilled in children's work in order that personnel will not be upset by exigencies and pressures from other programs. There should be close coordination between the division of child welfare and other divisions of the state department of public welfare.

The child welfare division should have the following broadly defined functions: the protection and care of homeless, dependent, and neglected children and children in danger of becoming delinquent; the regular statutory duties of licensing, inspecting, and supervising private and public children's institutions; the provision of adequate child welfare services, by a skilled staff, to accomplish the functions mentioned.

The welfare board should have the power to make necessary rules and regulations for carrying out the functions established by law.

There is a difference of opinion on whether the law which sets up the service should be broadly written, leaving the details to be worked out by the administrative agency, or whether it should be quite specific and detailed. A law that would allow a wide interpretation of functions and powers, and that would deal as little as possible with the mechanics of administration, would have much to commend it. If the law is broadly written in its specification of powers and duties, and little question about the extent and nature of the departments concerned remains, those responsible for the development of the program can place a much more liberal interpretation on their functions. This plan will prove satisfactory if the department is staffed with qualified people who can be relied upon to give sound administration. Any form of organization will eventually invite disaster if not staffed with trustworthy people.

There has been a trend in some jurisdictions to decentralize certain state functions by delegating them to the county or district welfare units, and, in some places, to town units. The breadth of delegated responsibility should depend on the demonstrated competence of the child welfare staff. The unit needs to be large enough to make it feasible for qualified people to be employed. The aim is to bring the direct service as close as possible to the individual child to be served and yet to maintain a unit strong enough to provide service of high quality. Certain functions, such as the final recommendations to the court in adoption proceedings and service to institutions and agencies, should remain within the state office until the local unit is adequately staffed with personnel qualified to assume such responsibility. If decentralization within a state is complete, the state's real job becomes more one of leadership, direction, and supervision and less one of actual administration, except for the administration of state institutions for children. The approach, then, is less authoritative and is rather one of assistance to the counties.

State training schools for boys or girls should be administered by the division of child welfare. They constitute a source of treatment for the child whose care at home or in the community seems inadvisable, and they should be one part of a total child welfare program. It is of vital importance that institutional programs be related to the broader program of child welfare. Various national agencies and groups have stressed their position in favor of such a plan. These institutions are not penal institutions for the young, but they should be treatment centers and training centers for children with serious behavior problems. The after-care, or so-called parole, administered after a child's release from a juvenile training school should be handled by competent workers on the staffs of the respective training schools, since it probably will not be practical for some time to include this work among the functions of a local welfare office.

The division of child welfare, because of its primary concern with the protection of children, should have licensing authority over private placement agencies, whether they are engaged in temporary or permanent placements, or both. These agencies must be of such quality that the state division can certify them to license their own boarding homes. When a state authorizes agencies to place children, it should not find it necessary to reinvestigate individual homes used by them or adoptions of children placed by them.

The state organization should act as consultant to a private agency, rather than as an authority. Although no rule on the number of visits that should be made during a year can be specified, the state department should not discharge its responsibility for licensing agencies or institutions merely by making a routine annual visit and renewing or refusing to renew an annual license. Consultation service should be available at all times to assist agencies and institutions in developing satisfactory standards for care. The public department has responsibility for working with the private child placing agencies and organizations to effect higher standards of work and improve the quality of personnel.

Statewide private children's agencies, with limited funds and limited staff, need to confer with the state department and work out a joint, realistic program.

Guardianship should not be a state function. It should remain with the parents unless they are unfit; but if the parents do prove unfit, the best present-day practice for both child and family is guardianship by the local unit of government rather than the state. If local units of government are not ready to assume this responsibility, the state may assume it temporarily with the understanding that counties will be certified to do so when they are able to. It will prove possible to decentralize guardianship into local units if the state department's philosophy is in favor of increased local services. Certification should be granted on the basis of personnel qualifications, standards of performance, case loads, and so on. A system of certifying counties to exercise temporary guardianship, with permanent guardianship the responsibility of the state, is too arbitrary and lacking discrimination.

Private agencies should limit and define their functions. They cannot continue their operations unless community interest in their program is sufficient to supply funds. They should not depend on public funds to support their program, although they have a right to ask for public funds to do the work for which they are equipped and the local public unit is not.

In the past, the state's problem was how to induce county boards to provide a public welfare or child welfare unit. Most states enacted laws requiring the establishment of such county units, but these were of little effect. There was usually no financial assistance from the state.

After the passage of the Social Security Act, the provision on grants-in-aid to dependent children and child welfare services required sweeping changes in the relationships between state and county. The federal act required a state to participate financially in a statewide program, and a state agency had to be given the responsibility for effective administration of the program in the state. Consequently, since 1935, the public social services have undergone reorganization, and the states are now recognizing and assuming their full and proper responsibilities for the welfare of children.

One of the noticeable improvements is the current ongoing study and revision of state laws relating to children. Now each of the 50 states and two outlying jurisdictions has recognized in law its responsibility for the welfare and protection of children. Every state has either a department of public welfare or a separate division or bureau of welfare within some other state department to carry out welfare functions, including those of child welfare.

The stronger state welfare departments operate on the theory that community planning and community organization constitute a basic responsibility of the state agency.

In approximately half the states, county welfare agencies have fairly broad legal responsibilities for services to children who are dependent, neglected, or handicapped. Each of the 52 jurisdictions has a plan for administration of public child welfare services by local child welfare workers in at least some of the counties or other local subdivisions.

The child welfare laws of a state reflect the concern of citizens for the welfare of their children who, because they are minors, do not have a voice in making their wants known or having their needs met. The laws in themselves create beneficial conditions; they define safeguards for those needing special protection and they give authority for administrative action by a public agency. Money is the key to progress in providing an effective state child welfare program. Without money, the state cannot use its regulatory powers to safeguard the child.

Sound organization and structuring of public and private welfare programs would require an integration of functions not only *within* the individual public and private agencies—state and local—but also *between* public and private services, in order that each community may have the best for its children. Integration means to pull things together, to relate the various parts of the whole. This, if efficiently done by able staffs, will result in a simplified total welfare program for children, with all-inclusive service provisions.

Endorsing the philosophy which demands that the needs of the whole child be met, we favor the emphasis on and the unmistakable trend toward the coordination of all the forces designed to promote the welfare of the child. Any tendency in comprehensive planning to separate, to isolate, or to "pocket" any one social service program is unsound. The success of an entire child welfare program is inextricably interwoven with all programs of social services for all people in need of such services.

Under a unified program, all persons in need of social services, especially children, will be assured of equitable treatment. Thus benefits will not be restricted to those who fit into some defined category because they meet certain eligibility requirements quite apart from the consideration of their needs; examples of such requirements are citizenship for old age assistance, permanent residence requirements for aid to dependent children and public assistance, and, in some states, certain residence requirements for child welfare services.

It is essential that children's needs be portrayed vividly and fearlessly, since the children cannot do the job themselves. Child welfare workers must urge people to think and see and understand why social effort, social change, and social legislation in behalf of children are imperative.

Although trends toward better provision for child care antedated the passage of the Social Security Act, the developments in child care since 1935 are much more significant than the antecedent improvements. However, we still have to meet many needs. In neither family welfare nor child welfare services have we begun to penetrate the complicated matter of family relationships. The area of family relationships is one that cuts across practically all services in public welfare, and it is a serious and mounting problem as evidenced by the steadily rising divorce rate.

In devising and refining a general philosophy of service for children, we can use social security legislation as a focal point for analyzing and evaluating the trends in both public and private services in child welfare. Currently, we are beginning to focus attention on the total well-being of the child, and to emphasize cooperative planning with courts, schools, public health services, and federal, state, and local agencies and departments, as well as with private and lay organizations concerned with the welfare of children. In this way, a total comprehensive program of service for children will be developed.

TRENDS IN PUBLIC ASSISTANCE

Largely because of Old Age, Survivors, and Disability Insurance, large numbers of persons who would otherwise be needy have been removed from public welfare. The effect has been to leave the public assistance program with a large number of able-bodied recipients, mostly women receiving funds under the Aid to Families with Dependent Children program. However, in recent years the decision on the part of the public to put the welfare mother to work has become prominent. The 1967 Amendment to the Social Security Act provides that all appropriate persons shall be referred to the work incentive program.

What is not clearly understood by proponents of the amendment is that most of the working mothers involved earn very low wages when they work, and that a considerable amount of costly training is necessary to improve their work skills. Of course they also assume that (1) the women can assimilate skills of sufficient magnitude to make them and their children economically self-sufficient; (2) skills of such magnitude can be ingested in short training courses; and (3) such programs are cheaper to the taxpayer than continued payments under AFDC to untrained mothers.

If a woman is one of the two million mothers in this country who is the sole provider of her family, and because of the training or work provision of the act, is eventually forced out of the home to work, what is to happen to her children? It is not always easy to use a day care center if one is available. It may be easier to leave children with a neighbor or alone at home unsupervised. The wages a mother receives are not always large enough to enable her to pay a baby sitter or an agency and her transportation costs to and from work or a child care center. The original philosophy of grants under Aid to Families with Dependent Children was to keep the mother in the home with her children.

Another proposed welfare change is in the planning stage, and is being advanced by the Department of Health, Education, and Welfare. The department is considering a new means of determining and redetermining eligibility for categorical relief. Instead of a detailed eligibility study of each applicant, a public welfare department would investigate a random sample of applicants, and conduct a follow-up investigation on a different random sample of recipients. It is hoped that this new method would allow public welfare workers to devote more time to social services for their clients and in addition would reduce the costs of most otherwise profitless investigations.

An old English plan that has been resurrected and discussed in recent years by various experts includes the outright supplementation of wages or other types of income. The supplementation would be in the form of either a negative income tax to those families whose income falls below the poverty line, or a children's allowance in the form of a family tax recoupment for each child.

Currently, many of the traditional rules of eligibility for public assistance are disappearing or are being questioned. The Supreme Court declared residence requirements for recipients of public assistance unconstitutional in 1969. The medical assistance (Medicaid) legislation, enacted in 1965, limits relatives' responsibility to spouse for spouse and parent for a minor or disabled child. States having "man-in-the-house rules," which deprived many otherwise eligible children from receiving assistance payments under Aid to Families with Dependent Children, were told by the Supreme Court in 1968 to discontinue this practice.

The long-standing Elizabethan tradition of local responsibility for needy persons has been challenged by city, state, and federal officials. Many people favor federalization of public assistance because of more adequate client grants. In turn, state and local officials see federalization as a help in balancing their budgets.

In January, 1971, Congress extended for three years the food stamp program, which was due to expire. The bill authorizes $1,750,-000,000 in appropriations for the first year. However, in the new law was added a provision requiring all able-bodied adults to work or register for work in order for their families to obtain stamps. The old law contained no work requirement. Approximately nine million poor Americans have been receiving food at discount prices by paying various amounts for stamps that have a higher face value when redeemed at food markets.

Under the new law, the only exemptions from the work requirement are mothers with dependent children and students enrolled in schools. However, mothers and children will lose their eligibility for food stamps if the father, or an older sibling, refuses to work.

The work rules require able-bodied persons between the ages of 18 and 65 to register for and accept a job if it is offered, as a condition of eligibility for receiving food coupons. If one member of a family does not take such a job, the entire family unit is disqualified from receiving food stamps. The job has to pay either the federal or state minimum wage or a floor of $1.30 an hour, and employment in a plant affected by a strike lockout is not acceptable. Critics have referred to the work clause as serfdom and a guarantee for cheap agricultural and domestic labor.

Under the new bill, a family of four with a monthly income of $200 would pay $60 a month to get $160 worth of stamps to buy food. Free food stamps would be issued to families with income of less than $30 a month.

THE CHILDREN OF THE WORLD

The children of today are the world's citizenry of tomorrow. The fate of the future welfare of our nation and of the world lies in their hands. As a result of the development of improved communications and rapid transportation, nations are growing closer to one another, and what happens to children anywhere becomes of vital concern to us.

We need the widest viewpoint possible. If children abroad lack basic needs, we can no longer afford to say, "Oh, those conditions exist in Europe, or in Asia, or in Africa, but they won't affect us here." They definitely do affect us, as do fluctuations in international economic systems.

Many Americans realize that this country cannot detach itself from problems involving the welfare of children throughout the world. This realization has reached into virtually every corner of the United States. As a consequence, many small groups in our urban and rural populations have organized, in various ways, to aid individual children or groups of children abroad—quite apart from the efforts of national and international organizations.

Increasing numbers of Americans are beginning to realize that we cannot be conscious only of the good things our country can do for its children. We cannot be a responsible people, with hope for a better world order, free from oppression and prejudice, unless we work for better standards of child care throughout the world. In short, all children are in a very true sense our children.

It is impossible to determine accurately the number of children throughout the world who are now in need—the children who are starving and sick, homeless, mentally ill, emotionally scarred, suffering from unbelievable misery, and lacking any opportunity for family life, education, or recreation. Since World War II there have been conflicts and disputes, both within and between nations, that have brought disaster to children, particularly in parts of Asia, Africa, and Europe.

The mature population of the world is powerless to change the past or to recompense these children for the hardships they have had to undergo and are undergoing. We must rely on the present to effect such retribution and prevention as we can. If we devote as much fierce effort, planning skill, energy, and initiative to create a chance for them as was spent in waging the wars that reduced them to such a direful state, something may be done to insure them a good future.

We, in the United States, can see to it that the machinery, already set in motion for the improvement of their conditions, is kept turning.

The Declaration of the Rights of the Child, drawn up in 1923 by the Save the Children International Union, of Geneva, was ratified by the General Council of the union on February 28, 1924. It has since been adopted in many different countries and, on September 26, 1924 the Fifth Assembly of the League of Nations passed a resolution endorsing the declaration and inviting states and members of the league to be guided by its principles in the work of child welfare. The declaration, commonly known as the "Declaration of Geneva," states that men and women of all nations, recognizing that mankind owes to the child the best that it has to give, declare and accept the following as their duty, beyond and above all considerations of race, nationality, or creed:

1. The child should be given the means for its normal development, both materially and spiritually.
2. The child that is hungry should be fed; the child that is sick should be helped; the erring child should be reclaimed; and the orphan and the homeless child should be sheltered and succored.
3. The child should be first to receive relief in times of distress.
4. The child should be put in a position to earn a livelihood, and should be protected against every form of exploitation.
5. The child should be brought up in the consciousness that its best qualities are to be used in the service of its fellow men.

The League of Nation's successor organization, the United Nations, acted on behalf of children in 1946. Earlier that year, in August, as the Council of the United Nations Relief and Rehabilitation Administration was concluding its activities in Geneva, it suggested that certain policies continue to be followed. The council members were anxious about what would happen to the millions of children in Europe and China who had depended upon UNRRA for food and other assistance. They suggested, in a resolution, the creation of an international fund to use remaining UNRRA assets for the benefit of children and adolescents. The distribution of aid was to be on the basis of need, without discrimination because of race, creed, nationality status, or political belief.

As a direct result of this resolution, the United Nations General Assembly, on December 11, 1946, established the United Nations International Children's Emergency Fund—now known, with the same initials UNICEF, as the United Nations International Children's Endowment Fund. This Fund was to be administered by an Executive Board, composed of representatives of 26 nations, and an Executive Director appointed by the Secretary-General of the United Nations.

The first function of the Fund was to be emergency feeding of children and pregnant women. It was estimated that 30,000,000 children were in need in European countries, and an equal or greater number in China and the Philippines. It was hoped that a budget of $450,-000,000 could be provided for 1947, to be made up of $32,000,000 from UNRRA, at least $100,000,000 from the United States, and the balance from other governments. The United States Congress, however, appropriated only $40,000,000, and other governments scaled down their contributions accordingly.

The Executive Board of the new organization held its first meeting on December 19, 1946, in New York City. Miss Katherine Lenroot was the member from the United States. The board unanimously chose as its first chairman Dr. Ludwik Rajchman of Poland, a physician who had been for 18 years a director of the health organization of the League of Nations, and who had suggested setting up the Fund. On January 8, 1947, an Executive Director was chosen; he was Maurice Pate, an American businessman and wartime director of the Prisoners of War Section of the American Red Cross.

The Fund was to be utilized and administered, to the extent of its available resources, for the following purposes, as defined by the resolution creating it:

a. for the benefit of children and adolescents of countries which were victims of aggression, and in order to assist in their rehabilitation;

b. for the benefit of children and adolescents of countries receiving assistance from the United Nations Relief and Rehabilitation Administration;

c. for child-health purposes generally, giving high priority to the children of countries that were victims of aggression.

In 1950, after Europe had recovered from the effects of World War II, the program was changed to emphasize long-term aid for child health projects and training projects for child welfare personnel in the world's underdeveloped regions, with a view to helping governments set up health projects to benefit children.

In October, 1953, the United Nations decided that the Fund should continue as a permanent international child welfare organization. By 1954 the Fund was helping 75 countries in Asia, Africa, the Middle East, and Latin America.

The Fund requires that the government or voluntary agency in the country being helped shall "match" the Fund's aid by providing local supplies of certain foods and a staff to assist in distribution, and also by furnishing staff for local medical and child welfare services. In 1954, recipient countries were more than matching Fund aid; they were stretching limited budgets to provide, on the average, $61 for every $39 put up by the Fund.

The Fund is empowered to provide food, clothing, and medical care for children caught in natural catastrophes, such as famines, droughts, floods, earthquakes, and volcanic eruptions. It also encourages, by assistance for limited periods, long-range campaigns against diseases—efforts that promise to benefit children and mothers for many years.

When a priest in Brazil was asked what the Fund had done for the people in his remote area, he pointed to his church steeple and said; "It used to toll the death of a baby three or four times a week. Now it tolls only three or four times a month."

In Paris, the Fund aided the French in establishing an International Children's Center, which provides training, research, and demonstration projects in maternal and child health services for doctors, nurses, social workers, and other personnel.

In Calcutta, the Fund supports a postgraduate training center for nurses and physicians at the All India Institute for Health and Public Hygiene.

These are only a few examples of the work being done. The Fund is helping governments build basic health services in many areas for people that had never suspected the existence of such things. In some of these areas the health center offers more than medical care. It may boast a club in which an expectant mother can learn to sew and to prepare a baby layette at unbelievably low cost, and learn some fundamentals about nutrition and baby diseases. Lectures, each with an appropriate movie, aid this instruction. In another club at the center, the mother may learn the basics of healthful homemaking.

In one section of a South American country, the Fund inspired so much community interest in health that the people planned a series of benefits to raise funds for a number of projects. These projects included the building of a large market in town; the establishing of a kindergarten, including a center for training young women to handle groups of preschoolers; the enlarging of the elementary school; and the staffing of a new children's hospital.

In March, 1960, the Executive Board of UNICEF made note of the fact that ten years had passed since the Fund has shifted its main emphasis from emergency relief to aid for long-range programs for children in developing countries. The Executive Board at its 1961 session broadened UNICEF aid to include the fields of education, vocational training, guidance and social services. Assistance in these fields was to be based on the need priorities in different countries.

In 1963 the staff of UNICEF reported that aid had been given to training projects in all fields receiving assistance within a particular country. The training projects varied from the creation of postgraduate departments to the practical training of workers in mass campaigns.

Apart from United Nations and other governmental efforts, much work is being done for child welfare abroad by a number of private groups in the United States. These groups include private social agencies, church organizations, service clubs, and others with an international viewpoint and scope. Information about them may be obtained from the Advisory Committee on Voluntary Foreign Aid and from the American Council of Voluntary Agencies for Foreign Service. The National Social Welfare Assembly serves as a coordinating body for public and private agencies giving international social services to foreign countries.

From the experiences of all the organizations mentioned above we may draw a few concluding remarks.

In trying to determine the type of environment needed for the full development of children and youth as stable citizens, and then attempting to provide that environment, we must recognize that there are appalling discrepancies between what we know the world's children need and what they actually get. Our goal, then, in the United States (where the discrepancies are smaller but nevertheless real) as well as in the rest of the world, is to equip children to live happily and securely in environments that are less than ideal.

We want children to have comfortable homes, three square meals a day, a place to play, a good school, and adequate medical care. These are all good things in themselves and the ability to supply them must be one test of our democracy. But we must keep a sense of perspective and proportion and make certain that material advantages do not become ends in themselves, but continue to be considered primarily as means; and that these advantages and the experiences in home, school, play, and other relationships will be such that they foster our children's growth into free cooperative human beings.

Nations are now so closely bound together that none can plan its own tomorrow without giving heed to the welfare of the world. We of the older and present generation have learned this fact only at the price of great suffering on the part of millions. We have proved ourselves unequal to the task of achieving a world of plenty, and freedom from fear, want, disease, and ignorance. We must pass on this task to the youth and children of today and tomorrow. Drawing from the bitter experience of our past efforts in these areas, we of the older generation must do what we can to help them.

We cannot boast of having kept faith with youth when we have subjected it to such great traumas of body and soul. Yet we can try again. In fact, for the good of all, we *must* try, as long as the responsibility remains ours. We, as Americans, with such wisdom as we have and with the will and the abundance of our resources, must use our power and influence to strengthen our own and the world community.

We can only hope that the younger generation will have the strength and resilience to surmount some of the difficulties that it has so effectively dramatized in action, word, and print.

Our government was designed "to promote the general welfare and to secure the blessings of liberty to ourselves and to posterity." In our present highly interrelated society and world, we cannot do this for ourselves and our descendents without doing it also, in large measure, for those of other nations.

The National Commission on Children in Wartime made a statement in April, 1945, that is still applicable: "Let us resolve now . . . that we will build courageously, imaginatively, ungrudgingly, and without discrimination as to race, color, creed, or national origin, services which will reach out to all our children and youth wherever they live and whoever their parents may be."

This is the challenge we face as child welfare workers.

We cannot fully analyze and discuss the future needs of children, or plan realistically for their welfare, without taking into consideration the dynamics occurring within nations. Some of the leading variables associated with worldwide change are found in the areas of population, economics, culture, and sociologistics.

SOCIAL CHANGE AND CHILD WELFARE

It is estimated that the world's population grew from 1,550,000,000 in 1900 to 1,907,000,000 in 1925 and 2,497,000,000 in 1950; it reached 2,691,000,000 in 1956 and 2,900,000,000 in 1960. It is anticipated that by 1975 the world will have a population of 3,800,000,000. We have not only been experiencing an increase in population but also in the rate of growth. For the period of 1900–1925 the world's population rate of growth was 23.2 percent. For the period of 1950–1975 it is expected to be 53.0 percent.

In 1950 there were 910,000,000 children in the world, with 704,-000,000 living in less developed countries. In 1975 the total number of children is expected to exceed 1,400,000,000, with 1,130,000,000 in less developed countries. The population increase is due to the rapid decline in mortality that has taken place throughout the world since the 1920's. This decline is traceable to such factors as improved public health practices, the availability of more food, better nutrition, improved health care, and the conquest of childhood diseases in many countries.

The consequences of rapid population growth are relative, but in less developed countries they are generally unfavorable owing to the fact that economic expansion on a given plane of living is unable to keep pace with population growth. As a result, society becomes increasingly unable to cope with the problem of hunger. In addition, in many of these countries, there is a shortage of arable land, agricultural technology, and investment capital. As a result the total picture is not encouraging for children and their welfare in many countries that are considered underdeveloped. Without a significant reduction in birth rates or a very rapid increase in national incomes in the less developed world, the outlook is dim for both children and adults. If the rate of population increase in many countries continues to exceed its economic growth, living conditions that are already wretched will deteriorate even more. Population expansion, increasing year by year without concomitant economic expansion, will inevitably aggravate the problems of poverty, hunger, and ignorance for children in many nations.

The contrast between the underdeveloped countries and countries with higher standards of living is manifested in many areas of life. One area includes the services that might be undertaken to solve selected child welfare problems. In countries with high standards of living we find considerable social legislation along with many public and private social agencies dealing with child welfare problems. The number of children in dire need in western countries is quite small, and thus more can be done for them with the available social and economic resources. But in the underdeveloped countries, where the needs of children are most acute and widespread, it would be difficult to improve the socio-economic conditions unless one could increase perceptibly the standard of living. Considerable financial help is needed for the basic problems of poor countries, and only meager resources are available.

The problems of children in countries with low standards of living differ in scope and magnitude from those of children in more prosperous countries. Juvenile delinquency, for example, exists in both types of nations, since it is a fairly universal phenomenon. The difference lies in its significance: it is extremely important in highly developed societies, but in poor countries, it is overshadowed by the many more basic problems faced by children and youth there.

The solution to a low standard of living is a general economic advancement for a population. However, pending such a solution, some of the effects of poverty may be relieved by providing certain social services. In all countries, the slum is one of the most serious manifestations of poverty, whether it is found in rural or urban areas. Regional and urban planning, based on relevant economic and social factors as well as on the mobility of the regional population, would be the ideal approach to solving effectively the problem of development and expansion of slum living. If such an ideal solution is impossible, less complicated programs would include environmental sanitation, playgrounds, day care centers, housing programs, health services, and education and welfare programs. These services will not obliterate the primary condition causing poverty but they will, in a modest way, help alleviate the needs of poor children.

Communicable diseases are the leading causes of sickness and death in countries with low standards of living. However, in recent years great progress has been made in the field of public health, as a result of the application of modern medical techniques. Nevertheless, death rates among children are, in some underdeveloped countries, ten times higher than death rates in advanced countries. Health conditions in most underdeveloped countries are extremely poor. Poor environmental sanitation spreads disease, and malnutrition lowers a child's resistance to disease.

Hunger is still one of the most important factors contributing to the suffering of children in many underdeveloped countries. It is also prevalent, though less so, in areas of some of our more advanced countries. Serious disorders in children are caused by certain nutritional deficiencies. In recent years the world's food supply has increased, but the quality and quantity of food available to many children is below what is needed for a normal diet. In countries in which the food supply is poor, the children, not the adults, generally suffer the most.

We need long-range programs to improve the nutrition of children not only in countries with low standards of living but also in those more advanced countries in which food is not adequately distributed. In underdeveloped countries, the larger part of the program would have to be directed toward improved general production of food.

More specific measures would include the following:

1. Steps would be taken to protect the future health of children; pregnant women would be provided with adequate health services, a balanced diet, and protection from overwork.

2. Obstetric services would be expanded in all societies. This expansion may be very difficult in countries and regions in which high birth rates are increasing and in which there is not more than one physician for every 50,000 inhabitants.

3. The health of children who are working would be protected by law in all societies. They would be forbidden to work under hazardous conditions.

4. The essentials of health and nutrition would be made part of elementary education so that children, upon reaching adulthood, would know the fundamentals of being a good parent.

5. Free school lunch programs would be established and expanded.

6. Programs to supply milk or other high-protein and vitamin-rich foods to young children would be established.

Programs of social services are important for the welfare of children in any society. However, they cannot solve the problems caused by rapid economic or social change. Nevertheless, they should be included in any social action programs that are planned for the alleviation of community problems.

The primary objectives of child welfare services are to promote the welfare of the child in his family and to offer protection for the maladjusted, neglected or abandoned child.

In general, the underdeveloped countries of the world have no social security systems. They also lack social legislation in the area of welfare. It is felt that, if public welfare services were available in those countries, they would ease the difficult changes from traditional to new ways of life that the people are experiencing, and thus they would protect the integrity of the family. In addition, the parents might be helped to gain employment, and might be educated in the essentials of health, proper nutrition, good child care, and home economics.

Other services that may be undertaken or expanded are guidance, education, and family counseling. Maternal and child welfare services should be established where needed. In many areas, nurseries and day care centers are needed for young children of working mothers.

Social services for children in rural areas of the world have been lacking for years. There is need for rural community development, literacy movements, campaigns for the improvement of education, agricultural modernization, nutrition programs, maternal clubs, and child welfare programs.

Legislation should be passed to give illegitimate children civil status in all countries of the world.

Abandoned children who subsist as beggars, bootblacks, or cigarette vendors need reception and training centers for their rehabilitation. Children of refugee groups and immigrant children need social and medical assistance.

A large proportion of the world's children work. Some of the occupations are in agriculture, industry, mining, handicrafts and itinerant trades. Although it is widely accepted that a minimum age for child employment should be established in the Geneva Declaration of the Rights of the Child, and although many legislative bodies have indeed established a minimum age, we find that it is violated throughout the world. In most countries, children begin to work between 12 and 16 years of age.

In many countries, working children are required to do exhausting tasks. In addition, they are underpaid and are without the minimum social and economic protection.

The majority of working children are employed without prior physical examinations, and no health services are provided for them. Some children work from six to eight hours a day without a weekly day of rest. This situation is usually found in agriculture and in the handicrafts.

There are serious defects in vocational training in this country and in many others. Elementary education is prerequisite to vocational training but is not sufficient in itself for entrance into a trade. Less than half the world's children receive any kind of vocational training. Few receive the training in agriculture that is necessary for rural modification. In urban areas, the education that children receive is just enough to divert them from the manual trades, and as a result they are forced to join the unemployed ranks of lower-echelon white-collar workers.

Governments have often approved social legislation calling for measures far more extensive than those that could, in all reasonable probability, be carried out or enforced. Most countries have not yet reached the stage at which they can meet the expense of extended social security or social service benefits.

The study of the future needs of children is a first step in the formation of a plan for the improvement of the conditions of children.

Countries with the highest standard of living must reassess their social services for children, from time to time, to determine their current relevance and to find out what old needs are still unmet and what new ones have arisen. The necessity for such appraisal and planning is greatest for the underdeveloped countries, because the potential of their children is needed for the future development of these nations.

The economic, political, and social implications of plans to meet the future needs of children have to be realistically considered. The balanced development of any society must be concerned not only with its economic resources but also with its human resources. Plans to create a present and future national policy of a country should also include plans to meet the needs of children.

Children should be prepared to have a useful and productive function in the future life of a nation. However, the present needs of children—centering on health, food, education, and shelter—cannot be ignored, if the child is to have a responsible role in the future of his country. It is up to each nation and its people to determine its own priority of future needs and to decide on its own plan of action. A government that embarks on a blind pursuit of economic goals, without taking into consideration the fact that children and their welfare represent the future potential of a nation, could very well lead a society to disaster.

SOCIAL MOVEMENTS AND CHILD WELFARE

Besides the structural changes in state, domestic, and international child welfare organizations that may influence the future of the child, there are certain selected social movements which, if successful, will also leave their impact on the future welfare of children. One of these movements is women's liberation, and another is the revolt of youth in our country against some of our traditional values.

In the past ten to 20 years several notable trends and developments in the United States and in certain other countries have occurred. Only time can tell if these happenings are the harbingers of true social movements and social change, or phenomena of an ephemeral nature. Likewise, any meaningful pronouncement on their significance for the future of child welfare must be deferred at this time.

Widespread publicity on the behavior of certain groups protesting selected contemporary values is not a fundamental ingredient of social change. Such publicity may be reporting the beginning of social change, but it may also be reporting only the heightened social awareness surrounding the protesting behavior of a relatively insignificant group. In other words, different behavior in itself neither signifies the beginning of social change nor results in social change, no matter how great the contemporary publicity may be. Nevertheless, the principles underlying the women's liberation and youth movements may indeed contain the germ of some lasting impact on our society and on the field of child welfare.

The two movements have many dimensions. For the purposes of this section, we will briefly discuss some of the obvious ones and their possible impact on child welfare.

The Women's Liberation Movement

Among the objectives of this movement are the attainment of wages and work opportunities that are equal to those available to men. Housewives are also demanding more time for out-of-the-home activities. Accompanying this demand is one for more day care centers for the children of all socioeconomic groups, starting with the centers for the youngest of children. If these requests are realized, we should find more women working outside of the home and a boom in day care centers. If more positions with equal pay opportunities are opened to women, the birthrate may as a consequence suffer. The future birthrate will probably diminish in any event, owing to the popularity and convenience of oral contraceptives, and to the general public reaction to environmental pollution and the growing density of population in this country.

Legalized abortion is another right that women demand as a part of the feminine principle. Until recent times, abortion has been regarded as the concern of society and thus did not fall into the realm of individual rights. The argument today is whether a woman has the right to choose between bearing a child and having an abortion, regardless of the interests of society.

In a society and world that is rapidly becoming overrun with people and their polluting proclivities, the voices of past and present countless women are currently being listened to. At present, at least three states have made the conditions under which abortions can be legalized more liberal than ever before. Whether legalized abortion as an individual right will sweep the country as a successful social movement remains to be seen. There is still formidable opposition to be contended with.

The long-term significance of legal abortion to child welfare is difficult to assess, because it might be affected by numerous variables. For example, if legalized abortion were taken advantage of by a disproportionate number of middle-class housewives, the social results may not be easily predicted; we could speculate on what might happen if our society produced an oversized proportion of lower-class children, but past predictions have not held up.

The benefits of legalized abortions for the individual mother or the unmarried mother can be readily imagined. Also, if legalized abortion becomes widespread, presumably the majority of children brought into our society will be wanted, and thus introduced into a potentially happier life.

The Youth Movement

Some of the beliefs underlying this movement are the following:

1. Social values that support an industrial-military complex should be questioned and challenged.
2. Sexual relations, in or out of marriage, are an individual matter, and of no concern to society.

3. Adherence to the Protestant ethic of work and ambition, as values in themselves, has no place in a rational world.
4. The relevance of higher education in a society that has exploited the fauna, the flora, and its people for material gain should be reexamined critically.
5. Religion has failed to condemn the injustices of this world and must become less dependent on the established order.
6. People should return to the simple life of primary living in communes.
7. All human beings are equal, regardless of race or sex.
8. The essential qualities of living are love, kindness, help, compassion, and social and legal justice for mankind.

We have no way of knowing how widespread the youth movement has become. From time to time we come across cases of communal living, peace parades, campus disorders, motorcycle gang warfare, and disturbances led by street people. Young people are involved in all these activities and others, but whether a really cohesive social movement is under way is questionable. Rather, a number of legitimate protests and outcries have been raised by a number of young people who have focused their energies on certain interests and issues.

The protests of youth have been heard by various organizations in our social structure, but at present one cannot yet detect any resulting social change. Youth has been granted some representation on committees or in other organizational categories, mostly so that their point of view may be heard, or the protestations of their peers assuaged. Because of the large proportion of our population that its members make up, youth is a potential force, but as yet its influence has been minimal, perhaps because (1) any social change is slow, and (2) they are not well organized. The youth movement may eventually influence the field of child welfare, but only time will tell.

Supplementary Readings

Batchelder, Alan B. *The Economics of Poverty*. Wiley, New York, 1966.

Bornet, Vaughn Davis. *Welfare in America*. University of Oklahoma Press, Norman, Oklahoma, 1960.

Burgess, Elaine, and Price, Daniel O. *An American Dependency Challenge*. American Public Welfare Association, Chicago, 1963.

Chambers, Clark A. *Seedtime of Reform: American Social Service and Social Action*. University of Minnesota Press, Minneapolis, 1963.

Coll, Blanche D. *Perspectives in Public Welfare*. U.S. Department of Health, Education, and Welfare, Washington, D.C., 1969.

Derthick, Martha. *The Influence of Federal Grants*. Harvard University Press, Cambridge, 1970.

Ferman, Louis A., Kornbluh, Joyce L., and Haber, Alan, Eds. *Poverty in America: A Book of Readings*. University of Michigan Press, Ann Arbor, 1965.

Freedman, M., et al. *Getting Hired, Getting Trained*. Department of Health, Education, and Welfare. Washington, D.C., 1966.

Harrington, Michael. *The Other America: Poverty in the United States*. Macmillan, New York, 1962.

Herzog, Elizabeth. *About the Poor*. U.S. Children's Bureau, Washington, D.C., 1967.

Katz, Carol Hecht, Ed. *The Law and the Low Income Consumer*. New York University School of Law, New York, 1968.

Levenson, Rosaline, Ed. *The Revolution in Public Welfare: The Connecticut Experience*. The University of Connecticut, Storrs, Conn., 1966.

Levitan, Sar A. *Programs in Aid of the Poor for the 1970's*. Johns Hopkins Press, Baltimore, 1969.

National Industrial Conference Board. *Education, Training, and Employment of the Disadvantaged*. National Industrial Conference Board, New York, 1969.

Pearl, Arthur, and Reissman, Frank. *New Careers for the Poor*. Free Press, New York, 1965.

Reissman, Frank. *The Culturally Deprived Child*. Harper and Row, New York, 1962.

Sicault, Georges. *The Needs of Children*. Free Press, New York, 1963.

Therkildsen, Paul S. *Public Assistance and American Values*. Division of Government Research, University of New Mexico, Albuquerque, 1969.

Wickenden, Elizabeth. *Social Welfare in a Changing World*. U.S. Department of Health, Education, and Welfare, Washington, D.C., 1965.

Wilensky, H. L., and Lebeaux, C. N. *Industrial Society and Social Welfare*. Free Press, New York, 1965.

Appendices

The Children's Charter

*The 1930 White House Conference on Child Health
and Protection, recognizing the rights of the child
as the first rights of citizenship, pledged itself
to these aims for the Children of America.*

I   For every child spiritual and moral training to help him to stand firm under the pressure of life.

II   For every child understanding and the guarding of his personality as his most precious right.

III   For every child a home and that love and security which a home provides; and for that child who must receive foster care, the nearest substitute for his own home.

IV   For every child full preparation for his birth, his mother receiving prenatal, natal, and postnatal care; and the establishment of such protective measures as will make child-bearing safer.

V   For every child health protection from birth through adolescence, including: periodical health examinations and, where needed, care of specialists and hospital treatment; regular dental examinations and care of the teeth; protective and preventive measures against communicable diseases; the insuring of pure food, pure milk, and pure water.

VI   For every child from birth through adolescence, promotion of health, including health instruction and a health program, wholesome physical and mental recreation, with teachers and leaders adequately trained.

VII   For every child a dwelling place safe, sanitary, and wholesome, with reasonable provisions for privacy, free from conditions which tend to thwart his development; and a home environment harmonious and enriching.

VIII   For every child a school which is safe from hazards, sanitary, properly equipped, lighted, and ventilated. For younger children nursery schools and kindergartens to supplement home care.

IX   For every child a community which recognizes and plans for his needs, protects him against physical dangers, moral hazards, and disease; provides him with safe and wholesome places for play and recreation; and makes provision for his cultural and social needs.

X   For every child an education which, through the discovery and development of his individual abilities, prepares him for life; and through training and vocational guidance prepares him for a living which will yield him the maximum of satisfaction.

XI   For every child such teaching and training as will prepare him for successful parenthood, homemaking, and the rights of citizenship; and, for parents, supplementary training to fit them to deal wisely with the problems of parenthood.

XII   For every child education for safety and protection against accidents to which modern conditions subject him—those to which he is directly exposed and those which, through loss or maiming of his parents, affect him indirectly.

XIII   For every child who is blind, deaf, crippled, or otherwise physically handicapped, and for the child who is mentally handicapped, such measures as will early discover and diagnose his handicap, provide care and treatment, and so train him that he may become an asset to society rather than a liability. Expenses of these services should be borne publicly where they cannot be privately met.

XIV   For every child who is in conflict with society the right to be dealt with intelligently as society's charge, not society's outcast; with the home, the school, the church, the court and the institution when needed, shaped to return him whenever possible to the normal stream of life.

XV   For every child the right to grow up in a family with an adequate standard of living and the security of a stable income as the surest safeguard against social handicaps.

XVI   For every child protection against labor that stunts growth, either physical or mental, that limits education, that deprives children of the right of comradeship, of play, and of joy.

XVII   For every rural child as satisfactory schooling and health services as for the city child, and an extension to rural families of social, recreational, and cultural facilities.

XVIII   To supplement the home and the school in the training of youth, and to return to them those interests of which modern life tends to cheat children, every stimulation and encouragement should be given to the extension and development of the voluntary youth organizations.

XIX   To make everywhere available these minimum protections of the health and welfare of children, there should be a district, county, or community organization for health, education, and welfare, with full-time officials, coordinating with a statewide program which will be responsive to a nationwide service of general information, statistics, and scientific research. This should include:

(a) Trained, full-time public health officials, with public health nurses, sanitary inspection, and laboratory workers
(b) Available hospital beds
(c) Full-time public welfare service for the relief, aid, and guidance of children in special need due to poverty, misfortune, or behavior difficulties, and for the protection of children from abuse, neglect, exploitation, or moral hazard.

For every child these rights, regardless of race, or color, or situation, wherever he may live under the protection of the American flag.

Pledge to Children

_By the Midcentury White House Conference
on Children and Youth, 1950_

To you, our children, who hold within you our most cherished hopes, we the members of the Midcentury White House Conference on Children and Youth, relying on your full response, make this pledge:

From your earliest infancy we give you our love, so that you may grow with trust in yourself and in others.

We will recognize your worth as a person and we will help you to strengthen your sense of belonging.

We will respect your right to be yourself and at the same time help you to understand the rights of others, so that you may experience cooperative living.

We will help you to develop initiative and imagination, so that you may have the opportunity freely to create.

We will encourage your curiosity and your pride in workmanship, so that you may have the satisfaction that comes from achievement.

We will provide the conditions for wholesome play that will add to your learning, to your social experience, and to your happiness.

We will illustrate by precept and example the value of integrity and the importance of moral courage.

We will encourage you always to seek the truth.

We will provide you with all opportunities possible to develop your own faith in God.

We will open the way for you to enjoy the arts and to use them for deepening your understanding of life.

We will work to rid ourselves of prejudice and discrimination, so that together we may achieve a truly democratic society.

We will work to lift the standard of living and to improve our economic practices, so that you may have the material basis for a full life.

We will provide you with rewarding educational opportunities, so that you may develop your talents and contribute to a better world.

We will protect you against exploitation and undue hazards and help you grow in health and strength.

We will work to conserve and improve family life and, as needed, to provide foster care according to your inherent rights.

We will intensify our search for new knowledge in order to guide you more effectively as you develop your potentialities.

As you grow from child to youth to adult, establishing a family life of your own and accepting larger social responsibilities, we will work with you to improve conditions for all children and youth.

Aware that these promises to you cannot be fully met in a world at war, we ask you to join us in a firm dedication to the building of a world society based on freedom, justice and mutual respect.

So may you grow in joy, faith in God and in man, and in those qualities of vision and of the spirit that will sustain us all and give us new hope for the future.

Films on Children

Acting With Maturity (Second Edition)
Explains that dating, family life, friendship, and school present young people with situations that may provoke them to immature behavior. Points out that reactions show that a person's feelings are as important as his actions, and that decisions require thinking before acting.

CORONET FILMS   1968

Adolescence
A group of young people, not juvenile delinquents, have been brought to the police station on a trespassing charge. The film comments on the varying attitudes of the accuser, the police officer, and a high school teacher, pointing out that the example of the adult is in large part responsible for the development of the teenager. From the About People series.

NATIONAL EDUCATIONAL TELEVISION, INCORPORATED   No date

Afraid of School: A Case of School Phobia
A six-year-old boy refuses to go to school even after his parents have tried bribery, persuasion, and spanking. His parents seek psychiatric help at the children's hospital. The film discusses the boy's fears, and shows how, with the help of his parents, he is finally able to face school.

ROBERT ANDERSON   1965

Alcoholism and the Family: The Summer We Moved to Elm Street
Discusses the problems of alcoholism. Examines the relationships among the members of a family during times of turmoil.

NATIONAL FILM BOARD OF CANADA   1968

Beginning Responsibility: Being a Good Sport
Acts of poor sportsmanship during a game of checkers lead Paula and

Woody into an argument. To suggest how this and other conflicts might be resolved, the film shows situations involving other youngsters and explores the underlying motives that lead to various types of poor sportsmanship.

CORONET FILMS   No date

Bob at Home

Portrays an educable mentally retarded child in his home environment. Shows how a positive relationship will help the child to develop various practices like telling time, crossing a street with care, helping at home, having fun with his family, and thinking of the needs of others. From the MGS Educational Series, No. 2.

MGS PRODUCTIONS, INCORPORATED   1964

Boy to Man

Deals candidly with the secondary and primary sexual changes of adolescence in the male. Produced under medical and psychiatric supervision. Animation.

CHURCHILL FILMS   1962

Children of Change

Depicts the special stresses and strains placed on children whose mothers work outside the home, and on the mothers who must adjust to two full-time jobs. Creates an awareness of the scope of the problem and offers one workable solution—day care centers.

MENTAL HEALTH FILM BOARD   1960

Dance Little Children

Discusses the pressures teenagers are under today. Describes an outbreak of syphilis in a typical American city. Discusses the parents' responsibility, and possible causes and solution related to the outbreak.

KANSAS STATE BOARD OF HEALTH   1961

A Different Kind of Neighborhood

Concerns the conflicts confronting a 14-year-old boy when he moves from a tenement community to a housing project. Provides insight into both the social and the psychological aspects of urban renewal.

UNIVERSAL FILMS   No date

Discipline and Self-Control

Explains that self-control is developed in children by discipline which is firm, consistent, friendly, and sympathetic. Suggests that good discipline is provided by the teacher who is warm, accepting, and assured, and shows the teacher how he can set a good example and avoid discipline problems.

DU ART FILM LABS, INCORPORATED   No date

The Family: The Boy Who Lived Alone

A boy decides to run away from home. Even though he enjoys being alone, he needs the security and love of his family, and he returns home with the help of the police.

ENCYCLOPEDIA BRITANNICA EDUCATIONAL CORPORATION   1968

Follow the Leader
Shows a pattern of behavioral forms emerging from the interaction of children placed in role-playing situations.

WCAU TELEVISION   1965

Four Children
Tells the story of four Head Start children, presenting an intimate look at the homes that influence them.

CAPITAL FILM LABS   No date

Goof
The story of a lonely and unhappy boy whose desperate efforts to gain attention make him extremely unpopular with other children. Emphasizes the necessity for recognizing and appreciating the worth of others regardless of their behavior.

ACI PRODUCTIONS   1968

How Babies Learn
Shows some important developmental advances during the first year of life. Stresses that learning is influenced by interpersonal environment, particularly the mother-child relationship, and by the physical environment in which the baby lives. Part of a government research project on infant learning.

DR. B. CALDWELL   1965

Indian Boy of the Southwest
Toboya, A Hopi Indian boy, tells about his life. He describes his home, his school, and the trading post.

WAYNE MITCHELL   1963

Julia
An open-discussion film which examines the problems involved in working with the handicapped child in the classroom. From the Critical Moments in Teaching series.

HOLT, RINEHART, AND WINSTON   1968

Learning From Disappointments
When three children are not chosen for the roles they wanted in the school history pageant, they overcome their disappointment through good sportsmanship, by choosing another goal and trying again.

CORONET FILMS   1961

Learning To Use Your Senses
Encourages children to verbalize sensory perceptions. Points out that people use their five senses automatically, and explains how to learn about the environment by using the senses.

ENCYCLOPEDIA BRITTANNICA EDUCATIONAL CORPORATION   1968

The Long Childhood of Timmy
Studies the life of a family of eight, which includes eight-year-old Timmy,

a mongoloid with a mental age of four years. Records the relationships and feelings which develop as a result of Timmy's retardation.

AMERICAN BROADCASTING COMPANY TELEVISION   1967

Losing Just the Same

The story of a Negro mother and her ten children who live on welfare but who dream of a world of Cadillac prestige and middle class status. A commentary on poverty in an urban Negro ghetto. From the NET Journal Series.

NATIONAL EDUCATIONAL TELEVISION, INCORPORATED   1966

Making a Map

Shows how desirable concepts are developed in a special elementary school classroom for the educable mentally retarded child. Depicts a boy and his classmates working together to construct a map of their classroom. Discusses concepts of direction and space orientation. Pictures the emphasis that is placed on having work ready on time, accepting help, and taking turns. From the MGS Educational Series, No. 3.

MGS PRODUCTIONS, INCORPORATED   1964

Many People Help Bob

Shows how desirable concepts are developed in a special elementary school classroom for the educable mentally retarded child. Depicts a boy and his classmates working together in preparing a map display for the principal. Discusses the development of various concepts in classroom and school orientation. From the MGS Educational Series, No. 4.

MGS PRODUCTIONS, INCORPORATED   1964

The Missing Queen

Tells the story of Kathy, who is wrongly accused of stealing a valuable stamp and who can't decide whether or not to tell her teacher the name of the person she thinks may have stolen the stamp. From the Breakthru Series.

TELEVISION, RADIO, AND FILM COMMISSION OF THE METHODIST CHURCH   1962

Morocco: Chaoui Faces His Future

Chaoui, a Moroccan youth, must decide whether to quit school and return to the farm or acquire an education that will benefit him and his country. Shows the customs and traditions of the villages, as well as the need for better farming methods.

UNITED WORLD FILMS   1966

The Parent: Part 1

Interviews three pairs of parents to discover what they expect from their children, and what their hopes are for them. From the Search for America Series, Part 1.

NATIONAL EDUCATIONAL TELEVISION, INCORPORATED   No date

The Parent: Part 2

Interviews parents as they discuss the relationship between them and their children, the responsibilities their children assume, and the kind and amount of encouragement they should provide their children. From the Search for America Series, Part 2.

NATIONAL EDUCATIONAL TELEVISION, INCORPORATED   No date

Patterns For Health

Discusses the establishment of early health habits for the preschool child, and shows how this early training develops patterns found in the well adjusted adult. Covers general as well as specific health needs of the four- to five-year-old child.

UNITED STATES OFFICE OF ECONOMIC OPPORTUNITY   1967

Phoebe: Story of a Premarital Pregnancy

Dramatizes the mental and emotional reactions of a teenager who discovers she is pregnant.

NATIONAL FILM BOARD OF CANADA   1965

Purple Turtle

Shows kindergarten children at work with various art mediums. Captures the intensity, delight, and skill with which four- and five-year-olds take to paint. Shows why art is one of the most important means of development.

ACI PRODUCTIONS   1966

Reinforcement Therapy

Presents three experimental programs that apply learning theory or operant conditioning to the treatment of severely disturbed autistic children, to the training of retarded children, and to the treatment of chronic schizophrenic adult parents.

SMITH KLINE AND FRENCH   1966

Steve Petchanek

The story of an educationally disadvantaged high school boy whose school counselor recognizes him as intellectually gifted. Shows how home visits, comments of teachers, and test data are used to help him in the self-development of his giftedness.

JARVIS COUILLARD ASSOCIATION   1966

Talking Together

Parents and teachers discuss how their exchange of ideas during the year was important to the development of the children. From Head Start's *At Home* Series.

UNITED STATES OFFICE OF ECONOMIC OPPORTUNITY   1967

Time Is For Taking

Gives insight into the world of the retarded child by portraying children in everyday situations at a residential camp for the retarded. Shows how problems develop and are solved by skillful counselors.

STUART FINLEY FILMS   1964

A Very Special Day: An Adventure at Coney Island
>A young boy, though ridiculed by his friends, feels obligated to help a girl who is lost. The film is designed to encourage discussion on the responsibility and the value of friendship.
>
>UNITED WORLD FILMS 1966

A Visit With the School Custodian
>Shows how desirable concepts are developed in a special elementary school classroom for the educable mentally retarded child. Describes the children's visit with the school custodian, and shows how they benefit from his work. The film teaches children good manners for a visit and the importance of keeping themselves and school property neat and clean. From the MGS Educational Series, No. 7
>
>MGS PRODUCTIONS, INCORPORATED 1964

A Visit With the School Nurse
>Shows how desirable concepts are developed in a special elementary school classroom for the educable mentally retarded child. Describes a class visit with the school nurse. Explains the role of the nurse in the school, the value of good health habits, and the importance of basic first aid information. From the MGS Educational Series, No. 6.
>
>MGS PRODUCTIONS, INCORPORATED 1964

The Way Back
>Records the story of the physical and emotional rehabilitation of a girl with a spinal cord injury. Shows how techniques used in her rehabilitation emphasize the team approach by professional people helping her to recover.
>
>REHABILITATION INSTITUTE OF CHICAGO 1964

The Way It Is
>Presents the chaos of the Ghetto school and reports on a New York University special learning project in Junior High School 57, Brooklyn. Shows visits with parents, teachers' meetings, and project workers in classrooms. Reports on the partial success of the project. From the NET Journal Series.
>
>NATIONAL EDUCATIONAL TELEVISION, INCORPORATED 1967

What Do I Know About Benny
>An open-discussion film which examines the problem involved in determining the academic aptitude of a child and in helping his mother to accept the results. From the Critical Moments in Teaching Series.
>
>HOLT, RINEHART AND WINSTON 1968

When I'm Old Enough . . . Goodby
>Discusses the problems faced by a young boy who drops out of high school. Emphasizes the value of proper guidance and the importance of the student's seeking this guidance.
>
>STATE EMPLOYMENT SERVICES 1962

Why Wait
>Illustrates methods of testing small children for various degrees and types of

deafness. Stresses the importance of early detection so that a child may be educated by special methods to compensate for his handicap.

MONTANA STATE UNIVERSITY   1961

Working To Learn Is Fun

Shows how desirable concepts are developed in a special elementary school classroom for the educable mentally retarded child. Depicts a boy and his classmates reviewing the value of past assignments and class visits and working on individual projects. Discusses the need to complete a task, ask for help, and leave the classroom in order before going home. From the MGS Educational Series, No. 9.

MGS PRODUCTIONS, INCORPORATED   1964

Your Junior High Days

Discusses the problems of transition from elementary school to junior high school. Emphasizes that all seventh graders face common problems. From the Junior High School Guidance Series.

MC GRAW-HILL TEXTFILMS   1964

Publications of Interest to Child Welfare Workers

American Child, National Child Labor Committee
American Journal of Mental Deficiency
American Journal of Orthopsychiatry
American Journal of Psychiatry
American Journal of Sociology
American Sociological Review
Annals
Catholic Action
Channels
Child Study, Journal of Parents' Education
Child Welfare, Child Welfare League of America
Children, U.S. Children's Bureau, Department of Health, Education, and Welfare
Crime and Delinquency
Federal Probation, U.S. Bureau of Prisons
Highlights, Family Service Association of America
Jewish Social Work Quarterly
Journal of Education for Social Work
Journal of Social Work, official publication of National Association of Social Workers
Mental Hygiene, National Association for Mental Health
Public Welfare, American Public Welfare Association
Recreation, National Recreation Association
Rural Sociology

Social Forces
Social Research
Social Security Bulletin, U.S. Department of Health, Education, and
    Welfare
Social Service Review
Sociology and Social Research

The I-Theory and Juvenile Delinquency

Since juvenile delinquency cannot be considered by any stretch of the imagination to be a clinical entity, few of the hundreds of empirical studies made in recent years, or few of the tens of theories in current vogue, even remotely support one another, even when replicated. This lack of concurrence is due to the complexity of the phenomena under study. However, the chief weakness is found in the fact that juvenile delinquency consists of many behaviors, and research or theory built upon one variable or narrow premise at best can explain not the whole phenomenon but merely a segment. A general theory of juvenile delinquency would help to place these theories and empirical findings in some kind of meaningful perspective. The I-theory of juvenile delinquency appears to provide such a frame of reference.

Without elaborating on the relationship of the I-theory to selected theories, findings, and forms of juvenile delinquency, we will present the theory in a series of propositions with a limited number of illustrations. The theory may serve as a reference point for the theoretically oriented reader in perusing the material on juvenile delinquency found in Chapters 8 and 9.

Theory is a model of certain findings, knowledge, and principles within a given field. More often than not it fails, proves to be unrealistic, or is useless to the student and the practitioner. On the other hand, it may have the virtue of calling the student's attention to important or neglected variables in a given set of phenomena, or of offering some semblance of order to a multiplicity of findings and axioms found in a given field.

The term theory is generally employed to denote the analysis of data in an effort to discover assumed underlying general principles. Social theory, which attempts to explain juvenile delinquency, is a search for abstract principles that will make concrete empirical social phenomena understandable, and will lead to an explanation and understanding of social relationships.

The theoretician is principally interested in describing the process by virtue of which phenomena exist. He attempts to discover a coherent body of principles that will enable him, not to foretell the nature of coming events, but to predict that, given certain conditions and relations, other events will follow. The *I*-theory (Introspection-Internalization-theory) is an attempt at describing the process underlying juvenile delinquency, and it may be succinctly expressed in the following series of propositions.

1. The problems of human behavior are of two types: (1) those relating to group life, and (2) those relating to the social development of human personality. The *I*-theory incorporates both types into its explanation of juvenile delinquency. It points out that these problems are interrelated in empirical reality, and that the individual is that much a product of social life and a member of society to the extent that he strives to form himself inwardly and outwardly as a personification of the purpose, aims, and values of society, or one or more of its subsystems.

2. Delinquent behavior results from the same processes as other behavior. It recognizes that both personality and social relationships must be taken into account in the explanation of delinquent behavior. From a scientific point of view, there is no advantage in contaminating the intrinsic nature of particular lines of conduct by introducing arbitrary standards into the processes of interaction from which modes of conduct emerge. Accordingly, the thesis of the *I*-theory is that the individual juvenile delinquent is a product of the same processes that produce the nondelinquent child. The difference between delinquent and conventional behavior is that the first type is judged officially by society to be undesirable. A theory of juvenile delinquency should thus explain all social behavior.

3. The use of "society" as a concept is acceptable only when it is explicitly stated that it is a completely verbal one, a dynamic happening or a process. Society cannot exist by itself. It requires interacting individuals to support its existence. The *I*-theory is interested in the behavior of interacting men and is concerned with concrete, factual conditions that actualize interaction in time and space.

4. Society consists of an involved and tangled network of social relationships between men, or of influences of men upon men. Society is a chain of occurrences flowing along with time. It refers not to a static entity but to a process; it refers not to human beings but to what goes on among associates. Just as life is not a thing but a process of living, so society is not a thing but a process of associating.

5. If society is made up of a web of vibrating, rhythmic, and changing social relationships that constitute a dynamic whole, and is a process of being, it follows that its interacting individuals must also be originators, reciprocators, and receivers of interaction. If society is a dynamic web of social relationships, its members are no less dynamic in engaging in these relationships. Juvenile delinquency, if it is to be explained sociopsychologically, will

have to be explained in dynamic terms that are in keeping with the nature of society.

6. Through the process of socialization, the individual tends to internalize certain norms and ideals. Socialization is a term that denotes the process through which the individual goes in acquiring patterns of behavior, habits, attitudes, and ideas of the social system into which he is born. The *I*-theory premises that an internalized value is one that determines an individual's behavior in all social situations that activate the value. For example, many individuals, through the process of socialization, have internalized the value of not eating human flesh. Under no conditions will these individuals eat human flesh, even if they are faced with starvation. The theory maintains that a social value is any datum that has empirical content accessible to the members of some social system and that may or may not be an object of activity.

7. Individuals have the power of making selections from the values presented by their social system. They are not mere automatons of a group, and they are capable of forming their own unique configuration of social values. Consequently, individuals do not internalize all the ideal values of society or of its subsystems. In the absence of internalization of values, behavior may be regulated by group pressures.

8. The behavior of an individual in a given social situation may be due to the presence or absence of group pressures or to internalized values. If a particular value is temperamental, the individual will respond to it only in activating social situations that involve group pressures. If the value is internalized, the individual will respond to it in all social situations, invoking it regardless of the presence or absence of group pressures.

9. Social behavior in general and juvenile delinquency in particular results from the interaction of an individual's temperamentalized-internalized value system and social situations that have been evaluated in terms of the value system. An individual's experience in a social situation is never one-sided. What his value system at any moment in time has become will determine how the social situation is experienced. In other words, when a juvenile with a temperamental value of omission or commission, which has been defined by society as being contrary to its official norms, interacts with a social situation that he considers as activating and complementing the value, behavior defined as juvenile delinquency results.

10. Most individuals have relatively few internalized values, and their various values are dispersed along a continuum representing various degrees of approach to internalization. The theory claims that the closer a value is to internalization, the more unusual will be the social situation that will complement and activate the negative aspects of the value and thus move the individual into action. Thus an individual may go through life as an outwardly honest man, since the highly unusual opportunity to steal a million dollars—the limit at which he will act counter to his value of honesty—has never presented itself. All individuals react to situations in terms of their value system.

11. As the child matures, certain of his internalized values may become temperamental, and vice versa, owing to sociopsychological experiences, maturation, education, unique experiences, and differential association. However, the individual's value system appears to become more rigid with time, especially if his experiences tend to be limited to a network of relatively stable social relationships.

12. The process of maintaining order in society is one of conditioning the individual so that his values will be in harmony with the basic values of society. However, the basic norms of a society can never account for the particulars of every social situation, but they prescribe principles within the wider range of conduct, leaving to the individual the decision of evaluating the social situation.

13. Juvenile delinquency results when the following interacting conditions are present: (1) a juvenile with a temperamental value of omission or commission; (2) a social situation that activates the value; and, (3) resultant behavior that is defined officially by society to be delinquent.

14. All life in a society is a compromise between the needs of the individual and the needs of the group. The development of social systems represents an attempt to fix and perpetuate these compromises. Social systems control the reciprocal behavior between individuals and between the individual and the group through ideal patterns of behavior. These patterns are derived from behavior and, in turn, are modified by behavior. All social systems in a society show a fairly close adjustment both in the forms of behavior prescribed by single patterns and between various patterns themselves. Social systems influence the attitudes and behavior of individuals who share its component ideas. All social systems include certain patterns which are at variance with the larger systems of a society or with some of its own subsystems.

15. The simplest abstraction of a social system consists of a behavior pattern controlling the reciprocal interaction of two individuals in occurring social situations. The concept of systems can also be extended, so that it can be visualized as having contact with, and being a part of, other wider systems, the resulting representation being one of systems within systems.

16. Each social system is limited by a boundary, and the location of this boundary will vary from time to time according to a problem's reference point. The boundary may be latent or temporarily inoperative, to be activated only when certain types of problems that require attention arise.

17. A considerable number of the values found in a given society may be classified as universals, in that they are found in all social systems in every society. All systems have many values in common, but certain systems also have values that are not universal, and some values are particular only to certain systems.

18. In a given social system, all values involved do not have the same valence that they may have in society as a whole or in comparison with other social systems. The reaction of a system's members to the violation of a

given value depends on the system's valence of the value in question, the frequency of the deviation, and the number and status of the violators in the system. In other words, the difference in valence of values found between systems means that certain types of behavior may be committed in some social systems of a society, but not tolerated in other systems within the same society.

19. Not only do certain systems pose opportunities for deviant behavior by virtue of their differential array of values that are not consistent with society's, but every system offers its own members with temperamental values opportunities for deviant behavior at the expense of the system itself. For example, if children in a Sunday school class do not steal books, the school will not keep its Bibles under lock and key, thus presenting the child with a temperamental value a chance to steal a Bible for home use.

To summarize the last two propositions, we may point out that we have at least two social situations that offer opportunities for deviant behavior: (1) *external systems deviation*, which allows individuals, while interacting in certain systems, to violate values highly regarded in other systems; (2) *internal systems deviation*, which is possible in all social systems and depends on the conformity of a high proportion of their members to its value system; a high degree of compliance creates the continued opportunity for deviant behavior since a high degree of outward group compliance does not call for the imposition or the activation of formal controls.

The significance of the *I*-theory for juvenile delinquency and child welfare lies in the methods used in the rehabilitation of the offender through social casework or correctional counseling.

It may be pointed out that the foregoing propositions not only offer a broad theoretical basis for the general practice, in correctional counseling, of dealing with the inner (or psychological) and outer (or sociological) aspects of an offender's problem, but they also provide the basis for broader therapeutic explorations into the background of the client's social relationships.

Justice for Children

The Congressional Record of December 9, 1970, carries a speech made by Senator Walter F. Mondale of Minnesota that is entitled, "Justice for Children."*

Prefacing his speech with concern for the implementation of the recommendations of the 1970 White House Conference on Children, Senator Mondale proceeds to give an excellent summary of the unmet needs of thousands of children in the United States of today.

Although students of child welfare will want to read "Justice for Children" in its entirety, the following six excerpts from Senator Mondale's speech illustrate the magnitude of some of the pressing problems in child welfare that are found currently throughout our country.

[1]

Our national myth is that we love children. Yet, we are starving thousands. Other thousands die because decent medical care is unavailable to them. The lives of still other thousands are stifled by poor schools and some never have the chance to go to school at all. Millions live in substandard and unfit housing in neighborhoods which mangle the human spirit. Many suffer all of these mutilations simultaneously.

In every society some people are consigned to the scrap heap—the ir-

* *The Congressional Record.* Proceedings and Debates of the 91st Congress, Second Session. Vol. 116, No. 197.

retrievably handicapped, the incurably ill, the incorrigibly criminal, the hopelessly uneducable.

But, in America we have needlessly allowed the scrap heap to pile up and up.

The most obvious victims of course are the 10 million children living in poverty and the untold millions maimed by racism.

But the scrap heap is not outsized merely because of poverty and racism.

Have we reduced the victims of physical handicaps to the irreducible minimum? Not when 45 percent of the children born in U.S. hospitals do not receive the prenatal care which could prevent some of the handicaps in the first place. Not when there are 3.7 million handicapped children who are not receiving the special educational services they require.

Have we reduced the victims of mental illness to the irreducible minimum? Not when there are 1.3 million children who need mental health services but are not getting them.

Have we reduced the victims of mental retardation to the irreducible minimum? Not when there are 1 million educable mentally retarded children who will never get the help they need to reach their full potential.

The victims are most emphatically not just the poor and the minorities.

Consider the victims of bad health care. It is not surprising, perhaps, that the infant mortality rate in Coahoma County, Miss., which is nearly two-thirds poor, is over twice the national average. But it may give pause to realize that the infant mortality rate in Westchester County, N.Y.—one of the wealthiest counties in America—is just about equal to the national average, a national average which is higher than at least a dozen other countries. No, the victims of bad health care are not just the poor.

Consider the victims of the tremendous shortage of preschool child development programs. Research shows that approximately 50 percent of a person's intellectual development takes place before he is 5 years old. Head Start and day care reach only one child in 10 among the poor, and the figures for children in other income groups are not much different. It is not just the poor who are missing out on crucial stimulation during the preschool years.

Consider the victims of our schools. The child of the ghetto may attend a school without textbooks, where the teacher thinks he is incapable of learning, where the paint peels and the plaster cracks, but the child of the suburbs finds less and less to engage him in school as well. Of 17 million school age children identified as "educationally deprived" by HEW, less than a third come from poverty families. "You have to have grown up in Scarsdale to know how bad things really are," one observer says. It is not just the poor who are the victims of our school systems.

Consider the victims of drug abuse. Millions of children—not just the poor—are having their lives twisted by the pandemic spread of drug abuse. Recent studies in suburban schools reveal that up to 75 percent of high school students have experimented with marihuana. Last year in Fairfax County, Va., there were more heroin cases discovered among young people than in the previous 5 years combined. The users come from among the highest income families in the county, including the sons and daughters of doctors and colonels. It is not just the poor who are the victims of drug abuse.

The children whom we are daily consigning to the scrap heap come from every income group, every racial group, every geographical area in our Nation. And every child consigned to the scrap heap is a useful life lost to the country, and indeed a lifetime of costs to the taxpayers in welfare, prison, or other expense.

The fact is that this is a problem in which the "real majority" has a deep and vital stake. It has become fashionable to suggest that the "real majority" somehow has concerns and views which are different from the poor. I disagree.

Fifty-five percent of Americans live in families with incomes of less than $10,000 a year. Whether the problem is schools or health care or preschool programs or what happens when a child is physically handicapped or mentally disturbed, all Americans share the same problems. And the sooner we can come to the shared realization that this is in fact the case, the sooner we shall create in America the atmosphere which our children need and deserve in which to grow up.

[2]

Who are the victims of our neglect?

First. The migrant child. Nearly a million are children who live in families which subsist primarily by doing migrant or seasonal farmwork. There is no child in America more powerless to change his future, more powerless to escape the cycle of poverty into which he has been born.

In addition to the problems which confront every poor child, the migrant child suffers the consequence of constant rootlessness. The image of traveling together as a family is perhaps one of the most cherished of the American culture. But for the migrant child, travel only means a new shack, a new field to work in, and a new school, if any. Travel only increases the pace with which his life is destroyed. The very rootlessness of his life is a monstrous curse.

Born into extreme poverty—the average earnings of each farmworker from farm labor are less than $1,000 a year—the child not only is physically unable to attend school regularly, but he begins working at a very early age to supplement meager family earnings. He not only suffers from malnutrition, but his learning perspective is geared to a neverending cycle of back-breaking work—bending, lifting, and carrying. By the time he is 10 or 11 he has stopped going to school and is beginning to have to cope with life as an adult.

By the time is 14 or 15 he is often married. Soon his health deteriorates —his teeth and skin begin to rot and his back shows the damaging effects of stoop labor. His ability to earn is permanently impaired. He is in constant debt, getting in deeper and deeper as life goes on. The grower and the crew leader advance him groceries and other necessities against his wages, and he never comes out ahead. He is powerless—both politically and economically —to affect his situation. The cycle is well on its way again.

Migrants are the poorest paid, the most underfed, the least healthy, the worst housed, the most undereducated, and perhaps the most abused human beings in our society today. What goes on from generation to generation is the awful wholesale destruction, physically and psychologically, of hundreds of thousands of American children—migrant children.

It was Michael Harrington who told us 10 years ago, in revealing "The Other America" to his fellow citizens, that while we had a poverty problem in this country, it did not exist on a scale or in an intensity comparable to other nations. We learned during the 1960's that he was wrong. We found that there were families in Mississippi and elsewhere who literally had no cash income. We saw, because a few Senators and some media people cared that there are children in America who have bloated bellies and running sores that will not heal.

There still are. It is not so fashionable in 1970 to talk about them. Hunger, it seems, was last year's issue. The other day someone remembered that President Nixon promised a free school lunch for every poor child by this Thanksgiving. It has not happened. Urgently needed reforms in the food stamp program have been in controversy for more than three and a half years and have still not been enacted. And all the while, there are still bloated bellies in Mississippi. I know it is hard to remember that every day. It is an uncomfortable thought, but in these days of our senses being assaulted with so many outrages, we have acquired an incapacity for further shock.

[3]

The Indian child. Perhaps the greatest poverty in America exists among American Indians. Add to this the welfare dependency and hopelessness which generations of paternalistic Federal trusteeship have brought, and the trap which confronts the Indian child is at least as dangerous and powerful as that which ensnares the migrant child.

We have heard it before, but we forget that annual Indian per capita income is only $1,500, less than half of the national average, that infant mortality is almost twice the national average, that 90 percent of Indian housing is substandard, and that suicide rates on the typical Indian reservation are more than double the national average.

As in other areas, the situation is not quite as bad as it was 10 years ago. The major reason is a rising generation of Indian young people of greater awareness and competency, who are not only committed to improving life

424   APPENDICES

in their communities, but are acquiring some of the skill and political sophis-
tication that is necessary to bring change.

But the American Indian is still governed by a Congress which too often
is more interested in protecting the land and water interests of the white
man than in making a better life for the Indian. And power relationships at
the local level are still not significantly different.

Three out of five Indian children attend local public schools—schools
which are funded by Federal funds under the Johnson-O'Malley Act and
the impacted school areas legislation. But this money is often spent for
purposes which do not benefit Indian children, and the Indian child is more
often than not assumed by the school system to be slow, lazy or dumb.
Indian students on the Muckleshoot reservation in Washington are automatically retained an extra year in the first grade of their public schools,
and the Nook-Sack Indians of western Washington are automatically placed
in a class of slow learners without achievement testing. No wonder massive
early dropouts from school occur, and high rates of suicide and alcoholism
ensue.

A third of the Indian children are in schools run by the Federal
Bureau of Indian Affairs. Some of these are in boarding schools, including
some 7,000 Navajo children under the age of 9, some of whom have frozen
to death trying to escape and get home during the winter. About 1,200
Alaskan natives presently go to Federal boarding schools in Oregon and
Oklahoma, thousands of miles from home. Two-thirds of the Indian children
entering BIA schools have little or no skill in English, but less than 5 percent
of the teachers in BIA schools are native to the culture and the language of
the children they teach. Only 773 Indian children in the entire country were
reached by the Federal bilingual education program in a recent year.

It has been our national assumption that Indians do not know how to do
anything for themselves. Reservations are in general managed by white
employees of the BIA, and Indian young people everywhere are indoctri-
nated with the idea of their incompetency.

The Indian child is also victimized by one of America's most dangerous
and mean assumptions—that there is only one language in America, and
that others are not worthwhile and will not be countenanced. Courses on
Indian heritage and culture are nonexistent in both Federal and local public
schools, and children are in every way made to feel that their own heritage
and culture is inferior and worthless.

[4]

The Chicano child and the Puerto Rican child. The list of victims prolifer-
ates. There are nearly 10 million Americans whose first language is Spanish,
and whose heritage is a Spanish language culture. There are many who have
Portuguese, Chinese, French, Japanese, and other culture and language

heritages. Like the Indian child, the Chicano or Puerto Rican child or other linguistically and culturally different child is daily penalized by the forced application of homogeneity, the assumption that diversity is intolerable.

Until recent years the Chicano—or Mexican American, as the Anglo culture dominated him—was a forgotten minority of huge proportions. Politicians sought his vote, but after the election things went back to business as usual. Nationally, he was eclipsed by the greater numbers and earlier political awareness of the black community. He was thought to be submissive and unquestioning of authority. His child was among the more invisible of our victims.

Now we know a little more about how things are. We have had some national attention to the Chicano as a farmworker, through the organizing efforts of Cesar Chavez with the help of the media. The growing Puerto Rican minority in New York City and elsewhere has begun to surface. The barrio of East Los Angeles has erupted in violence. A network television documentary has shown a newly born Chicano child dying of prenatal starvation within a stone's throw of the multimillion-dollar Hemis-Fair entertainment complex in San Antonio.

The Nation has begun to hear some tales from the victims who survived. We now know that 50 to 90 percent of Chicano and Puerto Rican children, depending on the area, come to school speaking only Spanish. Many of them, we find, are put in classes for the mentally retarded simply because they cannot cope with standardized English language intelligence tests.

The Senate Select Committee on Equal Educational Opportunity which I chair has heard some extraordinary personal testimony: A near Ph.D. Puerto Rican in educational administration at Harvard who was classified as retarded in elementary school; a Chicano Ph.D. in clinical psychology who spent several years in mentally retarded classes as a child; and a Puerto Rican woman lawyer who was told she has an IQ of 20 in elementary school. These are among the handful of victims who survived.

Others are not so fortunate. As many as one out of five Chicano children never go to school. Of those who do, one out of four drop out by the eighth grade. Less than half graduate from high school. In one school district in California 99 percent of the children in kindergarten are Chicano but only 30 percent of the graduating seniors are Chicano. Of 7,000 school-age Puerto Rican children in Boston, seven graduated from high school this past June.

Why? Not only are intelligent children treated as uneducable, but Spanish-speaking children are often forbidden to speak their native language in school and in many cases are even punished for doing so. In a south Texas school, children are forced to kneel on the playground and beg forgiveness if they are caught talking to each other in Spanish. In an Arizona elementary school, children who answer a question in Spanish are required to come up to the teacher's desk and drop pennies in a bowl—one penny for each

Spanish word spoken. "It works," the teacher boasts. "They come from poor families, you know."

Of course, the ways in which the Chicano and Puerto Rican children are victimized go on and on—the poor health care, the poor housing, the lack of job opportunities, and there is again the all-pervasive powerlessness. When Cesar Chavez began to organize, he found the law enforcement officials of the communities in California where he was working squarely on the side of the growers. When Chicano high school students in a small town in Texas demonstrated against school conditions, some were beaten by Texas Rangers, and those who were old enough were reclassified 1-A by the local selective service board. The sense of hopelessness, of inability to change conditions, is a major barrier to change. But again, if there is any basis for hope, it comes not alone from any increased commitment among Anglo politicians, but also from a rising generation of dedicated and able Chicano and Puerto Rican leaders. In Texas the Mexican-American Youth Organization, denounced as "militant" a year ago, helped form a new political party and elected a member to the school board in Crystal City. In New York Herman Badillo has been elected to Congress. All over the country Chicano and Puerto Rican young people are on the move, sometimes with tactics which cooler heads deem unacceptable or unwise, but always with a commitment and perseverance which are profoundly admirable.

As with Indian children, if the White House Conference were to be fully relevant, one would have expected to find more extended and specific reference to the daily damage we are doing to the children of Spanish-speaking Americans.

The poor white child. Two-thirds of the poor children in America are white. This is a fact which should have great political implications, but it is too often ignored or forgotten.

The greatest concentration of white poverty is, of course, in Appalachia. Things have not changed very much since the days when John Kennedy campaigned in West Virginia and was so deeply moved by what he saw there. In Appalachia today more than three-quarters of a million young people sit in the hollows and hills facing lifelong unemployment if they remain at home, and lacking the skills to do much of consequence [if] they leave. Over 900,000 children under 6—nearly half of the preschool children in the region—are poor. Less than one of 20 of Appalachia's poor children is in Headstart. Only 6 percent of Appalachia's children receive welfare assistance.

The way things work is quite simple, though perhaps the truth is a bit hard to face. The outside economic interests which control the region no longer have any need for the labor of the men who live there. Coal mining is gone or largely automated. Children are neglected because social services are not thought to be important for people of no economic value. There are no jobs for the fathers, either privately or governmentally created. There is no welfare if the man is living at home with his family. And the schools for the children are badly underfunded. Local authorities remain unwilling or unable to tax the outside large corporations. So the school construction needs of the 13 Appalachian States represented 42 percent of the total school construction needs in the entire country in a recent year.

[5]

Some of the victims whom I have mentioned live in cities. But any child who lives in one of the large central cities of America is a victim in ways which transcend his race and even his economic status.

The air he breathes—polluted by automobiles, powerplants, industrial plants, and home heating—makes him far more subject to disease than his suburban or rural counterpart.

The congestion in which he lives has clinically observable effects on his mental state. It is not surprising, for example, that studies find an astonishing incidence of mental illness in New York City, where the population density is almost 1,000 times that of the country generally, and an even greater incidence in central Harlem, where density is near 10,000 times the national average.

But that is only the beginning. In most instances, the urban child must face and deal with the worst aspects of America's institutions. The child attending school in one of the 20 largest school systems in the country is almost a year behind the national norm for the rest of the country. The health problems faced by the urban child are equally as horrifying.

Venereal disease has gone beyond the epidemic stage. Infant mortality in the ghettos and barrios is often four times the national average. And drug addiction is now rampant in all parts of every major city. For a child of the city, his powerlessness and isolation from the mainstream of America are more obvious at an early age; his disconnection from society's major institutions, schools, police, religious institutions, business and industry is more blatant. Lack of space, poor housing, density, and inadequate opportunities strain family relationships even further.

Every institution which confronts the urban child is the biggest, most unresponsive form of that institution our country has to offer.

The schools are dropout factories. In the ghetto schools, children as they get older fall further and further behind national norms in every skill.

The city hospital is totally dehumanizing. The patient waits 2 to 4 hours in a clinic to see a doctor he has never seen before and is likely never to see again.

The welfare is at its most bureaucratic and degrading. The landlord is an absentee or a public housing authority as bureaucratic as the slumlord is neglectful. The credit merchant overreaches, and repossesses the moment payments fall behind.

[6]

The handicapped child. There are more than 7 million handicapped children in America—emotionally disturbed, mentally retarded, physically handicapped in one of a variety of ways, or suffering from special learning difficulties. Nearly 5 million of these children are receiving no special educational services or other help.

Some are poor, but most are not. Most are children whose problem is not irremediable enough to cause them to be discarded into a public residential institution, but for whom the public schools have no appropriate programs and private services are either unavailable or too expensive.

We have, plainly and simply, failed these children. They are the victims of our neglect.

Consider the child who is in a residential institution either for the mentally retarded or for the mentally ill. Typically, it is old, crowded, understaffed, filthy, sterile, strewn with feces, devoid of hope, filled with blank faces. There are retarded children there who are educable if special education services are available. There are disturbed children who are curable if psychiatric services are available. There are neglected and abandoned children who are there simply because there is no other place to put them, and who will remain there until they are 16 and then be dumped on the street, propelled to the scrap heap by a society which did not care enough to make life possible for them.

Here again, our treatment is both inhumane, and senseless. It would save money to save lives. The annual cost of foster care is about one-eighth the cost of institutionalization. The lifetime cost of educating an educable handicapped or retarded child is about $20,000. Institutionalizing him will cost well over $200,000. And the Nation's handicapped children have potential earning power of $15 billion if they receive the special education and services necessary for them to realize their personal and economic potential.

Index